LONGITUDINAL DATA ANALYSIS USING STRUCTURAL EQUATION MODELS

LONGITUDINAL DATA ANALYSIS USING STRUCTURAL EQUATION MODELS

John J. McArdle
John R. Nesselroade

AMERICAN PSYCHOLOGICAL ASSOCIATION
WASHINGTON, DC

Copyright © 2014 by the American Psychological Association. All rights reserved. Except as permitted under the United States Copyright Act of 1976, no part of this publication may be reproduced or distributed in any form or by any means, including, but not limited to, the process of scanning and digitization, or stored in a database or retrieval system, without the prior written permission of the publisher.

Published by
American Psychological Association
750 First Street, NE
Washington, DC 20002
www.apa.org

To order
APA Order Department
P.O. Box 92984
Washington, DC 20090-2984
Tel: (800) 374-2721; Direct: (202) 336-5510
Fax: (202) 336-5502; TDD/TTY: (202) 336-6123
Online: www.apa.org/pubs/books
E-mail: order@apa.org

In the U.K., Europe, Africa, and the Middle East, copies may be ordered from
American Psychological Association
3 Henrietta Street
Covent Garden, London
WC2E 8LU England

Typeset in Goudy by Circle Graphics, Inc., Columbia, MD

Printer: United Book Press, Baltimore, MD
Cover Designer: Berg Design, Albany, NY

The opinions and statements published are the responsibility of the authors, and such opinions and statements do not necessarily represent the policies of the American Psychological Association.

Library of Congress Cataloging-in-Publication Data

McArdle, John J.
 Longitudinal data analysis using structural equation models / John J. McArdle and John R. Nesselroade.
    pages cm
 Includes bibliographical references and index.
 ISBN-13: 978-1-4338-1715-1
 ISBN-10: 1-4338-1715-2
 1. Longitudinal method. 2. Psychology—Research. I. Nesselroade, John R. II. Title.
 BF76.6.L65M33 2014
 150.72'1   dc23
                        2013046896

British Library Cataloguing-in-Publication Data
A CIP record is available from the British Library.

Printed in the United States of America
First Edition

http://dx.doi.org/10.1037/14440-000

CONTENTS

Preface ix
Overview 3

I. Foundations 15

Chapter 1. Background and Goals of Longitudinal Research 17
Chapter 2. Basics of Structural Equation Modeling 27
Chapter 3. Some Technical Details on Structural
            Equation Modeling 39
Chapter 4. Using the Simplified Reticular Action
            Model Notation 59
Chapter 5. Benefits and Problems Using Structural Equation
            Modeling in Longitudinal Research 67

II. Longitudinal SEM for the Direct Identification of Intraindividual Changes 73

Chapter 6.   Alternative Definitions of Individual Changes 75

Chapter 7.   Analyses Based on Latent Curve Models 93

Chapter 8.   Analyses Based on Time-Series Regression Models 109

Chapter 9.   Analyses Based on Latent Change Score Models 119

Chapter 10. Analyses Based on Advanced Latent Change Score Models 133

III. Longitudinal SEM for Interindividual Differences in Intraindividual Changes 141

Chapter 11. Studying Interindividual Differences in Intraindividual Changes 143

Chapter 12. Repeated Measures Analysis of Variance as a Structural Model 151

Chapter 13. Multilevel Structural Equation Modeling Approaches to Group Differences 159

Chapter 14. Multiple Group Structural Equation Modeling Approaches to Group Differences 167

Chapter 15. Incomplete Data With Multiple Group Modeling of Changes 177

IV. Longitudinal SEM for the Interrelationships in Growth 185

Chapter 16. Considering Common Factors/Latent Variables in Structural Models 187

Chapter 17. Considering Factorial Invariance in Longitudinal Structural Equation Modeling 207

Chapter 18. Alternative Common Factors With Multiple Longitudinal Observations 221

Chapter 19. More Alternative Factorial Solutions for Longitudinal Data 231

Chapter 20. Extensions to Longitudinal Categorical Factors 239

V. Longitudinal SEM for Causes (Determinants) of Intraindividual Changes 253

Chapter 21. Analyses Based on Cross-Lagged Regression and Changes 255

Chapter 22. Analyses Based on Cross-Lagged Regression in Changes of Factors 271

Chapter 23. Current Models for Multiple Longitudinal Outcome Scores 281

Chapter 24. The Bivariate Latent Change Score Model for Multiple Occasions 291

Chapter 25. Plotting Bivariate Latent Change Score Results 301

VI. Longitudinal SEM for Interindividual Differences in Causes (Determinants) of Intraindividual Changes 305

Chapter 26. Dynamic Processes Over Groups 307

Chapter 27. Dynamic Influences Over Groups 315

Chapter 28. Applying a Bivariate Change Model With Multiple Groups 319

Chapter 29. Notes on the Inclusion of Randomization in Longitudinal Studies 323

Chapter 30. The Popular Repeated Measures Analysis of Variance 329

VII. Summary and Discussion 331

Chapter 31. Contemporary Data Analyses Based on Planned Incompleteness 333

Chapter 32. Factor Invariance in Longitudinal Research 345

Chapter 33. Variance Components for Longitudinal Factor Models 351

Chapter 34. Models for Intensively Repeated Measures 355

Chapter 35. Coda: The Future Is Yours! 367

References 373

Index 401

About the Authors 425

PREFACE

George Orwell wrote a lot of important books. At one point, he also considered the reasons why people write books at all. One conclusion he reached was that this task was typically undertaken to deal with some demon in the author's life. If this is true, and we have no reason to doubt Orwell so far, then we thought it might be useful to consider the demons that drive us to take on this seemingly thankless task. The best explanation we have come up with involves at least three motives.

We have led a workshop on longitudinal data analysis for the past decade, and participants at this workshop have asked many questions. Our first motive in writing this book is to answer these questions in an organized and complete way.

Second, the important advances in longitudinal methodology are too often overlooked in favor of simpler but inferior alternatives. That is, certainly researchers have their own ideas about the importance of longitudinal structural equation modeling (LSEM), including concepts of multiple factorial invariance over time (MFIT), but we think these are essential ingredients of useful longitudinal analyses. Also, the use of what we term *latent change scores*, which we emphasize here, is not the common approach currently being used by many other researchers in the field. Thus, a second motive is to distribute knowledge about MFIT and the latent change score approach. Most of the instruction in this book pertains to using computer programs effectively.

A third reason for writing this book is that we are enthusiastic about the possibilities for good uses of the longitudinal methods described here, some described for the first time and most never used in situations where we think they could be most useful. In essence, we write to offer some hope to the next generation of researchers in this area. Our general approach to scientific discourse is not one of castigation and critique of previous work; rather than attack the useful attempts of others, we have decided to applaud all the prior efforts and simply lay out our basic theory of longitudinal data analysis. We hope our efforts will spawn improved longitudinal research.

Our weeklong workshop with the same basic title as this book has been sponsored every year since 2000 by the Science Directorate of the American Psychological Association (APA). This APA workshop is based on an earlier workshop on longitudinal methods started at the Max Planck Institute (MPI) for Human Development in Berlin in 1986 (at the invitation of the late Paul Baltes). This book presents the basic theory of longitudinal data analysis used in the workshop. A forthcoming companion book, titled *Applications of Longitudinal Data Analysis Using Structural Equation Models*, will present the data examples and computer programs used in the workshop.

The current LSEM workshop continues to be sponsored by APA and is now led by Dr. Emilio Ferrer and Dr. Kevin Grimm at the University of California at Davis each summer. And near the end of each new workshop, one of the authors of this book still gives an invited lecture. In this way, the features of our original LSEM workshop live on.

We have found that the concepts of "change analysis" are wide ranging. We know this book-length treatment will not be definitive, and we just hope it is viewed as another step along the way. These particular steps were developed during a time when both authors were teaching faculty of Human Development at The Pennsylvania State University (PSU) and subsequently colleagues at the Department of Psychology at the University of Virginia (UVa), the dates of this collaboration ranging from about 1985 to 2005. During that time, we taught 10 summers of APA-sponsored workshops at UVa (2000–2009), and we learned some valuable lessons about longitudinal research. For example, we learned we needed to separate the basic concepts of "growth and change" in our own approach to data analysis (see McArdle, 2009). We also learned about the importance of adequate measurement models (see McArdle & Nesselroade, 2003). It also became apparent that the more the computer programs changed, the more they stayed the same (to be discussed). Perhaps it is obvious that our collaboration would not have been possible unless we were encouraged to work together, so we thank both PSU and UVa for all the time they allowed us to think about these issues.

There are many specific people to thank for our collaboration. At the top of this list we must mention our wives, Carol Prescott and Carolyn Nesselroade. These two unusual people gave us critical support that helped us produce this book, and they continue to allow us the time to work on these matters. Of course, we have tried to incorporate their ideas into this text as best we can, and about all we can say now is "thanks." We know this is really not enough.

Next in line we thank our wonderful colleagues and graduate students at UVa, including (in alphabetic order) Steven Boker, Sy-Minn Chow, Ryan Estabrook, Emilio Ferrer, Kevin Grimm, Paolo Ghisletta, Fumiaki Hamagami, Thomas Paskus, Nilam Ram, Lijuan (Peggy) Wang, and Zhiyong (Johnny) Zhang. Many of these students suggested changes in the materials, and we tried to use everything they suggested. In particular, Aki helped us edit the prose you see here and provided most of the figures. Other important students include Ulman Lindenberger (now MPI, Berlin director) and Karl Ulrich Mayr (now full professor, University of Oregon). We make special mention of Drs. Ferrer and Grimm, who have contributed to this material in more ways than one and who, as mentioned earlier, lead the LSEM workshop (now at the University of California at Davis) each summer. There are many others who deserve credit for their comments and questions. All these graduate students are making important contributions on their own right now, and this is especially rewarding for us.

As stated earlier, our professional colleagues at UVa were essential to this effort, and the short list of important supporters includes Richard Bell, Mavis Heatherington, Richard McCarty, Dennis Profit, Jerry Clore, and Sandra Scarr. Other colleagues who supported our efforts and made an important difference in our thinking were many well-known scientists—Paul Baltes (PSU, MPI), Ray Cattell (UI, UH), John Horn (DU, USC), Ron Johnson (UH), Bill Meredith (UCB), Rod McDonald (OISE, UI), and Bill Rozeboom (UCA). There is simply no way to adequately thank this unique group of scientists for taking the time to confide in us things they had just discovered and what they actually thought about these things. These people are no longer alive, but we hope their research and their thoughts live on here. We also thank many members of the Society of Multivariate Experimental Psychology for their continuing support of the development of these ideas. Finally, we thank all the many participants of our APA-sponsored workshops and the APA Science Directorate and APA Books staff for the time and effort they put in toward challenging us to produce a coherent piece about clearing up some basic concepts about longitudinal research.

In sum, this book is intended as a tribute to the many contributions and the ideas of many, many others.

LONGITUDINAL DATA ANALYSIS USING STRUCTURAL EQUATION MODELS

OVERVIEW

Longitudinal data are difficult to collect, but longitudinal research is popular. And this popularity seems to be growing. The reasons why researchers now appear to be enamored with this approach will be questioned, but there is no doubt the collection of longitudinal data is on the rise. With this comes the subsequent need for good data analysis methods to analyze these special kinds of data. Structural equation modeling (SEM) is a valuable way to analyze longitudinal data because it is both flexible and useful for answering common research questions. However, the most appropriate SEM strategy to use will depend on the specific question you are trying to answer.

Baltes and Nesselroade's (1979) seminal chapter identifies five basic questions or purposes of longitudinal SEM (LSEM):

- direct identification of intraindividual changes,
- direct identification of interindividual differences in intraindividual changes,

- examining interrelationships in intraindividual changes,
- analyses of causes (determinants) of intraindividual changes, and
- analyses of causes (determinants) of interindividual differences in intraindividual changes.

We note that "changes" were referred to as "differences" in Baltes and Nesselroade's (1979) original text.

In this book, we present the most useful strategies and techniques for each of these five purposes. We do not offer all kinds of models, just the selected set of SEM models we have actually put to use. Two important but underused approaches are emphasized: multiple factorial invariance over time (MFIT) and latent change scores.

We focus on the big picture approach rather than the algebraic details. We realize that excessive amounts of linear SEM algebra can get in the way of big picture thinking, so we have tried to minimize the required algebra and calculus herein. Thus, we have limited the algebra and calculus to separate exhibits. We think the defining equations can be studied in some depth as our main message is presented. To facilitate student learning, a forthcoming companion book will give several fully worked out examples, including computer scripts.

The remainder of this overview introduces basic topics that are central to this book. We begin by briefly explaining our approach as developmental methodologists and how this informs the design and timing of our measures. Next, we discuss the purpose of SEM in general and LSEM in particular. Finally, we explain how the rest of this book is organized in relation to Baltes and Nesselroade's (1979) five purposes of LSEM.

OUR APPROACH AS DEVELOPMENTAL METHODOLOGISTS

Who are developmental methodologists anyway? And why should anyone listen to them? These are two questions that have been of interest to us for a long time, probably because we fit into this small category of scientists!

Methodologists study the many ways researchers evaluate evidence. It is clear that some formal methods are better than others, and the key role of the methodologist is to point this out to others. There is no real need for a methodologist to actually find any facts (i.e., collect empirical data), and this seems to put these people in a special category. One would think this makes the task much easier. But it is also clear that other people seem to find it very hard to listen to a person who does not know all the troubles and nuances of doing "real" research. So, in this book, we will not use computer simulation to prove our points here; we have done so elsewhere, but only to check on the accuracy of the programs. Instead, we will only present real data. And it is probably best if the person suggesting what to do has some experience with the specific problem at hand. One of the clearest statements of our general approach has been written about before:

> Tukey argued that there have to be people in the various sciences who concentrate much of their attention on methods of analyzing data and of interpreting results of statistical analysis. . . . They have to use scientific judgment more than they use mathematical judgment, but not the former to the exclusion of the latter. Especially as they break into new fields of sciencing, they must be more interested in "indication procedures" than "conclusion procedures." (Cooley & Lohnes, 1971, p. v)

So we view ourselves as data analysts and not as statisticians. This will become evident as you read more details here. We now add the term *developmental* to this distinction. There are many words used to define developmental, but here we will simply concentrate on "changes over time." These changes, of course, could come from a system where a very small amount of time has passed, such as the observation of a person over a few minutes, or some part of day, or the observation of a person over many weeks, or the observations of many people over many years. In this definition, the specific times are not critical, and they can occur in early childhood, or late adulthood, or both. What is important is the nature of change that can be captured and what aspects of change cannot.

So we will also try to represent what is known in the field of developmental methodology by being very explicit about the design and timing of our measures, and we will apply the methods we advocate to real data. Our hope is that some of you will use these methods right now and others will improve these methods for future work. Either way is certainly okay with us.

WHY USE SEM?

So why do we use SEM, or SEM programs, at all? Well, it is not true that we use SEM because of the path diagrams—many traditional models can be represented using path diagrams, and, although it is not clear to many, we really do not need to use SEM tools to use SEM concepts. Also, some of the standard multivariate tools are now very easy to use. But there are three good reasons why we use SEM for data analysis.

First, we use SEM because we have a priori ideas about individuals and groups that we want to examine in real data. Some of these ideas are well beyond the standard analysis of variance (ANOVA) and the so-called general linear model framework. We would certainly like to know if we are wrong about these a priori ideas, so we certainly appreciate much of the ongoing work on SEM estimators, statistical indices, and overall goodness-of-fit indices.

Second, we use SEM because we want to consider the inclusion of unobserved variables in our models, that is, latent variables. We often think about latent variables in our theories—variables that are not directly measured or measurable—and we want to represent them in our models of these theories. In this sense, the inclusion of latent variables is for clarity, not for obscurity. It is also clear that the accurate representation of observed variable distributions may require more complex measurement models than the typical normality assumptions.

Third, we use SEM because we would like to have empirical assistance selecting the "true" or "correct" model, or at least an adequate model, for a set of data. We believe we can tell we have found an adequate model when we estimate parameters that do not differ with different samplings of person or variables or occasions (i.e., the parameters are invariant). In the terms of linear regression, we do not always want the model with the highest explained variance for the current set of data, but we do want the model that is most likely to replicate over and over again.

Since these three goals seem reasonable and continue to be part of most behavioral science research, SEM combined as both a concept and a tool is now very popular, and multivariate data analysis is likely to remain this way for a long time to come. But perhaps it is now clear that the typical SEM was not specially defined for the issues of longitudinal data analysis, much less dynamic SEM, so what we offer in this book is a different variety of SEM than that typically displayed in the SEM journals (e.g., see the journal *Structural Equation Modeling*).

And, although we do add much here about reporting indices of fit (e.g., chi-square, root mean square error of approximation), we do so for the dual purposes of clarity and communication, and we also think very little of the typical search for the "best-fitting model." We think that this kind of search can be of benefit to a single publication effort, but it holds little promise for evaluating the replicability or invariance of effects over multiple experiments. Additionally, we view the consideration of a measurement model to be a fundamental aspect of experimental design, and a poor measurement model can lead to failures that often go undetected. Our experiences suggest that any model is best built up from component parts, and this leads us to consider the separation of different aspects of any model into submodels for evaluation. Thus, instead of searching for the best-fitting model, we favor an SEM approach designed to carry many results from one analysis to the next. We carry out SEM analyses by fitting all models in pieces rather than starting with a simultaneous solution.

WHY USE LSEM?

Although SEM has both benefits and limitations, there are many good motivations to use contemporary SEM for longitudinal analyses. Among many benefits, we can see a required clarity of process definitions, ease of programming of complex ideas, clear tests of parameter equivalence, and generally appropriate analyses of otherwise inaccessible ideas. A few of these SEM techniques even lead to novel ideas for objective data analysis, including easy ways to deal with ordinal measurements. For example, perhaps SEM path diagrams provide a clearer way to think about longitudinal analyses. Unfortunately, among many LSEM limitations that remain are the need for large and representative samples of persons for reasonable estimation and also for a normal distribution of residuals (or uniquenesses) to create appropriate statistical tests. These are not easy requirements to present graphically. But, most importantly, we need to state what is to be examined about dynamic influences in advance of the data analysis, on an a priori basis. In this way any SEM requires the kind of clear and penetrating thinking seldom achieved in behavioral science. In common practice, we get stuck using the SEM models in ways that are far simpler than is possible if some ingenuity is applied.

The LSEM approach differs from earlier approaches to longitudinal data analysis. Several decades ago, longitudinal analyses were based largely on principles derived from linear growth models and formalized in terms of ANOVA techniques (e.g., Pothoff & Bock, 1975; Roy, 1964). These concepts were extended with the creation of randomized blocks and Latin squares (see Fisher, 1925; Winer, 1962) designed for plants and nonhuman animals. Of course, this can be much more complicated in human research. For these reasons, in research on human aging, we often separate cross-sectional "age differences" from longitudinal "age changes" (as in McArdle, 2009). Many recent analyses of developmental data analysis use information gathered from both cross-sectional and longitudinal selections in what are termed *panel studies* (Hsiao, 2005), but the questions seem much broader. Nevertheless, ANOVA-type analyses, based largely on plants and nonhuman animals, flourished in the behavioral sciences, and they still seem to do so today.

Some recent presentations on longitudinal data analysis are based on statistical procedures that combine these seemingly separate estimates of age differences and age changes (for references, see McArdle, 2009). One way to do this is to create an "expected trajectory over time," where the expected values are maximum likelihood estimates and formal tests of hypotheses are encouraged (e.g., Hsiao, 2003; Miyaziaki & Raudenbush, 2000; cf. McArdle & Bell, 2000). New computer programs for what are termed *latent curve* or *mixed-effects* modeling allow parameters to be estimated and are used in making predictions and inferences. This book, however, is based on our earlier work on LSEM. We need to have some ways to understand longitudinal data, and several theoretical statements have been formalized into "models" with useful statistical properties. These models allow us to consider alternative substantive ideas, to fit these alternatives to data, and hopefully to make an informed choice about which alternatives are most useful. Key failures of any kind of analysis come when a researcher reflexively applies methods without thinking about what they may mean and then by not recognizing when the model predictions fail to look like the data.

What we basically want is a longitudinal structural equation model (LSEM) that has a minimal number of estimated parameters and fits the observed data well. In the case of longitudinal data, it would also be useful if the model made predictions about future behaviors of individuals and groups. There is no doubt that this can be a demanding task for anyone, and we may not succeed. In fact, this entire SEM approach may fail, and we will simply conclude that it is not possible to do this.

This also means, in our view, the current SEM approach is far less revolutionary than the past work. SEM is simply a natural generalization of most prior work. However, we do think the new SEM techniques are not really much better than the prior ones (cf. Raykov & Marcoulides, 2006). In this sense, the classical techniques still form basic guideposts, and there are many worthwhile aspects of the older classical calculations. We will mainly use SEM because it can be used to make concepts clear and it is now very convenient.

One matter about which we want to be very clear at the outset is the distinct way we make inferences about causal influences when we use randomized assignment to groups versus when we have nonrandomized assignment to groups. The former is now becoming more popular as randomized clinical trial (RCT) research (see McArdle & Prindle, 2008), and this is reasonable because the RCT approach leads to exceedingly simple inferences: Fisher (1925) cleverly and definitively showed that when individuals were randomly assigned to conditions, the effect of the condition could be easily and unambiguously estimated from the mean differences. This is a clear-cut case of the statistical model of inference being forced to be correct by design (i.e., with large enough sample sizes, N, the error terms can be assumed to be uncorrelated with the predictors, so all resulting parameters are unbiased).

The same cannot be said of situations where the data have been collected without regard to the person selection: the persons are simply observed as they progress through time, so this data collection design is often termed observational data (Cochran & Cox, 1950). This basic distinction between randomized and observational data has separated many research traditions (see Cronbach, 1957). Unfortunately, this is almost always the case in longitudinal data collections where no randomized conditions are used at all, for either practical or ethical reasons, but dynamic effects that would be estimated from randomized conditions are still sought (see Shrout, 2011). Obviously, this self-selection of persons is a big barrier for good longitudinal research. But we agree with R. B. Cattell (1966c), who basically asserted that there exists a continuum of experiments when we have data and substantive questions for which we do not know the answer. He suggested, in these cases, that we mainly need to put a premium on good measurement and good data analysis. After all, we do think that astronomy is a science, which is chockfull of scientific experiments (as did Cattell, 1966d).

The LSEM approaches presented here are obviously not all that can be done using the more generic SEM concepts. We treat these as starting points for other ideas, and we leave many advanced issues for a subsequent presentation (see McArdle & Hamagami, 2014a). But the SEMs we do present are highlighted here because they are a reasonable match to the goals of longitudinal data analysis proposed by Baltes and Nesselroade (1979). With this in mind, we will try not forget the most important lessons of the past. At the same time, we do need to invent new ways to collect optimal sets of data required for powerful tests of hypotheses about development. These are among the most important challenges for contemporary and future longitudinal research, and our hope is that some of the SEM ideas presented here can be instrumental in reaching that goal.

PREVIEW OF THIS BOOK

This book consists of seven parts with five chapters each. Part I (Chapters 1–5) presents an in-depth discussion of the goals and other background information on longitudinal research, including SEM and research designs. Parts II through VI are the heart of the book and cover models for Baltes and Nesselroade's (1979) five objectives of longitudinal research.

Part II (Chapters 6–10) explains how to analyze information about the changes within a person. Baltes and Nesselroade (1979) used the term *intraindividual differences*, but we will speak of *within-person changes* (McArdle, 2009). Because we now think "change" is most easily and most appropriately indexed by the use of a simple change score, although others have questioned this logic, this approach is formalized in our first true model definition in Part II. The careful reader will notice we make some effort to show how this simple change approach to data analysis can be useful, both in calculation and interpretation, and we try to separate the controversial aspects from the noncontroversial aspects. This use of simple change score approach can be considered as our first suggestion about using longitudinal data analysis.

Part III (Chapters 11–15) explains how to analyze differences between groups of persons in the way people change. This terminology differs from that of Baltes and Nesselroade's (1979) original text, which used the phrase "intraindividual differences in interindividual differences." Now there are at least two reasons for altering the prior terminology: (1) The term *within persons* is traditional ANOVA terminology to designate the separation of scores from the same person. (2) This is in contrast to components that are between persons. By separating these terms into within and between persons, the term *differences* can then be reserved for models that imply the separation of different individuals. In general, we will focus on concepts about "the differences in the changes," and we hope this generally confusing set of verbal terms will still make sense. The representation of group differences in change processes can be accomplished using the variety of methods that the literature now refers to as latent curve, mixed-effects, multilevel, or even multiple group modeling. We will try to clarify the options in these alternatives. This separation of terms can be considered our second suggestion about using longitudinal data analysis.

Part IV (Chapters 16–20) explains how to analyze multiple outcome variables. This is not typically done by others in this area, and single variables seem like enough. In this book, we have used this objective as a vehicle for discussing the important concepts of multivariate measurement. The use of common factors as a way to summarize information can be considered the third requirement of our longitudinal data analysis approach, and this was certainly our intention. Practical problems in the fitting of any statistical model with longitudinal data begin with scaling and metrics. These ideas can be examined at the item level by forming a scoring system for any desired construct using classical concepts from item response theory (see Lord, 1952; McArdle, Grimm, Hamagami, Bowles, & Meredith, 2009; McArdle & Hamagami, 2003). Other key scaling issues include the exact timing of observations (e.g., Boker & McArdle, 1995; Gollob & Reichardt, 1987) because, as is often the case, any variable transformations can alter the statistical patterns. Optimal measurement collections are a major challenge for new empirical research and are worthy of much further discussion (McArdle, 2011d). Indeed, the multivariate perspective (see Cattell, 1966b, 1966d) when combined with SEM permits tests of hypotheses of common concepts we ordinarily take for granted. We will try to show how recent developments in SEM can lead to useful concepts, such as scale-free measurement and invariant common factors, and we are especially keen on what can be accomplished with models of MFIT. We will also try to show how this can helps us achieve the error-free changes we seek. This part emphasizes our commitment to the common factor model.

Part V (Chapters 21–25) explains how to analyze the causes of intraindividual changes. This part suggests that there are many alternative longitudinal models that can be fitted to different kinds of longitudinal data. It will surprise many readers, but only a selected set of these models take into account the specific ordering of responses. In these LSEMs, it will be important to recognize that models of individual differences among dynamic variables lead to hypotheses about individual trajectories over time. That is, the difference (or change model here) model leads to the trajectory expression in the same way the differential equation model leads to the integral expression (see Boker, 2001; Oud & Jansen, 2000). To make this tractable and practically useful, we present models of discrete timing and pose several alternative models about time-based dynamics at the individual level; then we illustrate how we can turn these into structural equation models. Any dynamic interpretation requires a focus on time-dependent parameters in the models rather than the time-independent correlation of the time-based scores, and this puts extra emphasis on the explicit definition of time and time lags (e.g., Gollob & Reichardt, 1987; McArdle & Woodcock, 1997). This part emphasizes our suggested commitment to time precedence and a dynamic approach.

Part VI (Chapters 26–30) explains how to analyze the causes of interindividual differences in intraindividual changes. This part considers the possibility that there are group differences in the prior dynamic models. Although this probably seems obvious, it is hardly ever examined, and we try to show how it could be done. Once again, the representation of group differences in change processes can be accomplished using the variety of methods the literature now referred to as latent curve, mixed-effects, multilevel, or multiple group modeling. But in these LSEMs it is also important to recognize that models of group differences among dynamic variables do not necessarily reflect dynamic processes for the group. The LSEM analyses presented here are limited because they make specific assumptions about latent changes in measured individuals and groups (as in McArdle & Prindle, 2008; Meredith & Tisak, 1990; Muthén & Curran, 1997). The current literature also seems to pursue a lot of exploratory data analysis models, including what are now referred to as *latent class mixture models* or even *SEM Trees*. Although these analyses can be a very useful at appropriate times, we will not discuss these models here (but see McArdle & Hamagami, 2014b). Thus, Part VI emphasizes our commitment to, and suggested use of, allowing group difference in dynamics.

Finally, Part VII (Chapters 31–25) integrates the previous chapters and elaborates on several of the book's main topics, including incomplete data designs, uses of individual time series, and meta-analysis problems but we do so without concrete examples. We also suggest the use of recent computer programs (see our forthcoming companion book, *Applications of Longitudinal Data Analysis Using Structural Equation Models*), but these are fairly standard applications now, so we focus on models where the computer code is publicly available (i.e., R). In our companion book we also will present code that we think is widely used (e.g., Mplus). This code will obviously change over the next few years, but we do not expect many alterations in the underlying ideas of either book.

All notations in this book are based on LSEM and are listed in Exhibit 1.

EXHIBIT 1
A Brief List of Abbreviations (Notation) Used in This Book

English letters

Letter	Description
b	Raw regression weight
c	Canonical score
D	Observed change score
e	Error or residual
E	Expectation operators of means and covariances together
f	Function value of fit index
F	Measurement factor score
$F[t]$	Measurement factor score at time t
$F1[t]$	Measurement factor score 1 at time t
$F2[t]$	Measurement factor score 2 at time t
(g)	Superscript to indicate group, g = 1 to G
j	Subscript to indicate specific measure
k	Subscript to indicate specific measure
L or L^2	Likelihood as a single index of model fit
m, M	Subscript to indicate measure or means vector observed
n, N	Number of observations: n in group; N in total sample
O	Observed means and covariances together
$P[*]$	Latent curve component score based on observed X[t] scores
$Q[*]$	Latent curve component score based on observed Y[t] scores
t, T	t = specific time; T = total times (occasions of measurement)
$u[t]$	Unique score at a specific time
$X[t]$	Observed score at time t of variable X (usually defining independent variables)
$Y[t]$	Observed score at time t of variable Y (usually defining dependent variables)
$z[t]$	Unobserved residual score

Symbol	English translation	Description
		Greek letters
A	Alpha	RAM matrix of all one-headed arrows (directed parameters)
α	alpha	Intercept term in the change equation
β	beta	Regression weight in the change equation
γ(j,i)	gamma	Coupling parameter; e.g., indicates coupling from score i[t] to change in score j[t + 1]
δ	delta (lower case)	Change score
Δ	delta (upper case)	Change score operator
ε	epsilon	Error or residual score
ζ²	zeta squared	Disturbance variance ($\zeta(m)^2$) or covariance $\zeta(i,j)$
η[t]²	eta squared	Reliability coefficient [at time t]
F	Filter	RAM filter matrix of units and zeros (to determine observed from all variables)
ι	iota	Intercept
λ, Λ	lambda, Lambda	Factor loading (or matrix)
μ	mu	Expected mean vector of observed variables
ν	nu	Mean of latent variable (or common factor)
ρ	rho	Correlation
σ	sigma	Standard deviation (σ) or variance (σ²)
Σ	Sigma	Summation operator or expected covariances
Σ_τ	Sigma	Expected covariance matrix of observed variables
τ	tau	Threshold estimate for categorical variable
φ	phi	Factor variance $\phi(k)^2$ or covariance $\phi(i,j)$
χ²	chi-square	The distribution of sums of squares used as an index of model fit under a normality assumption
ψ²	psi squared	Unique variance ($\psi(m)^2$) or covariance $\psi(i,j)$
ω[t]	omega	Basis coefficient in the latent model [at time t]
Ω	omega	RAM matrix of all the two-headed arrows (slings; undirected parameters)
O	Omicron	Prediction from moving average in time series

(*continues*)

EXHIBIT 1
A Brief List of Abbreviations (Notation) Used in This Book (Continued)

Symbol	Description	Example
		Other symbols
[.##]	Standardized estimate	[.38] - Standardized value of 0.38
[integer]	Subscript to indicate time (occasion of measurement)	V[2] - Verbal composite score at Time 2
{ }	Notation to indicate component	Q{0} - Score on level factor
*	Deviation score	d*
italic	Latent variable	F
UPPER CASE	Observed variable	Y
		Abbreviations for types of models
ANOVA	Analysis of variance	MANOVA — Multivariate analysis of variance
BLCS	Bivariate latent change score	MFIT — Multiple factorial invariance over time
CUFFS	Curve of factor scores	
DCS	Dual change score	MLCS — Multivariate latent change score
DIOG	Dynamic invariance over groups	QMS — Quasi-Markov simplex
		RAM (RAMpath) — Reticular action model
FOCUS	Factor of curve scores	RANOVA — Repeated measures analysis of variance
LCM	Latent curve model	
LCS	Latent change score	TCS — Triple change score
		TSR — Time-series regression
		TVC — Time-varying covariate

I
FOUNDATIONS

1

BACKGROUND AND GOALS OF LONGITUDINAL RESEARCH

A party of order or stability, and a party of progress or reform, are both necessary elements of a healthy state of political life.
—J. S. Mill

One thing about which fish know exactly nothing is water, since they have no anti-environment which would enable them to perceive the element they live in.
—Marshall McLuhan, *War and Peace in the Global Village*, 1964

This first quote above, by John Stuart Mill, was supplied by our knowledgeable colleague, Steven M. Boker, for a chapter written some years ago (Nesselroade & Boker, 1994). This is an apt opening quote for this chapter for a couple of reasons. First, it simultaneously recognizes the concept of stability and the concept of change. Both concepts are important; indeed, they are both critical. Without a concept of stability there would be no need for a concept of change and vice versa. One way the reader may have sometimes heard the second quote phrased as "We do not know who discovered water, but we are pretty sure it wasn't a fish." This is intended to mean that humans are "tuned" to appreciate variation rather than sameness. The former registers on our sensory mechanisms and stimulates us, whereas in its extreme form we soon become unaware of the latter. Silence is a wonderful adjunct to sound sleep but, judging from the plethora of audio devices in operation, it is a major bane of today's teenager's waking existence.

---

http://dx.doi.org/10.1037/14440-002
Longitudinal Data Analysis Using Structural Equation Models, by J. J. McArdle and J. R. Nesselroade
Copyright © 2014 by the American Psychological Association. All rights reserved.

More to the point, if there were nothing but constancy, there would be no need to develop and use longitudinal methods. An emphasis on variability, coupled with an acceptance of the fact that the individual is the primary unit of analysis in studying behavior virtually "forces" the researcher to seek some form of longitudinal (repeated measurements) information. How else can one access variability in behavior at the individual level (Nesselroade & Molenaar, 2010a, 2010b, 2010c)?

The second, and more important sense in which the Mill quote is apt, is that it establishes a dynamic between the two concepts: political "reality" resides in neither party; rather it is in the relationships the two parties bear to each other. Much of the longitudinal modeling about which you will be reading may tend to emphasize either change or stability over the other, mainly because that is where our science is historically. But there will be chapters explicitly devoted to presenting how one models the more dynamic features of longitudinal data. This is an important distinction and the direction in which we believe the future of behavioral science modeling lies.

DEFINITION OF LONGITUDINAL RESEARCH

"The study of phenomena in their time-related constancy and change is the aim of longitudinal methodology." Baltes and Nesselroade (1979) advanced this sentiment in a book that one of us edited and for which a historical overview chapter was written. This definition and the five rationales for longitudinal research that Baltes and Nesselroade developed help to define the scope of longitudinal research and provide key underpinnings for the remainder of this book. We repeat these principles now because we think they are important.

When Baltes and Nesselroade (1979) set out to delimit what longitudinal research was about, they encountered considerable uncertainty in the literature. A couple of examples of some of the comments regarding longitudinal research they found were "There is no hard and fast definition of what constitutes a longitudinal study" (Hindley, 1972, p. 23) and "Longitudinal is a general term describing a variety of methods" (Zazzo, 1967, p. 131). These expressions of ambiguity were in some ways discouraging but, on the other hand, it was challenging to try to provide a more systematic and positive working definition. They produced the following:

> Longitudinal methodology involves repeated, time-ordered observation of an individual or individuals with the goal of identifying processes and causes of intraindividual change and of interindividual patterns of intraindividual change [in behavioral development]. (Baltes & Nesselroade, 1979, p. 7)

As we move toward developing and presenting the five rationales for longitudinal research, this definition fleshes out the essential nature of longitudinal research that we eventually settled on a little bit more. In the present book, we consider quite a wide range of longitudinal research possibilities—from some single subject designs to panel designs of various kinds. We have found the above definition a helpful guide in trying to answer the question "Just what are the main arguments for why longitudinal research is important?"

For Baltes and Nesselroade, longitudinal research was closely tied to developmental questions, and we have "lifted" the following figures from something that Baltes wrote (see Figure 1 in Baltes & Nesselroade, 1979). We chose them because they illustrate well the theoretical ideas about what one might be observing longitudinally in the study of development.

There are several features of Figures 1.1 and 1.2 that we want to call to your attention. The idea being expressed in Figure 1.1 is that, across a life span, for many different kinds of behavioral phenomena, there does appear to be considerable evidence for an increase in between-persons variability with age. At a very practical level, people at younger ages, on average, are a lot more like each other in many respects than they are at older ages. At the same time, there are some variables for which individuals' trajectories tend to go up with age, others for which they tend to go down, and some that are more complicated than that. But the point is, if one puts together a lot of the information that we now have that is descriptive about the ways people change over time, there is a wide variety of possibilities. Obviously,

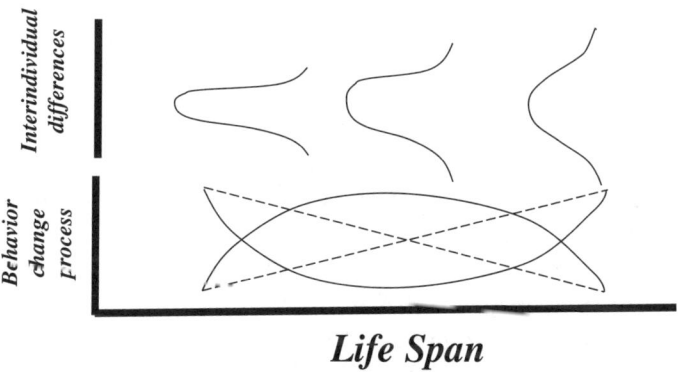

Figure 1.1. Selective examples of life-span developmental processes. Age-correlated increases in interindividual variability in the upper part. From *Longitudinal Research in the Study of Behavior and Development* (p. 16), by J. R. Nesselroade and P. B. Baltes, 1979, New York, NY: Academic Press. Copyright 1979 by Elsevier. Adapted with permission.

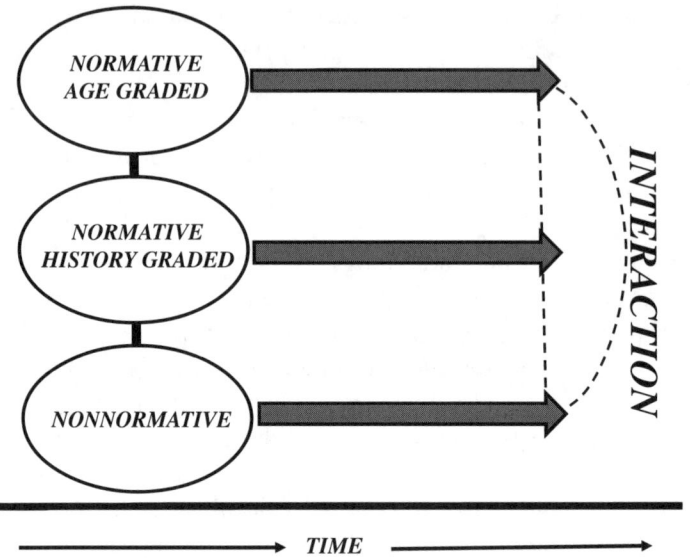

Figure 1.2. Illustration of three major influence systems on development: normative age graded, normative history graded, and nonnormative. From *Longitudinal Research in the Study of Behavior and Development* (p. 19), by J. R. Nesselroade and P. B. Baltes, 1979, New York, NY: Academic Press. Copyright 1979 by Elsevier. Adapted with permission.

this variety of form and function places a tremendous burden on researchers to measure, to model, and to represent adequately such a rich variety of phenomena. Therefore, we need a lot of different tools to model and understand longitudinally what development or other kinds of processes across time involve.

Figure 1.2 reminds us of there are numerous, complex reasons why we change over time developmentally. Some of these reasons are orchestrated by our own selves, some by societal institutions, and still others are seemingly unorchestrated but still occur, and with lasting effects.

We now turn to the five main rationales for conducting longitudinal research that were presented by Baltes and Nesselroade (as listed earlier). These five rationales, we argue, are the primary reasons why one engages in longitudinal research. The structural equation modeling analyses are simply ways to carry out these analyses. The terminology used then is admittedly somewhat cumbersome now, but it is usefully descriptive and will be referred to often in the remainder of this book. Let us examine each of the five in turn in a slightly different way.

FIVE RATIONALES FOR CONDUCTING LONGITUDINAL RESEARCH

Direct Identification of Intraindividual Change

As noted earlier, there is one way to get at change (variation) at the individual level, and that is by measuring the same individual at least twice. It is an obvious point in some ways but, for various reasons, it was a good place to begin in developing these rationales for conducting longitudinal research. Intraindividual change occurs in many forms. For example, it may involve changes in level, amplitude, or frequency. Or, it may involve interbehavioral changes. For instance, physical abuse of others may be supplanted by verbal abuse as one ostensibly becomes more socialized.

Still other kinds of changes are found in the literature such as are designated by terms such as the differentiation hypothesis of cognitive development (Olsson & Bergman, 1977; Reinert, 1970). The theory holds that as organisms age, their cognitive structure becomes more differentiated. So, for instance, instead of being equally good or bad at all cognitive tasks, an individual may be a standout in verbal behavior and only mediocre in mathematics. Pertinent to the focus of this book, even though differentiation is an individual development concept, it is typically studied via cross-sectional designs and group data analyses.

As the reader is likely to be aware, this may or may not be defensible. The relative merits of substituting cross-sectional research for longitudinal efforts have long been argued. In order for cross-sectional comparisons to be good approximations to what one can study longitudinally, either the cross-sectional data must meet the condition that different-aged subjects must come from the same parent population at birth, it must be possible to match subjects across age levels, or different-aged subjects must have experienced identical life histories or else these conditions must be shown to be irrelevant. In most cases, it seems to us that longitudinal designs will not be supplanted easily.

Direct Identification of Interindividual Differences in Intraindividual Change

The basic idea here is relatively simple. If one is studying interindividual differences in the traditional sense, one is, by definition, making comparisons across individuals. But when one's focus is on comparing patterns of intraindividual change rather than single scores or levels across individuals, longitudinal information is necessary for defining those change patterns among which differences are sought.

EXHIBIT 1.1
The Expression of a Generalized Learning Curve

Consider the mathematical expression that follows (data from Tucker, 1958, 1966):

(1) $$Y[t]_n = \omega[1]Q[1]_n + \omega[2]Q[2]_n + \cdots + \omega[k]Q[k]_n + e[1]_n$$

This decomposition leads to a way of talking about what is happening on the left-hand side (the actual performance Y[t]) in terms of general patterns of change, that is, intraindividual change patterns—the unknown group weights (ω[k]), but also the individual level information in the latent variables (Q[k]).

Let us briefly illustrate something that is going to come up again and again in the material to follow. Consider the mathematical expression in Exhibit 1.1. This expression was taken from one of the earliest articles now recognized as a progenitor of latent curve modeling, Tucker (1966). In this article, Tucker presented what he called generalized learning curve analysis. We point this out for the following reason: This is a way of identifying simultaneously both the general group structure and the individual differences structure within one framework. This was originally presented by Tucker (1958, 1966) as a principal component analysis of the raw data, rather than of the deviation scores or covariances, because he wanted to preserve the trial-to-trial differences (gains) in performance. What you will see later under the topic of latent curve modeling, including latent growth curve modeling and latent change score modeling, offers a variety of refinements on this general approach.

Analysis of Interrelations in Behavioral Change

This third rationale pays homage to the multivariate perspective on behavior (Baltes & Nesselroade, 1973; Cattell, 1966; Nesselroade & Ford, 1987), which recognizes that determinants have multiple consequences and consequences have multiple determinants. A meaningful way to try to study these manifold relationships within a multivariate perspective involves the formation of various kinds of linear combinations according to some criterion by which the defining weights are chosen. Canonical correlation, linear discriminant function analysis, and other multivariate analysis techniques rest on this basic principle. Factor analysis, including its use in creating measurement models, involves simultaneously examining the interrelations of multiple factors and multiple variables. Clearly, if one wants to study the interrelations in behavioral change—how behaviors change together over time—one needs longitudinal information.

Analysis of Causes (Determinants) of Intraindividual Changes

Here the essential idea is that almost any notions we have of causal connections involve some kind of time-dependent observations. At a minimum, one must observe the entity/entities at least twice in time, preferably more, to draw inferences regarding determinants of change. We realize this is a statement about observational data, and we will not make any special claims to understanding causality (but see Part V of this book). In fact, this concept holds at both the individual level but also in examining what causes people to differ in the way they are. Models for this goal are relatively novel, and they are termed *dynamic*. Because this is a main reason for this book, this goal will not be pursued now.

Analysis of Causes (Determinants) of Interindividual Differences in Intraindividual Change

All individuals do not change in the same way. Why? The search for explanations for why there are interindividual differences in intraindividual change patterns also requires us to attend to causes or determinants. Here, too, in order to make inferences regarding causal relations one needs at a minimum two different observations. Whether the same repeated measurement occasions used to define the intraindividual changes can also be the basis for inferences regarding causation is a matter of the research design used and the nature of the resulting data. These matters also will be examined in detail in the remainder of this book.

LINKAGE BETWEEN THEORY AND METHODOLOGY

The conduct of rigorous longitudinal research is a demanding enterprise, and keeping the five rationales in mind provides a way for us to approach more systematically the discussion of the finer points of longitudinal methods and modeling. The problems and pitfalls to be avoided in designing longitudinal work are discussed in detail in many different sources (see, e.g., Baltes, Reese, & Nesselroade, 1977; and Laursen, Little, & Card, 2012).

A useful criticism that Campbell and Stanley (1963) pointed out in their original article about simple longitudinal studies is that they are *pre-experimental*. That is taken by many as a pejorative term, especially if one is trained in classical experimentation. Because the fact is that for much of the work behavioral scientists do, participants cannot be randomly assigned to treatment conditions. This is certainly true in traditional longitudinal designs, so one has to be aware at least of the various threats to the validity of such designs. In relation to the Campbell and Stanley (1963) arguments, however, the complicating problem is that for process and developmental questions, often what is seen as a threat to internal validity in simple longitudinal designs is also the very phenomenon of interest to us (i.e., maturation). This issue will be discussed at various points in this book.

In one of his last articles, the late Joachim F. Wohlwill (1991) identified his view of the relationships between method and theory in developmental research as partial isomorphism. Here is his basic point and we think it is a crucial one: Wohlwill observed that many of us were taught to believe that theory should drive method and people who knew only methods ought to have some sense of chagrin for their lack of appreciation of theory. Wohlwill then pointed out that what really happens is that sometimes theory is out ahead, demanding new methods, but sometimes method is out ahead, pushing theory. He described it very much in the same dynamic terms as suggested in the quote by John Stuart Mill at the beginning of this chapter. The reader may want to keep this in mind as so much of this book is devoted to methods.

As valuable as they are, methods do not get us anywhere by themselves. Progress in a discipline eventually comes through the interplay of forces rather than because one dominates the other. Even if you have no interest in theory, it is still incumbent on you, the reader, to "push" those who do care about theory just as it is the theoretician's obligation to demand newer, more appropriate methods be made available for testing theoretical propositions. One way of stimulating this dialog is to provide methods—along with the suggestion that there is something interesting to do with the data. Here is something that has the potential of showing this kind of relationships or detailing that kind of relationships. As scientists, we think that is the duty of all of us, not just those trying to write better theories, to try to keep this interchange moving ahead.

Finally, before jumping into the deeper water, we want to say just a bit about the concept of causal lag for the simple reason that, during the course of making his or her way through this book, the reader is going to repeatedly encounter the concept. There will be discussions at various points about such notions as intervals. For example, how often should one measure over a given span of time? If one wants to "tie down" a process of some sort, are there optimal points of measurement? If one is really trying to connect putative causes with putative effects, how do you do that, in terms of the sequence of observations of your measurement? The reader will see that these represent a complicated set of issues, but there are at least some aspects that can be dealt with in a pretty straightforward way.

The idea of lag now becomes very important in the longitudinal research and modeling context, perhaps much more so than we have realized in the past. It is complicated in part by the fact that when one considers multivariate systems and latent variables, the possibility arises that various pertinent variables do not have the same optimal spacing or optimal lag in regard to their dynamics and their relationships to other variables. We cannot promise you that you will reach the end of the book with the answers to these questions, but we can promise you that you will be more sensitive to them.

Let us try to summarize a few key ideas at the beginning. Our task in this chapter was partly to get readers up to speed. First of all, the longitudinal ideal is emphasizing a temporal perspective in research questions involving one's data. That is one of the underlying "golden threads" running through the entire book. Longitudinal data most directly provide the information we need for making sure that a temporal perspective can be implemented in thinking about the phenomena of interest to us. Process and systematic change—These ideas do not stand a chance of being explored effectively, we will argue, without adopting a temporal perspective that includes some kind of longitudinal orientation. Longitudinal data provide exceptional opportunities to study and model interesting phenomena. They offer different opportunities than do other kinds of data, and at the same time, they present different kinds of challenges. Our focus for the book is on exploring many of these opportunities provided by longitudinal data—and their associated challenges.

2

BASICS OF STRUCTURAL EQUATION MODELING

One purpose of this chapter is to present an accessible overview of recent research on what are termed *structural equation models* (SEM; following McArdle & Kadlec, 2013). We will define our own notation (see Chapter 4), which we hope will be useful for longitudinal research at a level intended for graduate students in the behavioral sciences, some possibly taking a SEM class currently. Thus, if the reader knows a lot about SEM already, this chapter (and the next two) can be skipped without much loss. While formal training in algebra or calculus is helpful, it seems it is not really required to apply such methods. But we think it is important to provide more details on the reason we use SEM as a generic approach to deal with the current longitudinal problems. We are not the first to come to this conclusion, and the concepts illustrated earlier by Goldberger (1973) seem reasonable now because they focused on primitive elements in SEM.

---

http://dx.doi.org/10.1037/14440-003
Longitudinal Data Analysis Using Structural Equation Models, by J. J. McArdle and J. R. Nesselroade
Copyright © 2014 by the American Psychological Association. All rights reserved.

The popular term *SEM* can be used to represent many different kinds of multivariable techniques. Statistical analyses as seemingly diverse as multivariate analysis of variance, exploratory and confirmatory factor analysis, manifest and latent variable path analysis, multidimensional scaling, time-series analysis, behavioral genetic analyses, and so on, all can be organized under the same SEM heading. This generalization is useful because in all such cases, we consider SEM a reflection of three key ideas in modern statistical data analysis (in reverse order): (a) The term *model* is used to represent a theory in terms of propositions about the relationships between variables; (b) the term *equation* means that the relationships between variables are expressed in a formal fashion using the explicit rules of algebra; and (c) the term *structural* is used to suggest that these algebraic equations form a specific restrictive pattern about real data consistent with the model, and hence the theory.

This implies that in some way SEM is useful for testing theories with real data. It is typical to presume that one or more of the observed variables (X) acts as an input to another set of variables (Y). For simplicity, it is typical to eliminate the intercept (β_0) and calculate a single linear regression coefficient (β_1) to describe an X → Y relationship. This simple expression is presented in Exhibit 2.1 and is drawn as a path diagram in Figure 2.1.

EXHIBIT 2.1
Defining a Linear Regression

We typically write the simple linear regression expression (from many other researchers; Fox, 1997):

(1a) $$Y_n = \beta_0 + \beta_1 X_n + e_n$$

where the Greek letters are used to represent population parameters to be estimated; the intercept (β_0) and slope (β_1) and the residual scores (*e*) are not directly observed (so they are written in italics). We also typically assume

(1b) $$E\{X\,X'\} = \sigma_x^2,\ E\{e\,e'\} = \sigma_e^2,\ \text{and}\ E\{Xe'\} = 0.$$

where β_0 is the *intercept* term—the predicted score of Y when X = 0, where β_1 is the *slope* term—the expected change in the predicted score of Y for a one-unit change in X, and the *e* term is the *residual error*. Here the *E* is a symbol used for the expected values.

We can note that the expectation symbol *E* is used as a shorthand for the usual summation symbol Σ taken over a finite sample size *N*. Given this, the combined expression above (Equation 1) is considered the structural equation model for the observed scores.

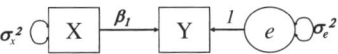

Figure 2.1. A simple linear regression model with no intercept. Estimates are typically calculated as $\beta_1 = \sigma_{yx}\sigma_{xx}^{-1}$, $\sigma_e^2 = \sigma_y^2 - (\beta_1 \sigma_{xx} \beta_1')$.

DRAWING THE COMPLETE PATH DIAGRAM

It may now be obvious that all of the parameters in the first equation we use here are not represented in the standard path diagram of Figure 2.1. That is, there are new parameters for the variance terms but none for the means or intercepts (see Exhibit 2.1). This is true because the original path diagrams of Sewell Wright (1921) were intended only for covariants of variables (i.e., with mean zero, variance one), and the standard drawing, as it turns out, is going to be a big limitation in the analysis of longitudinal data.

In this specific case, path diagrams of longitudinal data were originally used with time series-based autoregression models, and these models seemed to reflect actions or predictions moving forward in time (e.g., to be described in Chapter 6). At that time, it was very unclear if any movement was actually taking place in the data or if anyone was actually doing any traveling at all (no, no one is really traveling). Subsequent work showed how these diagrams can be effectively used in the context of growth and change with latent variables (e.g., Chapter 6, this volume; McArdle, 1986, 2009; McArdle & Anderson, 1990; McArdle & Epstein, 1987; McArdle & Woodcock, 1997). The utility of simple path diagrams as tools becomes clearer as we deal with more complex examples.

To align the path diagram as closely as possible with the necessary algebra, we have developed a slightly different graphic notation termed *RAMpath* (McArdle & Boker, 1990; Exhibit 2.1; and Chapter 4, this volume) that we initially hoped would be easy to convey. But this can become decidedly more complicated because researchers have already well-developed ideas about how such models should be presented.

We now ask all readers to consider the simplicity of what we propose. In all cases, we first separate variables into only two classes: All observed variables are drawn as squares, and all unobserved variables are drawn as circles. These rules imply that the residual terms need a circle around them, and this is exactly what is done in Figure 2.1. Next, we include two-headed arrows to represent the variance terms that are missing (and these represent the main diagonal of one of the model matrices). This is also done in Figure 2.1. The means and intercepts will be added later (see Figure 2.4). But we will use this RAMpath analysis notation (of Chapter 4) throughout.

STANDARD ESTIMATION OF LINEAR MULTIPLE REGRESSION

To illustrate the points just made in more detail, let us assume we have measured several persons (N) on two variables (Y and X) and, for some reason or the other, we want to describe their functional relationship as X → Y. This expression is considered the "structural equation model for the observed scores." For simplicity, we can eliminate the intercept (β_0) and calculate a single linear regression coefficient (β_1) to describe this X → Y relationship. By assuming that the residuals are independent of the predictors, we know (from calculus) that the best estimate of this coefficient has a specific numerical value ($\beta_1 = s_{YX} s_{XX}^{-1}$) that is considered as the best estimate (i.e., best linear unbiased estimate). The reasons for this solution are presented in Exhibit 2.1.

There is one verbal alteration worthy of further consideration. Because we are not dealing with the same people over time in standard regression, we now consistently alter the term *change* when applied to the slopes to be a *difference* in the slopes. That is, the unknown weights in a regression are the expected differences in the outcome due to a one-unit difference in the predictors. This seems like a trivial alteration now, but the reason we advocate it will become clear in later longitudinal contexts.

GOLDBERGER'S BIASES IN REGRESSION

We can use these well-known results to calculate the regression coefficient, and we use this to define the other statistical features of the regression model (Fox, 1997) and follow other aspects of the initial SEM treatment by Goldberger (1973). By assuming that the residuals are independent ($E[X,e] = 0$) of the predictors, we know (from calculus) that the best estimate of this coefficient can be found by multiplying the observed covariance of Y and X (σ_{YX}) by the inverse (or division) of the variance of the X variables (σ_{XX}^{-1}). This is exactly the same as dividing out the variances and covariance of the predictor variables (X) from the relationships between the criterions (Y) and the predictors (X). This is a closed form estimation based on using the standard or "normal" equations (see Exhibit 2.3). This simple calculation probably cannot be explained enough. This basically means the regression weight is the effect of X on Y "as if" there were no variation in X. Of course, there is variation in X, but we want to know what it would be like if some of this were not there. For this reason, this is termed a *statistical control* to distinguish it from an *experimental control*. In the typical situation, there is variation in X (or among multiple Xs) so we view this as a *statistical adjustment* to the

EXHIBIT 2.2
Steps in Estimating a Linear Regression

In the standard regression model (of Exhibit 2.1, Equation 1; following Goldberger, 1973; Fox, 1997, among many others), we have a typical two-part model where

(1) $\qquad Y_n = \beta_0 1_n + \beta_x X_n + e_n$, with $E\{e\ e'\} = \sigma e^2$

Given that the error terms are identical and independently distributed (IID), we can assume they do not count any further. This allows us to calculate some of the expected variances and covariances, and this will lead directly to the best linear unbiased estimate (BLUE) of the regression term as

(2a) $\qquad (Y_n - \mu_y) = \beta_1(X_n - \mu_x)$ or

(2b) $\qquad (Y_n - \mu_y)(X_n - \mu_x)' = \beta_1(X_n - \mu_x)(X_n - \mu_x)'$ so

(3a) $\qquad (Y_n - \mu_y)(X_n - \mu_x)'\left[(X_n - \mu_x)(X_n - \mu_x)'\right]^{-1} = \beta_1$ or

(3b) $\qquad \beta_1 = E[YX']\,E[XX']^{-1}$ or

(3c) $\qquad \beta_1 = \sigma_{yx}\sigma_{xx}^{-1}$

That is, the BLUE regression term is simply the observed covariance of Y and X divided by the observed variance of the Xs.

If these assumptions are correct, we also have the BLUE intercept defined as

(4a) $\qquad \mu_y = \beta_0\mu_1 + \beta_1\mu_x + \mu_e = \beta_0 + \beta_1\mu_x$ so

(4b) $\qquad \beta_0 = \mu_y - \beta_1\mu_x \quad \text{or} \quad \mu_y - (\sigma_{yx}\sigma_{xx}^{-1})\mu_x$

Since we know the observed variance and have the BLUE of the predicted variance, we can estimate the error variance as

(5a) $\qquad \sigma_Y^2 = \beta_1^2\sigma_X^2 + \sigma_e^2$ so

(5b) $\qquad \sigma_e^2 = \sigma_Y^2 - [\beta_1^2\sigma_{XX}^2]$

This means we can write

(6a) $\qquad Y_n = \beta_1 X_n$ or

(6b) $\qquad (Y_n X_n') = \beta_1(X_n X_n')$, or

(continues)

EXHIBIT 2.2
Steps in Estimating a Linear Regression (Continued)

(6c) $$(Y_n X_{n'})[(X_n X_{n'})]^{-1} = \beta_1 \text{ or}$$

(6d) $$\beta_1 = E[YX']E[XX']^{-1} \text{ or}$$

(6e) $$\beta_1 = \sigma_{YX}\, \sigma_{XX}^{-1}.$$

We note that the inverse operator is used so that X may include many predictor variables. It is now possible to simply write the key structural expectation of the XY covariance as

(6f) $$\sigma_{YX} = \beta_1 \sigma_{XX}.$$

In any sample we have the estimated population values, so

(6g) $$s_{YX} = \beta_1 s_{XX}, \text{ and}$$

(6h) $$\beta_1 = s_{YX}\, s_{XX}^{-1}.$$

In simple regression, we can see exactly why the slope formula in Equation 6e (or 6h) works: The structural form expressed in Equation 6e when divided by the value of σ_{XX} (or with the X variance removed) also leaves us with the new regression coefficients (6f, β_1) written in terms of observations (s_{YX}, s_{XX}).

EXHIBIT 2.3
Issues in Estimating a Case 1 Regression Model With Bias

Let us assume that the following is the correct model (data from Goldberger, 1973):

(1) $$Y_n = \beta_{YX} X_n + \beta_{YZ} Z_n + e_n$$

This new theoretical model implies that when we calculate the linear regression based on the expectation of the observables only (i.e., as $\beta_1 = \sigma_{YX}\, \sigma_{XX}^{-1}$), we will end up calculating the incorrect value because

(2a) $$\sigma_{YX} = \beta_{yx}\sigma_{xx} + \beta_{yz}\sigma_{zx} \text{ so}$$

(2b) $$\beta_1 = (\beta_{yx}\sigma_{xx} + \beta_{yz}\sigma_{zx})\sigma_{xx}^{-1} \text{ or}$$

(2c) $$\beta_1 = (\beta_{yx}\sigma_{xx}\sigma_{xx}^{-1}) + (\beta_{yz}\sigma_{zx}\sigma_{xx}^{-1}) \text{ or}$$

(2d) $$\beta_1 = (\beta_{yx}) + [\beta_{yz}(\sigma_{zx}/\sigma_x^2)]$$

under the assumption that the new residual terms (e) are identical and independently distributed (IID). Here it is obvious that the estimated β_1 does not equal the population β_{yx} unless the second term ($[\beta_{yz}(\sigma_{zx}/\sigma_x^2)]$) is zero. This can be true if either the new variable has no effect on the outcome ($\beta_{yz} = 0$) or the new variable is uncorrelated with the other predictor ($\sigma_{zx} = 0$).

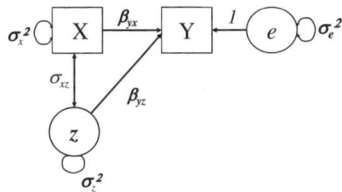

Figure 2.2. The population model is a regression but with a latent predictor. If $\beta = \sigma_{yx} \sigma_{xx}^{-1}$ then $\beta_1 = \beta_{yx} + [\beta_{yz} \cdot \sigma_{zx}/\sigma_x^2]$, estimate = correct + bias.

observed data, and most times this will be substituted for the term *statistical control*. Of course, this regression is one of the simplest models we will discuss, and we hope that it will become clear that not all SEM calculations are so easy, but they all use this same basic logic.

The initial SEM treatment by Goldberger (1973) considered a first alternative to the original model—the potential biases due to a missing predictor in a SEM. Let us assume the correct structural model is drawn here as Figure 2.2. That is, the correct model for the outcome is multiply determined, but here we assume we do not really know this fact. This is the same as a linear regression for the observed data (Y and X are measured), except we have included an unobserved variable (z, drawn as a circle) that has an effect on the outcome (Y, with β_{yz}), and it is allowed to be correlated with the other measured predictor (X, with σ_{yx}).

The key feature now is that this model has a structure of observed covariances that is slightly different from the standard linear regression model of Figure 2.1. That is, when we obtain the typical regression estimate (β_1), we will have an incorrect or biased estimate of the true regression coefficient (β_{yx}) to the degree there is any nonzero effect of z on Y (β_{yz}) together with any nonzero correlation of z and Y (σ_{zx}). The missing z variable can be any other variable, of which there are probably many, so this kind of bias is likely to occur with real data.

This kind of *missing predictor variable* bias can create changes of sign and is not strictly bounded. It is clear that one solution to this dilemma is just to measure z and include it in the model together with X in a multiple regression. This is certainly a good idea, but good luck finding these variables! This is the reason why regression coefficients are altered when additional variables are included in the overall prediction model. This also means that when we find that the parameter remains the same no matter what other variable is included, we assert parameter invariance and think that we have found the structural parameter. The suggested solution, as usual, is to fit the correct model (Figure 2.3) directly to the observed data

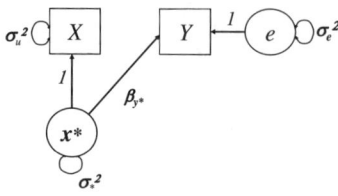

Figure 2.3. The correct model is a regression with an unreliable predictor. If $\beta = \sigma_{yx}\sigma_{xx}^{-1}$ then $\beta = \beta_{y*}[\sigma_*^2/\sigma_x^2]$.

using SEM techniques. In practical terms, this solution requires both the available data (measurements on X, Y, and Z) in addition to the regression tools.

As another alternative, Goldberger considered the biases due to the unreliability of a predictor in a structural equation model. Let us assume the correct model is one where the input variable that we measure (X) is decomposable into a true score ($x*$ in Goldberger's notation) that produces the outcome (Y) and also an unreliable part (u) that does not. This relationship and can be expressed as the structural model in Exhibit 2.4, and it could be drawn as well (but not here; see McArdle & Kadlec, 2013).

This implies that the effect of having unreliable predictors pushes the true value of the regression coefficient downward by the size of the unreliability ($1 - [\sigma_*^2/\sigma_x^2]$). It is useful to know that the estimated coefficient will always be smaller than the true coefficient, and this bias will not alter the sign of the coefficient, but this is actually not a desirable result. The suggested solution is to fit the correct model to the data, even though this requires more empirical data.

As a next case, let us consider the biases due to the unreliability of an outcome in a structural equation model. Let us assume the correct model is one where the outcome variable that we measure (Y) is decomposable into a true score ($y*$) that is produced by X and an unreliable part (u) that is not. This is also not drawn here although it could be (McArdle & Kadlec, 2013). This turns out to be an important separation later but, indeed, unreliability of measurements is clearly one of the big issues in SEM. It follows that data with unreliable outcomes does not alter the true value of the regression coefficient. But the size of the unreliability will affect the error variance (which will increase by the size of the unreliability $\sigma_e^2 + \sigma_u^2$). Thus, the standardized coefficient and the explained variance will be lowered, and this is also not a desirable result. The suggested solution is to fit the correct model directly to the data, again requiring more data and more programming.

EXHIBIT 2.4
Issues in Estimating a Case 2 Regression Model With Bias

Let us assume the correct model is one where the input variable that we measure (X) is decomposable into a true score (x^*) that produces the outcome (Y), and also an unreliable part (u) that does not (data from Goldberger, 1973). This is drawn in Figure 2.4 and can be expressed as a structural model:

(1a) $$Y_n = \beta_{y*} x_n^* + e_n$$

where

(1b) $$X_n = x_n^* + u_n$$

If this is assumed to be the correct model, but we calculate the value using standard regression formulas (i.e., $\beta_1 = \sigma_{yx} \sigma_{xx}^{-1}$), we would be incorrect. That is, using standard regression we find

(2) $$\sigma_{yx} = \beta_{y*} \sigma_*^2 \text{ and } \sigma_{xx} = \sigma_*^2 + \sigma_u^2$$

$$\text{so } \beta_1 = (\beta_{y*} \sigma_*^2)/(\sigma_*^2 + \sigma_u^2)$$

$$\text{or } \beta_1 = \beta_{y*} [\sigma_*^2/(\sigma_*^2 + \sigma_u^2)]$$

$$\text{or } \beta_1 = \beta_{y*} [\sigma_*^2/\sigma_x^2]$$

Here, the estimated regression (β_1) does not equal the true regression (β_{y*}) unless the true score variance (σ_*^2) is equal to the total variance (σ_x^2). This can happen when there is no measurement error ($\sigma_u^2 = 0$).

The biases due to the unreliability of both predictors and outcomes are an important part of SEM, so let us consider something not fully explored by Goldberger (1973). If this kind of a model is assumed to be the correct model but we calculate the standard regression formulas, we find the effect of having unreliable predictors and outcomes means that both the true value of the regression coefficient will be biased downward by the size of the unreliability ($1 - [\sigma_*^2/\sigma_x^2]$) and the standardized coefficient and explained variance will be lowered. The suggested solution is to fit the correct model directly to the data, but this is not always possible. That is, to create a unique solution, we can use multiple indicators of the true variables (y^*, x^*).

The final case considered by Goldberger was the most complex, as he considered the biases due to the possible feedback of effects in a SEM. Here, he assumes the correct model can be represented by a set of recursive

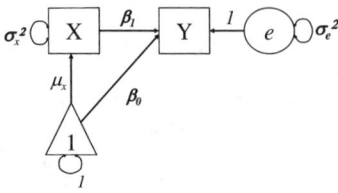

Figure 2.4. A simple regression model with an intercept. $\beta_1 = \sigma_{yx}\sigma_{xx}^{-1}$, $\beta_0 = \mu_y - (\sigma_{yx}\sigma_{xx}^{-1})\mu_x$, $\sigma_e^2 = \sigma_y^2 - (\beta_1\sigma_{xx}\beta_1)$.

linear equations where the variables that we measure (X and Y) both presumably have an effect on one another. If a feedback loop is assumed to be the correct model, but we calculate the value using standard regression formulas, we find the effect of having a true feedback loop among the predictors means the true value of the regression coefficient will be biased in complex ways. Thus, this general problem is not actually solved when we do a regression analysis and assume we try to calculate the true effect. The suggested solution is to fit the correct model directly to the data, but we now know feedback does not have a unique solution with just two measured variables (O. D. Duncan, Haller, & Portes, 1968; Hauser, Tsai, & Sewell, 1983).

Although we have not highlighted this issue yet, the same general approach can be used to examine the intercept term (β_0) in regression, and this can be illustrated in the path diagram of Figure 2.4 (and Exhibit 2.5). To estimate the intercept parameter at the same time as the usual regression slope, we can include a constant term in the model as a measured predictor,

---

EXHIBIT 2.5
Issues in Estimating a Case 6 Regression Model

Let us assume the standard regression is correct. Once we estimate the regression slope (β_1), this leads to the estimates of other unknown parameters (adapted following Goldberger, 1973), such as

(1) $$\sigma_e^2 = \sigma_y^2 - (\beta_1 \sigma_{xx} \beta_1')$$

and

(2) $$\beta_0 = \sigma_y - \beta_1 \sigma_x,$$

so the same bias will exists in the intercept as in the regression coefficient.

---

labeled 1, and include it in the diagram as a triangle to indicate its special feature: it is constant. It follows that we need to include this constant into the model of expectations, but this is easily done by augmenting the covariance matrix with a mean vector or by estimating the model from the average cross-products matrices (after Rao, 1965). This approach, using means and covariances together, forms the basis of many of the more complex models that will be discussed here (McArdle, 1986, 1994, 2007a, 2007b, 2009).

But, and this is important, and the inclusion of means alone does not alter the prior biases raised by Goldberger (1973). Thus, and maybe not so surprisingly, the intercept is biased as well as the slope. One solution to these problems is to represent the model in terms of the true parameters, and this often requires more measurements to be included.

3

SOME TECHNICAL DETAILS ON STRUCTURAL EQUATION MODELING

In this chapter, *structural equation modeling* (SEM) is broadly defined as a set of techniques that can solve part of the problems posed by Goldberger (1973). The increasing use of this SEM approach to data analysis is described. We will first show how SEM techniques are used increasingly in the behavioral and social sciences. Second, some technical features of SEM are presented to illustrate its key benefits. Some classical issues are described that highlight issues SEM researchers usually find to be important, and the big appeal of SEM comes when it offers some hope to deal with these issues. Third, we consider the inclusion of common factors as latent variables in path models that can be incorporated into SEM, and we claim that the inclusion of common factors is what really makes SEM different from other statistical approaches. Fourth, we describe how SEM calculation works, and this gives rise to various indices of goodness-of-fit. In the final section, we answer specific questions about SEM practices and include a discussion of issues for future SEM uses.

http://dx.doi.org/10.1037/14440-004
Longitudinal Data Analysis Using Structural Equation Models, by J. J. McArdle and J. R. Nesselroade
Copyright © 2014 by the American Psychological Association. All rights reserved.

AVAILABLE SEM COMPUTER PROGRAMS

SEM is a reflection of the computer revolution and there are several current computer programs we could use. We list a few of the most available SEM programs in Exhibit 3.1. As we can see here, there are now many SEM computer programs, each with its own style and approach, but there are a few common features of these computer programs that are worthy of further discussion. For example, and it certainly does not seem to be clear, but all SEM programs essentially provide the same answers to the same problems.

There are many important variations about how a SEM can be compactly expressed to the particular program, and there are many variations on how the parameter estimates and goodness-of-fit indices should be chosen as best, and there are a few variations of what output is needed and what is not needed. But, for the most part, all of the available SEM computer programs do the same calculation with the same model and the same data. Actually, this is really what we want them to do, and they are not very different from the way we think about programs for the t test or the analysis of variance (ANOVA). But for some reason SEM programming seems different. What we know is that any SEM program can be used to carry out the analyses promoted here.

This means we can choose the classical programs: the linear structural relations model (LISREL); the many other free programs such as lavaan, Rprogram, Mx (Neale, Boker, Xie, and Maes, 1999), or OpenMx; the programs with the most structural options such as Mplus (Muthén & Muthén, 2005); or the programs that are part of a statistical system that we already know, such

EXHIBIT 3.1
Some Available Computer Programs for Longitudinal Structural Equation Modeling (circa 2011)

LISREL: Original and most well-known program and notation, by Jöreskog and Sörbom (1979)
Mx: The first general and freely available program, by Neale, Boker, Xie, and Maes (1999)
Mplus: The most expensive but most general program, by Muthén and Muthén (2005)
Other structural equation models that are part of standard statistical packages:
  AMOS (SPSS), CALIS (SAS), EQS (BMDP), GLIM (STATA), and RAMONA (SYSTAT)
Freely circulated R programs: SEM, lavaan, and Open-Mx
Other programs are not marketed as SEM, but can give equivalent results: SAS MIXED, lme, NLMIXED, nlme, MLwin, WinBUGS, and LatentGOLD.

Note: If the structural equation model is identical and the data are identical, all programs listed above should give exactly the *same results for the same model*. Of course, programs differ in some ways that may be important to a user (e.g., data entry, model syntax, model options).

as SAS-CALIS and SPSS-AMOS (J.L. Arbuckle & Wotke, 2004). There are even other reasons why we would choose one program over the other. For example, LISREL, CALIS, and Mx assume a parameter is zero until it is listed. Or we may like it that Mx and AMOS create their own kinds of path diagrams. Unfortunately, these are not exactly the kind used here. These types of issues will not be considered further here because they are changing daily. That is, we will allow any SEM program to do the required calculations for our model with our data because we are fairly sure there is only one answer.

Any SEM representation of the model scores is used to create expectations about the basic summary statistics—means and covariances—of the observed data. This is important because these expectations can be compared with the data observations to form a test of goodness-of-fit; that is, expected means (μ) compared with observed means (**m**) and expected covariances (Σ) compared with observed covariances (**S**). The simple convention that can be seen here is that the expected statistics are based on some model estimates so these are written as Greek letters, whereas the observed statistics are written using the more familiar Arabic symbols. This highlights one of the big limitations of SEM—we only compare means and covariances, so any other potential model versus data differences (i.e., skewness or kurtosis) are assumed not to be critical. Although this should be seen as a severe limitation, this is also true of many other popular data analysis techniques, such as multiple regression and ANOVA, principal components and factor analysis, and canonical correlation and canonical regression. We can now view SEM as simply a natural generalization of this work.

EXAMINING SEM THEORIES

Given these statistical limits, many scientific theories can be represented as testable models. Most importantly, SEM gives researchers a way to represent theories as models using latent variables that are not directly measured. This is easy to do and is a major benefit of SEM because many key constructs in the behavioral sciences simply cannot be directly observed and measured. Of course, hypothesis testing is not always rigorous and is not always possible because our theories can quickly require more elaborations than are part of the available data. We are consoled only because we will know that our model, and hence our theory, is far beyond evaluation by our available data.

If we create a structural equation model on an a priori basis, we can then determine how well the expected model fits the observed data by calculating a variety of a priori defined goodness-of-fit indices. Unfortunately, any truly confirmatory analysis requires a great deal of prior information. For example, to really test any model, we would need to have point hypotheses about all the group (i.e., fixed) parameters (i.e., the one-headed arrows). This is not the typical case, and we often settle for testing the pattern or structural hypotheses of the parameters (i.e., is a specific correlation equal to the product of two parameters?). Under these less rigid but reasonable conditions, if we further assume all residuals are normally distributed, we can compare the model-based likelihood-ratio with a chi-square distribution and determine the probability of observing such an event—this model for these data—at random. Now all we need is to have some well-developed criteria for the decision process in testing. That is, to use this procedure directly, we need to decide what we are willing to accept as a random misfit (e.g., probability of misfit $\geq .05$) or to we may want to highlight the nonrandom misfits (probability of misfit $< .05$).

This statistical approach, of course, is virtually identical to calculating a probability of misfit value in an ANOVA or regression context, although a typical SEM often has many more parameters, so it is not surprising that all the assumptions and inference problems are similar as well. That is, we need to deal with the difference between "statistical significance" and "substantive importance" (McArdle, 1998). Although some people think SEM has alleviated most statistical problems, it certainly has not. Poor-quality data will not miraculously provide robust results, just as cause-and-effect relationships cannot easily be formed from observational data. What SEM has done, and in a classical way, is to allow the representation of complex theories as complex models and the basic expressions of models in terms of equations, so they can easily be used to examine ideas about the structure of a data set. What SEM has not done up to this point is resolve the decision-making process about what is random and what is not. But this is actually a hidden blessing because, presumably, this job is still up to the investigator. We think this is appropriate because this is where all good scientific judgments are made. Incidentally, we should recognize that not all SEMs are based on a priori theory, and basically all we now encourage SEM researchers to try to do is to tell us what they actually did (McArdle, 2011d).

When we consider SEM in this fashion, we find SEM is all around us, and it has been here for a very long time. The broad ideas of SEM, as both concept and tool, probably started with the common factor analysis model of Spearman (1904; Horn & McArdle, 1980, 1992, 2007), and this led to extensions such as the path analysis concepts of Sewell Wright (1918, 1934) and the variance components ideas of R. A. Fisher (1919, 1925; Li, 1975). These SEM ideas seemed to be dormant in academic research for about 50 years, and only recently were revived by a combination of the efforts of quantitatively minded sociologists (O. D. Duncan, 1975; Goldberger & Duncan, 1973; Hauser & Goldberger, 1971) and psychologists (e.g., Werts & Linn, 1970). The early SEM seemed to be largely based on its conceptual and theoretical advantages rather than on the creation of analytic tools. But it also seems fair to say that these SEM concepts have enjoyed a revival in the last few decades, partially based on the generation of new SEM tools (see Exhibit 3.1).

CONFIRMATORY FACTOR ANALYSIS AND THE POPULAR LISREL MOVEMENT

The current forms of SEM really took on a life of their own when these ideas were placed into the context of what was termed a confirmatory factor analysis with latent variables (Jöreskog, 1970b; McDonald, 1985b). This approach was probably best represented in the general framework termed LISREL (Jöreskog, 1973a, 1973b; Jöreskog & Sörbom, 1979; Wiley, 1973). In the LISREL approach the researchers were interested in creating a general approach to data analysis, but one that was far more general than the ANOVA-based general linear model (Bock, 1975; Muller & Stewart, 2006). LISREL advocates seemed to suggest that we should always consider an analytic framework that included hypotheses about "unobserved" variables based on both means and covariances (McArdle & Hamagami, 1989; Figure 3.1 and Exhibit 3.2).

In simplest terms, the LISREL concept suggested that the econometric concept of multivariable regression could be merged with the psychometric

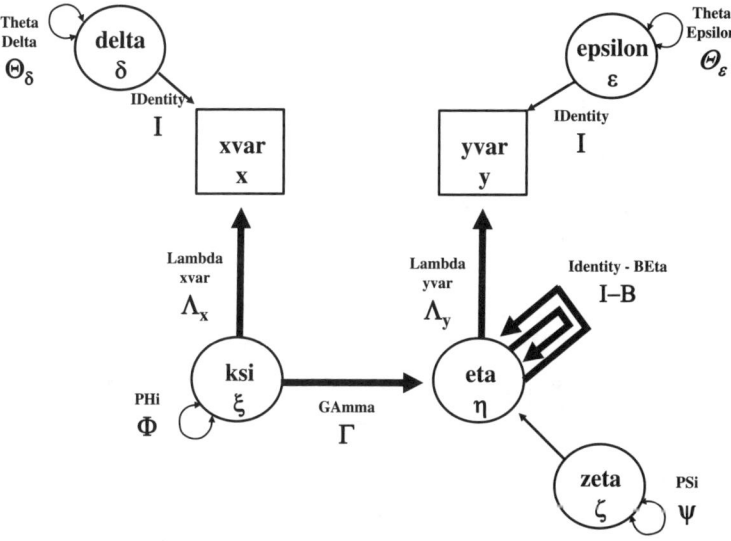

Figure 3.1. The linear structural relations model concept as a path diagram. From "A review of Hayduk's 'Structural Equation Modeling With LISREL: Essentials and Advances,'" by J. J. McArdle and F. Hamagami, 1989, *Applied Psychological Measurement, 13* (1), p. 110. Copyright 1989 by SAGE Publications. Reprinted with permission.

EXHIBIT 3.2
Specifying a General Structural Equation Model Using LISREL Notation

Part I: Defining LISREL variables:
X = observed "independent" variables (also termed X-side variables),
Y = observed "dependent" variables (also termed Y-side variables),
ξ = unobserved common factors of X-side variables,
η = unobserved common factors of Y-side variables,
ε = unobserved unique factors of X-side variables,
δ = unobserved unique factors of Y-side variables,
ζ = unobserved disturbance factors of Y-side variables.

Part II: Defining LISREL parameter matrices:
Λ_x = X-side matrix of factor loadings,
ϕ^2 = X-side matrix of common factor covariances,
Θ_ε = X-side matrix of unique covariances,
Λ_y = Y-side matrix of factor loadings,
Ψ^2 = Y-side matrix of common factor covariances or disturbances,
Θ_δ = Y-side matrix of unique covariances,
Γ = regression matrix where the Y-side common factors are a function of the X-side common factors, and
B = regression matrix among the Y-side common factors.

---

concepts of common factors (e.g., Wiley, 1973). That is, in the LISREL approach we may have many X variables (i.e., independent, inputs, predictors, exogenous, or right-hand side) and many Y variables (i.e., dependent, outputs, endogenous, or left-hand side), and as usual, the X variables can affect the Y variables with specific coefficients. However, instead of simply calculating multiple regression coefficients for entire sets of predictors and outcomes, the LISREL model allowed researchers to pose hypotheses about the relationships between unobserved common factors with common factor scores; specifically, unobserved common factors of X-side variables could be thought of as based on common factor scores (termed η, although not estimated), and Y-side variables could also have common factor scores (termed ξ, although not estimated). The Y-side factors could then be regressed on the X-side factors, possibly with additional constraints such as some regression coefficients being zero. These equations for the scores could be represented in eight different matrices (as defined in Figure 3.1 and Exhibit 3.2). This fairly complex LISREL concept allowed researchers to place their theories in terms of unobserved constructs and still provide tests of goodness-of-fit using observables. This was the great breakthrough of the LISREL logic. The use of Greek letters, for both parameter matrices and, somewhat surprisingly, for unestimated latent variables, initially proved to be a barrier toward general understanding. But this barrier was soon forgotten as the

LISREL momentum built. As it turns out, the Greek lettering and the eight matrix concept was not really a great breakthrough of the LISREL logic.

It seems to us that the LISREL concept (see Figure 3.1, Exhibit 3.2) would not have gained such momentum if it were not associated with a working computer program—but this SEM concept was matched with an elegant SEM tool! In fact, the flexible computer programming of the first versions of LISREL (see Exhibit 3.1; Jöreskog & Sörbom, 1979; McDonald, 1985b) allowed the unknown elements in the eight matrices of parameters to be (a) fixed at known values, (b) free to be estimated, or (c) estimated but equal to a different parameter. This new computer-programming tool was a true innovation, came directly from the work of Jöreskog (1969; see Lawley & Maxwell, 1971), and matched other substantive areas where many new ideas for data analysis were emerging and being used (e.g., Nesselroade & Baltes, 1984).

The SEM-LISREL approach allowed researchers both to think more clearly about what they were saying and, at the same time, fit models to data in ways that could not be done previously. This is viewed as a combination of concepts and tools. SEM-LISREL could be considered useful for its conceptual advances or because it added important tools (computer calculations) for behavioral scientists. For these kinds of reasons, it has been difficult to summarize all the advantages of SEM in one way (e.g., see Stapleton & Leite, 2005).

One thing that is clear is that the notion of confirmatory or a priori hypothesis-driven modeling represented powerful conceptual thinking. At the time LISREL was initiated, there was much work on the generic testing of hypotheses about specific multivariate patterns of group means, including repeated measures (see Bock, 1975; O'Brien & Kaiser, 1985). However, these statistical tests of mean differences were carried out within a severely limited framework for hypotheses about covariances (see Rao, 1965). Thus, the SEM-LISREL program was a tool that permitted analyses well beyond the standard framework of estimation and tests of mean differences in the ANOVA-based general linear model.

Due to the broad generality of the SEM-LISREL idea, and in spite of all the unfamiliar and occasionally odd choices of Greek terminology (i.e., Was there any real benefit in labeling the unobserved, unestimated, common and unique factors with Greek letters?), the SEM-LISREL concept and the related computer program became very popular because SEM-LISREL allowed seemingly unlimited ways to estimate and test hypotheses about both means and covariances. For these reasons, SEM-LISREL was studied and used in great depth (see Jöreskog & Sörbom, 1979; see also Horn & McArdle, 1980; Meredith, 1993; Meredith & Horn, 2001) and is still popular today.

CREATING SEM EXPECTATIONS AND ESTIMATES

The way we create model expectations is not exactly clear to many researchers, but it is a fundamental technique. What we generally do is place values (or symbols) as elements of the model matrices and then use matrix algebra to generate the expected values. This is required and is done automatically by all of the computer programs, but not enough emphasis is placed on this calculation. Let us revisit an earlier thought—a SEM representation of the scores is used to create model expectations about the means (μ, for means **m**) and covariances (Σ, for covariances **S**) of the observed data. This is most important because it is these expectations that can be compared with the data observations to form a test of fit. The formal basis of LISREL notation was designed to produce a set of expected values (symbolized as E) from the eight-matrix notation (see Exhibit 3.2). In many ways, this was exactly like creating sums of squares for ANOVA.

Now that we have set up the SEM for linear regression we can examine several ways to obtain reasonable values for the parameters. In general, what we are trying to do is to find a set of parameters for the estimated relationships hypothesized that come as close to our observed relationships as possible. That is, we want to find those values that minimize some prespecified function of the observables, and we know this function could take on many different forms. So this definition of our goal can be accomplished in many ways, including by the direct result of calculus. Assuming we have created a functional goal, we need an iterative approach to model estimation, and we now use the procedures outlined in Exhibit 3.3 to estimate model parameters.

There are a series of important proofs that show how this iterative approach (based on Exhibits 3.2 and 3.3) can be used to estimate the best possible values for all model parameters (see Browne, 1984). Of course, this all presumes we have the correct model for the data, and if there is anything we are certain about, it is that we do not know the correct model for our data! This is true of multiple regression models for sure, but it is also true of many other forms of longitudinal modeling where we must make a great deal of assumptions. Of most importance now is that this iterative approach can also be used when we do not know what values are optimal by straightforward algebra or calculus. This is often the case when we have more complicated structural equation models, involving latent variables, recursive relationships, or both. We will deal with some of these more complex models in a later section.

There are many expressions that we can use to formalize the previous statements. These can be copied from any SEM textbook, and three particularly good ones are Loehlin (1987, 2004), McDonald (1985b), and, more recently, Kline (2005). Here you will find in-depth discussions of the "likelihood of the data" compared with the "likelihood of a model." At this

EXHIBIT 3.3
Estimation of Parameters for Longitudinal Structural
Equation Modeling (circa 2011)

1. Create a set of starting values: Make an educated guess for every parameter value. These can all be unities (ones) or zeros, or they can be created in different ways based on previous findings from the substantive area of interest. If the analyst does not do this, the computer program can simply provide them (and see McDonald & Hartmann, 1992).
2. Calculate the function at this iteration: Take the values for every unknown model parameter and put these values into the positions of the matrix. We can see we will create some differences between these guesses and the observations, and we can create a total function value for the overall model at this point.
3. Use some technique to find better values: Here there are several options to obtain an improved guess at the parameter values. If we are relying on standard structural equation modeling, we would calculate the next best values by fundamental calculus: We estimate the first- and second-order derivatives of the parameters with respect to this function (and this can be complicated), and we then use the ratio of first and second derivatives as the most desired change in each parameter. Of course, if we use a Bayesian-type estimator (i.e., WinBUGS; Lee, 2007; Ntzoufras, 2009; Zhang, Hamagami, Wang, Grimm, & Nesselroade, 2007), we might instead just simulate new scores for every latent variable and see how well these new values fit the data.
4. Put the new values into the calculation: After we obtain a new set of changes in the parameters, we can create new parameter values. We then plug these back into the matrix expressions, and we do the basic calculations (Steps 2 and 3) all over again.
5. Terminate this process when we cannot do any better: We terminate the iterative sequence when we do not get a big enough change from one iteration to the next. We term this convergence, but we usually do not know if we can improve the model fit further.

point, we could just copy some of the key parts for further discussion (as in Cooley & Lohnes, 1971), but what we actually plan to do here is far simpler. Mainly what we will do is to report the results of some of these ideas. To make this more transparent, we will typically separate what are termed group or fixed effects (typically in matrix of one-headed arrows, **A**) from individual or random effects (typically in matrix of two-headed arrows, Ω). As we will show, this fundamental distinction between individuals and groups turns out to especially useful in understanding and carrying out longitudinal research.

STATISTICAL INDICATORS IN SEM

There are many statistical features that have been considered in prior research on SEM. A typical structural equation model has fewer parameters than observed covariances, so any model can be said to have degrees of freedom (*df*). Each *df* represents one way the model can be incorrect about the expectations. That is, the *df* represent ways the model does not need to look like the observed data, and the more of these *df*, the stronger the a priori nature of the model. This is not very controversial, but it could be. For example, it is clear that in some models a specific parameter is more critical than another parameter. However, in the standard statistical literature, all parameters have the same formal basis. This is likely to change in the future.

Any overall goodness-of-fit index typically requires some idea of the desired relation of the data observations (**m**, **S**) and the model expectations (μ, Σ). Some function of the distance between observations and expectations is chosen, and we can calculate individual "misfits." It would be good if we could have some idea in advance of data analysis about which models fit and which do not. Various alternatives have been discussed by, among many others, Horn and McArdle (1980). To summarize these issues now, we will simply state that if we want the model to reflect a good fit to the data, we want the expectations to be close to the observations and hence, small misfits. Of course, the term *close* can mean many things to many different people, so we need to define this in further detail. Variations on this theme are presented in Exhibit 3.4.

In simple regression, we often attempt to minimize the squared distance between the observations and the expectations: the least squares function (i.e., $\Sigma[O - E)^2]$). But there are other reasonable alternatives to consider. For example, we may want to find the value that minimizes the squared distance of the observations and the expectations divided by the squared observations (i.e., $\Sigma[O - E)^2/O^2]$). This is one expression of the principle of generalized least squares (GLS). Alternatively, we may want to find the values that minimize the squared distance of the observations and the expectations divided by the squared expectations (i.e., $\Sigma[O - E)^2/E^2]$). This is one simplified expression of maximum likelihood estimates (MLE), but it is somewhat surprising that many researchers seem to use this MLE approach even with relatively small samples.

In contemporary SEM analysis, we think that a great deal of emphasis, probably too much emphasis (see Kaiser, 1976), is placed on statistical indices of overall model fit. Surely the model is not very good when it does not fit the data at hand. Although there are printed statements about the "probability of perfect fit," these are typically based on the comparison of random deviates and a priori intentions. Because it is really hard to judge either, this implies there really should be no rigid rules for this kind of comparison. However, publications and reviewers often have something different to say, and they may require the traditional levels of significance (e.g., $\alpha < .05$ or $\alpha < .01$). But since we are usually concerned that any probability index is asking for

EXHIBIT 3.4
Statistical Indicators in Structural Equation Modeling

When we define a model on an a priori basis, the "probability of perfect fit" can be obtained by assuming the misfits are all normally distributed (Browne, 1984). Searching for the generalized least squares estimator or maximum likelihood estimates, we obtain the misfit based on the means and covariances that are available, written as

(1) $$f = fun\{(\mathbf{m} - \boldsymbol{\mu}) + (\mathbf{S} - \boldsymbol{\Sigma})\}$$

where the specific function (*fun*) is not fully defined yet (Horn & McArdle, 1980). However, if we do define this function using multivariate normal theory (Cooley & Lohnes, 1974), then comparing the difference between the obtained likelihood with a chi-square distribution of random misfits can be accomplished by simply writing

(2a) $$\chi \sim L^2 = f * (N - 1)$$

with

(2b) $$df = \{m(m+1)/2 + m\} - p.$$

where m indicates the number of measured variables and p indicates the number of freely estimated parameters. If the obtained misfits do not behave like random misfits and the chi-square is relatively high for the associated degrees of freedom (df), we conclude the model does not fit the data. Thus, in the typical way, the chi-square itself is an index of distance of the best-fitting version of the theory to the observed data given the number of observations (N).

One index that compares model misfit to model complexity is the root mean square error of approximation (or ε_a; Steiger, 1990; Browne & Cudeck, 1993), which can be defined for any structural equation model as

(3) $$\varepsilon_a = \left(L^2 - df\right)^{1/2} / \left[df(N-1)\right]^{1/2}.$$

and interpreted as an index of average misfit per df per person.

A slightly different approach to creating an index for average sums of squares and cross-products is used by many others. This starts by creating a misfit index where we define a baseline model misfit according to the df misfit for a specific sample of individuals (N) as

(4a) $$M_0 = f/df_0$$

and any alternative model with more parameters, usually based on changes, for the same data as

(4b) $$M_m = f/df_m$$

so we can define a simple proportional index of reduced misfit identical to that of Tucker and Lewis (1973) as

(4c) $$\rho_m = (M_0 - M_m)/(M_0 - 1/[N-1])$$

and using this, we can simply calculate how much any specific model fits compared with its own null baseline.

As can be seen in both types of calculations, the key ingredients are the model likelihood (L_m^2), the misfit function (f), the model df (df_m), and the sample size used (N). All other indices of misfit are based on these unique numbers so they should be reported.

too many unwarranted assumptions, we may choose to estimate other indices of fit.

In every statistical analysis (e.g., regression), there is a trade-off between model accuracy (e.g., fit) and model parsimony (e.g., numbers of parameters estimated). Fit indices based on penalties are now popular, including Aikaike's An Information Criterion (AIC) and Schwarz's Bayesian Information Criterion (BIC). One such index even has a confidence boundary, so we can even evaluate the probability of close fit using the root mean square error of approximation (RMSEA or ε_a; e.g., Browne & Cudeck, 1993; Steiger, 1990). One set of author(s) suggested that we ensure that this index is less than a specified value (e.g., $\varepsilon_a < .05$), but this may not be needed. Any such cutoff criterion just needs to be greater than zero and be considered in comparison to the other reasonable models available. Since this is likely to be a different choice for each investigator, this index serves more of a heuristic value than a statistical one. In addition, we often do not define the model on an a priori basis, because we have used some key aspect of the data to help us choose a model, and so we often say we are "modeling." If so, we probably need to be careful to simply report our exact modeling approach, and we should not try to generate a probability statement at all (see McArdle, 2011d). Perhaps this is the final goal, as stated earlier: "From this point of view the statistical problem is not one of testing a given hypothesis but rather one of fitting models with different numbers of parameters and of deciding when to stop fitting" (Jöreskog, 1969, p. 201).

So what we suggest should be done in each LSEM analysis is to make sure each model is properly defined and can be written in terms of a L^2 with a specific number of df. This should be included both for clarity and communication. A wide variety of contemporary fit indices can and should be calculated from these basic misfit indices, and some researchers may prefer one or the other of these (for a full elaboration, among many others, see Burnham & Anderson, 1998, or Claeskens & Hjort, 2008). We can primarily illustrate this contemporary approach with our own calculation of the RMSEA (e.g., ε_a; Browne & Cudeck, 1993). A variety of other models can be suggested by theory or practice, and these will be fit to the same data as alternatives. If the models are "nested," then the parameters that are deleted or the parameters that are added can be evaluated for their contribution to the change in fit (comparing it to a χ^2 distribution). The "best" overall model for any set of data might not be sought out, but the scatter plot of model misfits L^2 versus df should yield a set of models that are "very good," a different set of models that are "average," and a different set of models that are "not good" (as in McArdle & Nesselroade, 1994). This leads to three sets of models fitted to the same data, and depending on our program of research, we would then highlight these sets.

It is also useful to point out that these statistical issues are not new. Very early on, some researchers have noticed some problems with using statistical logic. For example, Tucker and Lewis (1973) suggested the following:

> With the further developments of high speed digital computers and of effective computer programs by Jöreskog [1967] maximum likelihood factor analysis has become quite feasible for application. Experience with maximum likelihood factor analysis has been developing with these applications. This experience indicates a dilemma in the application of the likelihood ratio statistic to decisions concerning the factor analyses. . . . The problem with the use of the likelihood ratio statistic, or any other similar statistic, involves the form of the decision procedure. The statistical hypothesis is that the factor analytic model with a specified number of common factors applies strictly for a population of objects. Rejection of this hypothesis most surely will occur for a very large sample of objects at any usual level of significance. This rejects the scientific hypothesis. A reversal as to role of the statistical hypothesis and alternative hypothesis has occurred from the common use of decision procedures in scientific investigations for which the scientific hypothesis is the alternative hypothesis and is to be accepted when the statistical hypothesis has been rejected. (Tucker & Lewis, 1973, p. 2)

These authors further suggested some simple fit indices, such as the calculation of a model-based reliability coefficient where they examined the amount of fit obtained in the off-diagonal elements of the model expected matrix (their F_m) divided by the number of degrees of freedom in the model (df_m). They basically suggested that an overall estimate of fit for any model (ρ_m) could be obtained by substitution of observed values of these statistics:

> The resulting reliability coefficient may be interpreted as indicating how well a factor model with m common factors represents the covariances among the attributes for a population of objects. Lack of fit would indicate that the relations among the attributes are more complex than can be represented by m common factors. (Tucker & Lewis, 1973, p. 3)

These basic concepts can be useful here for several reasons. First, we know that misfit reduction is the essential ingredient in all model comparisons, and the use of division for essential comparisons (in ρ_m) seems very simple, and it is. Second, we do not want to apply too much statistical inference to these ideas (i.e., we do not deal with confidence intervals) mainly because we do not want to rely on the normality of residuals assumption. But, we can still focus on the generic issue of asking how much our alternative models, as much as we may like them, actually add goodness-of-fit to some initial baseline model (we may use ρ_m).

The specific estimate of any model parameter has some important features that follow the functional form (as in Horn & McArdle, 1980). For example, if we estimate some models using the ordinary least squares (OLS) function, sometimes termed the unweighted least squares we can say we have best linear unbiased estimates or BLUE (see Fox, 1997). If we estimate with a more complex function, such as generalized least squares (GLS) or maximum likelihood estimation (MLE), then we can say we have GLS or MLE. Under any weighting scheme, the standard error of the parameter can also be calculated and used to create a confidence boundary for the parameter (t = est/se[est], where a z is often used to symbolize this t relatively large samples), and this ratio is thought to be useful in model interpretation. In many cases, researchers ignore parameters that are not more than 2 standard errors away from zero, but they often do not say why they do this. Of course, this is a rather crude evaluation of the individual virtue of a parameter in a model, assuming it is uncorrelated with other parameters, and this strategy, which is probably based on the use of the inherently arbitrary $\alpha < 0.05$ criterion (i.e., that is, $t > 1.96$ and this is fairly close to $t > 2$). To avoid further problems here, what we will do here is round off values of the confidence boundary values unless they are less than two.

A NOTE ON STATISTICAL TESTING

One of the best things about SEM is that it carries with it all the solutions to problems of statistical inference that we came to appreciate in testing with the t test, ANOVA, and regression. The worst aspect of SEM is that many of the basic problems in statistical reasoning have come along too, and these have not yet been resolved.

For example, the meaning of a single parameter (p) in a model with multiple parameters does not seem to be fully understood. In most cases, this is an attempt to isolate the effect of input variables X on outcome variables Y as if all other effects were held constant (often termed controlled). Statistical controls are obviously different from experimental controls in the number of assumptions that need to be made.

Next comes the saliency of a single parameter. In most statistical model this is usually estimated by taking the ratio of the parameter estimate to its own standard error (i.e., the second derivative ratio). This is entirely reasonable, except, as in any multiple regression, we must also assume the error term that is associated with this parameter is normally distributed. This may or may not be the case. This assumption seems to be compounded when we take this ratio and make a decision about whether it is zero or not. This is often done by using a cutoff of the arbitrary value of two as mentioned earlier. Since the model parameters may be correlated, and this is not taken into account in the usual z-ratio, the better way to do this would be to force the parameter to zero and examine the loss of fit of the new model to the overall data. So we will do this.

This brings us to what seem to be the biggest set of assumptions: the single model fit index. In all cases here, we give the L^2 for a particular model fit to a particular set of data with associated df. This seems reasonable, and as it gets larger, we are further away from fitting and creating an adequate model. But we note that for this L^2 to follow a chi-square distribution (χ^2) with the associated df and obtain a probability for the model given the data, the residuals from the model fit are collectively required to be normally distributed. Since, in most case, these assumptions are probably not true, we cannot usually use this a priori probability.

These statistical issues in statistical equation models are really no different from what we would find with other more standard data analysis models (i.e., the t test, ANOVA, regression), so we live with the uncertainty. One of the basic problems with all the models we will present here is the standard assumptions that we must make. To the degree that these assumptions are wrong, so is the rest of the analysis. For example, we typically assume linearity, additivity, normality of residuals, and homogeneity of replicates. Of course, we do not know of any better approach, but see Wilcox, 1998.

We are well aware that these are simple assumptions that may not work in reality. For the first two we have proposed various alternatives that can assist us in understanding our data. That is, the alternative models under the heading of latent changes can be seen as one way to deal with alternative assumptions about linearity and additivity. The normality of the IID residuals is a particularly complex phenomenon, but it seems needed for all basic model-fitting procedures. The observed data do not have to be multivariate normal, but the part we cannot see (the misfits) need to have the exceedingly simply structure of uncorrelated normal deviates. Because we do not think that we can assume it in many cases, we have not used the statisticians' lamplight: the probability of the null case. Indeed, we can see the L^2 as an indicator on its own, and we do not really need to make a decision in a single case. Again, we do not now know of any better approach.

NOTES ON STATISTICAL POWER

The classic definition of *statistical power* is the ability of a researcher to detect the direction of an effect using a null hypothesis test of significance (see Cohen, 1988). In the typical equation, power or $(1 - \beta)$ is the percentage of Type II errors that we are willing to accept on an a priori basis. Traditionally acceptable Type II error rates have fluctuated from area to area within psychology, with a minimum proposed level being 20% and a more desirable level being 80% (Cohen, 1988). Others still have indicated that higher levels of power are necessary for good psychological studies—in the 95% "equipotent" range (Muller & Benignus, 1992; O'Brien & Muller, 1993). This prior research outlines considerations when planning studies and calculating effective sample sizes given the phenomenon under investigation. There is not much in the prior literature on the nonnormal cases, although this is needed and probably is coming.

The issue of power in multivariate studies presents us with an opportunity to use available data more effectively (e.g., Schmitz, Cherny, & Fulker, 1998). One overarching theme that seems relevant here is that good research requires an analysis of power in advance of model analyses (Baguley, 2009; Hoenig & Heisey, 2001). Of course, the history of psychology is littered with ideas and theories that have been less than fruitful because of null results (Maxwell, 2004). By focusing on data that are available, our effect sizes, and thus our initial hypotheses, might be biased because of the amount of underpowered studies within psychology. In an attempt to reconcile this apparent dearth in the literature, Thomas (1997) proposed the use of a proactive approach to studies of power. It is important to note that the implementation of power is just as crucial as following proper ethical standards (i.e., McArdle, 2011d). That is, we do not want to carry out any underpowered study. It now seems common to calculate power using a reactive approach, but this actually does little to make a case for adequate sample sizes because power for such tests is based largely on the fitted model probability value (Hoenig & Heisey, 2001). Some have proposed research designs based on priors and updated posteriors once results are obtained, instead of recalculating and repackaging a result. Of course, if we have them, we can use priors to determine measures and models. But if the sample size is not explicitly calculated beforehand, then any power analysis after the fact is not fully informative because we cannot do anything except report the result.

Needless to say, we would like to have the ability to find effects that are really there, so power considerations are very practical. Another practical advantage of premeditated planning of research is that we are likely to work more efficiently. The cost-effectiveness of a study is important to its viability. Given that funding is limited in research, it would benefit researchers to know whether they would receive more bang for their buck if they got more participants versus more replicate measures (D. B. Allison, Allison, Faith, Paultre, & Pi-Sunyer, 1997). It also does not seem fruitful to spend time on experiments that are bound to failure (i.e., due to low power).

A more recent aspect of study design has been the optimality of study size and duration through minimizing SEMs to their most basic forms (Oertzen, 2010). In addition, an emphasis on reliability of measures and within-person variation of analysis of covariance designs of SEM produces strong, testable models based on theory. In experimental design we can see the benefit of streamlining and preparing for studies so optimal outcomes are more likely on an a priori basis (i.e., significant probability values).

In all cases, to determine SEM power, we need the sample size (n), the size of the effect (d), and the Type I error rate (α). These steps are outlined in Cohen (1988) with rules of thumb for interpretation of the calculated effect sizes for many basic data analysis models (e.g., contingency tables, ANOVA, and regression). A simple reorganization of these variables will allow us to determine effect size or sample size if power is held constant. The concept of power goes beyond the standard practices of minimum group sample sizes and research rules of thumb; power is a way of determining how many people are needed to find an effect "that's really there" of a given treatment. In terms of this point of view, we put more importance on what the size of the effect we are looking for is than we had done before (Cohen, 1988). Studies are based on prior research findings, and we use these results to determine how to effectively measure our research question. In this way, proper statistical analysis of research carried out will provide definitive results on the theory under investigation.

There are many prior research articles attempting to understand how power is calculated in multivariate and longitudinal designs (T. E. Duncan, Duncan, & Strycker, 2013; MacCallum, Browne, & Sugawara, 1996; McQuitty, 2004; Muthén & Curran, 1997; Muthén & Muthén, 2002a; Raudenbush & Liu, 2000; Satorra & Saris, 1985; Schmitz et al., 1998; Tanaka, 1987; Yuan & Hayashi, 2003). These results demonstrate there are a lot of benefits to using an SEM analysis over traditional statistical methods. The ability to test specific hypotheses within the model as well as do traditional tests (i.e., ANOVA) within the same structure makes it a versatile tool. The use of factor models and longitudinal data requires an advancement of methods for dealing with power calculation beyond the initial method outlined by Cohen (1988).

To determine model fit in SEM, a few methods and procedures used should be introduced. A practical method of determining model fit is the use of the L^2 or χ^2 difference test (J. G. Anderson & Gerbing, 1988; Saris & Satorra, 1993; Satorra & Saris, 1985; Tucker & Lewis, 1973). In this method we definitely base all assumptions on normality of residuals, but we use nested models to provide test statistics about how certain pathways can be constrained within each sequence of models. Nested models are those that have the same exact structure but constraints are added or removed, which changes the number of parameters estimated. This changes the df for the model depending on how many constraints are added or removed. The change in L^2 model fits is compared with the change in df between those same models. The difference in L^2 scores of these nested models can then be compared to determine which model has the best fit. Even though the L^2 values of the nested models are correlated, the L^2 values of the difference between models are independent, allowing for a χ^2 test of significance based on the change in df (Steiger, Shapiro, & Browne, 1985), all under the assumption of normality of residuals.

Some examples of SEM power analyses have been extensive in analyzing the effects of covariance structure on resultant power. MacCallum, Browne, and Cai (2006) showed how nested models could be compared in SEM programs to yield reasonable power approximations for prospective studies. Several studies present standard methods for examining power in a latent growth model framework (Fan, 2003; Hertzog, Lindenberger, Ghisletta, & Oertzen, 2006; Hertzog, Oertzen, Ghisletta, & Lindenberger, 2008). These studies provide a set of guidelines to adapt our problem. In creating a set of nested SEMs with latent variables explicitly defined, we can test what sample sizes are approximated with a given effect size.

One tractable method seems to be that of Satorra and Saris (1985) as used by McArdle (1994). This is a two-step method based on the likelihood ratio test χ^2 value's noncentrality parameter. An implied model is fit with parameters fixed to obtain a covariance structure outputted based on the alternative hypothesis being true. The null hypothesis is then fit, and the noncentrality parameter is estimated. The df for the comparison model is calculated as the difference between the two hypotheses, and the critical value is the χ^2 value associated with the df. This is the value used in the noncentrality parameter function to determine power for detecting the effect in the alternative hypothesis (as in McArdle, 1994).

Alternatives to the L^2 tests are the likelihood modification and Wald test. The likelihood modification index is an estimate of the change in fit by freeing one parameter in the model. The Wald test uses the squared value of the t values for the parameter. Another way to compute statistical power in an SEM setting is to use Monte Carlo methods. The most influential of this type of method was proposed first by Steiger (as written up in 1990) and used by Cudeck and Browne (1993) and Muthén and Muthén (2002a). First, a population model is established with population values used to create a sample set. Second, a set of samples are fit to the model and model fits are obtained. Then the alternative model is fit, and the difference in model fits can be calculated and tested, just as in the two-step method by Satorra and Saris (1985). Another simple technique is to record the percentage of successful rejections of the null model by Monte Carlo simulation methods (T. E. Duncan, Duncan, & Strycker, 2013). These methods average the percentage of successes over many repetitions to minimize random anomalies in simulation of the data.

Other methods were described by MacCallum, Browne, and Sugawara (1996) for models including latent variables. This group proposed that the measure of close fit, the RMSEA, be used to calculate a model's power for a given effect size. The concept of close fit as given by the RMSEA measures how the model closely approximates the data, as opposed to the exact misfit given by the χ^2 measure. The noncentral distribution of RMSEA values for the null and alternative hypotheses are compared, and the power is the probability that we can detect a difference between these two distributions. The probability of power is a function of the noncentral distribution for the degrees of freedom, d, and the noncentrality parameter (λ), based on the χ^2 for the alternative hypothesis. This is compared with the critical value given by a specified level of significance, the α level. The calculated power is given as the area under the curve beyond the critical value. The null hypothesis is the calculated RMSEA values for our models from the simulation runs. This is then compared with a small difference in model fits that is specified beforehand. For example, if we want to know the probability that a null and alternative model are significantly different, we can test these values compared with a null model RMSEA fit = .05 with an alternative model RMSEA fit = .03. Although these specific values remain arbitrary, the concepts they represent are not.

There has not been much prior evaluation of the dynamic models presented here, but the principles are the same. A two-group dynamic model was defined in McArdle and Prindle (2008) and evaluated for statistical power in Prindle and McArdle (2012), and the basic ideas are all included. They studied one kind of dynamic model of the expected means and covariances across at least two groups: randomly assigned control and experimental groups based on two or more occasions. A good question can be asked because they were randomly assigned only at time 1. The purpose of this Monte Carlo study was to determine sample size recommendations for a basic set of dynamic model issues from other researchers. These authors concluded that the chi-square power of perfect fit calls for at least $n > 270$ individuals to detect moderate differences in the two-group case, whereas the RMSEA procedure of close fit seems to require as many as $n > 1,450$ participants. It is shown that parameters that provide input into the change score affects power versus those that come from indirect pathways.

CURRENT STATUS OF SEM RESEARCH

It is a bit difficult to know exactly who is using SEM for what purpose. One recent article by Stapleton and Leite (2005) attempted to summarize all current SEM syllabi in classroom usage, but many classic conceptual treatments were necessarily overlooked. There are also online blogs (e.g., http://www2.gsu.edu/~mkteer/semnet.html) and Internet websites devoted to the SEM enterprise, but the same could be said about almost any faddish idea. The early SEM research seems to have been focused on the development of the concepts, whereas more recent SEM research seems to be focused on the tools. In this book, we will go back a step and focus on the concepts not the current usage.

To consider this question of current SEM usage more seriously now, McArdle and Kadlec (2013) conducted a Google Scholar search, and our results are presented graphically there. Across disciplines, 22% of the articles on SEM were published during the 20th century, whereas 78% were published during the first decade of the 21st century. A large percentage of the articles (47%) were published in the social sciences/arts/humanities, followed by engineering/computer science/mathematics (27%), and then business/economics (21%). Moreover, these three disciplines have also showed a steady increase of articles on SEM between 2000 and 2009. Almost half of scholarly articles on SEM are being produced by social scientists, and most all of them seem to be using SEM mainly as a new tool. But it also seems that the SEM tools are now largely used in an appropriate fashion—to examine the utility of theoretical ideas about the effects of unobservable variables in terms of observable relationships.

A simple regression analysis (Figure 2.1 or 2.4) does not really stimulate us to use SEM in any way, but some aspects of the formal basis of SEM regression provide the needed motivation. In this case, the classic treatment of SEM by Goldberger (1973; in Goldberger & Duncan, 1973) is worth reconsidering. To paraphrase the earlier work, Goldberger initially suggested that the reason we do not use regression on all of our data analysis problems is that the simple linear model of regression is often incorrect and our typical results are biased. To be sure, it was well-known that nonlinear relations may exist and additional predictor variables may be needed. But, and this may surprise some readers who do not think of regression analysis as a concept, Goldberger starts with the idea that regression analysis is used to make a "statement about causes" (see also Pearl, 2000). Goldberger seems to make the case that our standard data analyses should not be a search for the "highest" explained variance (i.e., maximum predictability) but the "correct" explained variance (i.e., maximum replicability). Of course, we can only begin to think this is true when our parameters remain the same from one analysis to another. Goldberger termed this principle *invariance* (1973, p. 2). Indeed, the search for invariance of parameters has now become a very basic principle in SEM, and we use it here a great deal. In general, this means that any regression analysis can be incorrect for a number of reasons, leading to "biased" coefficients. Goldberger (1973) shows how SEM concepts and algebra can be used to consider the resulting biases, so his basic concepts will be used here with both algebra and path diagrams.

4

USING THE SIMPLIFIED RETICULAR ACTION MODEL NOTATION

It is fairly well-known that a specific matrix algebra formulation such as structural equation modeling (SEM)–linear structural relations model (LISREL; of Exhibit 3.2) is not the only way to create model expectations (McArdle, 2005). Without any loss of enthusiasm for the basic premises of SEM, it is fair to say that there were several knowledgeable researchers who suggested that the LISREL concept and computer program was not actually the best way to deal with such problems, and Roderick P. McDonald (1980) was among the most vocal (Loehlin, 1987, 1998, 2004; McDonald, 1985b). In McDonald's alternative approach, the newly available computer programming he created allowed an unrestricted level of higher order common factors that he termed *covariance structure analysis* (COSAN). The use of the resulting concepts and computer program produced exactly the same numerical values as LISREL, but it was not nearly as popular as LISREL, and this was unfortunate because COSAN was free software. The notation we will use here—the

---

http://dx.doi.org/10.1037/14440-005
Longitudinal Data Analysis Using Structural Equation Models, by J. J. McArdle and J. R. Nesselroade
Copyright © 2014 by the American Psychological Association. All rights reserved.

reticular action model (RAM)—is slightly different, because it uses a simplified algebra to match the diagrams (see Figure 2.4).

As stated earlier, it is not necessary to use any particular algebraic notation as long as the general SEM principles are followed. Nevertheless, our own interest in path diagrams also led to another innovation in the calculation schemes. Our prior use of COSAN proved instrumental in asserting that the eight-matrix notation, and the entire LISREL concept, was not the only correct way to carry out SEM (Horn & McArdle, 1980). In fact, a practical comparison of COSAN and LISREL applications led directly to the simplification known as RAM theory (McArdle, 1979, 2005; McArdle & McDonald, 1984).

RAM ALGEBRAIC NOTATION

It became clear to us (McArdle, 1978; McArdle & McDonald, 1984) that only three model matrices were necessary to consider any structural equation model: (1) a filter matrix (**F**) of completely fixed ones and zeros designed to distinguish the manifest variables from the latent variables in a model, (2) an arrow matrix (**A**) of potential one-headed arrows (regression coefficients and means) based on directional hypotheses, and (3) a sling matrix (Ω) of potential two-headed arrows based on nondirectional hypotheses. This resulting set of parameters is the RAM notation (McArdle & McDonald, 1984) with vectors (**p, u, q**) and model matrices (**A**, Ω, **F**). This is more simply termed *RAM specification* (McArdle, 2005), and we will use here it only because it matches the path diagrams exactly. RAM is fully defined in Exhibit 4.1, and the resulting expectations are given in Exhibit 4.2.

RAM GRAPHICS

Perhaps it is now obvious that this path diagram (e.g., Figure 2.1 or 2.4) are not plots of the raw data but topographical representations of some of the assumptions in the model of analysis; that is, the residual has no mean, no correlation with the predictor, and so on. These path diagrams do not say anything about the distribution requirements for the predictor X, primarily because X can have any distribution. But it also does not say anything about the distribution of the residuals, although we do know that the unobserved residual scores (e) need to be "normally distributed" for the statistical tests to be exact. Nevertheless, one might reasonably ask, do we need to know all this just to define a simple linear regression? The complete answer to this question really depends on what we are going to do next.

EXHIBIT 4.1
A Generalized Set of Rules Used To Define a Model
for Any Structural Equation Model

Distinguish types of variables: There are only observed variables (*M*, drawn as squares) and unobserved variables (*L*, drawn as circles). The summation of all variables is a list (of size *V* = *M* + *L*).
Distinguish type of parameters: There are only directed relationships (**A**, drawn as one-headed arrows) and undirected relationships (**Ω**, drawn as two-headed slings).
Define the filter matrix **F**: Create a (*M* by *V*) matrix of zeros, and enter unit values where the variables that is observed (in the row) is give the same name as the variable in the model (in the column).
Define the arrow matrix **A**: Create a square but nonsymmetric (*V* by *V*) matrix of zeros, and enter unit values where any variable is the outcome (in the row) of any other variable in the model (in the column).
Define the sling matrix **Ω**: Create a symmetric (*V* by *V*) matrix of zeros, and enter unit values where the variable in the model is connected (in the row) to any other variable in the model (in the column).

Note. From *RAMpath: A Computer Program for Automatic Path Diagrams* (pp. P15–P18), by J. J. McArdle and S. M. Boker, 1990, Hillsdale, NJ: Lawrence Erlbaum Publishers. Copyright 1990 by Taylor & Francis. Adapted with permission.

One caveat is that, because we have introduced the constant (triangle labeled 1) as part of this expectation, we end up with expectations for a combination of both a mean vector and a covariance matrix, or a matrix of first and second moments. This kind of calculation is actually well-known by another name; we have created an average sums of squares and crossproducts (SSCP) matrix expectation (Bock, 1975), and this is sometimes referred to as a *matrix of moments*. But we will use this matrix as a group summary in our basic fitting algorithm. However, since we will often be thinking about means and covariances separately to some degree, we need a convenient way to separate out the expected mean vector from this one. This can be accomplished in many ways. This is obviously the mean square plus the

EXHIBIT 4.2
Specifying Model Expectations for Any SEM
Using RAMpath Notation

Calculate all model effects **E**: Calculate the square matrix of total effects from one variable to another by writing $\mathbf{E} = (\mathbf{I} - \mathbf{A})^{-1} = \mathbf{I} + \mathbf{A} + \mathbf{A}^2 + \mathbf{A}^3 \cdots + \mathbf{A}^k$
Calculate all model expectations: Calculate the symmetric (V by V) matrix of all model expectations as **SSCP(V) = E Ω E′**
Calculate observed model expectations: Calculate the symmetric (M by M) matrix of all model expectations as **SSCP(M) = F SSCP(V)′ F′** or **F E Ω E′ F′**

covariances (i.e., the SSCP) listed in the prior equations. This SSCP matrix is used to summarize the expected information about the model-based raw scores. In this format it seems easier to see that the use of a constant has zero effect on the expected covariances, and the two-headed unit value on the constant is included to preserve the needed cross-product.

Given that we use RAM notation and we are sincere about completing our diagrams, we do not need any further steps. RAM notation represents the necessary and sufficient conditions for any structural equation model (for proof, see McArdle & McDonald, 1984). Once again, we should not forget that the main point of RAM notation is that these three matrices also were based on a one-to-one identity (or isomorphism) with the path analysis graphics (for details, see McArdle, 2005; McArdle & Boker, 1990). In various demonstrations, we have showed how this three-matrix approach produced exactly the same values as the eight-or-more-matrix approach (e.g., McArdle, 2005; McArdle & McDonald, 1984). This approach, in fact leads to a general statement of the model reconstruction (Exhibit 4.2) with an associated set of tracing rules (in Exhibit 4.3). We do not give details about these issues because these are simply reflections of the algebra.

EXHIBIT 4.3
A Generalized Set of Tracing Rules for Any Structural Equation Model

The following are after Wright (1918, 1921)—assuming RAMpath diagrams—by McArdle & Boker, 1990:

The RAMgraph: When defined using RAMpath rules can be briefly described in terms of a set of actions that represent the nonlinear structure of the model expectations.

The effect matrix **E** contains actions that are one-way tracings in a RAMgraph. Each element (**e**{x ... w}) is the action from any variable v(w) to any variable v(x) that passes through a one-way asymmetric sequence of r > 0 adjacent variables connected by r – 1 one-headed arrows **a**{i,j}.

Bridges **B** are sequentially defined two-way movements or tracings in the RAMgraph. The element **b**{x ... w:z ... y} is a tracing from any initial variable c(x) to any terminating variable v(y) that passes through a symmetric sequence of (a) one backward action **e**{x ... w} tracing backward from v(x) to v(w) connecting r > 0 variables, (b) one and only one sling (**s**{w,z}) connecting two mediating variables v(w) and v(z), and (c) one forward action (**e**{y ... z} = **e**{z ... y}′) traced from V(z) to v(y) connecting q > 0 variables.

Connections **C**: The complete linkage between pairs of variables is the sum of all nonparallel bridges between two variables. Thus, **c**{x,y} = **b**{x ... w: z ... y} **s**{y,z} **b**{z ... y: w ... x} also is termed the average cross-product or sums-of-squares. The bridges are nonparallel if they may be stated in a different notational sequence even though they may contain the same elements (i.e., **b**{x ... w: z ... y} NE **b**{x ... z: w ... y}.

Note. From *RAMpath: A Computer Program for Automatic Path Diagrams* (p. P11), by J. J. McArdle and S. M. Boker, 1990, Hillsdale, NJ: Lawrence Erlbaum Publishers. Copyright 1990 by Taylor & Francis. Adapted with permission.

We are suggesting that the existing SEM computer programs could be quite useful (e.g., LISREL, COSAN; see Exhibit 3.1), but all available matrices in these programs were not needed because only these three-parameter matrices were needed to produce all the correct model expectations (Σ). The big benefit of this simplified programming is that it made exceedingly complex models relatively easy to consider (e.g., Grimm & McArdle, 2005; McArdle, 2005; McArdle & Hamagami, 2003). Nevertheless, any structural equation model only consists of variables that are either measured (squares) or not (circles), and relationships that are either directed (arrows) or not (slings). All other statements about the reasons why a specific approach should be used (i.e., combining econometrics with psychometrics) could still be useful, but they are certainly not essential. Of most importance, because this separation of measurement and structural model does not always lead to the best longitudinal analyses—as with the earlier COSAN concept, it was no surprise that the RAM concept was not uniformly recognized by the scholars who had put so much time and energy into this incredibly complex LISREL concepts, notation, and programming. Perhaps the original RAM names were unfortunate choices, but the same could be said for the LISREL concepts (McArdle, 2005). Nothing was necessary but it was useful.

USING PATH DIAGRAMS AND RAM ALGEBRA

One very useful feature of SEM—the path diagram—was originally thought to be only a conceptual device. But the close relation of the algebraic equations to the subsequent path diagram is important, because it is useful, and may explain some of the popularity of SEM among novices (McArdle, 2005). However, because the path diagram does seem to convey information we, like others before us, will use it rather extensively here (O. D. Duncan, 1975; Heise, 1974). However, and unlike the others, in any path diagram used here, observed variables are drawn as squares, unobserved variables are drawn as circles, and (1) a constant (needed when means or intercepts are used) is included as a triangle. Using this notation, a path diagram of the traditional model of simple linear regression is depicted in Figure 2.4. This model can now be seen to have three additional variables: (2) an observed outcome (Y), (3) an observed predictor (X), and (4) an unobserved residual (e). We emphasize that there are actually four variables in this model, but the constant is usually not counted. The model also has three basic parameters: (1) a slope (β) indicating the difference in the expected outcome for every one-unit difference in the predictor, (2) the variance of the predictor (labeled σ_e^2), and (3) the variance of the residual (labeled ψ^2). From these last two variances we can calculated the explained variance in Y due to X (i.e., $R^2 = [\sigma_e^2 - \psi^2]/\sigma_e^2$), but the explained variance is not strictly a parameter in the basic model (we do not use it in computer scripts; see the companion book).

When we notice that the path diagram has only a few elements, it seems natural to do the same with the algebra (see Exhibit 4.2; McArdle, 2005; McArdle & McDonald, 1984). As a caution, what follows next is a brief algebraic presentation of RAM notation, and it is clearly not needed by everyone. In fact, we will really only use this once in the whole book, and we will concentrate our efforts on the path diagrams instead. However, the algebra and the diagrams are completely consistent, and the algebra really did come first, so all is not lost by restating the obvious features of the simple regression model, and this is done in Exhibits 4.4 and 4.5.

These kinds of path diagrams can be conceptually useful devices for understanding basic concepts or tools, and we use them often here. They also are conceptually useful because they allow a potentially complex multi-faceted theory to be portrayed in a single display. These diagrams are also

---

EXHIBIT 4.4
Specifying a Regression Using RAMpath Notation

Assuming we would like to create a simplified version of the LISREL model matrices so we can write any model that is properly drawn (i.e., using the RAMpath rules of path analysis). To do so, we first simply define all variables in the model (**p**) as a list or vector:

(1) $$\mathbf{p} = [Y\ X\ 1\ e],$$

and we can then write the linear relationships among all variables in a general way as the model as

(2) $$\mathbf{p} = \mathbf{p}\mathbf{A} + \mathbf{u}$$

where **u** is introduced as a set of unknown residuals, and we define a square and nonsymmetric matrix of regressions or one-headed arrows (**A**) in this simple regression example as

(3) $$\mathbf{A} = \begin{pmatrix} |0 & \beta_1 & \beta_0 & 1| \\ |0 & 0 & 0 & 0| \\ |0 & 0 & 0 & 0| \\ |0 & 0 & 0 & 0| \end{pmatrix}$$

and we can verify that there are exactly four non-zero one-headed arrows in the diagram, but their placement in this matrix (as column variables into row variables) is defined by the order they were placed in the **p** vector (in Equation 1).

EXHIBIT 4.5
Specifying Regression Expectations Using RAMpath Notation

At this point it is generally useful to restate the relationships among all variables (Exhibit 4.4, Equation 2) as

(1)
$$\begin{aligned} \mathbf{p} &= \mathbf{p}\,\mathbf{A} + \mathbf{u}, \\ \mathbf{p} - \mathbf{p}\,\mathbf{A} &= \mathbf{u}, \\ \mathbf{p}(\mathbf{I} - \mathbf{A}) &= \mathbf{u}, \\ \mathbf{p} &= (\mathbf{I} - \mathbf{A})^{-1}\mathbf{u}, \\ \mathbf{p} &= \mathbf{E}\,\mathbf{u}, \end{aligned}$$

where we introduced a square identity matrix (**I**) and the inverse operator (−1) to contain a matrix of total effects (**E**), which for this simple example is

(2)
$$\mathbf{E} = (\mathbf{I} - \mathbf{A})^{-1} = \begin{pmatrix} |(1-0) & \beta_1 & \beta_0 & 1 & |^{-1} = |1 & \beta_1 & \beta_0 & 1| \\ |0 & (1-0) & 0 & 0 & | & |0 & 1 & 0 & 0| \\ |0 & 0 & (1-0) & 0 & | & |0 & 0 & 1 & 0| \\ |0 & 0 & 0 & (1-0)| & & |0 & 0 & 0 & 1| \end{pmatrix}$$

While this can be an awfully confusing step (and is obviously trivial here because $\mathbf{E} = \mathbf{I} + \mathbf{A}$), what we have generally done is to rewrite all model variables (in **p**) as a linear function of their unknowns (in **u**). This now allows us to define the expected values of the unknowns ($E\{\mathbf{u}\,\mathbf{u}'\}$) using the placement of the two-headed slings (Ω) defined here as a lower triangular matrix with non-zero elements. In the simple regression example this is

(3)
$$E\{\mathbf{u}\,\mathbf{u}'\} = \Omega = \begin{pmatrix} |0 & & \text{sym.}| \\ |0 & \sigma_x^2 & & | \\ |0 & 0 & 1 & | \\ |0 & 0 & 1 & \psi_e^2\,| \end{pmatrix}$$

At this point we can verify that there are exactly three non-zero two-headed arrows in the diagram, and their placement in this matrix is defined by the order that we placed them in the **p** vector.

To complete the typical model specification, it is useful to separate (or filter out) the observed variables (squares or triangles) from the unobserved variables (circles). This is especially useful because we want to compare our model expectations (see below) with all *observed variables*. To do so, we first write the as subset of all **p** as

(4a) $$\mathbf{q} = \mathbf{F}\,\mathbf{p}.$$

(*continues*)

EXHIBIT 4.5
Specifying Regression Expectations Using RAMpath Notation *(Continued)*

To get from the observed **q** from all **p**, we can write a *filter matrix* (**F**), defined in this example as

(4b)
$$\mathbf{F} = \begin{pmatrix} |1\ 0\ 0\ 0| \\ |0\ 1\ 0\ 0| \\ |0\ 0\ 1\ 0| \end{pmatrix}$$

Again we can verify that there are exactly three observed variables in the diagram, and the placement of the unit values in this matrix is defined by the order they were placed in the **p** vector.

---

practically useful as a tool because they can be used to represent the input and output of any of the SEM computer programs. This is not true when people create their own notation, such as including (a) unit vectors without two-headed arrows, (b) multiple unit vectors, or (c) arrows into other arrows. In such cases, we are left to consider what this all means. But the SEM path diagrams do not only substitute for the SEM algebraic interpretations, so typically the path diagram is used as a conceptual device. Examples where this happens will be pointed out.

5

BENEFITS AND PROBLEMS USING STRUCTURAL EQUATION MODELING IN LONGITUDINAL RESEARCH

We now know that these overall principles of structural equation modeling (SEM) can be presented and used in many different ways. It is interesting that the popular linear structural relations model (LISREL) model did not actually restrict any theory from being fit, nor did it actually impose any practical restriction. In fact, LISREL notation gave us no new restrictions at all, but it still proved to be useful.

STATISTICAL MODEL TRIMMING

LISREL concepts were used in the simplification of otherwise complex models by Hauser, Tsai, and Sewell (1983), and this was really a tour de force of modeling. Unfortunately, they then termed their use of hypotheses as "model trimming" (p. 28). If we look carefully at their analysis, we find that what they actually did was to restrict various parameters of an otherwise

http://dx.doi.org/10.1037/14440-006
Longitudinal Data Analysis Using Structural Equation Models, by J. J. McArdle and J. R. Nesselroade
Copyright © 2014 by the American Psychological Association. All rights reserved.

unwieldy model on an a priori basis and interpreted their results based on changes in fit, and this surely seemed statistically defensible. In fact, it still does. However, in current usage (Chou & Bentler, 2002), the concept of model trimming seems to be based on eliminating what are empirically determined to be nonsignificant results from an a prior run of a model, often found by "specification searches" or "model modification indices." This approach is fairly simple to implement, but unfortunately it does not always lead to the true expression of a model—or even a better expression of a model (Brown, 2006; MacCallum & Austin, 2000). Not only is the basic LISREL concept forgotten, but also are some the most valuable lessons.

In fact, because key SEM parameters are very likely to be correlated with other parameters in the model, this use of the new trimming approach is highly suspect. The only procedure that has been justified on a statistical basis is for us to write a series of "nested" models and evaluate the change in fit. This is often done by setting a key parameter to zero, allowing the other parameters to take the place of the key one, and then by seeing if the model fit is significantly altered (using standard χ^2 comparison logic). If there is a great loss of fit, we can induce that the key parameter was important. Of course, now we must decide what is "important," and this probably should change with every problem because it represents a different body of research. Although this approach can be much more tedious, there does not seem to be a simpler way to carry out this evaluation in a statistically defensible fashion. By the way, we should not view this as a novel SEM problem—this is true in the analysis of variance (ANOVA) as well. If the model was defined on an a priori basis, without use of the available data, we can justifiably say we are "confirming." We think this should be done as a reasonable first step (McArdle, 2011a). If not, and we somehow use the available data to alter the model pattern and our approach to data analysis, then we are "exploring." For this reason we think exploration should always be done as a second phase of good modeling (McArdle, 2011b).

The latter is often a key feature of modern techniques in what is commonly termed statistical modeling, but it is not often stated very clearly. As we will show here, we certainly have nothing against exploring data to find clues for the best way to represent the data in terms of a model, and the resulting model may even replicate on another set of data. But the use of traditional a priori-based probability values in such a search procedure is of unknown validity, largely because we cannot define everything we would have done to get this far: the long list of explorations includes outlier detection, transformation of variables, use of modification indices, and introduction of new models based on serious displays of the data. This leaves little doubt that we are hardly ever doing purely confirmatory research, and this is perfectly acceptable, as long as we do not put too much faith in the calculated and printed probability values.

Another basic problem emerges: We use confirmatory models to make stronger hypothetical statements, but even after what might have been a long exploration, we would like to present our exploratory results as if they were all based on prior hypotheses. But they are not! It is disappointing to read about research where a good exploration is guided by and judged by a seemingly injudicious choice of an a priori significance test. This is simply unethical behavior that should be avoided at all costs (McArdle, 2011d). That is, there is nothing wrong with exploration, and we should all probably say so with a more clear conviction. We will certainly ask, "What is your theory about the changes?" but we will assume this is just a starting point for further analyses. Any result we obtain will be subject to cross-validation and constructive replication by others, but this is indicative of a widespread problem. This does not seem to be based on reticular action model (RAM) notation, which by itself is a bit static, but the use of RAM as an alternative surely gives us courage to question standard ways of thinking.

BOTH SEM AND LONGITUDINAL SEM CAN BE USEFUL

Up to this point, we have tried to set the stage for the utility of longitudinal SEM (LSEM) analysis, and we have been careful not to actually fit any LSEMs to real data or even tried to explain why we need to make specific analytic choices. There are many excellent examples of SEM in the growing literature (e.g., Ferrer-Caja, Crawford, & Bryan, 2002; King, King, & Foy, 1996; Kline, 2011; Widaman, 1985). We think it is fair to say that a key reason researchers have moved toward SEM is because of the a priori inclusion of latent variables representing common factors and an interest in overcoming biases (Lawley & Maxwell, 1971; Goldberger, 1973; McDonald, 1985b). In general, we include latent variables because we are trying to estimate the unbiased parameters of the models to be discussed from the data.

In the next few sections, we explore a few selected particular uses of SEM with latent variables in path models. We try to point out how this can create an advantage for SEM over other forms of data analysis. We illustrate a few alternative LSEM ideas published in the context of a real data analysis problem in "Latent Variable Analysis of Age Trends in Tests of Cognitive Ability in the Health and Retirement Survey, 1992–2004" by McArdle, Fisher, and Kadlec (2007). As we quickly found, aspects of the available theory and available data led us to use very different LSEMs than most people routinely advocate.

Because there are so many contemporary statistical models that can be said to have a SEM form, such as mixed-effects models (McArdle &

Hamagami, 1996), and can be fitted using SEM software, it is often best to say that SEM is an *idea* rather than a *technique*. In the terms used here, SEM is a *concept* rather than a *tool*. What we know is that one necessary feature of SEM is of the requirement for clear model specification. When we write out a structural equation model—any structural equation model, we really need to know what we are thinking. If we do not have any rigorous thoughts, then we also do not have any structural equation model. This type of exercise is very useful when creating more simulations for demonstrations (not presented here), for evaluation of software, or even for Monte Carlo simulation of complex mathematical–statistical issues. The SEM approach offers a level of precision not readily available to other approaches, and this is one reason it is so widely heralded. However, when it comes to actual data analysis, as shown here, the use of SEM does not always improve our understanding beyond that found by simpler and more standard methods (McArdle, 1991a). So perhaps SEM is best thought of as both a theoretical tool *and* a practical tool (McArdle & Kadlec, 2013).

BENEFITS AND PROBLEMS OF LONGITUDINAL PANEL DATA

The models to be defined here can all be used with what is often termed *longitudinal panel data* (Baltagi, 2010; Hsiao, 2003; Lazarsfeld, 1948), and this comes with both benefits and problems. These data are quite common in the behavioral science research literature because this kind of structure can arise if an initial cross-section of persons are followed up at some later time(s). The overall sample size, or density of observations (D), is basically the number of individuals (N) multiplied by the number of times they have been measured (T). For this reason it is common to assume everyone is measured at all occasions and simply state that, for each measure, $D = N \times T$. Many of the prior treatments of these data are primarily concerned with statistical estimation techniques, and we are obviously not.

We are concerned with data collections and data structures, however. These kinds of data can be described as data that are multiple slices, partly cross-sectional (N), and partly time series (T). So actually, most all statistical models and issues will apply to these data, as we will see. For example, panel data actually have multiple cross-sections, so it can be thought of in this way, but it also includes multiple time points per person (as in a time series), so we can think of it this way too. We will combine models from both perspectives in this treatment. Of course, the measured variables do not have to be "repeated," with essentially the same measurement characteristics, but we also will focus on specific models for these specific kinds of data.

The statistical *dependence* (or *clustering*) of the longitudinal observations is not usually considered a problem in typical statistical inference of cross-sections (although it creates real problems here, too!). Although this dependence, the fact that the same people are measured again, is a considerable problem to be overcome, it allows us to examine "changes" within a person, especially the reasons why variation exists in these changes, and this is a key message of our models. The SEMs we will pose include many different variations on this theme, but they always include within-person changes as a natural way to deal with these dependencies. The models we will pose also try to account for the unobserved variation or what is termed *unobserved heterogeneity* in these persons, and this is another key issue here. Sometime researchers like to say "the person acts as their own control," and although this delineation is technically unneeded, it is certainly of the right spirit. In fact, this can be seen as a clear benefit of most longitudinal research.

One big problem with longitudinal data is that some people do not participate at all occasions, and a problem that is not fully addressed here can be called the problem of attrition or dropout (but see McArdle, 2013). Of course, we are well aware that attrition happens in almost any real longitudinal data set of any duration, and considerable efforts have gone into posing solutions for these big problems (see McArdle, 2013; McArdle & Hamagami, 1992). In our case, we still want to examine changes within a person, so having fewer time points is certainly not desirable. Additional problems emerge if the participant dropout is related to the phenomena under study. So this is a very practical disadvantage of any longitudinal study, and it needs to be considered in more detail than we can provide here.

Another problem is that the SEM approaches we will suggest do not always work. Unless the SEM based on the mean and covariances is most appropriate for the scores at hand, the model is not guaranteed to "converge," and thus we will be left with no answers at all (see Exhibit 3.3); this also can emerge when we ask reasonable questions. Many people figure they can diagnose all the ills in these kinds of models, but this complexity grows and it can be enormous. So we will not always have the best answers to such questions.

But by far and away the biggest problem we have found with SEM for any data is the need to state hypotheses in advance of the data collection and analysis (see McArdle, 2011d). Such a priori theory, especially multiple alternatives, is simply not found in many cases of the kinds of individual changes that we like to consider, and we will find a need to explore the available data. This distinction between confirmatory and exploratory science follows much like Jacob's (2011) warning: "In today's vastly expanded scientific enterprise, obsessed with impact factors and competition, we will need much more night science to unveil the many mysteries that remain about the workings of organisms" (p. 767). He did not define day science as akin to the generic *confirmatory* approach offered here, but we will, and we will remember that night science *exploration* is actually what we will try to do in any case. We find we must still solve important problems and still must find ways to bring more of the fun of night science into the drudgery of day science. So our general advice here will be to examine multiple changes in multiple ways, and to fully realize this does not solve all problems. These problems are so common that they can be considered the norm in our work. And it can be a real problem when we do not know what is going to happen and we are just waiting (and wanting) to see. The prediction of the changes within a person is not as obvious as we may think.

So as we see it, longitudinal panel data are loaded with both benefits and problems. Let us pursue some of these next with SEM in mind.

II

LONGITUDINAL SEM FOR THE DIRECT IDENTIFICATION OF INTRAINDIVIDUAL CHANGES

6
ALTERNATIVE DEFINITIONS OF INDIVIDUAL CHANGES

It is relatively easy for anyone to say, "That person has changed." Indeed, we think some form of this expression is one of the most commonly used statements in the English language, or in any language for that matter. But to further characterize this individual change, we would like give it a quantitative metric. This can be presented as a simple change score, as we do so below. After doing this we will want to go further and express a model for these changes. We can, of course, simply state that the change we observe has an average (it has a mean) and it is not the same for everyone (it also has a variance). But what we really want to know is if there some characteristic of the person that alters the way we think about these changes. That is, the individual changes we describe may be the result of some other influences measured within the individual.

In this section of the book, we do not take on all these problems, and our initial concern is mainly how to organize information about the changes within a person. There are now many statistical and mathematical models

---

http://dx.doi.org/10.1037/14440-007
Longitudinal Data Analysis Using Structural Equation Models, by J. J. McArdle and J. R. Nesselroade
Copyright © 2014 by the American Psychological Association. All rights reserved.

for doing this, and we will describe some of these here. But we first emphasize that both the means and covariances are often important in models of change. A great deal of prior work on structural equation modeling (SEM) has been devoted to problems of longitudinal analyses. This SEM approach was thought to provide a practical way to deal with the complex issue of measurement error in longitudinal "panel" data (e.g., Heise, 1974; McArdle & Woodcock, 1997; Sörbom, 1975; Wiley & Wiley, 1970). Later on, this included the seminal work by Jöreskog and Sörbom (Jöreskog, 1970b, 1974, 1977b; Jöreskog & Sörbom, 1979; Sörbom, 1975) on formalizing and testing autoregressive simplex models using latent variables with LISREL. We will basically use all of these prior good ideas and show how these can be extended to the longitudinal context.

Although there can be many reasons why people change, there are only a few alternative versions of these reasons in typical usage. This is especially true when we only have longitudinal panel data (Hsiao, 2003), where the same persons ($n = 1$ to N) are repeatedly measured on only a few occasions ($T < 5$). We will deal directly with a few such models now, and we start the simple pre–post case (where $T = 2$; see Oakes & Feldman, 2001). We think these alternatives shed some light on the issues we face. Of course, the problem we will continue to face when we only have two time points is how to eliminate the measurement error. As it turns out, this will not be so easy to do.

To start, we can write a basic score deviation model as first done in Exhibit 6.1, where we illustrate our algebraic notation and illustrate the use of simple linear combinations. We can then symbolize the basic mean and variance as any variable. In this notation, any score is either observed (square) or unobserved (circle) or constant. In this graphic notation, a triangle (i.e., exactly half of a square) is used to indicate the special "assigned" vector of ones (1s). The mean of any score Y is included in any path diagram as a one-headed arrow from the constant to the score Y. Any variance of Y is included as a two-headed arrow connecting the variable Y to itself. For these reasons, we can draw the unusual but complete diagram in these terms. If this is not done, all parameters of importance to us cannot be drawn in the same diagram.

THE OBSERVED CHANGE SCORE CALCULATION

By far and away the most common metric for change is the use of the *difference* or *gain* or *change* score (D_y). We assume we have measured scores on the same attribute (Y) and at least two different time points (Y[1] and Y[2]), and we use a subscript n to designate different people (i.e., $n =$ to to N). If so, then the change can be quantified as done in Exhibit 6.2.

EXHIBIT 6.1
Defining the Model for a Deviation Score

To start, we can write a basic score deviation model as

(1) $$Y_n = \mu + Y_n^*$$

where Y_n is the observed score for person n, μ is the unit constant for the group, and Y_n^* is the deviation score ($Y_n - \mu$) around the mean for person n. This model can then be rewritten as a linear combination:

(2) $$Y_n = \mu 1_n + 1 Y_n^*$$

with a vector of ones (scores of 1 imply a individual constant) for the mean and a weight of one (where 1 is a group constant) for the deviations. We can then symbolize the basic variance as either

(3) $$\sum \{Y_n^{*2}\}/(N-1) = E\{Y^*Y^*\} = \sigma^2$$

where the notation of sums of squares (Σ^2) or expected values (E) or even population parameters (σ^2) is used.

Although this is not typical, the path diagrams we use for change models always include means and variances. Assuming the previous score deviation model

(4a) $$Y_n = \mu + Y_n^*$$

with variance expectations of

(4b) $$E = \{Y^* Y^{*'}\} = \sigma^2$$

and cross-products expectations of

(4c) $$E = \{Y Y'\} = E\left\{(\mu + Y_n^*)(\mu + Y_n^*)'\right\} = \mu^2 + \sigma^2$$

EXHIBIT 6.2
Defining an Observed Change Score

Let us assume we have measured scores on the same attribute (Y) and at least two different time points (Y[1] and Y[2]), and we use a subscript n to designate different people (i.e., $n =$ to to N). If so, then the change can be quantified as

(1) $$D_{yn} = Y[2]_n - Y[1]_n,$$

where no deviation score is implied.

This use of the observed change score (D_y) approach offers an exceedingly simple interpretation. That is, this implies that when the score is positive, the person has changed in a positive way, or gone uphill. Assuming this score is positive, it is often termed the *gain* score or *growth* score instead. But when the score is negative, the person has changed in a negative way or gone downhill. We usually call this the *loss* or *decline* score. If we had scaled this change score the opposite way, with score Y[1] subtracted from score Y[2], then the interpretation would be the opposite too. When the score is zero, the person has not changed at all. Since this is a characteristic of a single entity, we will strictly use the term *change* here. This basic calculation is not controversial, and for our own consistency, we will always subtract the latter value (Y[2]) from the former value (Y[1]).

THE CLASSIC CRITIQUE OF CHANGE SCORES AND ITS INITIAL RESOLUTION

There have been major critics on the use of difference or change scores (e.g., Cronbach & Furby, 1970; see Exhibit 6.3). In one critique, a typical model for a set of observed repeated measures is that we have an unobserved "true score" at both occasions (y), and an unobserved random error (e[t]) that is independent over each occasion. Furthermore, the scores are only correlated because they share the same unobserved true score (y). In this model the true score remains the same, and all changes are based on the random noise. If the previous model holds, then it is relatively easy to see that the simple difference score can be rewritten so it is only based on random noise. It now follows that the characteristics of the change score (i.e., mean, variance, correlations) are entirely based only on the changes in the random error scores. This also implies that the reliability of the change score is zero (see Exhibit 6.4). For these reasons the use of the simple difference or change score approach has been frowned on in much of developmental research. Indeed, the pronouncements of Cronbach and Furby (1970) were clear and important: "At the end of this paper the authors argue that gain scores are rarely useful, no matter how they may be adjusted or refined. . . . This argument applies not only to changes over time, but also to other differences between two variables" (p. 68), and "there appears to be no need to use measures of change as dependent variables and no virtue in using them" (p. 78). These clear messages were taken to heart by many developmental researchers.

Other researchers (e.g., Nesselroade, 1972; Nesselroade & Cable, 1974) used a slightly different variation on this basic theme. They defined an alternative model for a set of observed repeated measures with two unobserved true scores (y[t]) and random noise (e[t]). This alteration of the basic idea

EXHIBIT 6.3
Defining the Model of an Observed Change Score

Cronbach and Furby (1970) defined a typical model for a set of mean deviated observed repeated measures as

(1a) $$Y[1]_n^* = y_n + e[1]_n$$

and

(1b) $$Y[2]_n^* = y_n + e[2]_n$$

where y is an unobserved true score for both occasions (so it is printed in lower case and italics), and $e[t]$ are two unobserved random errors that (1) have mean zero, (2) are independent of the true score, and (3) are independent of each other. The brackets ([ ]) are used to signify the time t.

If the previous model (Equation 1) holds, then it is relatively easy to see that the simple difference score can be rewritten as

(2) $$\begin{aligned} D_{yn} &= Y[2]_n - Y[1]_n \\ &= (y_n + e[2]_n) - (y_n + e[1]_n) \\ &= (y_n - y_n) + (e[2]_n - e[1]_n) \\ &= e[2]_n - e[1]_n \\ &= \Delta e[t]_n \end{aligned}$$

so the resulting change is completely composed of random error.

Other researchers (e.g., Nesselroade, 1972, 1974) defined a different model for a set of observed repeated measures as

(3a) $$Y[1]_n^* = y[1]_n + e[1]_n$$

and

(3b) $$Y[2]_n^* = y[2]_n + e[2]_n$$

where $y[1]$ = an unobserved true score for the first occasion, $y[2]$ = an unobserved true score for the second occasion, and $e[t]$ are the unobserved random errors. The alteration of the basic idea of the underlying model is relevant. Using the same logic as used earlier, it is now possible to redefine this model as a change and write

(4a) $$Y[1]_n^* = y[1]_n + e[1]_n$$

and

(4b) $$Y[2]_n^* = y[1]_n + \Delta y_n + e[2]_n$$

where $y[1]$ = an unobserved true score for both occasions, Δy = an unobserved "true change" at the second occasion, and $e[t]$ are unobserved random errors.

(*continues*)

EXHIBIT 6.3
Defining the Model of an Observed Change Score   (*Continued*)

If and only if this second model holds, then the gain score can be rewritten as

(5)
$$D_{yn} = Y[2]_n - Y[1]_n$$
$$= (y[2]_n + e[2]_n) - (y[1]_n + e[1]_n)$$
$$= (y[2]_n - y[1]_n) + (e[2]_n - e[1]_n)$$
$$= \Delta y + (e[2]_n - e[1]_n)$$
$$= \Delta y_n + \Delta e_n$$

so now the change is partly due to the change in the true score and partly due to random error. This is intended to demonstrate that any alteration of the model makes a difference to the summary statements.

---

of the underlying model is relevant. Using the same logic as used earlier (in Exhibit 6.3), it is now possible to redefine this model as a change where the characteristics of this change score (mean, variance, correlations) are party based on the changes in the random error scores but also partly on the changes in the true score. In this approach, the relative size of the true-score gain determines the variance and reliability of the changes (see Exhibit 6.4). This implies that the change score may be a very good way to consider measuring change and researchers should consider them carefully, especially using a model of latent scores without accumulated errors.

It surely seems that researchers all over the field of developmental research have been taught that there are no true score changes and that this is the proper way to construct a model of change. This is a major difference of opinion we have with other developmental researchers. However, judging by the implicit usage of the observed change score in models such as ANOVA and other SEMs, it is possible the tide has somehow shifted (since 1970). In our view, the possibility that there are true change among latent variables (see Exhibits 6.3 and 6.4) seems like a more reasonable starting point, and even more likely in practice, and this leads to an entirely different conclusion—If there is an unobserved change in the true score, it will then be an important part of the observed change score.

The key practical issues, then, compel us to try to design experiments that reduce the size of the error, and hence, the contribution of the error terms to the analysis of change. We will investigate several ways to do so in later sections. But, and in general, we will herald the use of the simple change score throughout this book, especially when it is formed from invariant latent factors, largely because this type of change score will then be free of errors of measurement. In fact, we will make this kind of latent change score (LCS) the focus of all subsequent analyses.

EXHIBIT 6.4
Defining the Reliability of an Observed Change Score

The reliability of any score is defined as the ratio or variance proportion of

(1a)   reliability = variance of the true score/variance of the observed score,

or symbolically as

(1b) $$\eta^2 = \sigma_y^2 / \sigma_Y^2$$

As we demonstrate here, in classical work this statistic is often estimated by using the correlation or covariance of two scores.

In a model where there is no change in the true score (Cronbach & Furby, 1970), then the observed scores are only correlated because they share the same unobserved true score (y), and we can write

(2a) $$E\{y, y'\} = \sigma_y^2$$

$$E\{e[1], e[2]'\} = 0$$

$$E\{e[t], y'\} = 0$$

$$E\{Y[1]^*, [2]^{*\prime}\} = E\{(y_n + e[1]_n)(y_n + e[2]_n)'\} \sigma_y^2$$

In this kind of model the reliability of each observed score can then be calculated as

(2b) $$\eta^2[t] = E\{y[t], Y[t]'\} = E\{(y_n)(y_n + e[t]_n)'\} = \sigma_y^2 / (\sigma_y^2 + \sigma_e^2),$$

or as

(2c) $$\eta^2[1] = E\{y[1], Y[1]'\} = E\{(y_n)(y_n + e[1]_n)'\} = \sigma_y^2 / (\sigma_y^2 + \sigma_e^2),$$

and

(2d) $$\eta^2[2] = E\{y[2], Y[2]'\} = E\{(y_n)(y_n + e[2]_n)'\} = \sigma_y^2 / (\sigma_y^2 + \sigma_e^2),$$

so the reliability in this model is considered the same at each time point. In this case, the reliability of the changes can be calculated as

(2e) $$E\{D_y, Y[t]'\} = E\{(y_n + e[2]_n)(y_n + e[2]_n)'\} = 0/(\sigma_y^2 + \sigma_e^2) = 0$$

In a model where there is some change in the true score (Nesselroade, 1972) the observed scores are correlated because they share the same unobserved true score ($y[1]$), so we can write

(3a) $$E\{Y[1]^*, Y[2]^*\} = E\{(y[1]_n + e[1]_n)(y[2]_n + e[2]_n)'\} = \sigma_{y[1]}^2$$

(*continues*)

EXHIBIT 6.4
Defining the Reliability of an Observed Change Score   (Continued)

but we can also observe

(2a) $E\{y[1], y[1]'\} = \sigma^2_{y[1]}$

$E\{y[2], y[2]'\} = \sigma^2_{y[2]} = E\{(y[1]_n + Dy[2]_n)(y[1]_n + Dy[2]_n)'\}$
$= \sigma^2_{y[1]} + \sigma^2_{Dy[2]} + 2\sigma^2_{y[1]Dy[2]}$

$E\{y[1], y[2]'\} = E\{(y[1]_n)(y[1]_n + Dy[2]_n)'\} = \sigma^2_{y[1]} + \sigma^2_{Dy[2]} + 2\sigma^2_{y[1]Dy[2]}$

$E\{e[1], e[2]'\} = 0$

$E\{e[t], y[t]'\} = 0$

$E\{Y[1]^*, Y[2]^{*\prime}\} = E\{(y[1]_n + e[1]_n)(y[2]_n + e[2]_n)'\} = \sigma^2_Y$

In this kind of model the reliability of each score can then be calculated as

(2b) $\eta[1] = E\{y[1], Y[1]'\} = E\{(y[1]_n)(y[1]_n, +e[1]_n)'\} = \sigma^2_{y[1]}/(\sigma^2_{y[1]} + \sigma^2_e),$

and

(2c) $\eta[2] = E\{y[2], Y[2]'\} = E\{(y[2]_n)(y[2]_n, +e[2]_n)'\} = \sigma^2_{y[2]}/(\sigma^2_{y[2]} + \sigma^2_e)$

so they are not equal if there is systematic change in the true score. That is, the reliability of a measure is a function of the size of the true score variance. Similarly, the reliability of the changes can be calculated as a variance of rates as

(2e) $E\{D_y, Y[2]'\} = E\{(y[2]_n - y[1]_n)(y[2]_n, +e[2]_n)'\} = \sigma^2_{Dy[2]}/(\sigma^2_{y[2]} + \sigma^2_e) > 0$

This brings us to a major turning point in our longitudinal research. We could now describe all the problem associated with observed change scores, such as (a) unreliability of change as an outcome (Linn & Slinde, 1977; Rogosa & Willett, 1983), (b) the unreliability of change as a predictor (Cohen, Cohen, West, & Aiken, 2003), (c) the potential for regression to the mean (Cook & Campbell, 1979), or (d) combinations of all problems. On the other hand, we also realized we could simply bypass most of these problems by dealing with the unreliability of scores in terms of factor model parameters (as we did in McArdle & Nesselroade, 1994, 2003). The latter approach basically implies that all of our change scores will be latent. We describe how to implement this option here, but we do not deal with all the other reasonable critiques of observed change scores.

TYPE D CHANGE: SIMPLE CHANGES AS OBSERVED SCORES

In Type D change score models, we use the same repeated measures scores, the same data, but we can write the observed change score model in Exhibit 6.5. Here we have defined the change in terms of the most recent score subtracted from the prior score. Assuming we have defined a change score in this way can also simply define its means and covariances. To draw a path model in the same way, we just drop the Y[2] and add the D_y to the diagram, and this is done in Figure 6.1. This modeling approach is widely used by the proponents of the repeated measures analysis of variance (RANOVA; see Bock, 1975; Hertzog & Rovine, 1985; McArdle, 1977; O'Brien & Kaiser, 1985; Winer, 1962).

As just stated, the nonstandard (e.g., RAMpath) path diagram of this model is presented here as Figure 6.1. In this diagram the only two relevant variables are the initial score (Y[1]) and the observed change score (D_y). The key scores in this model are assumed to be measured variables so they are drawn as squares. The model parameters of the variance

---

EXHIBIT 6.5
Defining a Type D Change Score Model

In Type D change score models, we use the same repeated measures scores, the same data, but we can write the observed change score model as

(1a) $$Y[2]_n = Y[1]_n + D_{yn},$$

and then note that this is formally equivalent to defining

(1b) $$D_{yn} = Y[2]_n - Y[1]_n,$$

which we often do. Once again, we have defined the change in terms of the most recent score subtracted from the prior score.

Assuming we have defined a change score in this way can simply define a few key features of the means and covariances, such as

(1c) $$D_{yn} = \mu_D + D_{yn}^* \text{ and}$$
$$E\{D_y^*, D_y^{*\prime}\} = \sigma_D^2 \text{ and}$$
$$F\{Y[1]^*, D_v^*\} = \sigma_{1D}$$

An alternative but equivalent way to define this model is to write the linear combination

(1d) $$Y[2] = 1Y[1] + 1D_y,$$

which is the same as Equation 1a. Although this algebraic symmetry with a linear combination is utterly simple, it will be useful in more complex expressions later.

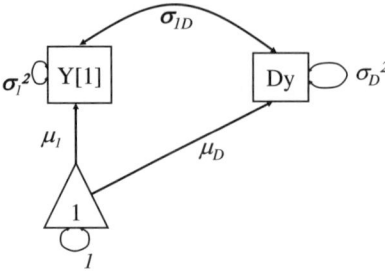

Figure 6.1. A path diagram of an observed change score.

of the first occasion (σ_1^2), the variance of the observed change score (σ_D^2), and the covariance of the initial scores and the changes (σ_{1D}) are drawn with two-headed arrows. Because the means are important as well, the unit constant (1) is reintroduced. The one-headed arrows indicate the mean of the initial level (μ_1) and the mean of the changes (μ_D). The two-headed arrow on the unit constant can be estimated (at 1) so the tracing rules of path analysis reproduces the average sums of squares and cross-products (McArdle, 2005).

The next diagram, Figure 6.2, adds the source of the change score (y[2]) as a latent variable with fixed unit values. Of course, Y[2] was measured and could be used, but it is not. Here we can more clearly see that the theoretically unobserved y[2] is a exact function of observed Y[1] and D_y. Since the fixed unit values here point directly at the latent y[2], this representation does not actually alter any model expectation for the observables. As it turns out, we can often assume that unobservables exist without altering any SEM.

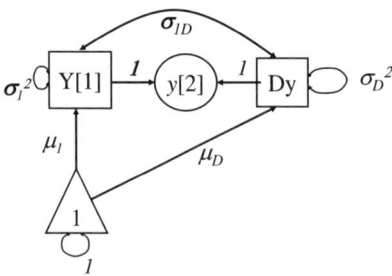

Figure 6.2. A complete path diagram of a change score model (to specify the origin of Dy). The circle is included simply as a reminder that the Dy variable comes from the y[2] = Y[1] + Dy expression.

TYPE A CHANGE: TIME-TO-TIME PREDICTION OF SCORES

In the Type A autoregression model, a linear model is expressed for over two occasions of measurement where the second observed score (Y[2]) is predicted from the first observed score (Y[1]). This is more formally described in Exhibit 6.6. This approach is used when the second score is measured after the first score, usually by a known time delay (termed a time lag, or Δt, here). What seems to matter for interpretation most here is the size and sign of the slope (β_1), and not the intercept (β_0), so this is often based on deviations around the mean (Y[t]*). The slope term (β_1) is often referred to as the difference in the predicted score of Y[2] for a one-unit difference in Y[1]. Indeed, the term *difference* is often used when we actually mean change within a person (as in McArdle, 2009). As in other regression models, *e* is a residual score, sometimes termed a disturbance, but it is uniformly considered an unobserved and random score that is uncorrelated with Y[1] but forms part of the variance of Y[2].

This model is redrawn in Figure 6.3 using typical covariance terms, and this is nearly a standard presentation of a regression model. However, because we want to add the mean (μ_1) and intercept (β_0) terms, we need to add a constant term (1) and then we can draw the full model as Figure 6.3. This more complete diagram now has the same properties as any linear regression model (see Chapter 2). In this typical representation, the ratio of the variance of *e* to the outcome variance Y[2] ($\sigma_e^2/\sigma_y^2 = 1 - R^2$) can be a useful index of forecast efficiency, and the explained variance ($R^2 = 1 - [\sigma_e^2/\sigma_y^2]$) can be formed in a similar way. As with any regression, the explained variance is not a parameter in the model, but is a ratio of parameters that are part of the model. This approach is widely used in both the analysis of covariance and time-series regression (Hsiao, 2003).

EXHIBIT 6.6
Defining a Type A Autoregression Model

In the Type A autoregression model, a linear model is expressed for over two occasions of measurement as

(1) $\qquad Y[2]_n = \beta_0\,\beta_1 + Y[1]_n + e_n$

where β_0 is the *intercept* term, or the predicted score of Y[2] when Y[1] = 0, β_1 is the *coefficient* or *slope* term, often referred to as the difference in the predicted score of Y[2] for a one-unit difference in Y[1]. Indeed, the term *difference* is often used when we actually mean change (McArdle, 2009). In most notation used here, Greek letters are used for the *estimated parameters*, and this includes the *fixed*, or *group* characteristics (β_0, β_1), and the *random*, or *individual* characteristics (ψ_ϵ^2) here.

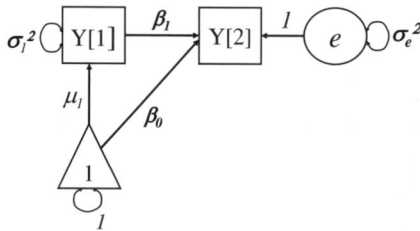

Figure 6.3. A cross-products based autoregression model for two repeated measures. The inclusion of constant 1 allows the intercept β_0 to be part of the regression equation for Y[2]. Mean deviates not used as scores.

The knowledgeable reader will note that we have created a *time-forward* prediction. That is, we use the timing of the observations to define our prediction equation (Y[2] as a function of Y[1]). This is typically done here because we are interested in a sequence of predictions over time, but we do note that the regression could work the same in reverse (i.e., Y[1] as a function of Y[2]).

TYPE DR: REGRESSION OF CHANGES

In the longitudinal case, now we might ask, "Where are the changes, represented in the autoregressive model just presented? Is the change part of the disturbance term?" But before we go off and make up an unusual story, one variation on this basic model may be useful. In what might be called a Type DR approach, we combine elements of the observed change score model in Exhibit 6.7 and Figure 6.4. We start with the Type D model, but we use the initial time score as a predictor of the changes so that the outcome is the change and the regression coefficients are used to describe the effect of the earlier scores on this outcome. The residual in this one (z) is different from regular linear regression because it is based on a prediction of the changes, but we often presume it has an independent residual variance (ζ^2) as well.

In this notation, we can now see that the previous expressions (Exhibits 6.6 and 6.7) are formally identical. This can be demonstrated by simple substitution. More importantly, this basically means that any model that uses change as an outcome can be considered exactly the same as the autoregression model with one parameter altered: the change regression (α_1) is one minus the autoregression ($\beta_1 - 1$). Incidentally, this is also true of the standardized scores. In other ways too, the numerical results should not differ. If other variables are added, the same is true.

We are not the first to notice this interesting parallel (e.g., see Kessler & Greenberg, 1981). In these terms we could call this alternative model a *residualized change score* expression (Tucker, Damarin, & Messick, 1966).

EXHIBIT 6.7
Defining a Type DR Regression Change Model

We start with the Type D model, but we use the initial time score as a predictor of the changes:

(1) $$D_{yn} = \alpha_0 + \alpha_1 Y[1]_n + z_n$$

so that the outcome is the change score and the regression coefficients are used to describe the impact of the earlier (in time) scores on this outcome. Of course, the residual here (z) is different because it is based on a prediction of the changes, but we can presume it has an independent residual variance (ζ^2) as well.

In this notation, we can now see that some of the previous expressions are formally identical. That is, if we substitute this Equation 1 into Equation 1 of Exhibit 1.0d, we obtain

(2) $$(Y[2]_n - Y[1]_n) = (\beta_0 + \beta_1 + Y[1]_n + e_n) - Y[1]_n$$
$$= \beta_0 + (\beta_1 - 1)Y[1]_n + e_n$$
$$= \alpha_0 + \alpha_1 Y[1]_n + z_n$$

where slightly different labels are used for the regression parameters.

Some researchers (P. D. Allison, 1990; Coleman, 1968) have cautioned that since the Y[1] is clearly a part of the change score D_y, then the parameters of this model (i.e., β_0, β_1, ψ^2) do not have the same properties as the usual regression model. That is, it is rather difficult to think of the prior score (Y[1]) being held constant when it certainly is not held constant because the same variable is the outcome. But, in our view, this is simply a property of all regression terms, and the key problem here is that we are talking about the same measure repeated over time.

Others have noted that the last two approaches can yield equivalent results, especially when dealing with only two occasions (Winer, 1971), and many have suggested that the choice is basically a substantive one (e.g.,

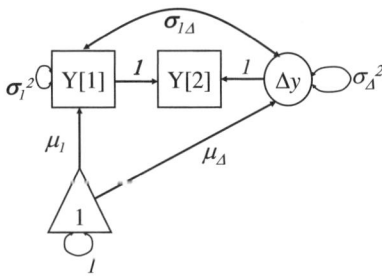

Figure 6.4. A path diagram of the latent change score. The Δy is an unobserved variable whose moments (μ_Δ, σ_Δ^2, $\sigma_{1\Delta}$) are implied by the formula Y[2] = Y[1] + Δy.

Fitzmaurice, 2001); that is, "Do you want to try to take into account the past or not?" As it turns out, this use of regression with a change score outcome is not exactly the same problem for our approach because our approach is not based on observed scores. Although the approach we do advocate is a bit different, and not used by many others, it is relevant to the discussion here.

TYPE Δ AND TYPE ΔR CHANGE: MODELING CHANGES AS UNOBSERVED SCORES

In Type Δ change score models, we use the same repeated measures scores from the same data, but we can write the latent change score model where the change is not directly observed. This LCS is drawn as Figure 6.5 and defined in Exhibit 6.8. This makes sense because we often collect data at two occasions and then imply a change between these two times. Here the two observed scores are considered as linear combinations, and the change is the constructed scores (Δ_y defined by a unit value), but it is not directly observed so it is considered as a latent variable. That is, to draw a path model in the same way, we just consider the Y[1] and Y[2] as observed and add the Δy to the diagram as a unobserved variable (i.e., a circle). From this approach we can add the means and covariances of the observed change scores. As done before, this model could include a predictor from the past, and the change regression could be rewritten as a residual latent change score. Although this approach is not now widely used and we have not actually seen it used by anyone except us (McArdle & Nesselroade, 1994), it is presented as a path diagram in Figure 6.5.

The characteristics of any latent change score (Δ_y) are "numerically identified" in exactly the same way as any other latent variable; we need to attach it to an observable with a fixed (usually positive) value. Here it is

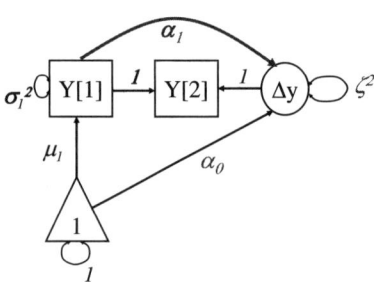

Figure 6.5. A path diagram for the regression of the latent change score. The Δy is an unobserved variable whose moments (μ_Δ, σ_Δ^2, $\sigma_{1\Delta}$) are implied by the formula Y[2] = Y[1] + Δy *and* Δy = α_0 + α_1 Y[1] + z.

EXHIBIT 6.8
Defining a Type Δ and a Type ΔR Regression Change Model

In Type Δ change score models, we use the same repeated measures scores, the same data, but we can write the latent change score model by rewriting the model as

(1a) $$Y[2]_n = Y[1]_n + \Delta_{yn},$$

where the change is not directly observed. This concept is formally equivalent to defining

(1b) $$\Delta_{yn} = Y[2]_n - Y[1]_n.$$

Here the two observed scores are considered in exactly this way, and the change is the constructed scores (Δ_y, from unit values), but it is considered as a latent variable. From this simple exhibit we can add a few key features of the means and covariances, such as

(2) $$\Delta_{yn} = \mu_{\otimes y} + \Delta^*_{yn} \text{ and}$$

$$E\{\Delta^*_y \Delta^*_y\} = \sigma^2_{\Delta y} \text{ and}$$

$$E\{Y[1]^* \Delta^*_y\} = \sigma_{1\Delta y}.$$

As before, this model could include a predictor from the past, and the latent change score regression, or residual latent change score, could be rewritten as

(3) $$\Delta_{yn} = \alpha_0 + \alpha_1 Y[1]_n + z_n.$$

---

attached to observed variable Y[2] with a fixed value of 1. The constraints used here are (a) an explicit unity for the regression of variable Y[1] toward Y[2] with (b) a zero explicit residual term.

This approach could be crucial because one model we will emphasize later uses of this kind of expression when the variables in question are themselves unobserved or latent factors, possibly representing common factors, and generally termed F[t] (in italics). These are scores that have not been measured but are implied by other variable restrictions (see Exhibit 6.9, to be described more fully in Part IV of this book). We will consider a model where we have a common factor score at any time (F[t]) that is itself indicated by a set of invariant factor loadings (λ) equal by the set of observed scores (Y[t]) and added to a unique factor score (u[t]). This unique score is considered to contain something specific to every variable (i.e., a specific factor) and something random (i.e., a random factor). More on this basic concept will be dealt with (and depicted) in the models of Part IV.

After this kind of measurement model is in place, we can derive the latent change scores (Δ_F) among common factors using the simple logic of fixed unit values, and these are now available for further inquiry. In this

EXHIBIT 6.9
Defining a Type Δ Factor Change Model

One model we emphasize later (see Type 3) uses of this kind of expression when the variables in question are themselves unobserved or latent variables, possibly representing common factors, and generally labeled here as $F[t]$. For example, we will write

(1) $$Y[t]_n = \lambda F[t]_n + u[t]_n$$

where we have a common factor score at any time ($F[t]$), indicated by a set of factor loadings (λ) multiplied by the set of observed scores ($Y[t]$) and added to a unique factor score ($u[t]$). After this kind of measurement model is in place, we can derive the characteristics of

(2) $$\Delta_{Fn} = F[2]_n - F[1]_n,$$

where the factors are now latent change scores (Δ_F), using the simple logic of fixed unit values, and these are now available for further inquiry. Of course, this approach requires the common factors to have the identical scaling at all occasions (λ), or else we could not treat this as a latent change score, and we need to verify this by additional model constraints.

---

framework we rather assume or test the hypothesis that all $F[t]$ are in the same metric or scale of measurement; that is, these factors are said to have multiple factorial invariance over time (MFIT). We will go into this in some detail later (see the models of Part IV in this book), but, for now, we can state that if a basic form of invariance can be said to exist, then the changes in the latent variables can be seen to have some very useful properties. For example, these latent or uncalculated change scores can be said to have the same simple interpretation as the calculated change scores. Furthermore, these latent change scores can be used to describe a wide variety of variables.

SUMMARY OF THE TWO-OCCASION MODELS

What we have just tried to demonstrate is that (1) given any two-occasion repeated measures data, we can write several alternative structural change models. (2) It is not easy to distinguish these models by goodness-of-fit tests, because these models can be exactly identified, rotated, and fit as well as one another. (3) Our interpretations of change from these models are fundamentally restricted by these initial choices, so choose carefully then to match the problem at hand. (4) Measurement error can have direct effects on lowering the determination of individual differences in changes. It also appears that (5) the models presented here, autoregression, observed change scores, and change-regression scores, cannot really be distinguished from one another when there are only two occasions of measurement ($T < 3$). But the last two models can have slightly different interpretations because the change-regression model takes into account prior differences and the simple change score model does not.

The confusion that this initial problem of change models has generated is almost beyond repair. First, many people are sure the direct use of change score information is incorrect, and it is not. Then, for example, these basic models of change are often clearly mixed up:

> There are two approaches to the prediction of change in such analyses, and in this book [sic] we use both. The first approach involves computing a change score by subtracting the "before" measure from the "after" measure, and then using the change score as the "dependent variable." The second approach uses the "after" measure as the "dependent variable" and include[s] the "before" measure as one of the "predictors" (i.e., as a covariate). In either case one could say that the earlier score is being "controlled," but the means of controlling differ and the results of the analysis also can differ—sometimes in important ways. (Bachman, O'Malley, & Johnston, 1978, p. 199)

This approach, representing both the change score model and the autoregression model, seems to be entirely democratic. The researchers really try to look at every aspect of the two-occasion problem hoping, as if by some miracle, the data will burst out and reveal themselves! But rather than be pejorative about researchers who are reasonably confused, let us look to the positive aspects of this problem.

One reasonable conclusion we can arrive at is that there are many useful models for change, but the key choice within any approach is to use the change score as the dependent variable. Then the remaining question is whether or not we want to use the initial score as a predictor of change. This can be a difficult question: "Do we want an answer as if everyone is actually allowed to be different at the first occasion?" If so, we should not enter the initial score as a predictor of change. But in fact we typically do we want an answer to the question "What if everyone were the same at the first occasion?" In this case, we should enter the initial score as a predictor of change. And although we must remember that there is always a substantive choice about the selection of relevant predictors, we also would probably not enter a redundant predictor that simply created a tautology. We need to consider each problem in its own context—and carefully.

In the rest of this book we typically do consider the outcome as a change score, and then we will almost always add that one of the potential inputs is the prior time score. Of course, if we have enough measured time points we may even want to approach the problem of "does the change in x impact the change in y?" To avoid problems with the usual residual change score analysis, we will use latent variables. Of course, we need not do this at all but, and in every case, the intercept and the residual terms will count as well. In most models, the explained variance is based on the same residual variance (σ_e^2), but it is compared in autoregression model with the variance at a later time (σ_2^2); however, in the change regression model, it is compared with the variance of the changes (σ_Δ^2). This change regression model (of Exhibit 6.7) will be considered for the most part because it is the only model that allows all aspects of the data to be considered at once. Any of these changes could be among latent variables as well (of Exhibit 6.8 or 6.9), and as we will show, this is a most useful way to proceed.

7

ANALYSES BASED ON LATENT CURVE MODELS

In 1985 an important innovation in longitudinal research was created by Bill Meredith (later published as Meredith & Tisak, 1990), who showed how the "Tuckerized curve" models (after Tucker, 1958) could be represented and fitted using a structural equation model based on restricted common factors. Although this was a general development of the repeated measures analysis of variance (RANOVA) problem (Bock, 1975; Fisher, 1925; Winer, 1971), it was not presented in that way by Meredith. This work led us to try to solve some persistent methodological and substantive studies of growth processes using structural equation modeling (SEM) techniques, including the use of path diagrams for growth models (McArdle, 1986, 1997; McArdle & Anderson, 1990; McArdle & Epstein, 1987; McArdle & Hamagami, 1991, 1992). These latent curve models (LCMs) have since been expanded and used by many others to isolate systematic trait-changes (O. D. Duncan, 1975; McArdle & Woodcock, 1997; Mehta & West, 2000; Muthén & Curran, 1997; Willett & Sayer, 1994).

http://dx.doi.org/10.1037/14440-008
Longitudinal Data Analysis Using Structural Equation Models, by J. J. McArdle and J. R. Nesselroade
Copyright © 2014 by the American Psychological Association. All rights reserved.

The contemporary basis of LCM analyses can also be found in the recent development of multilevel models (Bryk & Raudenbush, 1987, 1992; Goldstein, 1995) or mixed-effects models (Littell, Milliken, Stroup, & Wolfinger, 1996; J. Singer, 1998), but this will be emphasized here when we consider observed group information. The work by Browne and du Toit (1991) showed how the nonlinear dynamic models could be part of this same framework (Cudeck, du Toit, & Sörbom, 2001; McArdle & Hamagami, 1996, 2001; Pinheiro & Bates, 2000). Most recently, McArdle (2001) and Bollen and Curran (2004, 2006) have suggested a way to include autoregressive terms into these models. In particular, McArdle (McArdle, 2001; McArdle & Hamagami, 2001; McArdle, Hamagami, Meredith, & Bradway, 2001a) suggested the use of LCS as a practical basis for practical evaluation of dynamic models. We will elaborate on this model later in this part of the book.

LCMs DEFINED

To ameliorate some of the prior problems, a seemingly odd set of structural equation models was originally used. There are generically termed *LCMs*, and they can be fitted by either approximate RANOVA methods or exact SEM methods (from McCall & Applebaum, 1973; Meredith & Tisak, 1990; see also McArdle, 1986, 1988; McArdle & Epstein, 1987). This contemporary LCM approach typically starts by assuming we have a trajectory equation for each occasion as in Exhibit 7.1 and Figure 7.1. That is, the data at any time point are assumed to be the sum of (1) unobserved or latent scores representing the individual's initial level ($Q\{0\}$), (2) unobserved or latent scores representing the individual change over time or slope ($Q\{1\}$), and (3) unobserved but independent unique features of measurements ($u[t]$). In this model the arrows from the latent slopes to observed variables are a set of group coefficients ($\omega[t]$) or basis weights that define the timing or shape of the trajectory over time (e.g., $\omega[t] = t - 1$ for a linear model). The way the basis parameters are chosen for the LCM makes it possible to obtain different change interpretations.

The main requirement for estimation of this model is that we have at least one fixed value for each factor and one fixed zero to separate Factor 1 from Factor 2. For example, assuming we select all fixed values of 1 for the first component, we can write this without a multiplier (i.e., as $Q\{0\}$), and we can term it a *latent level*. We can fix the position of this level by placing a zero anywhere in the second set of loadings, and where we put this zero, the second factor has no influence. For example, if we place a fixed zero in the first position of the basis (i.e., $\omega[1] = 0$), we essentially are forcing the level to be at the first occasion of measurement, so we can term this the *initial latent level*. However, if we place a fixed zero at, say, the third occasion (i.e., $\omega[3] = 0$), then the latent level is at the third occasion, and this changes the estimated

EXHIBIT 7.1
Defining a Latent Curve Model

This contemporary latent curve model approach typically starts by assuming we have a *trajectory* equation for each occasion for each person formed as

(1) $$Y[t]_n = Q\{0\}_n + Q\{1\}_n \omega[t] + u[t]_n.$$

That is, the data at any time point is assumed to be the sum of (1) unobserved or latent scores representing the individual's initial level ($Q\{0\}$), (2) unobserved or latent scores representing the individual change over time or slope ($Q\{1\}$), and (3) unobserved but independent unique features of measurements ($u[t]$).

The standard "unconditional" model assumes that the latent variables are not dependent on any other variables so, at the next level we also define latent variable scores of

(2a) $$Q\{0\}_n = \mu\{0\} + Q\{0\}_n^*,$$

and

(2b) $$Q\{1\}_n = \mu\{1\} + Q\{1\}_n^*.$$

To reinforce the idea that the uniqueness has no means, we can also write

(3) $$u[t]_n = 0 + u[t]_n$$

---

covariances of the latent level and slope, but the goodness-of-fit is the same. Depending on the number of means (T) and covariances ($T*[T + 1]/2$), we typically evaluate how likely this model is for the observed scores. That is, these linear model parameters (all six) are all uniquely identified, so it has positive ($\{T+T*[T+1]/2\} - 6$) degrees of freedom (df) for testing its validity.

Basic factor analysis principles (see Part IV) are used in scaling the slope factor ($Q\{1\}$) by using different basis coefficient. This initial set of linear basis weights (i.e., $\omega[t] = [0,1,2,3]$) forces the mean of the slope and the variance of the slope to be in units derivable from the "Time of Testing" ($\omega[t] = 1,2,3,4$). This scaling implies that the mean reflects a one-unit change from Time 1 to Time 2, and a one-unit change from Time 2 to Time 3, and a one-unit change from Time 3 to Time 4. Another popular alternative yielding the same fit is based on a scaling of the weights as a simple proportion of the time elapsed (as $\omega[t] = [0/3, 1/3, 2/3, 3/3] = [.00, .33, .67, .1.0]$), and this implies as in later examples that the estimated mean, variance, and covariance of the slope are exactly three times larger to achieve the same expectations (and fit) for the observed data.

An unbalanced set of basis weights (as $\omega[t] = [0, 1, 3, 5]$ can be used to account for the observed but "unbalanced" time delay between occasions. This choice effectively scales the parameters of the slope so it is now in 1-year

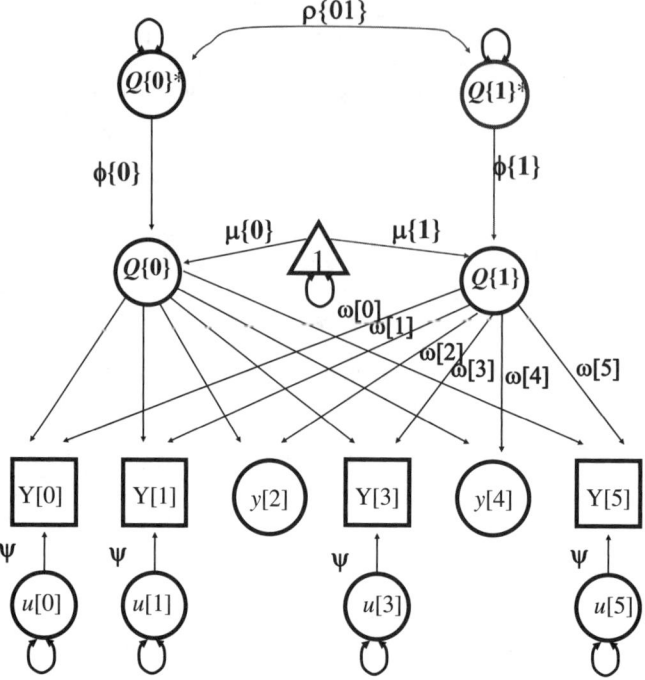

Figure 7.1. A path diagram of a generic latent curve model.

intervals (seen in the slope mean, variance, and covariance). We can alternatively use proportions here (i.e., ω[t] = [0, 1/5, 3/5, 5/5] = [.00, .20, .60, 1.0]), but the fit of any Age- or Grade-based model will be the same, because the estimated mean, variance, and covariance of the slope will be adjusted to achieve the same expectations (and fit) for the observed data. In this case the choice is mainly whether or not the slope to be used represents a 1-year change or changes over all these years. In most case, these choices are up to the analyst.

It is possible to fit model much more elaborate linear basis models as a way to reconstruct time. One of the most obvious ones is to use the actual age of the person at the time of testing. Of course, this requires us to know their age at each testing, assuming not everyone is the same age at testing, and perhaps no pair will have exactly the same age separations (McArdle, 1991b). There is no formal test of the difference in fit due to these kinds of alternative linear bases, because these alternatives (i.e., Time vs. Grade vs. Age) all have the same *df*. However, here there will be a change in fit due to each particular reconstruction of linear time, so we could fit each one of interest and look to see which fits the data better (as in McArdle, 2011c; McArdle & Bell, 2000).

Most importantly, in the LCM, we write the model expectations for the means, variances, and covariances as in Exhibit 7.2. What this shows is that

EXHIBIT 7.2
Defining the Parameters of a Latent Curve Model

In this model, we first define latent variable mean expectations of

(1a) $$E\{Q\{0\}, 1'\} = \mu\{0\},$$

and

(1b) $$E\{Q\{1\}, 1'\} = \mu\{1\}.$$

Next, we define latent variable variance expectations of the level factor

(2a) $$E\{Q\{0\}^*, Q\{0\}^{*'}\} = \phi\{0\}^2,$$

and the slope factor

(2b) $$E\{Q\{1\}^*, Q\{1\}^{*'}\} = \phi\{1\}^2,$$

and only one estimate for all the unique variances

(3a) $$E\{u\{t\}, u\{t\}'\} = \psi^2,$$

and one latent variable covariance expectation of levels and slopes as

(3b) $$E\{Q\{0\}^*, Q\{1\}^{*'}\} = \phi\{01\} = \phi\{0\}\phi\{1\}\rho\{01\}.$$

so we can express the results in terms of a correlation ($\rho\{01\}$) as well.
When these latent expressions are all defined, the observed variables should have mean expectations of

(4a) $$E\{Y[t], 1'\} = \mu[t] = \mu\{0\} + \mu\{1\}\omega[t],$$

variance expectations of

(4b) $$E\{Y[t]^*, Y[t]^{*'}\} = \phi[t]^2 = \phi\{0\}^2 + \phi\{1\}^2\omega[t]^2 + 2\phi\{01\}\omega[t]^2 + \psi^2$$

and covariance expectations of

(4c) $$E\{Y[j]^*, Y[k>j]^{*'}\} = \phi[j, k] = \omega\{j\}\phi\{1\}\omega[k] + 2\omega\{j\}\phi[01]\omega[k].$$

Of course, the fact that $\omega[t]$ is part of all observed variable expectations is notable.
Following McArdle (1986), we can also reconstruct the trajectory in the reliability of the latent score over time:

(5a) $$\eta[t]^2 = \phi[t]^2 / (\phi[t]^2 + \psi^2)$$

where

(5b) $$\phi[t]^2 = \phi[0]^2 + \phi\{1\}^2\omega[t]^2 + 2\phi\{0,1\}\omega[t]^2$$
$$= \phi[0]^2 + (\phi\{1\}^2 + 2\phi\{0,1\})\omega[t]^2$$

the LCM is a formal SEM hypothesis that links the observed means and the observed covariances by using the same parameters ($\omega[t]$). Variations of this model of the underlying raw scores can now be evaluated because they create restrictive hypotheses for both the means and the covariances. That is, if the observed means and covariances do not follow from the model assumptions, we will assume the model assumptions are incorrect.

As seen in the equations above, the added contribution of the LCM slope comes from its mean ($\mu\{1\}$), its variance ($\phi\{1\}^2$), and its covariance with the initial level ($\phi\{0,1\}$). As was pointed out earlier (see McArdle, 1986, among several others), these parameters will change depending on the scaling and hence, interpretation, of the latent variables. But two things for sure are that (a) any change in the fit of the means is due to the one parameter addition of the changing contribution of the slope mean and (b) any change in the variance and covariance contribution of the slope is due to the combination of the slope variance and covariance together. Thus, any test of the mean changes from the baseline is based on one *df*, whereas any changes in the covariance from baseline are based on at least two *df*. This is not an unusual idea, but it is an idea that is often overlooked; because the correlation between level and slope is an estimated parameter, it adds to the covariance prediction as well (see Exhibits 7.1 and 7.2).

Any judgment about the usefulness (i.e., improvement in fit) of slope variance is based on the addition of both the slope variance and covariance terms, because in this case they are really not separable. This implies, for example, that if we want to know if the addition of the slope term adds significantly to the model, then this takes three parameters to achieve (i.e., the mean of the slope, the variance of the slope, and the covariance of the level and slope). This compound term for the slope using both variance and covariance terms is invariant under any linear scaling of the basis coefficients, but the variance of the slope is not. In order to avoid confusion, we will call this compound parameters a *connection* rather than a covariance.

THE LCM AS A PATH DIAGRAM

One version of this type of model was presented as a path diagram in Figure 7.1. As before, all path diagrams are supposedly an exact translation of the defining matrix formulation (McArdle, 1986, 2005). In this case the initial latent level and slopes are often assumed to be random variables with fixed (or group) means ($\mu\{0\}$, $\mu\{1\}$) but random (or individual) variances ($\phi\{0\}^2$, $\phi\{1\}^2$) and similarly random covariances ($\phi\{01\}$). The standard deviations ($\phi\{j\}$) were originally drawn to permit the direct representation of the correlation ($\rho\{0,1\}$) instead of the covariance ($\phi\{0,1\}$; see McArdle & Hamagami, 1991).

This is not usually considered to be critical for estimation, but it can be (i.e., because the use of standard deviations limits the variances to be nonzero).

The inclusion of the slope as a variable is a key feature of any model where we want to evaluate hypotheses about the group means and covariances that require the same parameters of proportionality (i.e., the basis weights ω[t]). Indeed, this calculation of the LCM is an indirect way to evaluate the patterns of the score trajectories. One unusual and new feature of this model is the use of a constant to represent a measured variable that actually has no variation, i.e., the unit constant. The value of unity ("1") associated with the unit constant is needed to create appropriate expected sums of squares, and indeed, this is a model of average sums of squares and cross-products (SSCP), or moments around the means. The key reason this new option is added to the model is to allow us to make hypotheses about the group means and intercepts of the variables in the model. In this approach there is only one constant (per different group), and this always has a two-headed arrow attached to it representing the SSCP of the constant and is typically estimated at its starting value (i.e., unity, but it could be any positive constant).

The models we are talking about now can become very complicated very rapidly. So it is wise to build up some concepts from simpler models first. With this in mind, let us reconsider what we are saying by using Figure 7.2. This is an extremely simple-looking diagram that can actually be used to convey a lot of information. Here we presume that the phenomena of interest (Y[t]) has been measured at some occasions (the squares) but not at others (i.e., the circles). The reasons for this kind of unbalanced data are not always clear, and they are not always the same. But surely there is always a reason why this happens. By setting up an equal interval in time between our latent variables, we have a clear understanding that this has happened. Incidentally, in several prior examples, the measurements were not made at all (e.g., the circle could stand for "zero funding"). This is a case of "unbalanced" timing.

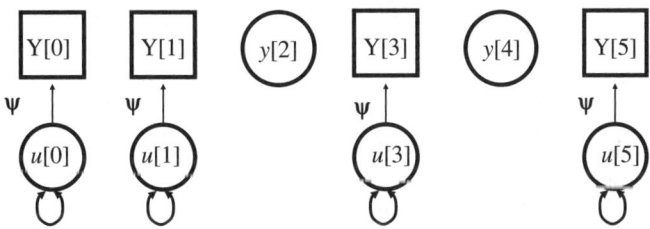

Figure 7.2. A path diagram of a no-growth–no-individual differences model. The scores at *y*[2] and *y*[4] are not observed, but this allows for an unequal spacing of observed occasions. Residual scores with equal error variance (ψ^2) are added at all measured occasions.

Of course, "planned missing data" (as in McArdle, 1994) are also often created in cases where no changes are assumed to be have taken place (i.e., no reason to measure before a week after the event, then 1 month, then 6 months, then 1 year, etc.). We will often ignore the information in the time lags of the observed variables, because this model allows us to consider information at a constant distance among all the variables.

The next element that is added is another latent variable ($u[t]$) associated with each measurement point. On a philosophical basis it could be argued that there should be measurement error even when the variables are not measured, but because this will have no effect on the fit here, we will not argue too much now. What we will do is represent this unique term as an unobserved variable (in a circle) with some variance where each is assigned to the two-headed arrow of unit length (so this is not labeled). Each uniquenesses also has an unknown but equal impact on the observed repeated score (labelled ψ). In terms of the observed variables, the variation that reaches each observed variable is the square of this loading ($\psi^2 = \psi\ 1\ \psi'$). This representation effectively constrains all variance to be "non-negative" and was once thought of as a big plus (see McArdle, Prescott, Hamagami, & Horn, 1998), but it was soon pointed out that variances that are actually zero may have a sampling distribution that can place them below zero (McArdle, 2006).

Figure 7.3 starts in exactly the same way, including a common factor (labeled $Q\{0\}$) with a specific structure. This is an unusual common factor because it requires all loadings to be equal to the unit value (so these are not labeled either). This new common factor is assumed to have a deviation from its own standardized version (labeled $Q\{0\}^*$) and a mean ($\mu\{0\}$) from the constant 1. Taken together this implies that all observed variables have the same mean ($\mu\{0\}$), the same variance ($\phi\{0\}^2 + \psi^2$), and the same covariance ($\phi\{0\}^2$). Thus, this is a model where the individuals are not the same at the beginning of the series, but nothing changes over time. We will always use this model as our baseline model with repeated measures data.

Figure 7.4 is intended to be a simplified version of the previous baseline model. Here, the latent variable spacing has been removed (i.e., this does not include circles for $y[2]$ or $y[4]$), and each deviation has been represented as a squared variance ($\phi\{0\}^2$ and ψ^2). All other model parameters are the same. If this compact form of the prior model were fitted and all the variances were positive, the fit would be the same as the prior model. This is simply presented here as a largely equivalent alternative representation.

Figure 7.5 starts from this point, with the prior common factor (labeled $Q\{0\}$) to the prior LCM (of Figure 7.2). But here we add another common factor (labeled $Q\{1\}$) with weights or loadings ($\omega[t]$) that are not equal to 1, and these are used to describe some shape of change over time (possibly $\omega[t] = t - 1$). As stated earlier, these are often termed a set of "basis coefficients,

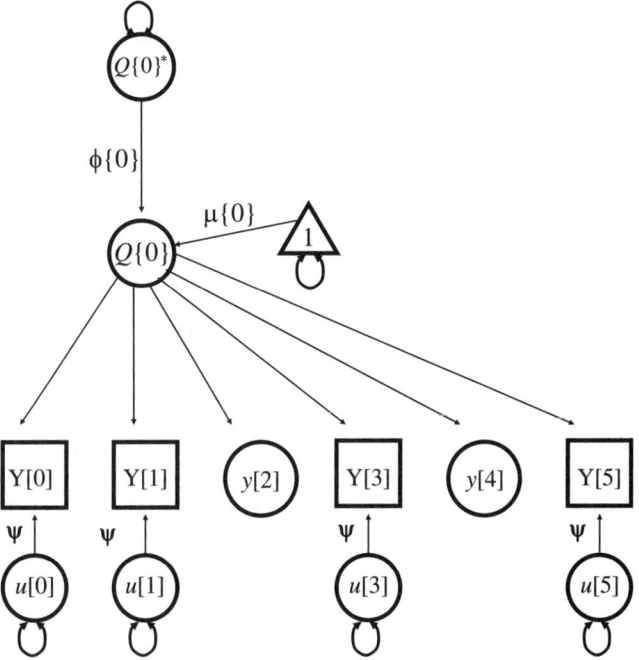

Figure 7.3. A path diagram of a latent curve model with "level" scores separated from "error" scores. The intraclass (person) correlation is $\eta^2 = \phi\{0\}^2/(\phi\{0\}^2 + \psi^2)$ and fixed unit values (not labeled).

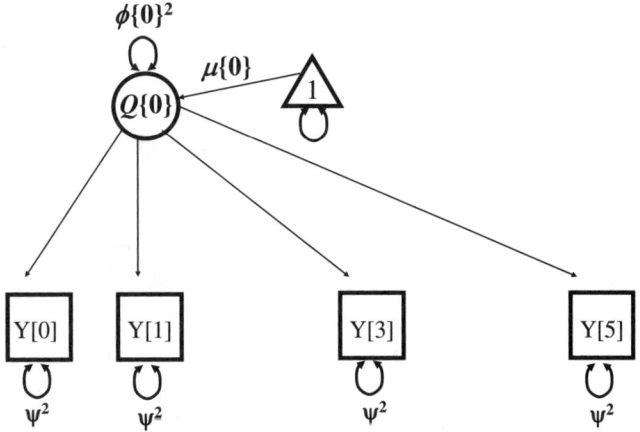

Figure 7.4. An alternative path diagram of an equivalent-level-only model.

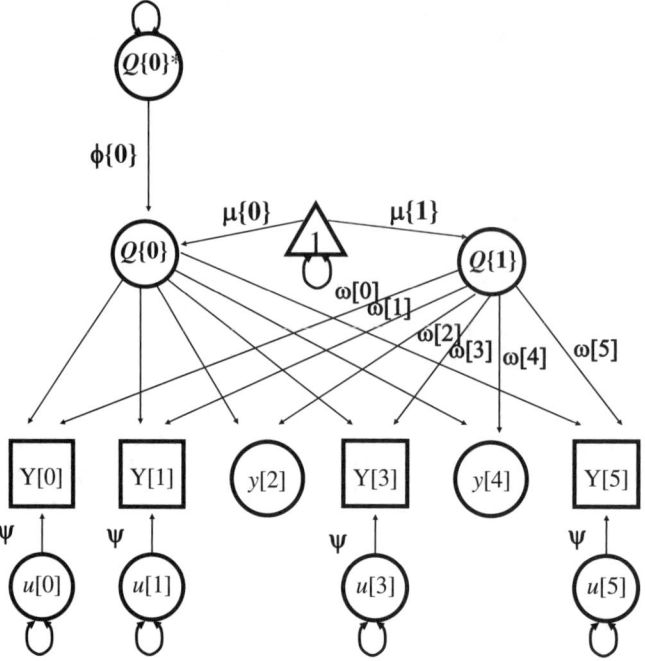

Figure 7.5. A path diagram of a latent curve model with levels and slope (later used for repeated measures analysis of variance).

weights, or saturations." This new common factor is assumed to have a mean ($\mu\{1\}$) but is not now assumed to add variance or covariance to the system. This is a model where the observed means are allowed to change as a function of the a priori basis, but where the covariances are the same as before for the baseline model. This seemingly odd-looking path model actually represents the RANOVA model (Fisher, 1925; McArdle & Epstein, 1987; Meredith & Tisak, 1990).

As we now see, the final LCM path diagram can also be interpreted in SEM terms as a two common factor with means, and this was done in Figure 7.1. The relationships between the latent levels $Q\{0\}$ and all observed scores $Y[t]$ are fixed at a value of 1. In contrast, the relationships between the latent slopes $Q\{1\}$ and all observed scores $Y[t]$ are assigned a value based on the time parameter $\omega[t]$ which, depending on the application, may be fixed or estimated. The latent variables are written in italics ($Q\{0\}$, $Q\{1\}$) because they are similar to the predicted scores in a standard regression equation; i.e., we do not use Greek notation because these scores are not estimated. For a variety of reasons to be discussed next, the unique components ($u[t]$) are defined as having constant deviations (ψ) and are uncorrelated with other components. In this longitudinal model the change score ($Q\{1\}$) is assumed to be constant within an individual, but is not assumed to be the same between individuals. Incidentally, the contribution of the initial McArdle and Epstein (1987) article on this topic was mainly to create a drawing of this LCM, so it became clear that it was a SEM and could be estimated and evaluated in the usual way (cf. Hertzog & Rovine, 1985; McCall & Applebaum, 1984; Meredith & Tisak, 1990).

UNIQUE VARIANCE ESTIMATES AND IMPLIED RELIABILITY

This LCM deals with the errors of measurements as a subset of the unique factor variance (ψ^2) so it is possible to say the latent level and slope described here are free from measurement errors. These level and linear slope scores are termed latent because they are estimated under this assumption of uncorrelated unique variables. Of course, this estimation assumes we have the correct model, and this is hardly ever a certainty. In any case, the implied numbering of the components (i.e., $Q\{k\}$) has nothing to do with the time involved and more to do with the model complexity.

An interesting question has been raised about the need for the unique variances to be identical. If the uniqueness represents the presence of independent influences, it could change over time. If it does, this means the ratios of the true score to the overall variance will change as well (McArdle, 1986). In an alternative way we can consider a trajectory in the reliability of the score over time ($\eta[t]^2$; see Exhibit 7.2), where the reliability at any time is a function of the true-score variance and the unique variance (and see McArdle & Woodcock, 1997). These intraclass terms can be easily calculated for any model. It may surprise some that the reliability of a variable can change over time, but this happens only when the variance of the common factors increases and the variance of the error of measurement stays the same. The latter is the definition that we use here (as used by Heise, 1970, 1974) as it was in RANOVA.

This issue of a changing uniqueness was considered but was not used by McArdle (1986), and a similar concept was also used later by Browne and du Toit (1991), who fitted a longitudinal model where the size of this unique term was increasing over time in a structured fashion. For unstated reasons, there now seems to be a tendency to allow these unique variance parameters to be entirely free, and thus change over time, without much thought about what this implies for expectations of repeated observations. This basically means we are not concerned with the observed variance terms. Perhaps researchers do not like the idea of the reliability of the scale changing with the occasion of measurement, but this change is a characteristic of the standard LCM, not of the scale itself. The set of assumptions for free unique variance is even the default in some new computer programs for LCM (e.g., Mplus), but this really seems like an unwise option. Of course, an improved fit can be obtained if we are not concerned about the observed variances (e.g., the main diagonal of the observed covariance matrix), but as we will show, this is not the only way to achieve better fit.

Mainly, an approach with varying measurement errors can be informative if researchers have an a priori reason for relaxing this constraint. However, if we want to mimic the other kinds of models in statistics (e.g., the separate linear regressions, the RANOVA, the multilevel model), it is most important that these uniquenesses are forced to be the same value so there is only one residual variance term. Of course, this is also partly because we believe that all changes over time should be part of the common latent variables in the system of equations. It is clear that several other researchers have found the independent uniqueness to be a useful parameter to estimate separately, but it is often not based on any formal hypothesis.

NONLINEAR QUADRATIC MODELING

Although a linear scaling of the basis function is now extremely popular (J. Singer & Willett, 2003), it is only one of many that can be used in latent curve modeling. This could be important because we do not think the changes are exactly linear in any case. For example, it is possible to add a lot of nonlinear complexity based on age or time to the simple growth curve models for the study of within-person changes. Wishart (1938) introduced a creative way to examine a nonlinear shape: the use of fixed power polynomials to better fit the curvature apparent in growth data. The individual growth curve (consisting of $t = 1, \ldots, T$ occasions) is summarized with a small set of linear orthogonal polynomial coefficients based on a fixed power-series of time ($\omega[t]$, $\frac{1}{2}\omega[t]^2$, $\frac{1}{3}\omega[t]^3, \ldots 1/p\, \omega[t]^p$) describing the general nonlinear shape of the growth curve. This model is formally expressed in Exhibit 7.3. In this way the quadratic model allows the changes to have a linear relationship with the changes in the basis. If the basis is defined as time ($\omega[t] = t$ or $t-1$), then the quadratic model assumes change is linear with time (Bock, 1975; Wishart, 1938).

The quadratic form of this basic model can be depicted as a latent path diagram as well. As we can see, this appears to be a bit more complicated because it requires a third latent component with a basis that is restricted to be a simple function of the first basis (i.e., $\frac{1}{2}\omega[t]^2$), but all of this is done so the implied change is linear with time (i.e., we add acceleration). Additional variance and covariance terms can be used to account for individual differences in these new latent variables. In order to clarify these expressions, ordinary least squares (OLS) quadratic regressions can be estimated for all the scores on an individual basis. Typically, we find that introducing some curvature allows the model to approximate the data points more closely. Of course,

EXHIBIT 7.3
The Model of Polynomial Growth in a Latent Curve Model

A second-order (quadratic) polynomial growth model implies that the loadings of the second component are fixed to be a function of the first components (i.e., the derivative is linear with time). This can be written as a latent trajectory as

(6) $$Y[t]_n = Q\{0\}_n + Q\{1\}_n \omega[t] + Q\{2\}_n \tfrac{1}{2}\omega[t]^2 + u[t]_n.$$

We do notice that when we take the differences between successive occasions in this model we have

(7) $$\begin{aligned}D[2]_n &= \{Y[t]_n - Y[t-1]_n\} \\ &= \{Q\{0\}_n + Q\{1\}_n \omega[t] + Q\{2\}_n \tfrac{1}{2}][t]^2 + u[t]_n \\ &\quad - Q\{0\}_n + Q\{1\}_n \omega[t-1] + Q\{2\}_n \tfrac{1}{2}][t-1]^2 + u[t-1]_n\} \\ &= \{Q\{0\}_n - Q\{0\}_n\} + \{Q\{1\}_n \omega[t] - Q\{1\}_n \omega[t-1]\} \\ &\quad + \{Q\{2\}_n \tfrac{1}{2}\omega[t]^2 - Q\{2\}_n \tfrac{1}{2}\omega[t-1]^2\} + \{u[t]_n - u[t-1]_n\} \\ &= Q\{1\}_n \{\omega[t] - \omega[t-1]\} + Q\{2\}_n \tfrac{1}{2}\{\omega[t]^2 - \omega[t-1]^2\} + \{u[t]_n - u[t-1]_n\} \\ &= Q\{1\}_n \Delta\omega[t] + Q\{2\}_n \tfrac{1}{2}\Delta\omega[t]^2 + \Delta u[t]_n \\ &= Q\{1\}_n \Delta\omega[t] + Q\{2\}_n \tfrac{1}{2}\Delta\omega[t]^2 \\ &= Q\{1\}_n 1 + Q\{2\}_n \tfrac{1}{2}\end{aligned}$$

Thus, the quadratic model allows the changes to have a linear relationship with the changes in the basis. If the basis is defined as time ($\omega[t] = t - 1$), then the quadratic model assumes the changes are linear with time (for details, see Bock, 1975; Bryk & Raudenbush, 1992; Wishart, 1938).

---

a model of growth data might require this form of a second-order (quadratic), third-order (cubic), or even higher order polynomial model fitted to the data. The polynomial family kind of nonlinear models is very popular (e.g., Bryk & Raudenbush, 1992; Wishart, 1938) and has even been seen as the generic solution to the problem of errors of measurement (e.g., Alwin, 2007), but as we see it now, it is not really simple. This more complex model is presented in Figure 7.6.

SELECTED LATENT BASIS EXTENSIONS

One reason researchers use the LCM logic is that it permits a rich variety of alternative extensions. For example, a different alternative to the linear growth model was brought to light by Meredith and Tisak (1990)—the model

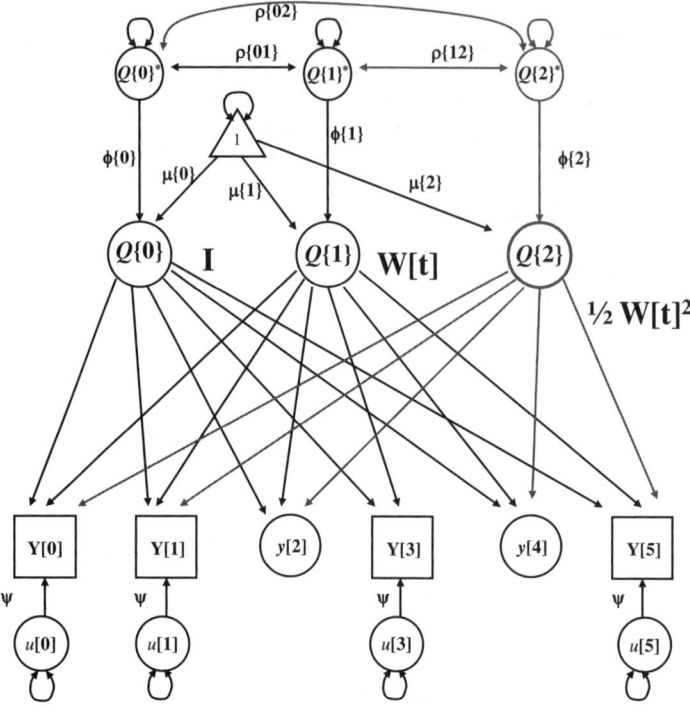

Figure 7.6. A path diagram of a quadratic polynomial as a latent curve model.

proposed by Rao (1958) and Tucker (1958, 1966) in the form of summations of "latent curves." These latent curves were free to vary over time and were not fixed at specific values. These innovative techniques were important because they added the benefits of the SEM techniques. SEM made it possible to represent a wide range of alternative growth and change models (McArdle, 1986, 1997; McArdle & Anderson, 1990; McArdle & Epstein, 1987; McArdle & Hamagami, 1991, 1992). Our use of this latent curve concept can be accomplished with only a minor adjustment to the LCM of Figure 7.1: We can allow the curve basis coefficients to take on a form dictated by the empirical data.

In this alternative LCM, we simply write a model for the same person at multiple occasions where the last two basis weights are fixed (at $\omega[1] = 0$ and $\omega[1] = 1$), whereas the others ($\omega[3]$ and $\omega[5]$) are free to be estimated. If this alternative fits just as well, the first and last coefficients could be fixed instead, and we could fit a latent basis with a proportion scale, that is, two are still fixed at $\omega[1] = 0$ and $\omega[5] = 1$, but $\omega[1]$ and $\omega[3]$ are estimated. The key requirements seem to be that (1) one of the coefficients defines this as different from the level (i.e., $\omega[t] = 0$) and (2) another positive value is used to fixed to define the scale of the slope (i.e., $\omega[t + j] = 1$). Once this is done, all other slope parameters can be estimated (i.e., $\omega[t + k]$ = free), as well as the level-slope covariance ($\phi\{0,1\}$), and the loadings can be estimated as below zero or above one (with estimated standard errors).

It follows that if the remaining basis parameters are allowed to be freely estimated, we can end up with different distances between time points (i.e., an optimal simple shape for the whole curve). The estimated vector of basis weights ($\omega[t]$) has been termed a *meta-meter* or *latent time* scale that can be plotted against the actual age curve for clearer interpretation as done in McArdle and Epstein (1987). In an important sense, this latent time is the time scale where the function is maximally linear (McArdle & Epstein, 1987; Rao, 1958; Tucker, 1966). Once again, the actual time of the observed measurement is known, but the time scale the persons are actually operating under is not known, and here it is estimated using group coefficients. This is admittedly an exploratory device, but it could be an important one, because using this approach we can test the idea of a single common curve that is not linear. There are many ways to estimate these model parameters in an LCM framework, but this is very difficult to do with OLS, so OLS is not actually used. We can even estimate these coefficients in quadratic form, although this is not often done.

The use of a latent time scale in LCM is interesting, and it should not be overlooked in the effort to simplify the model. One way to say this is that this is simply an effort to find the scaling of time that allows the other model parameters related to the slope to be linear. Because it is often the case that time points are chosen in an artificial fashion, such as measurement near birthdays or the 1-week, 1-month, or 1-year repeats, the observed scaling of time is often known but highly suspect (O. D. Duncan, 1966; Gollob & Reichardt, 1987). This latent basis estimation ensures that a linear curve concept is examined fully at the latent variable level. Of course, the resulting curve may rise and then fall, so it could yield a nonlinear optimal curve. Also, this model can be simpler (i.e., using fewer parameters) than the standard quadratic polynomial model because here we do not add another variable to the latent variable model but this is often not discussed.

In the same sense that the latent basis model can tell us a lot about the latent time scale, we would be wise to pay attention to these estimates. At worst the inclusion of these parameters will not change the fit and the linear model would be retained, or we are more assured that linear slopes are the way to go. At best, we can learn something about the optimal timing of linear data collections, because we can learn that the linear model is too simple for the data at hand. One possible downside is that we are adding an exploratory component to what otherwise might be a clear confirmatory strategy. If so, we should not use the probability values in the usual way.

Incidentally, the shape of the curve and the fit of the model should not be dependent on the time points chosen for scaling the slope. We should be able to put the fixed zero and fixed one in any position and still identify the same shaped curve. We could even identify the LCM with a fixed zero as the covariance between level and slope and estimate T − 1 loadings of the slope factor. Of course, if we do this we could obtain the same latent curve and the same fit.

MORE COMPLEX NONLINEAR REPRESENTATIONS

There is nothing that precludes a more complex representation in the form of the latent basis model as long as we have enough measurements. This is certainly one of the attractive features of the LCM. Any fixed set of parameters can be used to define patterns of ups and downs. Another shape we have previously experimented with is based on the use of exponential constraints (see the first expression of Exhibit 7.4; McArdle & Hamagami, 1996, 2001). We can test whether the best curve is exponential in shape, but we do know that a single rate parameter (π) can estimated from many time points. This new model can be compared with the others because it uses fewer free parameters, but when we do so, this is usually an exploration.

We can even fit or even the more complete quadratic expression, where $\omega[t]$ is an estimated latent basis and the second set of loadings (½ $\omega[t]^2$) are a restricted function of the first ($\omega[t]$) weights. Obviously there is much more that can be learned from fitting this kind of more complex SEMs. These alternative models are illustrated in McArdle and Hamagami (2014b).

EXHIBIT 7.4
More Complex Growth Forms in a Latent Curve Model

Another shape we have previously experimented with is based on the use of exponential constraints, such as

(1) $$\omega[t] = exp\{-(t-1)*\pi\}$$

where a single slope parameter is estimated (π) but is distributed as a nonlinear fashion over time (as in McArdle & Hamagami, 1996; McArdle et al., 2002).

We can even fit or even the more complete quadratic expression

(2) $$Y[t]_n = Q\{0\}_n + Q\{1\}_n \omega[t] + Q\{2\}_n \tfrac{1}{2}\omega[t]^2 + u[t]_n$$

where the $\omega[t]$ is an estimated latent basis and the second set of loadings (½ $\omega[t]^2$) are a restricted function of the first ($\omega[t]$) weights.

8

ANALYSES BASED ON TIME-SERIES REGRESSION MODELS

Another important set of structural models for repeated measures data of the panel variety have emerged from the time-series perspective (T. W. Anderson, 1957; Browne & Nesselroade, 2005; du Toit & Browne, 2001). Although data used in time-series analyses are typically relatively lengthy in duration (with $T > N$), we can still use some of the lessons in panel data situations (with $N > T$). These time-series regression models (TSRs) almost all essentially suggest, once again, that the "future is predicable from the past," and this is hardly an arguable point. Although this is rarely debated, it is not clear how we can use this as a main feature of our longitudinal analysis. The real question is what can be gained from this perspective, and we think this can be a lot.

http://dx.doi.org/10.1037/14440-009
Longitudinal Data Analysis Using Structural Equation Models, by J. J. McArdle and J. R. Nesselroade
Copyright © 2014 by the American Psychological Association. All rights reserved.

TSR MODELS DEFINED

We should not overlook the overall simplicity that can be obtained by understanding the present from the past. And here we can use anything measured in the past. Some details of this standard expression are listed in Exhibit 8.1 and Figure 8.1.

These models always have a time lag (Δt) that is defined by the application. Models with particular reasons for including specific time lags (i.e., seasonal adjustment) can be considered special cases where some lags are included and some are not. For example, it may be useful to consider the current behavior as a function of just the most recent two lags of data, where the data two lags back ($Y[t-2]$) have useful properties in understanding the current behavior ($Y[t]$). Given statistical assumptions about the disturbances as independent and identically distributed (IID; e.g., IID with multivariate normality), we can calculate all expected variances and covariances.

An important and basic version of this TSR model is written with only one time lag, and the variance term ($\varphi[t])^2$ is defined by the size of the independent disturbances $z([t])$. This means that an underlying model of change that is autoregressive has a pattern of change that leads to diagonals entries of the covariance structure that are proportional. The utility of TSR comes when we add more variables and examine cross-lagged models, but this simple time-series structure still resonates with some (McArdle & Epstein, 1987; Walls & Schafer, 2006).

The careful reader will also note that the model disturbances are considered to have special status in, say, the discipline of econometrics. Indeed, these are "random shocks" that are indicative of something that, in principle, could be measured. Thus, there is a formal distinction between these kinds of residuals and the psychometric concept of errors of measurement that cannot in principle be measured. We will come back to this issue in Part IV of this book.

An even simpler (i.e., more restrictive) version of this TSR is written with a single coefficient β at each time, so it does not matter what time delay we are examining, and we can have simpler expected variances and covariances. These are based on the simple idea that only one regression parameter (β) raised to the power of the time difference ($t-1$) is needed to provide a structural representation. Because of its inherent simplicity, assuming the "power structure" expectation based on time lags, this is often termed the *Markov simplex* (Jöreskog, 1970b). This can be simplified even further by assuming all disturbance variances are the same (ζ^2), as was done by many others (Wiley & Wiley, 1970).

In general, these models are fitted is a sequence of increasing complexity, where we consider lower order lags first and possible models based on autoregression and even moving averages. A first-order moving average can be added to any of the prior models by writing, say, a model (see Exhibit 8.2)

EXHIBIT 8.1
Defining Time-Series Regression Models

In this model we typically remove the group averages so we can examine deviations within a time ($Y[t]^*$), or

(1a) $$Y[t]^* = Y[t] - \mu[t]$$

The specific way this mean is estimated could be an important consideration, but we leave this for later. We then consider all prior scores as predictors of these deviations,

(1b) $$Y[t]_n^* = \sum \{\beta[\Delta t] Y[t - \Delta t]_n^*\} + z[t]_n,$$

where the time lag Δt is defined by the applications. This is a critical issue we discuss later.

Now it may be useful to consider the current behavior as a function of just the most recent two lags of data:

(2a) $$Y[t]_n^* = \beta[1] Y[t-1]_n^* + \beta[2] Y[t-2]_n^* + z[t]_n$$

where the data two lags back ($Y[t-2]$) have useful properties in understanding the current behavior ($Y[t]$). Given the disturbances are independent and identically distributed (iid), we can calculate that some of the expected variances and covariances as

(2b) $$E\{Y[t]^*, Y[t]^{*\prime}\} = \{\beta[t] \phi[t]^2 \beta[t]'\} + \{\beta[t-1] \phi[t-1]^2 \beta[t-1]'\} + \psi[t-1]^2 \text{ and}$$

$$E\{Y[t]^*, Y[t+1]^{*\prime}\} = \{\beta[t] \phi[t]^2 \beta[t]'\} + \{\beta[t+1] \phi[t+1]^2 \beta[t+1]'\}, \text{ and}$$

$$E\{Y[j]^*, Y[k>j]^*\} = \{\beta[j] \phi^2 \beta[j]'\} + \{\beta[k>j] \phi[k>j]^2 \beta[k>j]'\} + \cdots$$

One basic version of this basic time-series model written as

(3a) $$Y[t]_n^* = \beta[t-1] Y[t-1]_n^* + z[t]_n$$

where, given the disturbances are IID, we can calculate that some of the expected variances and covariances as

(3b) $$E\{Y[t]^*, Y[t]^{*\prime}\} = \beta[t-1] \phi[t]^2 \beta[t-1] + \psi[t]^2 \text{ and}$$

$$E\{Y[t]^*, Y[t+1]^{*\prime}\} = \beta[t-1] \phi[t-1]^2.$$

where the disturbance variance term, $\phi[t]^2$, is defined by the size of the independent disturbances $z([t])$.

An even simpler (more restrictive) version of this TSR is written with a single coefficient β at each time, and we would write

(4a) $$Y[t]_n^* = \beta Y[t-1]_n^* + z[t]_n$$

where, given the disturbances are iid, we can calculate the expected variances and covariances as

(4b) $$E\{Y[t]^*, Y[t]^{*\prime}\} = \phi[t]^2 = \beta \phi[t]^2 \beta' + \psi[t]^2 \text{ and}$$

$$E\{Y[t]^*, Y[t+1]^{*\prime}\} = \phi[t,t+1] = \beta \phi[t]^2 \beta', \text{ and}$$

$$E\{Y[j]^*, Y[k>j]^{*\prime}\} = \phi[j,k] = \beta' \phi[k,j] \beta'$$

Of course, the interested reader should consult other sources on time-series model expectations (Hsiao, 1981).

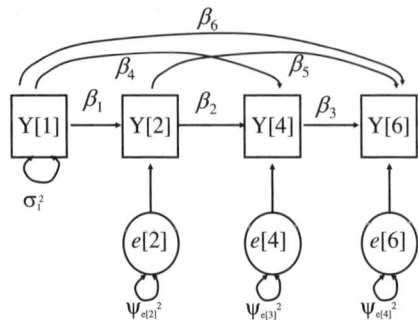

Figure 8.1. A fully recursive Markov chain model with time-based effects.

EXHIBIT 8.2
Advanced Time Series Regression Models

A first-order moving average can be added to any of the prior models by writing a time-series regression (TSR) model and then adding a relationship among the disturbances such as

(1a) $$z[t]_n = \Theta\, z[t-1]_n + e[t]_n$$

so the disturbance at a prior time impacts the next one and so on. (Note: Since the disturbances are assumed to have mean zero, no additional asterisk is used). These TSRs can be combined into an autoregressive moving average model (after Wold, 1949), and this can be seen to yield a more complex structural expectation of the variance at any time point as

(1b) $$\phi[t]^2 = \Theta\, \phi[t-1]^2\, \Theta' + \psi[t]^2$$

leading to observed variance expectations

(1c) $$E\{Y[t]^*, Y[t]^{*\prime}\} = \beta\, \phi[t]^2\, \beta + \psi[t]^2 = \beta(\Theta\, \phi[t]^2\, \Theta')\beta' + \psi[t]^2, \text{ and}$$

and observed covariance expectations

(1d) $$E\{Y[j]^*, Y[k>j]^{*\prime}\} = \beta\, \phi[j,k]\, \beta = \beta(\Theta\, \phi[j,k]\Theta')\beta + \psi[t-k]^2.$$

If these models are part of a data structure where the something has occurred at a certain point in time (i.e., and interrupt), then we can examine the model parameters before and after this "interrupt" and refer to our analysis using the term *autoregressive integrated moving average* (ARIMA; after Box & Jenkins, 1970). As before, the interested reader should consult other sources on time-series model expectations (see Hsiao, 1981).

---

plus a relationship among the disturbances so one disturbance affects the next one and so on. (Note: Because the disturbances are assumed to have mean zero, no additional asterisk is used). This TSR is intended for situations where some independent impact plays out over one extra time lag, but does not persist long afterward. These TSRs can be combined into an autoregressive moving average model (after Wold, 1980), and this can be seen to yield a more complex structural expectation such as Exhibit 8.2. If these models are part of a data structure where the something has occurred at a certain point in time (i.e., an interrupt), then we can examine the model parameters before and after this interrupt and refer to our analysis using the term *autoregressive integrated moving average* (after Box & Jenkins, 1970).

Some of the prior TSRs deal directly with measurement error. Of course, we can always fix the unreliability variance at some suggested level and fit the model around this fixed value (McArdle, 2001). In contrast, both Jöreskog (1970b, 1974) and Heise (1969, 1970) suggested that if $T > 2$ occasions of data were available, then the measurement error in a panel series could be estimated as part of a model, and it could be different at different occasions. To make this model identified, Heise (1969) seemed to be the first to add the constraint that the reliability of the variable would stay the same over time. Jöreskog (1970b) specifically termed his version the *quasi-Markov simplex*, and he drew something akin to the path diagram of Figure 8.5 (this diagram is drawn later). But he suggested that all parameters could not be estimated uniquely, and he provided an interesting example. Because he did not use equality constraints for his autoregressive parameters, only zero or one constraint, he suggested that only two of these parameters could be identified and estimated separately.

This basic issue was a TSR where the Markov relationship was among the true scores, written as Exhibit 8.3. Jöreskog (1970b) also showed how this model could be fitted by adding a few additional constraints. The goal of this model is to separate the change and the measurement errors, assuming the latent variable coefficient (β_f) was now of primary interest. Of course, Heise (1969) and Wiley and Wiley (1970) also suggested something very

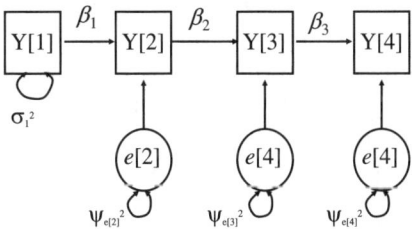

Figure 8.2. A first-order Markov simplex model with time-based effects.

EXHIBIT 8.3
Quasi Markov Simplex Models–Time Series Regression Models
With Measurement Error

This basic model was a time-series regression (TSR) where the Markov simplex relationship was among the common factors, and is written as

(1a) $$F[t]_n^* = \beta_f[t] F[t-1]_n^* + z[t-1]_n$$

with

(1b) $$Y[t]_n^* = \lambda F[t]_n^* + u[t]_n$$

but often this was simplified to the use of a single indicator ($Y[t]^*$), and the model was applied to true scores defined as

(2a) $$y[t]_n^* = \beta_f[t] y[t-1]_n^* + z[t-1]_n$$

with

(2b) $$Y[t]_n^* = y[t]_n^* + e[t]_n$$

---

similar, and these collective statements could be considered the first SEM approaches to deal directly with the simultaneous estimation of measurement error. Others suggested that a model with multiple indicators of a construct could be even more helpful (Nesselroade & Bartsch, 1977), but this suggestion was not taken seriously by many others (see the models of Part IV in this book). Nevertheless, this reduction of uncertainly was clearly the beginning of the longitudinal SEM effort in this direction.

PATH DIAGRAMS OF TSR

The simple path diagram of Figure 8.1 makes it clear that there are many SEM options for these kinds of time-series analyses. We will not draw all issues discussed in prior work. But, in this first diagram, one characteristic that is clear is that all variables in the past are used to produce (or predict) the future behaviors. The term *prediction* seems appropriate here, especially because we are assuming a time-dependent structure. But here we will reserve the word *prediction* for the a priori hypothesis that creates and expectation of a set of means and covariance. This specific kind of TSR is termed *fully recursive* because of the equations it generates (Wold, 1980), but this is not because of any feedback loops within time. Because it requires as many parameters to be calculated as there are observed correlations in the data, it is really not testing any major substantive idea. In this popular formulation we are not really able to test whether or not the past predicts the future, or even vice versa, but we can calculate the predicted values.

The diagram in Figure 8.2 has been modified by adding constraints. For example, we now say that the only predictors needed for future scores are the ones in the immediate prior occasion. That is, the first affects the second, the second affects the third, and the third affects the fourth, and that is all that is needed to predict the future values. In general, we can eliminate three parameters from Figure 8.1, and we can test this comparison of parameters as a formal hypothesis with three degrees of freedom (df). It has been emphasized that we are actually testing the importance of parameters that are not present, rather than the ones that are present. By fitting this alternative model, we can examine whether or not these restrictions seem reasonable for our data.

Each model can be written where the future deviation at a specific score at a time point (Y[t]) is predicted from the deviation at the prior score at an earlier time point (Y[t – 1]) using a linear regression model with one "fixed" group parameters (β) and a random set of independent disturbances ($z[t]$). This model could be fitted to the data directly, assuming the measured lags have some specific meaning, and this is done in Figure 8.3.

It also may be true that the time lags between occasions are not exactly equal and some model-based alterations are needed. Under the assumption that we want to follow the simplest Markov simplex pattern (i.e., with $\beta^{(t-1)}$), this leads us to the model of Figure 8.4, where two latent variables (y[2] and y[4]) have been introduced into the model to allow for the unequal or unbalanced set of observed scores (McArdle & Aber, 1990), now we can fit the appropriate constraints based on equal intervals of time.

As stated earlier, Jöreskog (1970b; 1974) seemed to make some special contributions to this kind of analysis by showing how a model with multiple occasions could be used to simultaneously estimate both reliability and

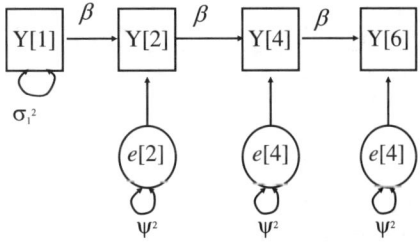

Figure 8.3. A Markov chain model with equal effects for manifest variables.

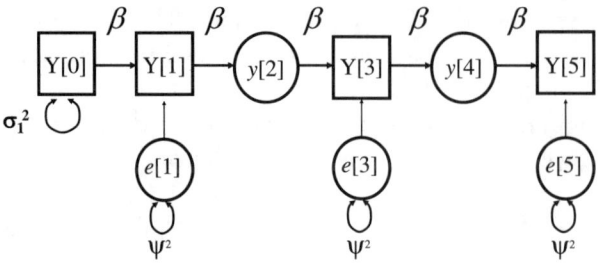

Figure 8.4. The equal-grade Markov model. The regression parameters are equated over equal intervals of time.

changes from a single univariate set of data, and he termed this a quasi-Markov simplex model, which is depicted in the path diagram in Figure 8.5.

Here it is clear that all influences over time are intended to be through the latent variable over time. This basic issue was surely influenced by the early work of Heise (1969, 1970) and Wiley and Wiley (1970). But the way Jöreskog introduced a latent variable within the time series was certainly elegant. He basically identified the model parameters by not estimating the first and last TSR, but he separated the errors of measurement from disturbances by these constraints. Many others have written about the utility of this model (e.g., Mandys, Dolan, & Molenaar, 1994; Werts, Pike, Rock, & Gandy, 1981). And, of course, the use of equality constraints in the prior model can be used to do even more with the total estimation. This often means the variance of the predicted scores increases over time, and if so, the reliabilities of the common factors can change as well.

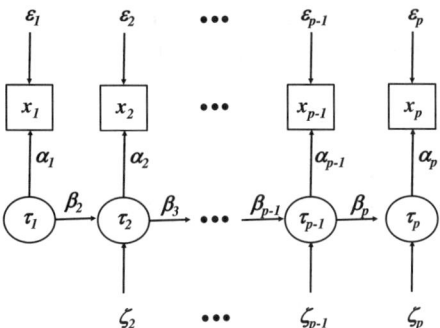

Figure 8.5. The quasi-Markov simplex model of Jöreskog. From *Contemporary Developments in Mathematical Psychology, Vol II* (p. 51), by D. H. Krantz, R. C. Atkinson, R. D. Luce, and P. Suppes (Eds.), 1974, San Francisco, CA: W. H. Freeman and Company. Copyright 1974 by Macmillan. Adapted with permission.

TIME-SERIES MODEL ASSUMPTIONS

Before going much further, let us note that there are some important conditions for these TSRs to be useful. We have emphasized an interpretation of these TSRs by typically assuming the time points are equally spaced, so any a coefficient could be substituted for another with the same specific time interval. This would allow us to have very few time-based parameters and represent a simple process indeed. Many social scientists choose to ignore this timing issue, by typically allowing any value for the first-order or higher order parameters, but this seems disingenuous at best. Of course, the observed data may also be "unbalanced" (as in McArdle & Nesselroade, 1994), and we may need to use unobserved variables representing the time points without data to deal with the problem (McArdle & Aber, 1990, as in Figure 8.4), but these are not the typical constraints defined for use in the TSR.

Another more typical restriction on TSR is an assumption of *stationarity*—that the variances (and covariances) remain the same over all times because the system has reached a steady state of equilibrium (Walls & Schafer, 2006). Equilibrium does not seem to be a reasonable assumption for many substantive problems about systematic changes, so when equilibrium does not occur, this particular TSR is probably not a good idea.

In addition, the means of the scores at each time are not considered, so they do not count against us here. This may sound foolish at first, especially to those coming from a strict ANOVA background, but there are many examples where these group-level (i.e., means) statistics are not a key element of the analysis. This problem does not create more model misfit, but it can be a problem when the change for the whole group is a key part of the substantive questions.

Perhaps it is now obvious, but the TSRs are not the same as the previous latent curve models (LCMs), in either their conception, goals, or model expectations (McArdle & Epstein, 1987). For example, in the LCM approach the means of the observed scores are an intricate part of the model fit, whereas in the TSR these do not really matter at all. Also, in the LCM approach no variable is actually considered to be a prior predictor (in time), and the time points might be shuffled about. The ordering in time is of critical importance in the TSR. At this point we are left to wonder which of these concepts is most useful. We will soon show how they both can be useful.

9

ANALYSES BASED ON LATENT CHANGE SCORE MODELS

The previous latent curve models (LCMs) and time-series regressions (TSRs) are only two approaches to the analysis of within-person changes that, while representing major modeling approaches, barely scratch the surface of all the possibilities (e.g., see McArdle, 2009; Walls & Schafer, 2006). The illustrations here are designed to show that any longitudinal structural equation model (LSEM), based on LCM-type models or TSR-type models, is used to make a prediction about longitudinal trajectory. Thus, many kinds of models have their place in the array of possible analytic frameworks, and empirical choices between models are not often so easy. It seems a bit like the choices between the model of analysis of changes and analysis of covariance of changes (as in Lord, 1967).

Some of these choices seem to be simply defined by the data. For example, we might have a data set where the individuals are measured repeatedly at many more time points (i.e., $T > N$). In this sense, a collection of complete cases at a few time points ($T < N$) within a panel study design is fairly easy

---

http://dx.doi.org/10.1037/14440-010
Longitudinal Data Analysis Using Structural Equation Models, by J. J. McArdle and J. R. Nesselroade
Copyright © 2014 by the American Psychological Association. All rights reserved.

to consider, even if the observed timing is unbalanced, and this has allowed us to go a bit further. In other studies we have far less data on more people (e.g., N = 204, T = 4) and we opt for the LCM approach, but using the self-imposed data design hardly seems like a good way to make a choice about a model for the data.

When faced with this problem in the past, we tried to merge the LCM and TSR. Figure 9.1 is a brief rendition of what was done by Horn and McArdle (1980) in the context of a common factor model. Basically, we thought we would simply fit a common factor model (e.g., an LCM) with a TSR simplex on the residuals. This seemed to match what was being done in other areas of statistical inquiry. In repeated measures analysis of variance (RANOVA), for example, the test of mean changes was often done assuming an AR(1) structure (Church & Schwenke, 1986). Other common factor models with multiple latent variables were considered in the area of biometric genetics (Boomsma & Molenaar, 1987). The recent autoregressive latent trajectory approach by Bollen and Curran (2004, 2006) can be considered a very similar merger of this type as well. But none of these LSEM approaches were very

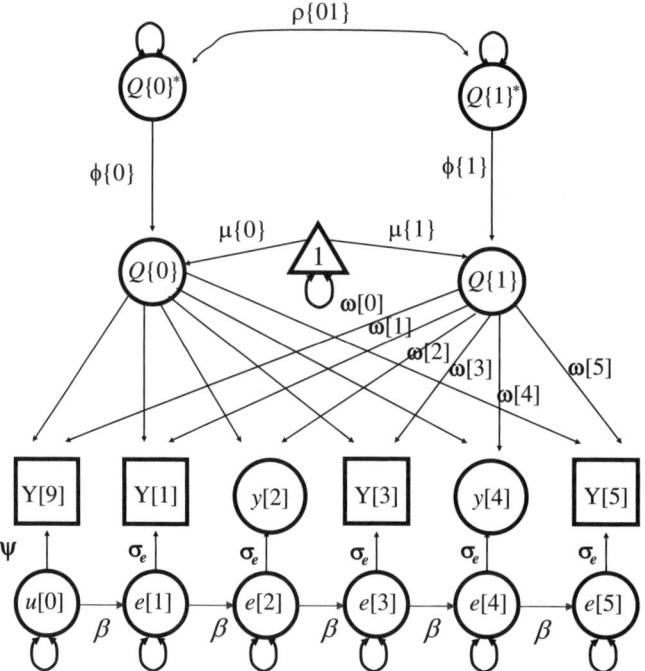

Figure 9.1. A path diagram combination of a latent basis model with an AR(1) structure. Adapted from *Aging in the 1980s: Psychological Issues* (p. 523), by L. Poon (Ed.), 1980, Washington, DC: American Psychological Association. Copyright 1980 by the American Psychological Association.

satisfying to us because they did not make the kind of intuitive or interpretive sense we wanted. We desired something more natural and easier to define.

Until now we have shown how the flexible LCM can be used to define the pattern of changes over time without random error (see Exhibits 7.1 and 7.2). Also, we have also shown how the TSR can be used to describe a Time- or Grade-based process where the prior scores are used to predict later scores and the latent variable is introduced so there can be an estimate of the reliability as well (Exhibit 8.1). But the question now is, "Can we combine these useful concepts?" The answer is yes, and this can be easily accomplished with a newer type of model.

THE LATENT CHANGE SCORE DEFINED

If we look back at the original scientific work on change analysis, we can find the original work of Sir Isaac Newton (or Gottfried Wilhelm Leibniz). Among many other discoveries, Newton suggested we first create an "integral" equation and then, to understand this function, we could write the "derivative" of a function. Of course, in much of his original work, Newton assumed we had the integral equation and was trying to work backward to find the appropriate derivatives. Now, we cannot find any writings where Newton considered longitudinal models for relatively short periods of time (i.e., panel data) or models with individual differences (although variables were separated from parameters) or even models with measurement error. But this was not specifically true of models written by others, and certainly by Nesselroade and Boker (1994). What they showed was that it was also possible to assume we first had the derivative of the data, in theory, in which case the resulting integral was a relatively easy calculation.

In what follows here we basically use the logic of writing a model for the latent change score (LCS) and use this model to imply a trajectory of scores over time. We will assume we are working with latent variables measured over shortened periods of time, and we will write out our theory for the simple difference equations: we will term these change equations here to isolate the distinction between and within persons. Then, following Newton, we will use these to write out the implied trajectory (rather than the integral) of these change models. The reason we will do this is because the trajectory that is implied from the change equation can be tested against real data, and we will want to do this.

Assuming we have the same repeated measures scores (Y[t]), we can write the LCS (Δy) for any person (n; see Exhibit 9.1). We can also add features of the means and covariances of these LCSs; however, because the Δy is not directly observed, but it is only implied as a feature of the model, it is not

EXHIBIT 9.1
Differential Functions to Change Functions Using Difference Operators

Among many other discoveries, Newton suggested we first create an "integral" equation

(1a) $$y[t] = f\{a, b, c, t\}$$

and then, to better understand this integral function, we could write the "derivative" of this function with respect to time using a classical continuous time (CT) approach

(1b) $$dy/d[t] = f\{a, b, c\}.$$

But here we can use the same process in a simpler fashion. Assuming we have the same repeated measures scores on Y[t], we can write the LCS for any person n using a discrete time (DT) conception as

(2a) $$Y[2]_n = Y[1]_n + \Delta y_n$$

where the Δy is an implied or latent change score. This interpretation can be verified simply by rewriting the model as

(2b) $$\Delta y_n = Y[2]_n - Y[1]_n$$

For now, we can also add features of the means and covariances of these change scores as

(2c) $$\Delta y_n = \mu_\Delta + \Delta y_n^* \text{ and}$$
$$E\{\Delta y^* \Delta y^*\} = \sigma_\Delta^2 \text{ and}$$
$$E\{Y[1]^* \Delta y^*\} = \sigma_{1\Delta}.$$

Because the Δy is not directly observed, but it only implied as a feature of the model, it is not possible to plot the unobserved change scores. Instead, we use the statistical information in the repeatedly observed scores to imply the statistics of the changes.

This DT approach (of Equation 2a) is used because it is far simpler than the CT approach (of Equation 1a) mainly because we assume that $\Delta t = 1$ for everyone, so Δt is not needed as a divisor in the change score. This leads to estimation differences between CT and DT and these will be discussed in Chapter 10.

---

possible to plot the unobserved change scores. Instead, we use the statistical information in the repeatedly observed scores to imply the statistics of the changes.

We need to have enough repeated measures data to be able to provide unique estimates of the error variance (ψ^2) or else we would not use the latent variable notation (i.e., Δy). We think it is fairly important that Heise (1969), Jöreskog (1970b), and Wiley and Wiley (1970) independently showed how when T > 3, this key separation of measurement error is achievable. This approach allows us to go beyond the usual two-occasion model (where T = 2) and examine hypotheses about any pairings of scores, and we can next write a set of alternative models for these latent changes. On an algebraic basis, we note that the assumption that all latent variables at the first level are one unit apart ($\Delta t = 1$) allows us to write the "rates of change" ($\Delta y[t]/\Delta t$) more simply as "individual latent changes" ($\Delta y[t]n$) or as the LCS approach.

Obviously, in this LCS approach, the specific model for latent change is a particularly open choice. We know that the observed data might have different time lags but, by assuming there is exactly one unit ($\Delta t = 1$) between each latent variable, we can write an expected trajectory over time with three unobserved parts: (a) an initial level, (b) a systematic accumulation of changes over time, and (c) an independent component. In this representation we can also say that the change score loadings are additive too.

LCS EXPECTATIONS

Of course, this approach may not be helpful, especially if something special happens in between any two points of time and we do not know about it. To the degree we can assume a simple change model, we can make an assumption of ergodicity (Molenaar, 2004) that the model parameters remains the same over some period of time. Of course, these assumptions can and should be challenged in empirical data analysis, but they can prove to be useful simplifying devices. In any case, the variances of the common factors ($\phi^2[t]$) could increase here, and if so, the resultant reliabilities ($\eta^2[t]$) could do so as well.

The models listed in Exhibit 9.2 are not exhaustive, of course, because, as we just said, any parameter suggested above could require a bracketed t as well (i.e., where the parameter is only valid for a specific time). But other considerations might apply as well. One of the most interesting aspects of this approach is that it makes it clear that these other assumptions exist. Another interesting aspect of this approach is that it allows many of the other models discussed here to be fitted as special cases. For example, the popular linear change model LCM is exactly the same as the typical additive LCS, whereas the popular autoregressive time-series model (TSR) is the same as one form of the proportional LCS. The least restrictive model among these seems to be exactly a combination of the prior model, and for this reason it was termed a dual change score (DCS) model as in McArdle (2001). This seems to be a typical approach to take: The search for the most general model, where everything else considered earlier was only a special case, was certainly a driving force behind many early structural investigations (McArdle, 2005).

EXHIBIT 9.2
Alternative Change Functions

By restricting the series to have the same structural basis among all latent observations that are one unit apart (i.e., $\Delta t=1$), this allows us to conveniently say

(1) $$\Delta y[t]_n = \Delta y[t]_n / \Delta t,$$

so the latent change score ($\Delta y[t]$) is directly interpreted as a rate of change in the latent variable.

Since we assume that $\Delta t=1$, for example, we can now suggest that these latent changes can be represented as

(2a) $$\Delta y[t]_n = 0, \text{ or}$$

(2b) $$\Delta y[t]_n = \alpha Q\{1\}_n, \text{ or}$$

(2c) $$\Delta y[t]_n = \beta y[t-1]_n, \text{ or}$$

(2d) $$\Delta y[t]_n = \alpha Q\{1\}_n + \beta y[t-1]_n, \text{ or}$$

(2e) $$\Delta y[t]_n = any \ other \ model.$$

We know that the observed data might have different time lags but, by assuming there is exactly one unit ($\Delta t = 1$) between each latent variable, we write an expected trajectory as

(3) $$Y[t]_n = Q\{0\}_n + \sum (j=1 \text{ to } t)\{\Delta y[j]_n\} + u[t]_n,$$

which has three unobserved parts: (a) an initial level ($Q\{0\}$), (b) a systematic accumulation of changes over time ($\Sigma(j = 1 \text{ to } t)\{\Delta y[j]_n\}$), and (c) an independent or unique component ($u[t]$). We can also write the usual latent basis that results from the accumulation as

(4) $$w[t] = \sum (j=1 \text{ to } t)\{\alpha[j]\}$$

so they can add up to form the usual weights for the latent basis.

The correlation of the latent level and slopes ($\rho\{0,1\}$) is, as in any trajectory-based model, (e.g., LCM), a function of where we place the latent level. So although it is unique, this correlation is not independent of the other parameters. We typically place the initial level this at the beginning of the series, but there are many other options we will not describe here (Grimm, 2012).

The mean and covariance structures that are expected from any of the models listed above can be complex, but these can be automatically calculated

EXHIBIT 9.3
Generic Change Expectations

The change model of any equation leads to a trajectory model for the latent scores that can be use to create expected means of

(1a) $\quad E\{Y[t], 1\} = \mu\{0\} + \sum (t = 1 \text{ to } T)\{\alpha[t]\mu\{1\}\}$

with an expected variance among observed scores at some point in time

(1b) $\quad E\{Y[t]^*, Y[t]^*\} = \phi\{0\}^2 + \sum (t = 1 \text{ to } T)\{\alpha[t]\phi\{1\}^2 \alpha[t]\} + \psi^2$

and an expected covariance among observed scores at different points in time $(T = k > j)$

(1c) $\quad E\{Y[j]^*, Y[k > j]^*\} = \phi\{0\}^2 + \sum (j = 1 \text{ to } k)\{\alpha[j]\phi\{1\}^2 \alpha[k]\}$

and these are the kinds of fairly complex expressions used to fit the model to real data.

---

from the structural equation modeling (SEM) programs or by special software. In one recent example, Grimm and McArdle (2005) use the MAPLE computer program (Maplesoft, Waterloo, Ontario, Canada; http://www.maplesoft.com) to generate model expectations based on symbolic values for a series of LCS models. When this is done, it becomes rather obvious that the key feature is that all expectations are formed by *accumulations*: that is, the expectation for the second occasion takes into account the expectation for the first occasion, and the expectation for the third occasion takes into account the expectations for the first and second occasions, and so on. But in general, we can use these models in the same way we use any other model—to examine the fit of the underlying structure of Exhibit 9.3 by comparing expectations with observables (for details, see McArdle & Hamagami, 2014b).

More important, the basic longitudinal SEM (LSEM) question has changed a bit. We suggest that we should not ask the typical question, "What over-time trajectory is implied by the model?" as many other researchers have suggested (e.g., Raudenbush, 2005; Raudenbush & Bryk, 2002). Instead, we should ask, "What underlying latent change model are we fitting?" In subsequent work we will try to show what this alteration in thinking can imply.

LCSs IN A PATH DIAGRAM

One of the best ways to explain our basic LSEM logic is to use path diagrams. In these models the latent changes need to be represented, and then the model of the changes needs to be attached. The models need to have the features of an accumulation over time. Now it should be clear that the diagram is simply an expression of the algebraic model. So if the diagram starts to look confusing, we suggest that a return to the algebra would be most useful.

To this end, we start with the diagram of Figure 9.2. In this figure we draw a model with no changes, as in Exhibit 9.4. This does show how we can add latent variables at a first level ($y[t]$) and add unique variance when the variables are measured. We can also place a fixed unit value between successive latent variables over time and add another latent variable ($\Delta y[t]$) to each of these. The unit constant is assigned to the latent intercept, so it has a mean ($\mu\{0\}$), and this mean is essentially distributed to all variables through the set of fixed unit regressions to all observed scores. However, because the LCSs have no predictors, there is no apparent change in the latent or manifest scores. Because nothing changes over time, we will use this as our baseline model.

We move to the diagram in Figure 9.3. In this figure we draw a model with additive changes. This model is the same as the prior model except now we include a second latent variable, termed a latent slope ($Q\{1\}$) with a mean ($\mu\{1\}$ or α), a variance ($\phi\{1\}^2$), and a covariance ($\phi\{0,1\}$) with the initial level. This

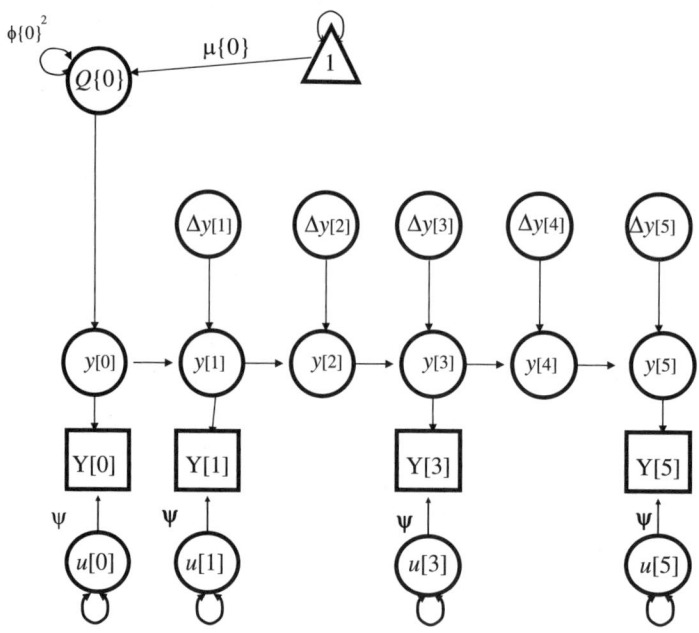

Figure 9.2. A reinterpretation of the no-changes baseline model using latent change scores. From *Structural Equation Modeling: Present and Future* (pp. 342–380), by R. Cudeck, S. du Toit, and D. Sörbom (Eds.), 2001, Lincolnwood, IL: Scientific Software International. Copyright 2001 by Scientific Software International. Reprinted with permission.

EXHIBIT 9.4
A No-Change Model Expectations

In one simplification of the LCS model we remove the slope. If so, then the variance around the latent mean ($\phi\{0\}^2$) also is accumulated through time in the same way, so now all measured variables have expected scores with means of

(2a) $\qquad E\{Y[t], 1'\} = (t \times 1) * \mu\{0\},$

and with an expected variance among observed scores at the same point in time

(2b) $\qquad E\{Y[t]^*, Y[t]^*\} = (t \times 1) \phi\{0\}^2 (t \times 1)' + \psi^2$

and an expected covariance among observed scores at different points in time ($T = j > k$) is the same for all time points

(2c) $\qquad E\{Y[j]^*, Y[j > k]^*\} = (j \times 1) \phi\{0\}^2 (j > k \times 1)'.$

Since nothing changes over time, this can be used as a baseline model for repeated measures.
 That is, if this model fits we can probably stop right here.

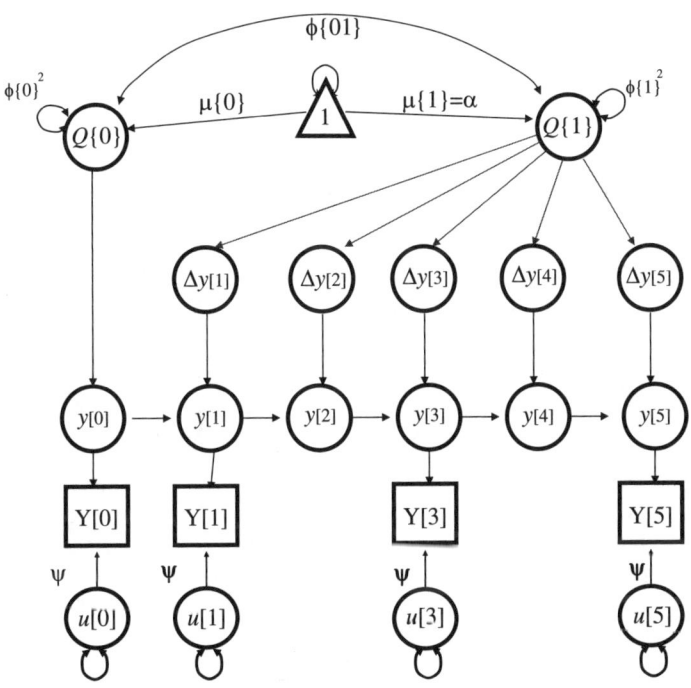

Figure 9.3. Representing a linear additive basis model using latent change score.

model has coefficients of unity from the latent slope to each latent change. This model is what we expect when we elaborate on the latent change of equation (see Exhibit 9.1). The first latent variable (y[0]) is only affected by the initial level (Q{0}), so it can be considered the same as that variable. However, the second latent variable (y[1]) is affected by the first (y[0]) and by the latent slope (Q{1}). Because the coefficients here are all of a fixed value of 1 pointing ahead in time, we can see that any changes in the second latent variable are conveyed to the third, and then to the fourth, and then to the fifth, and so on. This is the way we account for an accumulation of effects. In this model, the intervals of time are presumed to be equal, so the model also creates one change for Time 2 (y[1]), two of these changes by Time 3 (y[3]), three of these changes by Time 4 (y[4]), and so on. Indeed, this representation completely parallels the prior linear change model represented as a set of additive changes.

Figure 9.4 builds on this same idea but now suggests that there is a common slope, but the latent changes are not strictly defined as linear contributors. The coefficients here are not all of a fixed value of 1 pointing ahead in time because we can estimate two from the data at hand, $\alpha[3]$ and $\alpha[5]$. Still we can see that any changes in the second latent variable are conveyed to the third, and then to the fourth, and then to the fifth, and so on. This is the way we account for an

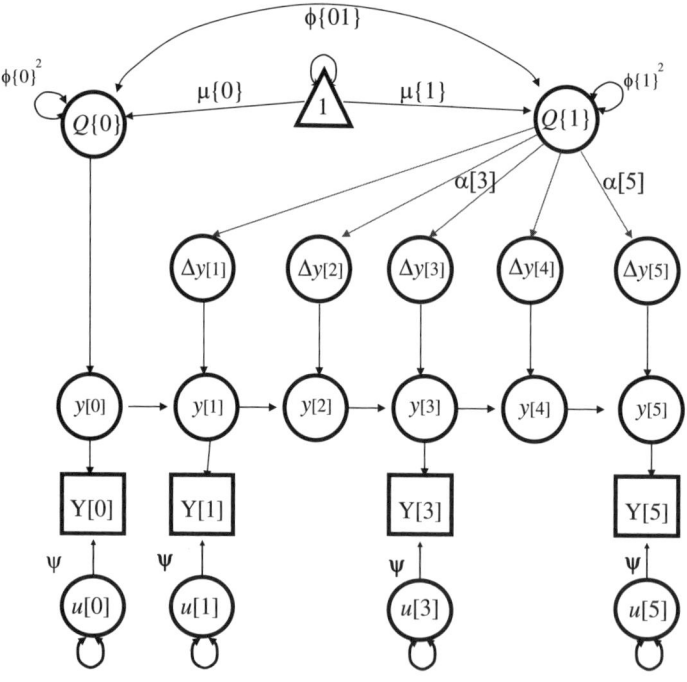

Figure 9.4. Representing a linear additive latent basis model in latent change score.

accumulation of effects. But in this model, the intervals of time are not necessarily equal, so the model also creates one change for Time 2 (y[1]), two of these changes by Time 3 (y[2]), three of these changes by Time 4 (y[3]), and so on. Of course, the estimated weights (α[3] and α[5]) could be negative, implying a decrement in the latent curve function. Indeed, this is a latent basis change model represented as an additive series of weighted changes.

The path diagram in Figure 9.5 builds on the TSR idea (of Figure 8.4), which now suggests that there is no common slope (i.e., no Q[1]), but there is a prediction of the later change from the earlier latent variable. This implies that latent variables earlier in time can generate variation later in time. This is completed in Figure 9.6 where have added two more parameters: the first is a residual disturbance termed z, which has no mean but is presumed to have an independent and equal variance in each latent change. This is done to exactly mimic the quasi-Markov simplex pattern we just described. But to make this model more interesting, we also consider the mean changes as part of this structure of scores, and this was never considered a part of the quasi-Markov simplex. This is a full representation of the TSR models (see Exhibits 8.1–8.3), and this is a model of proportional (or pure exponential) changes.

The next model of Figure 9.7 combines aspects of the prior two models, including the inclusion of both an additive effect from the slope, and a

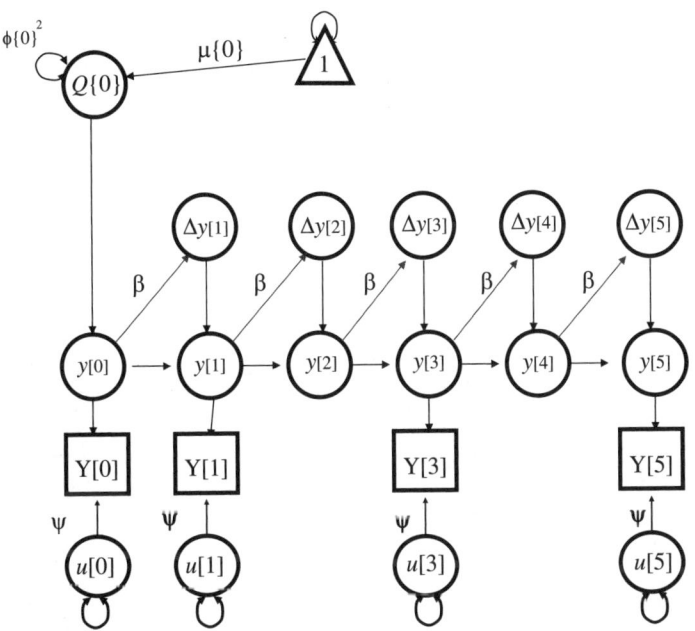

Figure 9.5. A latent change score interpretation of the proportional changes in the time-series regression simplex (see Figure 8.4).

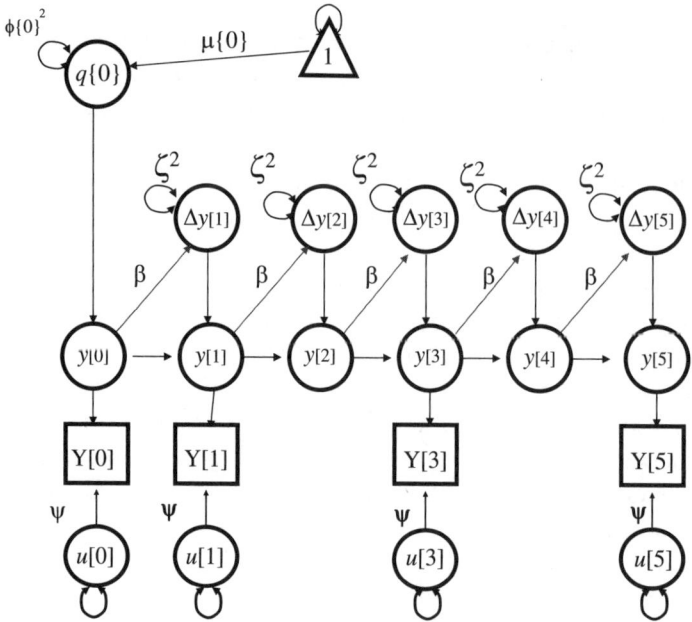

Figure 9.6. A more complete latent change score interpretation of the time-series regression simplex (compare with Figure 8.4).

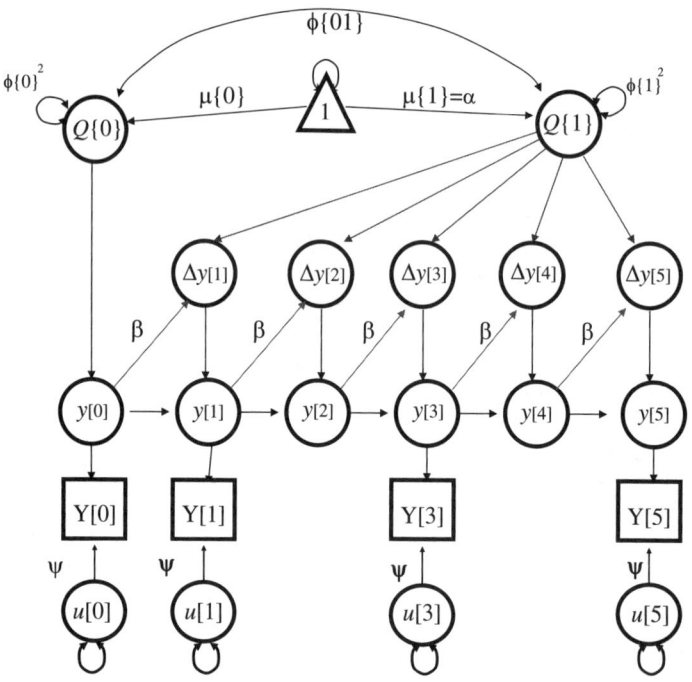

Figure 9.7. Representing a dual change score model.

proportional effect from the prior level of the latent variable. For this reason, we have termed this a *DCS model*. We note that this form of the model does not include the disturbance variance of the residual z (because it is hard to estimate separately), and it includes a changing mean expectation. These two aspects of this model do not exactly create the combination of the autoregressive TSR and the linear LCM. But we do expect this model could be useful if researchers do not know which parameter to fit (see above). Although we do not really have a favorite model here, the LCS approach seems easier to expand to more advanced concepts.

The plots of Figure 9.8 (following McArdle & Hamagami, 2001) show a theoretical subset of the family of expectations that can arise from different values of the DCS model parameters (α and β). Because it is not obvious, if one of these is fixed (or estimated) at zero (say $\beta = 0$), then we have an interpretation that is the same as if it were not there at all. But if both latent

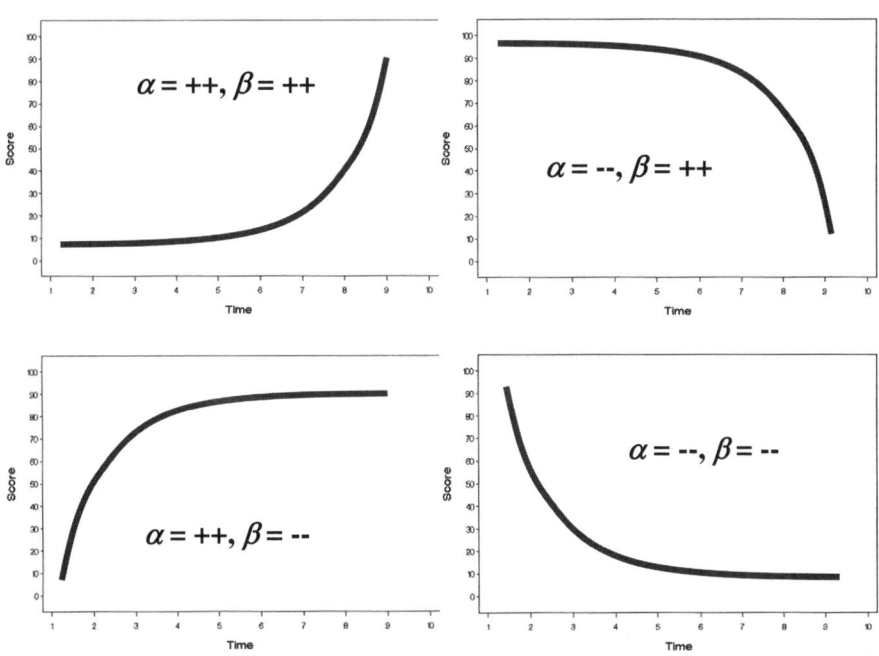

Figure 9.8. Alternative expected values from latent change score–dual change score parameters. From *Structural Equation Modeling: Present and Future* (pp. 15–16), by R. Cudeck, S. du Toit, and D. Sörbom (Eds.), 2001, Lincolnwood, IL: Scientific Software International. Copyright 2001 by Scientific Software International. Adapted with permission. From *New Methods for the Analysis of Change* (p. 147), by L. M. Collins and A. G. Sayer (Eds.), 2001, Washington, DC: American Psychological Association. Copyright 2001 by the American Psychological Association.

change parameters are positive ($\alpha > 0$ and $\beta > 0$), then we can use the DSC to fit a family of curves that start out low and rise rapidly. On the other hand, if they are both negative ($\alpha < 0$ and $\beta < 0$), we can think of the family of curves as starting out high and then going very low. If we find some differences in the parameters (e.g., $\alpha > 0$ and $\beta < 0$, or $\alpha < 0$ and $\beta > 0$), then we have the other kinds of curves shown here. The model expectation for the means and covariances over time is the net result of a combination of linear and exponential curves: All are possible using only the DCS version of the LCS.

10

ANALYSES BASED ON ADVANCED LATENT CHANGE SCORE MODELS

To start, we should mention that in prior work on the partial adjustment model (Coleman, 1968) it has been shown that it is not possible to uniquely identify both the mean of the slopes ($\mu\{1\}$) and the slope loading (α). This makes good intuitive sense because these parameters are both connected by one-headed arrows to the latent changes, so they are impossible to separate. The variation in the slopes ($\phi\{1\}^2$) could be considered variation in these model parameters, but the averages are not separable. Thus, we treat the two parameters of the mean ($\mu\{1\}$, α) as representing the same information.

We will not directly deal with the many advanced issues in latent change score (LCS) analysis (but see McArdle & Hamagami, 2004, 2014b). Instead, we will basically evaluate what we have done up to now, a strategy previously taken by McArdle and Hamagami (2001). At the same time, we also realize that some of the previous models do not fit most available data as well as we might have hoped, and we would like to make it all fit better. For example, one thing we could obviously do is relax the somewhat rigid assumption about the

---

http://dx.doi.org/10.1037/14440-011
Longitudinal Data Analysis Using Structural Equation Models, by J. J. McArdle and J. R. Nesselroade
Copyright © 2014 by the American Psychological Association. All rights reserved.

equality of all uniquenesses. This is a commonly used alternative in factor analysis, but we assume these are repeated measures and will not do this here. Another thing we could do is relax the assumption of equal parameters for equal amounts of time, but this is a key feature of future model prediction. In fact, we do neither of these here.

CONSIDERING A TRIPLE CHANGE SCORE MODEL

One alternative model that could be of interest to us now is one where we consider a dual change model with a latent basis model, which is similar to the latent change score model itself, one version (without disturbances) of which is depicted in the path diagram of Figure 10.1. This approach, defined in Exhibit 10.1, allows that the latent basis coefficients of change ($\alpha[t]$) are very much like those of all prior latent basis weights ($\omega[t]$), but here they provide information about the optimal amount of linear change that is useful in the intervals between latent variables in this model (this is the same information as the optimal distances of the latent variables as in the latent basis model, but here we judge the distance from the fixed value of 1 unit). Using this model, we can estimate the additive, proportional, and latent basis

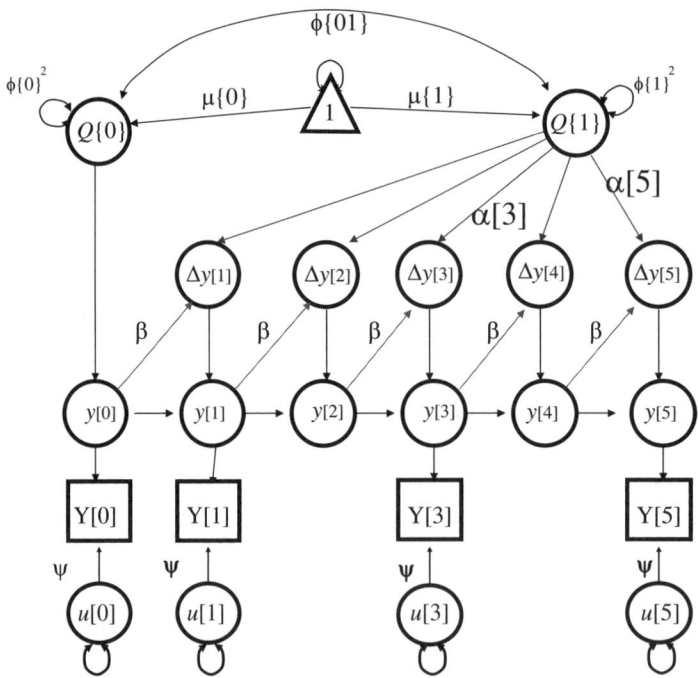

Figure 10.1. Theoretically representing a triple change score model.

EXHIBIT 10.1
A Model of Triple Change Scores

We could consider a series of changes where the time lag is not fixed at each interval, and this is written as

(1a) $$\Delta y[t]_n = \alpha[t] Q\{1\}_n,$$

or even where

(1b) $$\Delta y[t]_n = \alpha[t] Q\{1\}_n + \beta y[t-1]_n,$$

so the impact of some coefficients α[t] could vary over time. To make this uniquely estimable, we would need to force one of these α[t] at zero (to identify the initial level) and one of these at a positive fixed value (perhaps α[t] =1) to identify the slope.

---

coefficients. For this reason, we term it a triple change score (TCS) model. Since the dual change score (DCS) is still a subset of this model, this TCS model should fit as well, or better than the other models presented earlier.

This relaxation of equal time distances between latent changes was fitted here in an exploratory fashion: we simply considered it here by allowing the loadings of the latent changes on the latent slopes, following the same rules as discussed earlier (i.e., we require one zero and one fixed value). Of course, this requires more than two occasions of data. Although this kind of latent-basis latent change score (LCS; or TCS for that matter) model is not yet very popular, it has properties similar to the LCM with a latent basis (where, say, loadings ω[3] and ω[5] are estimated). We do this mainly because we want to reinforce the point that the maximum likelihood estimates (MLEs) that we obtain in any LCS are relative to the accumulation over all times, so instead of, say, a target value of 3 and then 5 for specific occasions, our target will always be a value of 1 for the interval between equally spaced time points of latent variables. The only free estimates for any parameter will be estimable in the intervals where we actually have observed data, so the time points where there are no data cannot contribute to the misfit or estimation. For example, if we had data at Times 0 and 1 but not Time 2 but then we had Time 3—as in the Wechsler Intelligence Scale for Children, Fourth Edition (Wechsler, 2004) example; (see McArdle & Nesselroade, 1994), and which we do in our first example in the applications. The LCM estimates were ω[t] = [= 0, = 1, 2, 2.5] we would obtain parallel LCS estimates of α[t] = [= 0, = 1, 1, 0.5]. In this sense, the specific amount of changes (α[t]) would accumulate to yield the same values as the overall weights (ω[t]; as in Exhibit 9.2).

The inclusion of the latent basis parameters of the latent curve model (LCM) into the LCS could be a more fundamental feature of these models, but it has not been so up to now. But if we think of the latent basis coefficients as *empirical time-adjustors*, it is clear that a latent basis can be added to any change model. For example, the more complex DCS might fit better in an adjusted time scale as well. So even though the DCS has a new parameter representing proportional change, it is considered the same at all time points, and the way the data were collected may not be in an optimal scaling. The addition of $T - 1$ more parameters could help the fit and help explain that the change model we estimate is "ergodic, but in a latent time scale." These, of course, are fairly novel ideas that need to be evaluated further.

A completely different possibility is to consider the disturbances from a TSR approach more seriously. These might be written as in Exhibit 10.2.

EXHIBIT 10.2
Further Latent Change Score Model Complexity

We could write

(1a) $\qquad \Delta y[t]_n = z_n$, or

(1b) $\qquad \Delta y[t]_n = \beta y[t-1]_n + z_n$, or

(1c) $\qquad \Delta y[t]_n = \alpha + \beta y[t-1]_n + z_n$.

To deal with other issues, we could write a model where there is a second set of lag parameters where

(2a) $\qquad \Delta y[t]_n = \alpha + \beta[1] y[t-1]_n + \beta[2] y[t-2]_n + z_n$, or

(2b) $\qquad \Delta y[t]_n = \alpha + \beta[1] y[t-1]_n + \beta[2] y[t-2]_n + \beta[3] y[t-3]_n + z_n$.

Other kinds of analysis are possible to fit with the second change scores as the outcome. These can be written as

(3a) $\qquad y[t]_n = y[t-2]_n + \Delta^2 y[t]_n$

so the second change is defined with fixed unit weights

(3b) $\qquad \Delta^2 y[t]_n = y[t]_n - y[t-2]_n$

and so we can write any model for the second changes, such as

(3c) $\qquad \Delta^2 y[t]_n = \alpha + \beta y[t-1]_n + z_n$.

Still other general representations can be written with the basis coefficients affecting the entire model as

(4) $\qquad \Delta F[t]_n = \alpha[t-1] \, fun\{LCS \, [t-1]_n\}$.

The explicit addition of a time-independent variance terms in the changes would be the same as the innovation variance or disturbance variance (ζ^2) described in the TSR earlier (in Chapter 8). Of course, we should again note that the LCSs from a DCS or a TCS do not have the same variance expectation, so this is not the reason to use innovation variance. On the other hand, innovations could be added because this is a notable feature in the prior estimation of the TSR quasi-Markov simplex and possibly is a good idea. Because we are now considering a slightly different model of changes, it could be used here as well.

Another variation in timing can occur because the unobserved but predictive latent lag is greater than one unit. Of course, this is possible, and the assessment of the empirically optimal lag for observed data is a routine part of TSR. This can be partly accounted for by the design of the observed measurements, or by changing the overall model and allowing prior time points to affect the changes later. To deal with these issues, we could write a model where there is a second set of lag parameters so the model basically implies that the latent change is a function of what happened both immediately before (as we had it earlier) and in the more distant past. This kind of setup has the virtue of taking the prior data into account as having both direct and indirect effects (O. D. Duncan, 1975). If these kinds of distributed lag models (but now applied to latent changes as the outcomes) were correct, the model with only one time lag (i.e., the immediate past as the only predictor) would not fit as well. This seems very common in all kinds of time-series and panel analysis (Hsiao, 2003), so it is likely to be useful here.

Perhaps the most interesting part of this representation is that the model can now be applied to higher orders differences (as in Boker & Nesselroade, 2002) or can allow higher order changes. One alteration we would use here is that when using a higher order model, we would only estimate measurement error model using the measured scores. In general, we can fit any model where the additive change score model would fit the data well if we had just picked a different time scale. This is the essence of the latent basis LCM described (see Exhibit 7.2). In such cases, we might want to estimate the model as an LCS with a latent basis in a different way. That is, for all occasions we could try to fit all of these timing concepts in a single model. There are obviously many more options that can be considered (McArdle & Hamagami, 2014b).

DISCRETE VERSUS CONTINUOUS TIME MODELS

One of the advantages of the discrete time (DT) approach used here is that it is simpler to understand. The basic concept is that we must use a latent score to create latent changes, and then the earlier prediction of the

LCS is really the focal issue. But there is no doubt that we can and should move to models of further complexity in the dynamics because, when we think about it carefully, the more complex models are far more realistic. No effect is really zero, and multiple determination probably takes on the form of more than one additional predictor. So this DT model should be considered as just another step along the way. Of course, the model we have chosen is already fairly complex. As we have seen, this complexity could be in the process itself, and any internal variable can affect the changes, or in its precursors measure variables. So we really might not know what else to do. It might also be that we have measured an arbitrary slice of the time course, so we cannot really set anything to be equal or zero. If we start with almost any within-person process, it may be most important to recognize that our time slices are typically arbitrary (e.g., on someone's birthday, last year at this time, 1 week, 1 month, or 6 months), and we do not exactly know what is the best time dimension to use. One way to overcome this problem is to allow time lags to be dimension under study, and a way to study the changes would be to assign individuals to a random time lag, as was advocated and then done by McArdle and Woodcock (1997).

Another way to deal with this and other similar problems is to use a continuous time (CT) model of change (for details see Arminger, 1986; Boker, 2001; Boker & Nesselroade, 2002; Oud & Jansen, 2000). This kind of model is important because it allows us to consider that the changes at any specific measured time lag can be represented in terms of effects at a common time lag (even $\Delta t = 0$ as estimated by the instantaneous derivative dt), by a set of transformations, and to test hypotheses about changes. This approach certainly takes care of varying time intervals for each person, and this is useful.

It appears that Bartlett (1946, as cited in H. Singer, 1993) was among the first to suggest, "for it is no use knowing how to calculate correlation coefficients if we do not know what they mean. Now, their interpretation depends on two interdependent things: The appropriateness of the theoretical scheme assumed and the magnitude of sampling fluctuations" (p. 527). He was also one of the first to deal with CT stochastic models on the basis of DT data. This can be very useful when we have lots of DT data but we want parameters for any time frame (i.e., a CT approach). Bartlett actually criticized the "unfortunate connection between the incidental observation interval and the theoretically relevant interval in conventional analysis." As he observed, "an employment index does not cease to exist between readings" (Bartlett, 1946, p. 31). In our context it seems that time units can matter and should be evaluated, but it is also true that Bartlett was among the first to advocate the use of latent variables as placeholders (later used by Horn & McArdle, 1980; McArdle & Hamagami, 1996, 2004).

In contrast to the DT modeling presented here, we now know that CT analysis can be used directly with differential equations to put dynamic effects in a CT framework. The use of CT with DT panel data appears to have been first considered by Arminger (1986), but he seemed to assume the exponential of a matrix was the same as the matrix exponential. It is not. This algebra was later corrected by Oud and Jansen (2000) in their CT estimation via structural equation modeling (SEM). The CT-SEM approach generally allows a consistent process to develop in infinitesimally small steps (i.e., at $dt = 0$), as long as each step represents the same phenomena. This CT approach is most useful because it clearly distinguishes the underlying dynamics from the DT observations. However, as will be obvious to almost anyone, the goodness-of-fit of such models, and the selection among alternative dynamic models, will only be testable and limited by the actual observations (i.e., DT) that we have. This implies we can always estimate CT parameters, but their accuracy will be dependent on both the data layout (Δt) and the model (SEM) chosen.

Very little effort is made to be critical about these CT-SEM models now, because they are hardly used at all. But assuming they will be used in the future, and we think they should be used, we will be somewhat critical here. First, as we have tried to demonstrate, the principles of measurement error need to be highlighted in any such model, and these are often overlooked for finer points and complexity of derivatives (Boker, 2001). Also, there is a need to link up the CT approach with the basic DT models of repeated measures analysis of variance (RANOVA) for comparison with a standard data analysis technique that is now so popular (see Chapter 12). It seems that this crucial step is largely overlooked by the current group of CT enthusiasts. Finally, because the measurement of everyone at the same time intervals is used most often in behavioral science research, even though this is not thought to be so wise by some (cf., McArdle & Woodcock, 1997), the CT models produce results that are effectively the same as the DT results. Another assumption used by both CT and DT is that every person is going through the same process, even if we can measure these people at different intervals of time. This assumption is hardly ever tested or testable. In essence, the DT approach can be most useful in testing some of the CT assumptions.

One of the potentially most satisfying aspects of this CT approach is in fact that the hypothesis-testing approach can be absolutely identical to that portrayed as DT here: A parameter that has been determined to be zero in DT is also zero in CT, because the likelihood function is the same. The same can be said of parameters that are presumed to be equal or invariant: The likelihood function and all testing are the same. This is not surprising since the observed data are the same in both cases. Also, time-independent parameters can be estimated using DT when many latent variable "nodes" are used (as in Horn & McArdle, 1980; McArdle & Hamagami, 1996). This is most important when we are trying to determine the basic trajectory of the events we have collected or if we are trying to test some hypotheses about consistency of effects. However, it is clear that what the CT models can do is (a) estimate parameter values for any time interval, (b) take into account measurement error, (c) allow individual differences in the time lags of measurement (i.e., allow Δt_n rather than create larger "bins" of time), and (d) establish predictions of a specific model at any time (inside or outside the measured intervals). When all of these issues are considered, the CT models can be very practical and very useful.

III

LONGITUDINAL SEM FOR INTERINDIVIDUAL DIFFERENCES IN INTRAINDIVIDUAL CHANGES

11

STUDYING INTERINDIVIDUAL DIFFERENCES IN INTRAINDIVIDUAL CHANGES

The second aspect of Baltes and Nesselroade (1979) that we use here is the suggestion that we consider analyses focused on differences between groups of persons in the way people change. This is another idea that leads to several novel longitudinal structural equation modeling (LSEM) alternatives. This is relatively simple from a model-based perspective: We could just say we assume the existence of two or more independent but observable groups of people and we want to know if these groups have the same parameters.

In this part we will describe several ways researchers have considered group differences and illustrate these methods. We consider three basic ways the available LSEM can be used to achieve these goals: (a) adding group contrasts in multilevel models (MLM), (b) isolating groups of persons and examining invariance of model parameters, in multiple group models (MGM), and (c) improved understanding of the self-selection to groups with incomplete data in special multiple group models. Each of these issues will be represented.

One key issue we will not deal with is exploratory classifications of person into groups (McArdle & Hamagami, 2014b). This can be accomplished a variety of ways (e.g., latent mixture models), but we will now stick to the problems with a priori groupings of persons.

What should become very clear is that the reasons why people are in groups in the first place is important to the inferences that can be made. If, for example, persons are randomly assigned to groups (as in McArdle, 2006), then any group differences can be attributed to the subsequent treatment. This is the hallmark of a randomized clinical trial (RCT) design (McArdle, 2007a; McArdle & Prindle, 2008; Prindle & McArdle, 2012). However, if people are not randomly assigned to groups, as in any observational data (McArdle & Nesselroade, 1994, 2003), there will be no way to untangle whether or not group differences are due to (a) events that started after data collection or (b) events that preexisted before data collection, or (c) events that are not measured at all. The same is true of situations where the observed longitudinal data we would like to have is, in fact, incomplete. Appropriate inferences always depend on how the people were selected for patterns of incompleteness.

Let us first add a measured variable (X) to characterize group differences directly using the previous linear expressions. This variable is assumed to take on one value for each person, and it can be categorical or continuous. If the variable was assigned to each person using a randomized procedure, we can make stronger inferences about the effects that we calculate.

SOME BASIC TWO-OCCASION GROUP MODELS

To start this process, it is very simple to write a linear model expressed for all persons (see Exhibit 11.1), where X is a binary variable—yes or no—defining group membership. If and only if (*iff*) the X is coded as in dummy variable form (0 or 1), we can write the simple conditional expression so we have the analysis of variance (ANOVA; or *t* test) model written as a linear regression. We can also use other forms of independent variable codes, such as effect coding, or even nonsense coding to obtain the same results. The choice of code for the independent groups does alter the size and sign of the regression coefficients. The explained variance of the model is the proportional amount of the outcome (Y[2]) due to the grouping (Cohen & Cohen, 1983).

In the analysis of longitudinal data, it is traditional to write a linear model that includes information about Time 1. This is usually done by writing a model where Y[1] is a predictor of Y[2] scores for the same individuals on the same variable at the second occasion. This direction is obviously a reflection of the timing of measurement. This model is presented in the path

EXHIBIT 11.1
Some Elementary Regression Models Including Group Differences

We can write a linear model expressed for all persons (for $n = 1$ to N) as

(1a) $$Y[2]_n = \beta_0 + \beta_1 X_n + e_n$$

where X is a binary variable—yes or no—defining group membership. If and only if (iff) the X is coded as in dummy variable form (0,1), we can also write the conditional expression

(1b) $$Y[2]_n[\ |X_n = 0] = \beta_0 + \beta_1 0_n + e_n$$
$$Y[2]_n[\ |X_n = 1] = \beta_0 + \beta_1 1_n + e_n$$

so β_0 is the *intercept* or mean for the group coded 0, and β_1 is the *difference in the intercept* or mean for the group coded 1.

It is traditional to write a linear model including information about Time 1 by writing

(2a) $$Y[2]_n = \beta_0 + \beta_1 X_n + \beta_2 Y[1]_n + e_n$$

where Y[1] are scores for a set of individuals on a first occasion and Y[2] are scores for the same individuals on the same variable at the second occasion. Assuming the X is once again coded as in dummy variable form (0,1), we can write the conditional model as

(2b) $$Y[2]_n[\ |X_n = 0] = \beta_0 + \beta_1 0 + \beta_2 Y[1]_n + e_n$$
$$Y[2]_n[\ |X_n = 1] = \beta_0 + \beta_1 1_n + \beta_2 Y[1]_n + e_n$$

so β_0 is the intercept for the group coded 0, β_1 is the difference in the intercept for the group coded 1, and β_2 is the *slope* for both groups.

One additional regression model for multiple groups is sometimes written as

(3a) $$Y[2]_n = \beta_0 + \beta_1 X_n + \beta_2 Y[1]_n + \beta_3 (Y[1]_n X_n) + e_n$$

where the "product" variable is created as $(Y[1]_n X_n)$. Assuming X is coded in dummy variable form (0,1) form, we can write

(3b) $$Y[2]_n[\ |X_n = 0] = \beta_0 + \beta_1 0_n + \beta_2 Y[1]_n + \beta_3 (0_n) + e_n$$
$$Y[2]_n[\ |X_n = 1] = \beta_0 + \beta_1 1_n + \beta_2 Y[1]_n + \beta_3 Y[1](1_n) + e_n$$

Here β_0 is the intercept for the group coded 0, β_1 is the difference in the intercept for the group coded 1, β_2 is the slope for everyone, and β_3 is the difference in the slope for the group coded 1. The last term allows the slope to be different over groups, and this is commonly called an "interaction" (Tukey, 1949).

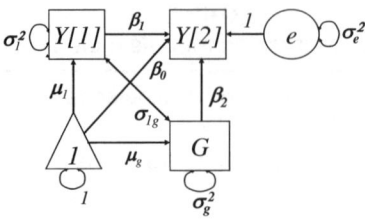

Figure 11.1. An autoregression model with group differences.

diagram of Figure 11.1. The parameters of the regression model, even fairly complex ones, are easy to interpret as group differences (see Exhibit 11.2).

This simple regression approach also includes models where a product term is used to allow the slope to be different over groups, and this is commonly called an interaction (see McArdle & Prescott, 2010; Tukey, 1949). If an interaction is present, we usually do not think that we have conditioned or controlled for the variation at Time 1. Perhaps our hope to control for Time 1 variation is why this more complete interaction model is hardly ever fit to real data (i.e., because it may be correct!). In any case, this representation of the complete analysis of covariance (ANCOVA) model with an interaction has been elaborated on before (e.g., Cohen & Cohen, 1983).

As another reasonable alternative for the same longitudinal data is that we can write the observed change model so the observed change scores (Dy) are defined to have an observed mean (m_d) and an observed deviation (D$\overset{*}{y}$) around this mean (see Exhibit 11.2). Given this standard starting point, we can now we add X as a dummy variable and rewrite the expression so the standard regression intercept ($v\{1\}$) is interpreted as the mean of the changes for the group coded 0, and the slope ($\gamma\{1\}$) is the difference in the average change score mean for the group coded 1 versus Group 0. One key difference between this change score approach and the prior ANCOVA approach is that we do not examine the prior scores (Y[1]) as a relative predictor (i.e., with an estimated slope β_1). Instead, the prior score (Y[1]) is thought to produce the second score (Y[2]) with a regression weight of unity. Here the observed change is our outcome by definition. As it turns out, this is the expression of what we often call a two-group repeated measures ANOVA (RANOVA) or the repeated measures *t* test (Bock, 1975; Fisher, 1925; Winer, 1971).

As before, we can add variables to this model, including an interaction. To accomplish the latter, we can first create to a product variable (the product is created as Y[1]$_n$ X$_n$; as in McArdle & Prescott, 1992), and so the intercept ($v\{1\}$) is the mean of the changes for the group coded 0, the slope ($\gamma\{1\}$) is the difference in the mean for Group 1 versus 0, and the other slope (β_3) is the difference in the slope for the group coded 1 versus 0. The last term allows

EXHIBIT 11.2
Some Elementary Change Score Regression Models

As another alternative for the same longitudinal data we can write an observed score change model as

(1a) $$Y[2]_n = Y[1]_n + D_{yn}$$

and

(1b) $$D_{yn} = m_d + D^*_{yn}$$

so the calculated change scores (D_y) are defined to have a mean (m_d) and a deviation (D^*_y) around the mean. Given this starting point, we can now we add X as a dummy variable and rewrite the expression

(1c) $$D_{yn} = v\{1\} + \gamma\{1\}X_n + z_n$$

a{1} is interpreted as the *intercept* in the change score for the group coded 0, and β{1} is the difference in the change score intercept for the group coded 1.

As before, we can add any variables to this model, including an "interaction." To accomplish this we can first create to a product variable (labeled $Y[1]_n X_n$) and write

(2a) $$D_n = v\{0\} + \gamma\{1\}X_n + \beta_2 Y[1]_n + \beta_3\{Y[1]_n X_n\} + z_n.$$

Now assuming X is coded in dummy variable form (0,1) form we can write

(2b) $$D_{yn}[\,|X_n = 0] = v\{1\} + \gamma\{1\}0_n + \beta_2 0_n + \beta_3\{Y[1]_n 0_n\} + z_n$$
$$D_{yn}[\,|X_n = 1] = v\{1\} + \gamma\{1\}1_n + \beta_2 Y[1]_n + \beta_3\{Y[1]_n 1_n\} + z_n.$$

Here v{1} is the *intercept* or the mean of the changes for the group coded 0, γ{1} is the *slope* for the group coded 0, β_2 is the *difference in the intercept* for the group 1, and β_3 is the *difference in the slope* for the group coded 1. The last term allows the slope to be different over groups, and this is commonly called an "interaction."

---

the slope to be different over groups, so this is commonly called an interaction. If an interaction is present here we do not assume we can "control" the variation at Time 1. In any case, this representation of the complete RANOVA model with an interaction has been elaborated on by many others (e.g., Cohen & Cohen, 1983).

Using the basic multiple regression models presented above, we have basically merged the idea of measured group differences in individual changes.

MORE GENERAL CLASSES OF GROUP DIFFERENCES

Of course, these are not the only alternative models we could consider. We can (a) add measured variables (X) that define group differences into the previous expressions, (b) use the group variable (X) to split the observed data into subsets for separate analyses, (c) define the unknown grouping variable (X) based on patterns of available data to deal with incomplete pieces, and/or (d) create latent groupings of people based on the pattern of available data. In any of these between-person models, the overall misfit can also be decomposed into individual components, and outliers can be examined at the individual level (e.g., McArdle, 1997).

The first question raised in this approach is slightly different: "Is exactly the same relationship observed within each group?" If this is the key question, the way we would answer it is to fit two separate models to the two-group data and see if they are the same. But if there are differences in observational data, we might like to know how much of these differences are due to the nonrandom selection of the persons. This can be examined by considering the effect on a regression model due to selection on the predictor scores (X). According to selection theorems developed first by Pearson and later elaborated on by Aiken, if this is this kind of sample selection exists, we should have a case where the first group (designated by superscript 1) would be directly compared with the second group (designated by superscript 2). It is not difficult to think about situations where there is explicit selection on the predictors; any experimental design (even RCT data) usually has this characteristic because we try to spread out the treatment effect over the predictors (possibly using random assignment), and then we try to see if the effect varies over the outcomes.

In general, we then expect that selection of persons on the predictor will have no impact on the X to Y regression weight (typically termed Y *regressed on* X), but could have a different effect on every other model parameter (including the means and covariances). This general idea can be formulized by writing the standard regression where all scores and parameters are allowed to have a superscript g (see Exhibit 11.3). This is very interesting, because there are many situations where we can think that the only way that people are selected is in fact on the predictors.

RESOLVING GROUP DIFFERENCES IN INDIVIDUAL CHANGES

We started with the prior equations because they actually go a long way toward pointing out why we could get different results from different models of the same data—the models are different! This point was clearly noted by

EXHIBIT 11.3
An Elementary Multiple Group Regression Model

We could have a case where the first group, written with a superscript 1, would look like

(1a) $$Y_n^{(1)} = \beta_0^{(1)} + \beta_1 X_n^{(1)} + e_n^{(1)}$$

whereas the second group (superscript 2) would have a model that looked like

(1b) $$Y_n^{(2)} = \beta_0^{(2)} + \beta_1 X_n^{(2)} + e_n^{(2)}.$$

This basic idea can be formally stated as

(1c) $$Y_n^{(g)} = \beta_0^{(g)} + \beta_1 X_n^{(g)} + e_n^{(g)}$$

where the g is a superscript and where we could add many predictors or have more independent groups in these kinds of expressions.

Lord (1967), who created what was later termed *Lord's paradox*. Most specifically, he wrote,

> A large university is interested in investigating the effects on the students of the diet provided in the university dining halls. . . . Various types of data are gathered. In particular the weight of each student at the time of his arrival in September and his weight in the following June are recorded. (Lord, 1967, p. 304)

Basically, Lord (1967) suggested we could then use a statistical model to examine weight gains over the freshman year in college students who were in one dining hall or the other. Of some importance here, the members of one Hall weighed more (and were taller) when they first entered college. In this example, the grouping variable is Hall, and the measured outcome variable is weight at Time 1 (the beginning of the first year) and Time 2 (the end of the first year). As reported by Lord, a univariate RANOVA was run, and the Halls showed no significant difference in weight changes. But, as he then also said, an ANCOVA was run using the same data, and one Hall's scores were significantly larger than expected, whereas the other Hall's were not. In his article, Lord simply stopped his analysis. In the terms used here, Lord demonstrated that the prior ANCOVA regression expressions could yield information different from the RANOVA expressions for the same data, and he was certainly correct. This was a famous problem that seemed to confuse researchers for many years (e.g., see Wainer, 1991).

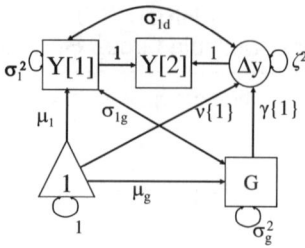

Figure 11.2. A latent change score model with group differences.

But the reason there could be a difference in results was due to the fact that these models were used to ask and answer different questions. The key point that could also be made is that if the prior score is used to predict the changes (as in ANCOVA), even if the outcome is later outcome (Y[2]) or changes (Δy), then all of the prior expressions in Lord's data collapse into a single solution. The entire paradox could be explained as, "Do we use Time 1 information to predict Time 2 changes?" If we conclude that the answer is always yes, then this compound model can be used as a complete resolution of Lord's paradox. Of course, in other research we might not always want to do this. Instead, we do not want to control for Time 1 variation before we look at Time 2 variations for one reason or another. This also can make sense in some situations. Indeed, it is somewhat surprising that an alternative outcome due to an alternative choice of a model was considered so paradoxical at the time (Wainer, 1991)! We hope that this SEM distinction is more obvious in Figure 11.2.

12
REPEATED MEASURES ANALYSIS OF VARIANCE AS A STRUCTURAL MODEL

As mentioned earlier, the second aspect of Baltes and Nesselroade (1979) was the suggestion that we consider analyses focused on "differences between groups of persons in the way people change." It is clear that the traditional term *within groups* (or changes) can be contrasted with *between groups* (or differences). This seems like traditional analysis of variance (ANOVA) terminology, and it is (Fisher, 1925; Winer, 1971). Of course, the use of the terms *intraindividual* and *interindividual* leads us to believe that Baltes and Nesselroade (1979) had a few other things beyond ANOVA in mind. In general, we will focus on "the differences in the changes," and we will use these other terms. We will show that any representation of group differences in change processes can be accomplished using the variety of methods the literature now refers to as *latent curves, mixed-effects, multilevels*, or even *multiple group modeling*. In our effort to clarify these alternatives we will start with the simple repeated measures ANOVA (RANOVA) model.

THE RANOVA ALTERNATIVE

One very popular latent curve model (LCM) alternative is the RANOVA model (Hertzog & Rovine, 1985; McCall & Applebaum, 1984), now more fully depicted as the path diagram of Figure 12.1. These basic models allow us to consider initial differences, for the individual and the group, and changes over time for the group. These differences and changes can be related to group membership, and this is often done using between-groups information. The model parameters can be fitted by either standard ANOVA or structural equation modeling (SEM) methods (from Bock, 1975; Meredith & Tisak, 1990; Winer, 1971; see also McArdle, 1977, 1986, 1988; McArdle & Epstein, 1987). This is one of the most popular models in the behavioral science literature so it seems like a good starting point for anyone with longitudinal data.

As we stated in an earlier part of this book, the standard LCM can be identical to the typical univariate RANOVA when the slopes are not allowed to vary (McCall & Applebaum, 1977). That is, RANOVA is very similar to the LCM because here we allow mean changes for both the levels and slopes. But RANOVA does not allow individual differences in the slopes (as in Figure 12.1 and Exhibit 12.1). Because of this simplification of the LCM,

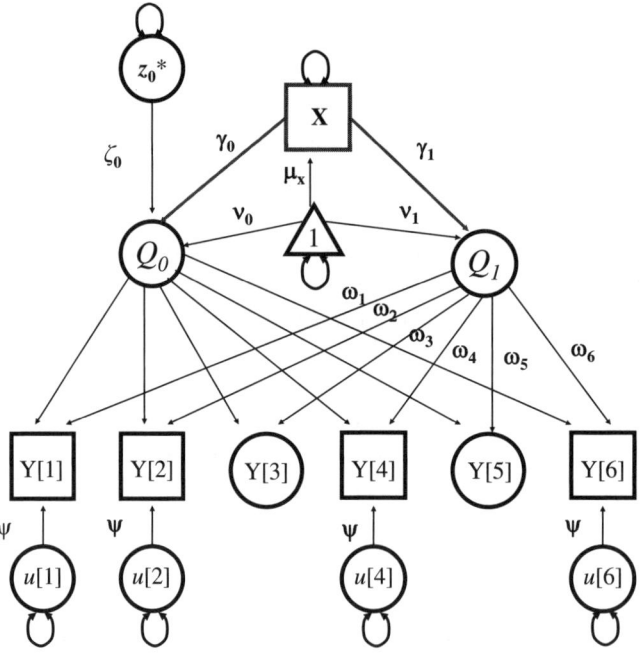

Figure 12.1. The repeated measures analysis of variance model with an external X variable affecting both the common levels and slopes.

EXHIBIT 12.1
The RANOVA Groups Model as a Restrictive Structural Equation Model

We can write a latent curve model (LCM) where

(1) $$Y[t]_n = Q\{0\}_n + Q\{1\}\omega[t] + u[t]_n$$

with mean changes allowed for both the level and slope *but with no allowance for individual differences in the slopes.*

Due to this simplification, the expected model expectations for the means is written exactly as the LCM as

(2) $$E\{Y[t], 1'\} = \mu\{0\} + \mu\{1\}\omega[t]$$

but the variance expectations are simpler and equal at all occasions

(3) $$E\{Y[t]^*, Y[t]^{*\prime}\} = \phi\{0\}^2 + \psi^2,$$

and the model covariances are simpler as well:

(4) $$E\{Y[j]^*, Y[j<k]^{*\prime}\} = \phi\{0\}^2$$

This also implies that the observed correlation over time is supposedly constant as well:

(5) $$\rho[Y[j], Y[j<k]'] = E\{Y[j]^*, Y[j<k]^{*\prime}\}/E\{Y[t]^*, Y[t]^{*\prime}\} = \rho$$

Due to these kinds of presumed equalities over time, this set of assumptions is termed *compound symmetry* (as in the generalized estimations estimate). If a repeated multivariate analysis of variance (MANOVA) model is used (as in Bock, 1975; O'Brien & Kaiser, 1985), then these covariance restrictions on the residuals are not assumed the original variables are allowed to be correlated in any way.

---

the expected model expectations for the means and covariances are far simpler that of the full LCM (Exhibit 12.2). This difference could be focused on the measured outcomes and not on their predictors.

This set of covariance assumptions (see Exhibit 12.2) are often given the label *compound symmetry* (Winer, 1971). The exact matrix assumptions are more properly termed "sphericity" (i.e., like a circle with equal eigenvalues), and several tests of this assumption have been created (Greenhouse & Geisser, 1959; Huynh & Feldt, 1970). The main thought is that with longitudinal data these covariance assumptions will fail and the significance tests of the mean of changes will be overstated, as suggested, for example, by McArdle (1977).

The LCM approach is fairly general because it offers a direct way to test the standard RANOVA as a simplified hypothesis (i.e., restricting the variance and covariance of the slopes to be zero results in compound symmetry).

EXHIBIT 12.2
The RANOVA Groups Model Including a Second Level

The traditional repeated measures analysis of variance (RANOVA) allows the potentially important addition of another group model at Level 2, and this can be written as

(1) $$Q\{0\}_n = v\{0\} + \gamma\{0\}X_n + z\{0\}_n$$

so the latent levels ($Q\{0\}$) are presumed to be partly altered by time-independent and ordered group information (X), possibly binary scores representing groups, with regression weights ($v\{0\}$, $\gamma\{0\}$) and independent and identically distributed (iid) disturbances ($z\{0\}$).

Similarly, for the slopes ($Q\{1\}$) we can write

(2) $$Q\{1\}_n = v\{1\} + \gamma\{1\}X_n$$

with potentially different regression coefficients ($v\{1\}$, $\gamma\{1\}$) but with no disturbance term. It is this final feature that makes this seem so odd because the group information supposedly explains all of the variation in the latent slope. But this should not be considered an odd diagram.

Although the standard ANOVA model may reflect a reasonable set of restrictive assumption in a number of circumstances, it may not be not reasonable with longitudinal data because of the individual variability in the slopes. In cases like these, one seemingly standard approach suggested for RANOVA is that we test the hypothesis of mean changes by "correcting" the degrees of freedom (*df*) in a model using an adjustment based on the failure of spherical assumptions (Greenhouse & Geisser, 1959; Huynh & Feldt, 1970). This is no doubt a useful corrective, but correcting the model *df* seems like an unusual way to proceed. In later work, we provide alternative longitudinal SEM (LSEM) approaches that avoid this correction.

GROUP DIFFERENCES ON THE LATENT VARIABLES

Most ANOVA treatments allow group differences, and RANOVA is certainly the same. RANOVA allows an important addition of another group model at different levels, and this is described in Exhibit 11.2. In general, the latent levels ($Q\{0\}$) are presumed to be partly altered by group information (X), with regression weights ($v\{0\}$, $\gamma\{0\}$) and with an independent and identically distributed (IID) disturbance term ($z\{0\}$). But the latent slopes ($Q\{1\}$) are presumed to be partly altered by the same group information (X), with regression weights ($v\{1\}$, $\gamma\{1\}$), but here there is no IID disturbance ($z\{1\}$). The latent variables are written in italics ($Q\{0\}$, $Q\{1\}$) because they are similar to the predicted scores in a standard regression equation. (Note: We do not use Greek notation because these scores are not estimated.)

In this general approach, the observed scores are at the first level, and the latent components are at a second level. As in any regression analysis, the coding and scaling of the between-person variable (X) and the within-person outcomes (Q{0}, Q{1}) will lead to different estimates of effects (ν and γ). That is, scaling of both the input and the outcome variables makes a big difference in regression and can make a big difference in RANOVA results as well.

THE SEM PATH MODEL OF RANOVA

RANOVA can be considered as a form of LSEM, and this form is depicted in Figure 12.1. Figure 12.1 starts in exactly the same way as before, but adds a common factor (labeled Q{0}) to the prior LGM of Figure 8.3. This other common factor is labeled Q{1}, with weights or loadings ($\omega[t]$) that are not equal to 1, and these are used to describe some shape of change over time (possibly $\omega[t] = t - 1$). In RANOVA it is quite typical to fix these basis coefficients to form a particular hypothesis, but this is not required. In RANOVA this new common factor is assumed to have a mean ($\mu\{1\}$) but is not assumed to add variance or covariance to the system. This is a model where the observed means are allowed to change as a function of the a priori basis, but where the covariances are the same as before for the baseline model. If we add the group information to the previous Figure 7.5, we end up with Figure 12.1. This seemingly odd looking path model actually can be used to represent most of the within and between components of the univariate RANOVA model (Hertzog & Rovine, 1985; McCall & Applebaum, 1984).

In the RANOVA (see Figure 12.1), the initial levels are often assumed to be random variables with "fixed" means ($\mu\{0\}, \mu\{1\}$) but with "random" variances ($\phi\{0\}^2$). The standard deviations ($\phi\{j\}$) may be drawn to allow the direct path diagram representation of the correlations (McArdle & Hamagami, 1991). This RANOVA path diagram can also be partly interpreted as a common factor model with means. The first latent factor score is a latent intercept or level score (labeled Q{0}), and the second latent factor score is a latent slope or change score (labeled Q{1}). The relationships between the latent levels Q{0} and all observed scores Y[t] are fixed at a value of 1. In contrast, the relationships between the latent slopes Q{1} and all observed scores Y[t] are assigned a value based on the time parameter ($\omega[t]$), which, depending on the application, may be fixed or estimated. For simplicity, the unique components ($u[t]$) are defined as having constant deviations (Ψ) and are uncorrelated with other components. Because there is no change expected in the common factor variance, there is also none expected in the reliability.

ADDITIONAL RANOVA ISSUES

There is often some discussion of the importance of having complete cases in RANOVA (O'Brien & Kaiser, 1979), but this is not actually required if estimated in this way (McArdle & Hamagami, 1991). This seems to be the fundamental difference between the approaches used by specific computer programs (i.e., R-code ANOVA and lme), but it is actually about the difference in assumptions about the corresponding residual terms. That is, if we make strict assumption about the residual terms (e.g., IID) then we can in fact estimate the parameters with incomplete data using other calculations (e.g., using R-code lme or SAS PROC MIXED or STATA xtmixed).

In any case, the RANOVA approach typically starts by assuming we have an equation for each occasion for each person formed as the sum of (a) unobserved or latent scores representing the individual's initial level ($Q\{0\}$) with a mean ($\mu\{0\}$) and a variance ($\phi\{0\}^2$); (b) fixed means representing the group change over time or slope ($\mu\{1\}$), in direct comparison to the general LCM, which has no slope scores ($Q\{1\}$); and (c) unobserved and possibly correlated unique features of measurements ($u[t]$). If the unique scores are required to be uncorrelated, we have this new kind of latent variable RANOVA model (Muller & Stewart, 2006).

RANOVA is not usually presented as an SEM alternative, but it can and should be done (T. E. Duncan, Duncan, & Strycker, 2013; Meredith & Tisak, 1990). RANOVA has a fairly flexible set of assumptions about the means over time. As in any LCM, the RANOVA model requires the loadings from the latent slopes to observed variables to be a fixed set of group coefficients or basis weights that define the timing or shape of the trajectory over time (e.g., $\omega[t] = t - 1$). This implies that a carefully selected set of basis weights (as $\omega[t] = [0,1,3,5]$) can be used to easily take care of any unbalanced time delay between occasions. In comparison to other models proposed here, RANOVA has a rather simplified set of covariance assumptions (i.e., compound symmetry), and these are not reasonable for many concepts of longitudinal changes. In the RANOVA longitudinal model, the latent change score ($Q\{1\}$) is assumed to be constant within an individual, but it is not assumed to be the same between individuals, so the expected correlation is the same no matter how many time points are used (as in typical generalized estimating equation [GEE] estimation). This can be examined, of course, and it should be: To the degree the RANOVA assumptions are reasonable, they offer very powerful tests of the mean changes over time.

One reasonable question about this basic statistical logic has come from RANOVA as a multivariate model (MANOVA; O'Brien & Kaiser, 1978). In these MANOVA models an optimally weighted linear combination is created for the particular question of interest, and this new linear combination is compared with all other linear combinations so we can evaluated its significance. To distinguish these types of models from univariate tests, we basically need more than two occasions of measurement ($T > 2$) and more than two groups ($G > 2$). When we have this situation, we can state a first multivariate hypothesis about the changes over time—the within-measure contrast: "Is there *any* linear contrast among the measures that would be significantly different from zero?" This is treated as a confirmatory hypothesis. This model for RANOVA obviously assumes that a test of the mean changes is useful with no implied covariance structure. In either RANOVA or MANOVA form, the additional between-group tests, we can examine the multivariate hypothesis about group differences—the between-groups contrasts. First, are there any linear contrasts that would yield a significant difference between groups? Second, are there any linear contrasts that would yield a change over time that would be significantly different over groups? Once again, these are treated as confirmations. There is no notion in the MANOVA tests that these linear combinations should be formed in the same predetermined way, so each contrast and test is interpreted independently. These are all tests of MANOVA mean differences evaluated for significance from zero given their observed variances and without further assumptions within groups.

If anything more than tests of mean differences are considered, it is not done with RANOVA. This implies that RANOVA should always be done first, because it is simplest, and then, no matter what result—univariate or multivariate—has been found, it should be followed up by more in-depth LSEMs. This seems like a reasonable approach as well.

There are many other models that can be fitted here, including polynomials (over Grade or Age or Time), but the basic results will not be altered, so we will not pursue these now. In fact, the overall confusion in the proper use of these alternatives, including the use of corrected *df* (corrected by the value of the sphericity ε), seems to have created a small cottage industry for repeated measures workers (Hertzog & Rovine, 1985; Maxwell & Delaney, 2004). Perhaps we should say that these models are merely tests of the mean changes, and nothing more, but it does allow an interesting set of covariances (i.e., compound symmetry or equal correlations). So we will ask a slightly different question: "Why calculate answers to the wrong question?"

Having come to the last point, we could stop here, but it seems worthwhile using these data to fit models that others do not consider to be part of the RANOVA, including hypothesis tests in the presence of incomplete data. This estimation of the independent residual variance is actually the key novel feature of this model. Incidentally, this SEM form of the levels and slopes, even if the slopes are fixed to be linear, means the levels and slopes are properly considered to be latent variables because we have estimated the residuals under the restriction of uncorrelated errors (W. Meredith, personal communication, 1992). Of course, what we are doing with the previous LCM is very similar, but now we have added a continuous predictor to use with the new latent variables. We could fit a model of the means (e.g., RANOVA) followed by a model of the covariances, but this seems a bit haphazard. We consider this issue in SEM terms next.

13

MULTILEVEL STRUCTURAL EQUATION MODELING APPROACHES TO GROUP DIFFERENCES

One of the most popular models currently used seems to be the inclusion of the between-persons predictor into an latent curve model (LCM) framework, by characterizing a static (one-time of measurement) group variable accounting for systematic variation in the latent levels and slopes. As in any regression analysis, the coding and scaling of the between-person variable will lead to different estimates of effects. This type of structural equation modeling (SEM) is depicted in Figure 13.1 and typically is called by terms that reflect the history of its development within a substantive discipline: This model is termed an *LCM* in psychology (Meredith & Tisak, 1990), a *multilevel model* (MLM) in education (e.g., Bryk & Raudenbush, 1992), a *mixed-effects model* (MEM) or a *random coefficients* model in statistics (e.g., Longford, 1993), and probably other things as well. For example, when this was done in the context of factor analysis, it was considered as an *external variable model* (McArdle & Epstein, 1987). To be fair, there are advantages to considering these analyses within each discipline. It may be useful to note that variations of this analysis

http://dx.doi.org/10.1037/14440-014
Longitudinal Data Analysis Using Structural Equation Models, by J. J. McArdle and J. R. Nesselroade
Copyright © 2014 by the American Psychological Association. All rights reserved.

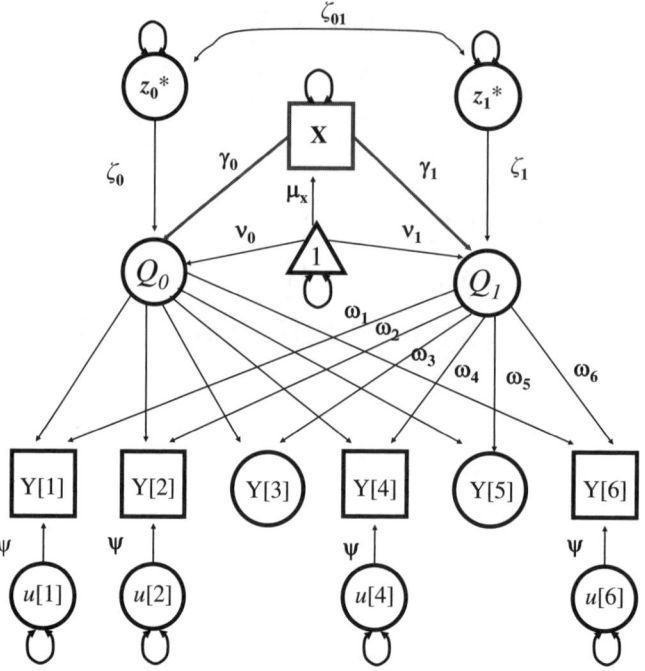

Figure 13.1. The LGM with an external *X* variable affecting both the common levels and slopes.

can be done using many computer programs, and the results will be identical (Ferrer, Hamagami, & McArdle, 2004).

Another strategy that is natural to SEM analyses is a multiple group modeling analysis. In this case, we can split the data into groups and freely examine group differences without further assumptions. The multiple group model (MGM) is not as widely used as the MLM, but it is rather easy to use and present, so we do so here. Although the MLM is compact and easy to understand and use, in the context of longitudinal changes the MGM may even be better.

MULTILEVEL MODELING OF CHANGES

The introduction of measured predictors of the latent variables is a natural aspect of latent variable path models, and it is no different here. In fact, this approach reflects the best thinking in what was once termed hierarchical modeling (Raudenbush & Bryk, 2002) and is now termed MLM (Goldstein, 1995). Here a set of the first-level variables (Y[t]) are used to form the latent level and slopes (Q{0} and Q{1}), and the second-level variables (X) are used as predictors of the latent levels and slopes. There should be no doubt that multilevel thinking has allowed much progress in the simplicity of the required calculations, especially in situations where there is a clustering of data, but there is also no doubt that this "new" approach does not automatically produce novel results (Ferrer, Hamagami, & McArdle, 2004; McArdle & Hamagami, 1996; Raudenbush & Bryk, 2002).

Nevertheless, two of the limits of this increasingly popular MLM approach quickly become evident. First, as in RANOVA, we need to assume that the variance and covariance of the residuals are identical over groups. This is not an easy assumption to satisfy in practice, so it is often ignored. Second, we need to assume that all changes due to groups are reflected in the means of the latent variables. Any changes in other forms of the statistics will not be highlighted here. Otherwise, these tests are the same as in any other form of the model (i.e., t tests).

MULTILEVEL MODELING DEFINED

The basis of the MLM is defined next. Indeed, it seems that the most popular model used now is the inclusion of the between-persons predictor into an LCM framework, and this static (one-time measurement) group variable (X), is used to account for systematic variation in the latent levels and slopes. This basic model can be written in the same way as the LCM of Chapter 7. We start with a first-level model of the change over the entire series that is exactly the LGM presented earlier. So we know that the basis weights can be all fixed or partially free to be estimated. But in the MLM, we now have the important addition of another group model at Level 2, usually written as a regression model where the outcome is the common latent variable (see Exhibit 13.1). In this approach, the observed scores are at the first level and the latent components are at a second level. Of course, the scaling of both the input and the outcome variables makes a big difference in regression, and it makes a difference in MLM results as well. This type of SEM is depicted in Figure 13.1, and the MLM expectations are in Exhibit 13.2.

CONSIDERING LATENT CHANGE SCORES

It is natural to transport this same type of analysis to other versions of models for change, such as time-series regressions (TSRs) or even latent change scores (LCSs). Since the LCSs can be used to create all the TSR models, showing how we can use this basic idea within an LCS framework is

EXHIBIT 13.1
A Multilevel Model Approach to Group Differences

In a multilevel model we now have the important addition of another group model at Level 2, usually written as

(1b) $$Q\{0\}_n = v\{0\} + \gamma\{0\}X_n + z\{0\}_n$$

and

(1c) $$Q\{1\}_n = v\{1\} + \gamma\{1\}X_n + z\{1\}_n$$

so the latent levels ($Q\{0\}$) are presumed to be partly altered by time-dependent ordered group information (X), possibly binary scores, with regression weights ($v\{0\}, \gamma\{0\}$) and an independent and identically distributed (iid) disturbance ($z\{0\}$). Similarly, the latent slopes ($Q\{1\}$) are presumed to be partly altered by the same group information (X), with possibly different regression weights ($v\{1\}, \gamma\{1\}$) and a possibly different iid disturbance ($z\{1\}$). As in any regression analysis, the coding and scaling of the between person variable (X) and the within person outcomes ($Q\{0\}, Q\{1\}$) will lead to different estimates of these effects.

---

relatively general, and one version of this appears in Exhibit 13.3. Here the latent variables of level and slopes are predicted by the external grouping variable. A path diagram of the resulting MLM-dual change score with measured group differences (X) is presented as Figure 13.2. Illustrations of both standard and nonstandard models follow.

EXPLAINED VARIANCE IN MLMs

There are many aspects of the prior MLMs that deserve further attention, and many of these issues are discussed in the relevant literature (e.g., Bryk & Raudenbush, 1992; Raudenbush & Bryk, 2002). But one persistent problem that emerges is how to evaluate the relative importance of the second-level predictors (Snijders & Bosker, 1999). One index that is useful is the explained variance at the second level ($R^2\{k\}$, with k = 1 or 2 here; see Exhibit 13.4). This can be strictly defined as the amount of variance in the levels and slopes that is predictable from knowledge of the second-level grouping variables.

In many cases, this straightforward interpretation poses no problems at all. But in some cases, we fit a sequence of models where the variability of each component changes with each model exhibit. If so, the general expressions (see Exhibit 13.4) always works within the context of any model, but it does not always work when we alter the meaning of the common factors

EXHIBIT 13.2
Multilevel Model Assumptions

In the structural equation model context we always add the mean expectations of

(1a) $$E\{z\{0\}, 1'\} = \mu\{0\}$$

and

(1b) $$E\{z\{1\}, 1'\} = \mu\{1\}$$

along with

(1c) $$E\{u[t], 1'\} = 0,$$

and this leads to observed mean expectations of

(1d) $$E\{Y[t], 1'\} = \mu\{0\} + \mu\{1\}\omega[t].$$

In a similar context we always add the simplified variance expectations of

(2a) $$E\{z\{0\}, z\{0\}'\} = \phi\{0\}^2$$

and

(2b) $$E\{z\{1\}, z\{1\}'\} = \phi\{1\}^2$$

along with

(2c) $$E\{u[t], u[t]'\} = \psi^2$$

and with the covariance expectations of

(3a) $$E\{z\{0\}, z\{1\}'\} = \phi\{01\}$$

and

(3b) $$E\{u[j], u[j<k]'\} = 0$$

and

(3c) $$E\{u[t], q\{k\}'\} = 0.$$

EXHIBIT 13.3
Multilevel Models of Latent Change Scores

We can write a dual latent change score model as

(1a) $\quad Y[t]_n = y[t]_n + u[t]_n \quad \text{and} \quad \Delta y[t]_n = y[t]_n - y[t-1]_n$

and this implies that the overall model for the scores can be rewritten as

(1b) $\quad Y[t]_n = Q\{0\}_n + \left(\sum \Delta y[k]_n\right) + u[t]_n.$

If so, we can write any model for the latent changes, such as

(2a) $\quad \Delta y[t]_n = \alpha Q\{1\}_n + \beta y[t-1]_n + z[t]_n.$

If we do this, we can rather easily add a predictor of the resulting levels and slopes as

(2b) $\quad Q\{0\}_n = v\{0\} + \gamma\{0\} X_n + z\{0\}_n$

and

(2c) $\quad Q\{1\}_n = v\{1\} + \gamma\{1\} X_n + z\{1\}_n$

where the usual regression coefficients ($v\{k\}$, $\gamma\{k\}$) are used to describe differences in the changes due to group membership (X). Of course, the assumption of different independent and identically distributed (IID) disturbances (z) could still be a potential confound.

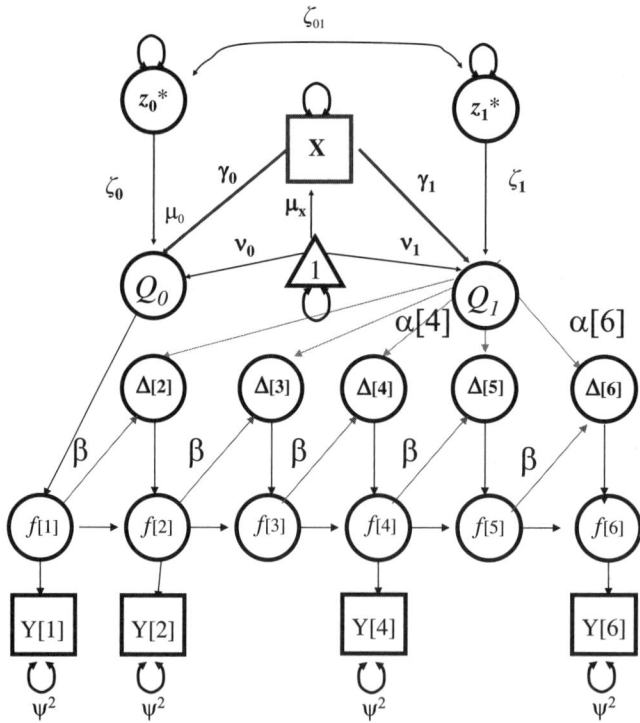

Figure 13.2. A triple change score model with multilevel modeling group differences.

EXHIBIT 13.4
Multilevel Variance of Second-Level Effects

We can always write

(3a) $$\phi\{k\}^2 = B\phi\{X\}^2 B' + 2B\phi\{XX'\} + \psi^2$$

so

(3b) $$R^2\{k\} = (\phi\{k\}^2 - \psi^2)/\phi\{k\}^2$$

for each latent component ($k = 1$ or 2 here), and the variance and covariance of the predictor variables (X) is defined in terms of regression (B) weights, and the disturbance variance (ψ^2) is what is remains to be predicted.

---

from one model to the next (Snijders & Bosker, 1999). In some case, we can alter what we mean about the meaning of the latent factor by manipulating the latent factor loadings, and this can reduce the size of the latent variance ($\phi\{j\}^2$), so the total variance achievable has changed as well. In cases where we do have the same common factors, the comparison of $R^2\{k\}$ from one model to the next will not be viable. However, in some cases the comparison of $R^2\{k\}$ from one model to the next will not be viable because we have changed the size of the common factors. Also, when we have multiple latent components, the covariance among these could be of relative importance, and we typically ignore this shifting quantity.

So, quite probably, we should not be thinking this way at all. Although we would like to apply first-order logic to the second-order statistics, maybe we should not. That is, the test of the model fit is the key index of whether or not the second-level variable can be used to account for all first-level information (though the components), and this is the testable feature of the model. So we really need to evaluate the loss of fit due to the inclusion of the second-level predictors. This can be done with likelihood statistics if we first allow all parameters to be predictors (M_0) and then we force all second-level parameters to have zero effect (M_1). The direct comparison of the first model to the second model (M_0 to M_1) is a test that the second-level variables were in fact predictive.

14

MULTIPLE GROUP STRUCTURAL EQUATION MODELING APPROACHES TO GROUP DIFFERENCES

A related question is whether or not something can be gained by splitting persons into nonoverlapping subgroups: a multiple group model (MGM) approach (McGaw & Jöreskog, 1971; Sörbom, 1979; Exhibit 14.1). This approach is slightly different, and we will explain how.

MULTIGROUP MODELING OF CHANGES

The regression case of multigroup modeling is illustrated in Figure 14.1, and the MGM for simple latent change scores (LCSs) is presented in Figure 14.2.

What surely can be gained by splitting data into nonoverlapping groups is some evaluation of the evidence for the equality of the meaning of the latent variables over groups. In Figure 14.2 we have separated the groups based on a training example, but any groupings are possible. Although this

EXHIBIT 14.1
Multiple Group Models as a Structural Equation Model

In the multiple group model approach to group differences we write a potentially separate model for each group. So for ($g = 1$ to G) we write

(1a) $$Y[t]_n^{(g)} = Q\{0\}_n^{(g)} + Q\{1\}_n^{(g)} \omega[t]^{(g)} + u[t]_n^{(g)}$$

and since there is a new constant in each group we can write the mean expectations as

(1b) $$E\{Y[t]^{(g)}, 1^{(g)}\} = \mu[t]^{(g)} = \{\mu\{0\}^{(g)} + \mu\{1\}^{(g)} \omega[t]^{(g)}\},$$

and the covariance expectations as

(1c) $$E\{Y[t]^{(g)}, Y[t]^{(g)}\} = \phi[t]^{(g)2}$$
$$= \{\phi\{0\}^{(g)2} + \phi\{1\}^{(g)2} \omega[t]^{(g)} + 2*\phi\{01\}^{(g)} \omega[t]^{(g)} + \psi^{(g)2}\}.$$

This implies that we allow potentially different latent means ($\mu\{0\}^{(g)}$ and $\mu\{1\}^{(g)}$), latent variances ($\phi\{0\}^{(g)2}$, $\phi\{1\}^{(g)2}$, $\psi^{(g)2}$), latent covariances ($\phi\{01\}^{(g)}$), and even latent basis coefficients ($\omega[t]^{(g)2}$).

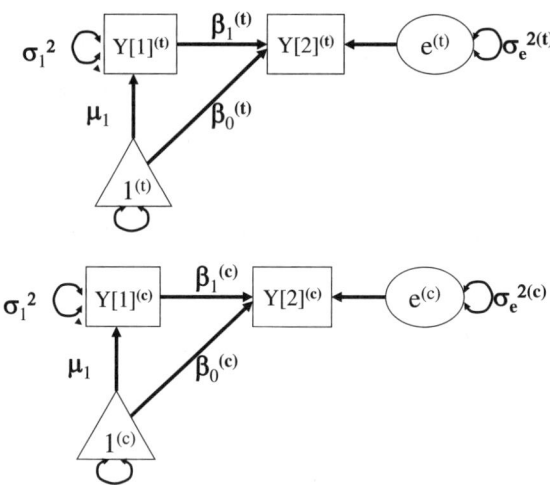

Figure 14.1. A multiple group autoregression model with selected group differences; T = trained group; C = complete data group.

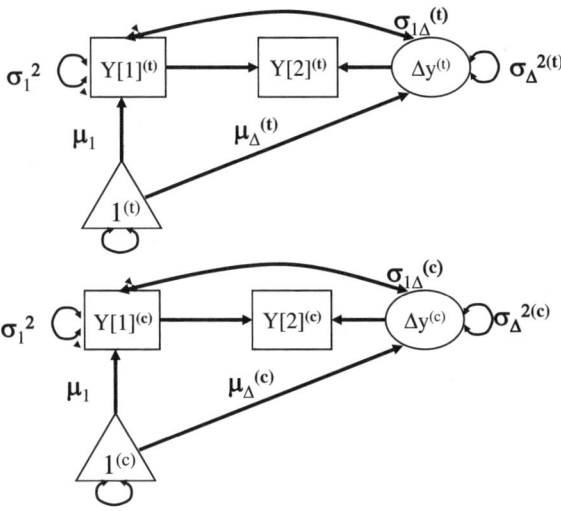

Figure 14.2. A multiple group latent change score model with selected group differences; T = trained group; C = complete data group.

seems to be the most important issue, we can actually expose two of the limits of the popular multilevel modeling approach. When using multilevel models (MLMs), the researcher needs to (a) select an overall model function for the entire group, and (b) the variance and covariance of the residuals of the latent variables are required to be the same over groups. This is not often stated, and if (a) or (b) is not possible, neither is the MLM, and the researcher is probably better off using an MGM approach. Nothing will be lost if the groups do not overlap because we can deal with the MGM model with MLM constraints (e.g., the variances all equal). At the same time, however, there are situations where the MLM approach is desirable. For example, we cannot use an MGM approach if the predictor variable are considered continuous (e.g., Age or Education), and we may want them to be used in that way.

Any analysis that does not require the previous constraints and can use a measured grouping variable to split the observed data into subsets for separate analyses, just like the MGM latent curve model illustrated in Figure 14.3. This approach explicitly recognizes that separate model frameworks are allowed, so not all persons need to have the same within-person change model. Although this is somewhat radical, it could be true, and what we end up with in another analysis would be very unclear. Although this is clearly evident, we will not pursue it here.

Instead, in the typical structural equation modeling (SEM) framework of Exhibit 14.2, we will simply check whether or not the model and the model parameters are identical across independent groups, based on multiple

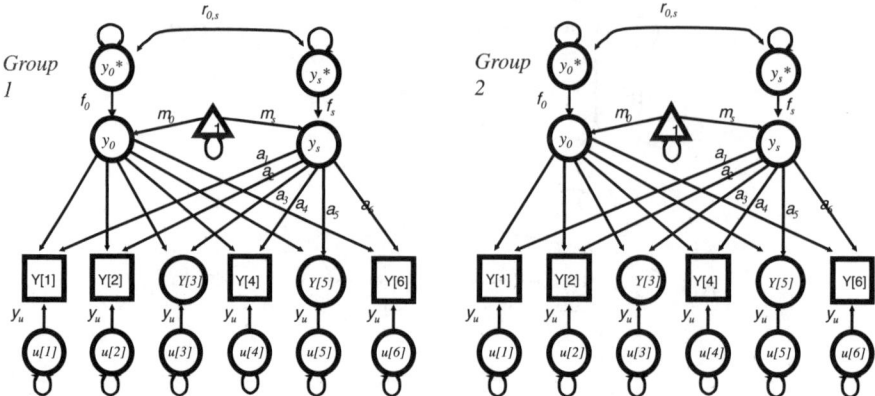

Figure 14.3. Multiple group latent curve structural equation models. The key question now is "are any parameters not meaningfully the same (invariant) over groups?"

EXHIBIT 14.2
The Maximum Likelihood for Groups Expression

In a single group model we write

(1) $$L^2 = fun\{(\mathbf{m}-\boldsymbol{\mu})+(\mathbf{S}-\boldsymbol{\Sigma})\}$$

where the observed means ($\mathbf{m}$) and observed covariances ($\mathbf{S}$) are directly compared to the expected means ($\boldsymbol{\mu}$) and expected covariances ($\boldsymbol{\Sigma}$) using some functional form (*fun*). As stated earlier, if this functional form comes from the multivariate normal distribution (as in Cooley & Lohnes, 1974), we can assume these deviations are normally distributed. When this is a reasonable set of assumptions, the model parameters are considered as *maximum likelihood estimates* (MLE) and this L^2 index can be compared to a central chi-square distribution (χ^2) with multiple degrees of freedom to examine the probability of misfit (i.e., given normal *iid* residuals).

Now in MGM a similar expression is used but here we write the weighted sum of

(2a) $$L^2 = \left(n^{(g)}/N\right)\sum(g=1\text{ to }G)L^{2(g)}$$

where, for each group, the misfit is only based on the means and covariances of that group, written as

(2b) $$L^{2(g)} = fun\{(\mathbf{m}^{(g)} - \boldsymbol{\mu}^{(g)}) + (\mathbf{S}^{(g)} - \boldsymbol{\Sigma}^{(g)})\}$$

This overall L^2 index can also be compared with a central chi-square distribution with multiple degrees of freedom to examine the probability of misfit of the multiple group model for all groups, given normal IID residuals.

group factor analysis (e.g., Horn & McArdle, 1992; Sörbom, 1979). As later expressed in Exhibit 14.3, this basically implies that we allow potentially different latent means ($\mu\{0\}^{(g)}$ and $\mu\{1\}^{(g)}$), latent variances ($\sigma\{0\}^{(g)2}$, $\sigma\{1\}^{2(g)}$, $\psi^{(g)2}$), latent correlations ($\rho\{01\}^{(g)}$), and even latent basis coefficients ($\Omega[t]^{(g)}$). The latter may be most important because this allows the shape of the function to differ over groups. This slope and the unique variances are not allowed to differ in the multilevel modeling approach.

THE MAXIMUM LIKELIHOOD FOR GROUPS EXPRESSION

The introduction of multiple group structural equation models, first promoted by Lawley and Maxwell (1963) as MGM-confirmatory factor analysis, then formalized by Meredith (1964a), and subsequently used by Sörbom (1975, 1979). Multiple group SEM turns out to be a remarkable

EXHIBIT 14.3
A Multiple Group Model for a Latent Curve Model With Two Groups

Assuming we have two groups (G = 2) on multiple measures, we can write

(1a) $\quad Y[t]_n^{(1)} = Q\{0\}_n^{(1)} + Q\{1\}_n^{(1)} \omega[t]^{(1)} + u[t]_n^{(1)}$, and

$\quad Y[t]_n^{(2)} = Q\{0\}_n^{(2)} + Q\{1\}_n^{(2)} \omega[t]^{(2)} + u[t]_n^{(2)}$.

We may now say the possible expected means differ over groups as

(2a) $\quad E\{Y[t]^{(1)}, 1\} = \mu[t]^{(1)} = \{\mu\{0\}^{(1)} + \mu\{1\}^{(1)} \omega[t]^{(1)}\}$, and

$\quad E\{Y[t]^{(2)}, 1\} = [[t]^{(2)} = \{\mu\{0\}^{(2)} + \mu\{1\}^{(2)} \omega[t]^{(2)}\}$,

and expected covariances differ over groups as

(2b) $\quad E\{Y[t]^{*(1)}, Y[t]^{*(1)}\} = \phi^{(1)2}$

$\quad\quad = \{\phi\{0\}^{(1)2} + \phi\{1\}^{(1)2} \omega[t]^{(1)} + 2*\phi\{01\}^{(1)} \omega[t]^{(1)} + \psi^{(1)2}\}$, and

$\quad E\{Y[t]^{*(2)}, Y[t]^{*(2)}\} = \phi^{(2)2}$

$\quad\quad = \{\phi\{0\}^{(2)2} + \phi\{1\}^{(2)2} \omega[t]^{(2)} + 2*\phi\{01\}^{(2)} \omega[t]^{(2)} + \psi^{(2)2}\}$.

As a key alternative, we may now say the two groups have the same basis weights or shape over time ($\omega[t]$) and constrain the model to be

(3) $\quad Y[t]_n^{(1)} = Q\{0\}_n^{(1)} + Q\{1\}_n^{(1)} \omega[t] + u[t]_n^{(1)}$, and

$\quad Y[t]_n^{(2)} = Q\{0\}_n^{(2)} + Q\{1\}_n^{(2)} \omega[t] + u[t]_n^{(2)}$,

leading to restrictions on the means and covariances over groups.

advance over classical analysis of variance thinking. That is, nothing at all needs to be lost here, because there can be one overarching MGM for the whole data set and parameters can be invariant over groups. A key to the success of the MGM approach comes from the early work by Jöreskog and his colleagues (Jöreskog & Sörbom, 1979; McGaw & Jöreskog, 1971; Sörbom, 1975, 1978). Basically, they showed how a single likelihood for a model could be subdivided into specific contributions of each separate group. In a single group model, we write a functional form for the likelihood (L^2) based on some difference between the observed means (**m**) and observed covariances (**S**) compared with the expected means (μ) and expected covariances (Σ) using some functional form (*fun*). As stated earlier, if this functional form comes from the multivariate normal distribution (as in Cooley & Lohnes, 1971), we can assume these deviations are normally distributed. When these are reasonable assumptions, this L^2 index can be compared with a central chi-square distribution with multiple degrees of freedom to examine the probability of misfit, given normal independent and identically distributed residuals (IID) residuals.

In MGMs a similar expression (see Exhibit 14.2) is used, but here we write the weighted sum of likelihoods ($L^{2(g)}$), where for each group, the misfit is only based on the means and covariances of that group. This overall L^2 index can also be compared with a central chi-square distribution with multiple degrees of freedom to examine the probability of misfit of the MGM for all groups given normal IID residuals.

McArdle (1997) used this MGM analogy and proceeded one more logical step and created an individual likelihood ($L^{2(n)}$) for each person: these misfits were plotted as a contribution to the overall misfit. From this plot we suggested that others could use these numbers to isolate model-based outliers (as shown in McArdle, 1997). It appears that this simple message is now being taken and is proving useful.

A TWO-GROUP MGM EXAMPLE

As an example, in an MGM model for two different groups of people (G = 2) defined by measured variables, we would write the group number as a superscript and consider a latent curve model for each group (see Exhibit 7.1). The key point is that the measured groups can be assumed to have a basic latent curve structure, but the parameters of these curves are allowed to be different.

Once the independent groups are formed from the measured variables in this way, we can use the constraints of invariance wherever we choose. That is, we may say the three groups have the same basis weights or shape over time ($\omega[t]$) and constrain the model. This then requires both groups to have the same shape over time ($\omega[t]$), and this is a typical constraint in multilevel modeling. Furthermore, we can even constrain the uniqueness over group ($\psi^{(g)2}$) to be the same, and this allows the means and covariance of the common factors to vary. This is also a typical constraint in multilevel modeling. This implies that the last set of restrictions are identical to the previous MLM, but we would not know if they were correct unless we forced them to be invariant in the MGM framework and examined the misfit.

These MGMs are identical to the MLMs when the proper constraints are put in place. If the means over time are the only aspect of the group differences, then the MLM approach seems easier to implement. Also, if the predictor is defined in a complex way (i.e., Continuous Age) and if it is not easy to form independent groups of persons, then the multilevel approach is very useful. That is, the key differences between the MLM and the MGM are the possible relaxation (a) of the basis coefficients and (b) of the unique variance terms.

Perhaps it is now obvious that if we can write a model for latent curves, we can do the same for latent change scores (LCSs). Of course, this is always the case, and the model we may consider now for independent groups (g = 1 to G) is written as Exhibit 14.4 and is drawn as Figure 14.4.

The parameters that are available for group differences are similar to those presented earlier. However, the group specific dynamic terms ($\alpha^{(g)}$, $\beta^{(g)}$)

EXHIBIT 14.4
A Multiple Group Model for a Latent Change Score Model With Many Groups

---

We can write

(1) $\quad Y[2]_n^{(g)} = Y[1]_n^{(g)} + \Delta y_n^{(g)}$ or $\Delta y_n^{(g)} = Y[2]_n^{(g)} - Y[1]_n^{(g)}$.

We can also write the means and covariances of these change scores as

(2a) $\quad \Delta y_n^{(g)} = \mu_\Delta^{(g)} + \Delta y_n^{*(g)}$

with

(2b) $\quad E\{\Delta y^{*(g)}, \Delta y^{*(g)\prime}\} = \phi_\Delta^{(g)2}$ and $E\{Y[1]^{*(g)}, \Delta y^{*(g)}\} = \phi_{1\Delta}^{(g)}$.

This implies we can also write a model of the latent changes with group designations as

(3) $\quad \Delta y[t]_n^{(g)} = \alpha^{(g)} Q\{1\}_n^{(g)} + \beta^{(g)} y[t-1]_n^{(g)} + z_n^{(g)}$.

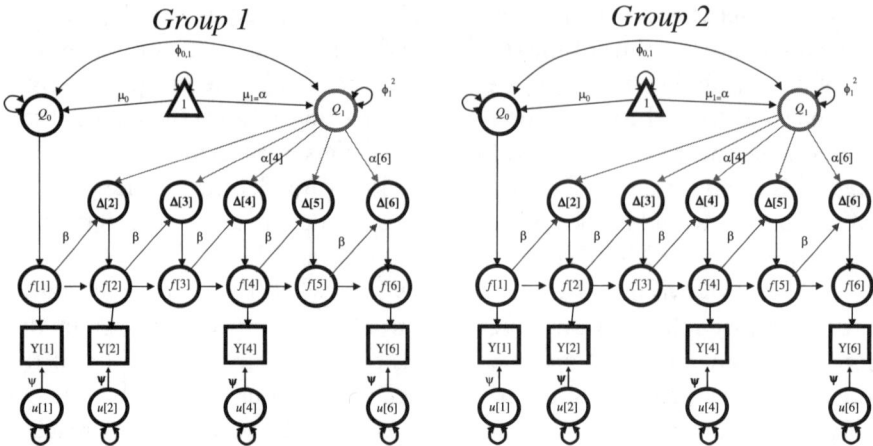

Figure 14.4. Multiple group latent change score models for multiple repeated measures.

are now available to change over groups as well. What should be done now is based on the substantive application, but the fact that any model parameter can be equated over groups is the fundamental feature of all models.

It is now possible to fit all variations of the group models using standard SEM software. There are many different models that can and should be fitted, and we will describe only a few of these. In order to focus in on the main results of a RCT study as one of our example applications, we describe both the MLM-SEM and MGM-SEM models based only on the LCS approach for univariate data (as done by McArdle, 2007a).

One possible reason for any misfit is that the intervals of time do not represent an equal spacing of time (i.e., 1 week, 1 month, and 6 months), but equal changes are the implied model of the use of constant dynamic parameters (e.g., as in Raykov, 1997a, 1997b). To examine this issue, we can try a variety of other bases, including using a more precise counting of weeks between tests (i.e., 0, 1, 4, 24), and the use of a power transformation. We can also fit a latent change model with free estimation of the optimal basis coefficients (i.e., 0, 1, 0.16, 0.04), because there may be some declines at later occasions but also that the dual change model was a reasonable starting point.

Another substantive model (not listed here) allowed all parameters representing the model to vary between the control and experimental group. In all models where the experimental and nonexperimental groups are defined to be the same (at pretest), all parameters can and should be equated.

The trajectories of the best-fitting model for the two groups on the key outcome scores can then written for both groups. This shows that an increased mean together with the variance over time is an expected result if some people learn faster than others within the Experimental group (or else the variance would decrease over time) and seems to be a reasonable way to describe the effect of the experimental manipulation (McArdle, 2001, 2007a). The trajectories of the best-fitting model for the two groups on other outcome scores may not show as much change, especially the variables that are not used in training. From all these estimates we can calculate the expected group trajectories and a multi-year latent change accumulation as the combination. If we are not using the same model for both groups, we might say the increases in one variable does not affect either variables (for more details, see McArdle, 2001, 2007a, 2007b; or the applications book, McArdle & Nesselroade, 2014).

15

INCOMPLETE DATA WITH MULTIPLE GROUP MODELING OF CHANGES

This use of multiple group factor invariance over groups (MFIG) model leads to an interesting observation. As it turns out, if we can assume multiple factors that are invariant over groups, then we do not need to measure every person on every variable in order to estimate most longitudinal structural equation models (LSEMs; for details, see McArdle, 1994).

The principle of multiple factorial invariance over groups (MFIG) used here can be expressed in several ways, but it is fairly simple to state that the latent variable loadings and the latent variable means (all of them) must be identical over groups. Also, it is simplest to say that the only differences between groups used here is that some variables are measured in some groups are latent (i.e., not measured) in other groups. In fact, the groups are to be defined by the pattern of available (i.e., nonmissing or complete) data. Obviously, the key feature in this approach seems to be the fitting of MFIG in situations where not all variables are measured in every group. The reasons why they are not measured can be crucial. But, in most cases, there is not enough information to identify the MFIG as tests, so these restrictions are fitted automatically rather than to yield an empirical test. In fact, in the typical case, there is no way to fit anything other than the MFIG constraints, so the MFIG is a set of necessary assumptions. Parameter estimation by maximum likelihood estimates (MLE) is also a needed requirement. Some new computer programs do not even emphasize that these multiple groups based on the pattern of incomplete data exist (see MPLUS; Muthen & Muthen, 2002).

USING THE MFIG PRINCIPLE TO DEAL WITH INCOMPLETE DATA

The first theoretical applications of this type seemed to have emerged in the early work of Lord (1955), who estimated the correlation among two scores for persons who were not measured on both variables (see also Cudeck, 2000). The first practical applications of this type of model with the new structural equation modeling (SEM) programs were fitted by Jöreskog and Sörbom (1977). This special device was quickly recognized and used by Horn and McArdle (1980), who promoted ideas about using this approach to deconstruct the Age–Time–Cohort dilemma by including "nodes" in models. They also discovered that all this work could be used to provide a multiple group model (MGM) approach for incomplete longitudinal data. In the longitudinal context, Marini, Olsen, and Rubin (1980) also suggested a very similar MGM-MLE approach. The same procedure was subsequently used by Rindskopf (1983), although he seemed to figure this out himself, and he termed it a "phantom" variable approach. The same logic of dealing with incomplete data by using added latent variables later appeared in P. D. Allison (1987) and in many subsequent presentations based on what was earlier termed full information maximum likelihood (FIML; Dempster, Laird, & Rubin, 1977).

Practical problems are encountered in any longitudinal study, including initial self-selection and dropout (or attrition). In prior work, a multiple group model (MGM) approach has been used (Jöreskog, 1971; McArdle & Hamagami, 1992) to deal with problems of "incomplete data" (Cudeck, 2000; Lord, 1955; McArdle, 1994), and this is important. In these situations, we can use the MGM-SEM approach, but here we define the grouping variable based on patterns of available data to deal with incomplete pieces (with the incomplete data simply drawn as circles in the path diagram). We then presume all parameters are invariant over all groups. This representation essentially mimics some key assumptions about longitudinal data (Little & Rubin, 1987; McArdle, 1994), but in some cases we can still obtain tests of fit that allow us to represent some of these assumptions as a testable hypothesis.

The actual way this works is that we first define groups of people who have the same pattern of complete and incomplete data, as presented in Exhibit 15.1.

EXHIBIT 15.1
A Multiple Group Model–Structural Equation Model Expression
for Dealing With Incomplete Data

First, each group is defined by the pattern of complete and incomplete data. That is, if person m only has data on p variables, then they are only grouped with other people who have similar data. In the standard multiple group model (MGM)–maximum likelihood estimates (MLE) framework, what we can do here is form two nonoverlapping or independent groups (see Figure 15.1): (1) one set of people with complete data ($\mathbf{q}^{(1)} = [Y\ X\ 1]$) and (2) a different set of people with only some of the data ($\mathbf{q}^{(2)} = [Y\ 1]$). But now we add a latent variable (x) into the second group, so all persons can have the same basic set of model parameters. In all cases, what we need to do is to restrict the model to have exactly the same placements and values of all one-headed arrows (A) and two-headed arrows (Ù), and then we filter ($\mathbf{F}^{(g)}$) the data in different ways. In the simple regression model listed above, we would write

(1) $$\mathbf{F}^{(1)} = \begin{pmatrix} |1 & 0 & 0| \\ |0 & 1 & 0| \\ |0 & 0 & 1| \end{pmatrix} \text{ and } \mathbf{F}^{(2)} = \begin{pmatrix} |1 & 0 & 0| \\ |0 & 1 & 0| \end{pmatrix}$$

leaving one (3 × 3) sums of squares and cross-products (SSCP) matrix for the first group and one (2 × 2) SSCP matrix for the second group, and these matrices might not have similar values.

Then in a typical MGM-MLE expression, we can write the overall likelihood as the weighted sum of the group likelihoods:

(2a) $$L^2 = (n^{(g)}/N) \sum (g = 1 \text{ to } G) L^{2(g)}$$

where, for each group, the misfit is only based on the means and covariances that are available within that specific group, and this is simply written as

(2b) $$L^{2(g)} = f_n^{*(g)} - 1\{(\mathbf{m}^{(g)} - \boldsymbol{\mu}^{(g)}) + (\mathbf{S}^{(g)} - \boldsymbol{\Sigma}^{(g)})\}$$

This overall L^2 index for all incomplete data groups can also be compared with a central chi-square distribution with multiple degrees of freedom to examine the probability of misfit of the invariant MGM-MLE for all groups given normal independent and identically distributed (IID) residuals.

Because only the data that are complete play any role in the calculation of the likelihood (in Equation 2), this is probably not best thought of as any test of the incomplete data, because that is not possible. But what this expression (Equation 2) does offer is a test of whether the complete data can be combined over multiple independent groups of observables. Any overall model can be chosen as long as the model parameters can be identified.

In general, the way this MGM-MLE procedure works is actually quite understandable and reasonable, although the required assumptions may be hard to meet. Let us take a very simple case: assume that we have the outcome variable (Y) that is present for everyone, but where the predictor variable (X) is missing for about one half of the individuals but is present for the other half. Assuming we want to fit a regression model to establish the prediction of Y from X, we might only use half of the data. This would be a reasonable starting point if we had done the variable selection by ourselves, but it may not be appropriate if there is some reason that the people have only part of the predictor scores (as in McArdle, 1994). For example, suppose we do not measure some of the data intentionally (e.g., due to cost). If we can assume that the regression model should apply to everyone—and this is a key model assumption—then we can certainly use the incomplete data techniques as depicted in Figure 15.1. Of course, the specific sample sizes for each group will need to be considered.

This example is intentionally simple, but Figure 15.1 essentially gives the overall idea of most incomplete data models. What we notice is that the second group is missing all information on X, but it still has the mean and variance of Y, so the covariance in the first group (used to form the regression coefficients) will need to be adjusted to make sure all model parameters are the same. The single set of parameters characterizing the entire group would then be obtained by estimating the parameters from two groups with invariant regression parameters, and the resulting MLE would be those that give the best estimate from a single population. If the data were missing in

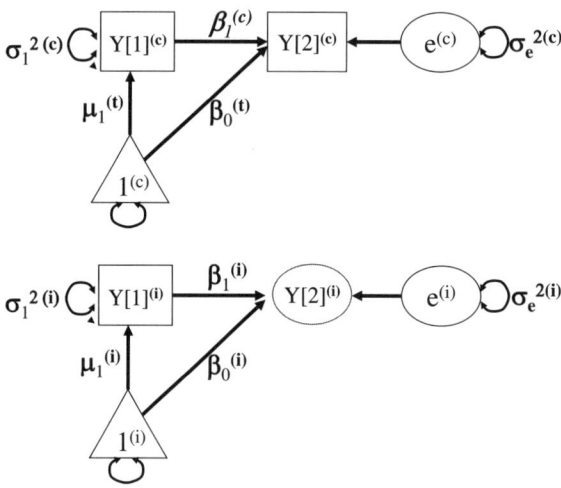

Figure 15.1. A multiple group autoregression model with incomplete data differences; C = complete data group; I = incomplete data group.

some way related to the measured data (i.e., selection on X or Y), then the result would be as close to the analysis that could be achieved if all data were present. If the data were selected in a way that was unrelated to the measured scores, then this will necessarily provide good estimates. But, in fact, it may not work at all, and we would not know it.

Of course, we could certainly have more subgroups based on other patterns of incomplete data. When we do this by variable sampling designs, we can even create a model of longitudinal attrition.

DEFINING A THEORY OF INCOMPLETE DATA

Rubin (1976) made some insightful comments about the definition of incomplete data. Basically, he proposed the following definitions of alternative kinds of data selection mechanisms, and we have presented this in a longitudinal context:

1. Missing Completely At Random (MCAR): This is the well-known thought that the dropout of any data point is randomly related to the phenomena of interest. In the longitudinal context this could be a random dropout at any occasion of measurement or be creating even more dropout over time.
2. Missing At Random (MAR): Dropout that is nonrandom but directly related to a measured variable. In the longitudinal context, this could be dropout at the second occasion because of the score that was obtained at the first occasion (as in McArdle & Hamagami, 1991). We could also base dropout on an observed variable that was measured at the first occasion, so it could be used in the analysis.
3. Not Missing At Random (NMAR): Dropout that is nonrandom and possibly directly related to an unmeasured variable. In the longitudinal context, this could be dropout due to a grouping category that could have been observed at the first occasion, but was not directly observed (McArdle 1994). For simplicity, we could simply say that if the observed score reaches a specific high or low level, then that person drops out.

The ideas presented by Rubin (1976) were not completely new, as he surely knew, and the terminology he suggested is certainly open to criticism, but this specific delineation is considered to be quite brilliant by many others today (Little & Rubin, 2002). Incidentally, Rubin was mainly interested in solving the incomplete data problems using multiple imputation (MI) techniques

(Little & Rubin, 2002; Rubin, 1976) anyway, and this is not exactly what we are doing here.

We can say that it was already clear that in practical longitudinal research the MCAR (Item 1) was often assumed, and the NMAR (Item 3) was often dismissed as possible but impractical. What we could do then, and now, is to see if there is any difference between the people who came back and those who did not. But the novel definition of MAR (Item 2), which when merged with MLE, made it possible to estimate the parameters of a longitudinal model even though some of the scores were selected and the mechanism was measured (P. D. Allison, 1987; Horn & McArdle, 1980; Marini, Olsen, & Rubin, 1980). The basic MAR idea was to use all available information to estimate any model parameter for a population of people, and the hope was that the model parameters would be corrected for any nonrandom selection model. More details will be presented on this basic idea in later sections, but the main claims for MAR seem to have already proven to be useful.

There is much good to be said about the technique known as MI (Rubin, 1976) because it seems to work so well. In this approach the incomplete values are estimated using the estimated parameters of a simple model (often a regression model), and these replacements are used to fit the LSEM. This is done multiple times to account for the random error variation: Different values are estimated for the incomplete data and the resulting parameters and fit of any LSEMs are then averaged to find the best values for the LSEMs as if the incomplete data were MAR. The assumptions of this MI-MAR seem the same as the MLE-MAR, but the results might differ a little bit. In fact, we have not been able to find major differences in using this option, so the MLE-MAR approach is the only technique presented here. The current LSEM programs provide relatively simple ways to deal with these issues, and researchers are taking advantage of these options (see, e. g., McArdle & Hamagami, 1991).

RECONSIDERING MASKED DATA

Other researchers have studied these problems in many different ways (Bell, 1954; Little & Rubin, 2002). What a brief demonstration based on "masking" data, or just not using it, could show is that even if longitudinal data are incomplete, they can all be fitted using the currently available LSEM programs. But what is not clear yet is if the answers provided in the MAR or NMAR cases are completely correct representations of the complete unmasked data. This could be critically important to appropriate inferences about change. If anything, our later demonstrations should be thought to add additional options to what we can do next. Unfortunately, we basically demonstrate that the choice among univariate models for individual changes is not so easy. Although some researchers seem to think we have a clear choice, this is not our conclusion. And of course, there are many more LSEMs that can be fitted to any data. So we will not belabor the process now, and instead of pursuing these key points about incomplete data any further now, we will move on and give some ideas about what other models we can fit with this novel LSEM technology. We will return to this basic issue in the last part here.

IV

LONGITUDINAL SEM FOR THE INTERRELATIONSHIPS IN GROWTH

16

CONSIDERING COMMON FACTORS/LATENT VARIABLES IN STRUCTURAL MODELS

The next question we often face in a longitudinal analysis is what to do when we have multiple outcome variables, as we often do. This problem is often overlooked in substantive research, because it is a difficult problem, but we think it can be very useful to consider because it is widely applicable. Now we are not talking about the completely exploratory use of many possible outcome variables until one seems to fit with a particular theory of change. Nor are we simply talking about the basic approach taken in what is termed exploratory factor analysis (EFA; e.g., Mulaik, 1971). While both topics are relevant here, the questions we ask begin with a surface look at the similarity of model estimates across variables, and then the deeper questions concern the time-dependent relationships of each variable to one another.

As stated earlier, the merger of structural equation modeling (SEM) concepts using the SEM tools is the basis of many real SEM applications. The SEM literature is filled with interesting forms of common factor analysis, from the randomized-experimental work of Blalock (1985a, 1985b) to

http://dx.doi.org/10.1037/14440-017
Longitudinal Data Analysis Using Structural Equation Models, by J. J. McArdle and J. R. Nesselroade
Copyright © 2014 by the American Psychological Association. All rights reserved.

the nonrandomized-observational examples in Rabe-Hesketh, Skrondal, and Pickles (2004; for more on the history of this division, see Cochran & Cox, 1950). In econometrics, these issues have been raised as "errors in variables" models using panel data (Baltagi, 2009; Griliches & Hausman, 1986; Hsiao, 2003). However, all such interesting applications include the concepts of latent variables (LV) in path models, so we extend this merger by highlighting features of our own.

We will use factor analysis as a generic term for describing the processes of describing, testing hypotheses, and making scientific inferences about unobserved variables by examining the internal structure of multiple variables (as in McArdle, 1994, 1996). We add the term *longitudinal data* to consider the special analyses based on the collection of information on the same individuals over some period of time, possibly even using repeated measurements. This bridging of longitudinal data with factor analysis is an attempt to provide clarity about the nature of the changes in the underlying factors in both the qualitative meaning of the factors over time and the quantitative differences in the level of the factors among people over time. Techniques for the integration of factor methods and longitudinal data actually form the basis of this book.

We start with the key historical developments in this area, describe the basic factor model, usually used for cross-sectional data, deal with the simplest case of repeated observations over two occasions, and then expand into factor analyses of more complex data collection designs. The models presented in this part of this book address other contemporary issues, including model fitting with incomplete data and future directions in factor analysis of longitudinal data.

To start, let us consider common factors/latent variables in structural models. During the past two decades there has been an increasing use of what is now termed confirmatory or structural factor analysis (SFA; see McArdle, 1996; Nesselroade & Baltes, 1984). The reason we do not usually call this approach confirmatory, unlike most everyone else, is because not only we will use this technology in situations where we have an a priori hypothesis, but also we may find ourselves in an exploratory mode of thinking. Indeed, we find this often is the case, and we simply want to be encouraged to state what we actually did (as in McArdle, 2011b). The clear benefit of SFA is that we can directly represent and test specific factor analytic hypotheses of interest. In contrast to the limitations of EFA, the standard factor extraction and the factor rotation are technical procedures not used in SFA.

COMMON FACTORS MEASURED OVER TIME

The SEM techniques described here have some common features. These SEMs can initially be used to make explicit tests of hypotheses about the likely number of common factors using precise statistical tests and allow precise and meaningful restrictions on parameters in any longitudinal model, including hypotheses about factor loadings and factor scores over time. More advanced structural equation models are used to test additional hypotheses about longitudinal data, including the analysis of factorial invariance. These models are important to developmental research because they can be used to evaluate quantitative changes in the scores of a factor over time as well as qualitative changes in the meaning of a measured construct over time. That is, although the same variables are measured at repeated occasions, we are not assured that the same constructs are being measured at each occasion. This lack of construct equivalence can occur when there is an experimental intervention between occasions or if the persons measured have developed in different ways. In the applications studied here, the matter of multiple factors with invariance over time (MFIT), as originally suggested by Nesselroade (1983) and later advocated by both McArdle and Nesselroade (1994) and McArdle (2007b). This will be highlighted here.

Factor analytic techniques have been developed and used by psychologists for most of the 20th century, and these methods have become especially useful in studies of individual differences. The key concept in any factor analysis is that a number of observed behaviors are a direct result of smaller number of unobserved or latent sources termed factors. This theoretical principle was used by Spearman (1904) in his early studies of the concept of general intelligence, and it has been applied in wide variety of empirical studies to isolate and identify latent factors representing parsimonious and reliable sources of differences between individuals and groups. In this sense, common factors in psychology share much with ideas from other areas of science: for example, the quarks and atoms of physics, the molecules and elements of chemistry, the genes and viruses of biology, and the unobserved planets and black holes of astronomy. These key scientific concepts are not directly observed, but we imply their existence from a large set of observed measurements.

To describe this general factor theory in the first article, Spearman (1904) created a technique for testing hypotheses about latent variables using only measured variables (for reviews, see Horn & McArdle, 2007, or McArdle, 2007b). He applied the first factor analysis model to a matrix of correlations from data collected on the school grades and mental tests of children, and indeed, he suggested that the single-factor model fit well (see Horn & McArdle, 2007). Over the next 25 years, Spearman posed more technical problems and invented many solutions for these difficult psychometric issues. He wrote a basic algebraic model for multiple observed variables based on a single common latent variable (LV), he considered different ways that the parameters in this model could be uniquely calculated, and he considered ways to evaluate the statistical goodness-of-fit of this model to empirical data.

In order to raise this general factor concept to a high level of a scientifically respectable theory, Spearman (1904, 1927) created a strongly rejectable model for the understanding of individual differences. In our view, most of the research that has followed Spearman's work on this topic has soundly rejected the simple idea of a single common source of intellectual differences among people, although we probably do need to recognize that many others have different views on this matter (Jensen, 1980; cf. Horn & McArdle, 2007). More important, in this early work on factor analysis, Spearman laid the basic foundation for all modern work in SEM. Indeed, there are many ways we can use LVs or common factors in SEMs (McDonald, 1985b, 1999).

At the outset, we must ask, "Are we just fooling ourselves when we add unobservables to a model?" Some people seem to think so (McArdle, 1994, 2007b), and it is not very hard to find rather poor examples of factor analysis in practice. We can also consider several alternative ways to estimate the model parameters in factor analysis (MacCallum & Tucker, 1991). But it is most useful to explicitly define what we mean here.

THE STRUCTURE OF COMMON FACTOR MODELS

Figure 16.1 is an SEM path diagram representing a single common factor as an LV, and this is detailed in Exhibit 16.1. The common factor score (the circle termed F) is not directly measured, but this common factor is thought to have its own variability (ϕ^2) and to produce the variation in each of the four observed variables (Y_m, m = 1 to 4) through the common factor loadings (λ_m). The common factor loadings have all the properties of traditional regression coefficients, except here the predictor is unobserved (McArdle, 1994). Each of the measured variables is also thought to have a unique variance (ψ_m^2) that is assumed to be uncorrelated with other

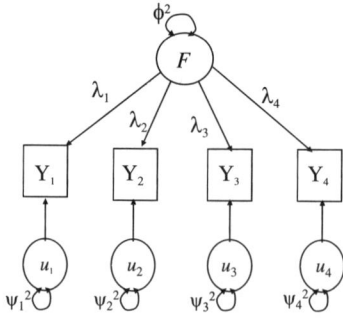

Figure 16.1. A path diagram of a standard one common factor model.

EXHIBIT 16.1
Defining a Common Factor in Structural Equation Modeling

The model for the observed variables at any time is thought to be

(1a) $$Y_{m,n} = \lambda_m F_n + u_{m,n},$$

where the observed variables (Y_m, m = 1 to M) common factor score (termed F) is not directly measured.

This common factor is thought to have its own variability (ϕ^2) so

(2a) $$E\{F, F'\} = \phi^2,$$

and each unique variable has its own variance,

(2b) $$E\{u_m, u'_m\} = \psi_m^2.$$

This implies that this variation reaches each of the observed variables through the respective common factor loadings (l_m), as either a variance

(3a) $$E\{Y_{m*}, Y'_{m*}\} = \sigma_m^2 = \lambda_m \phi^2 \lambda'_m + \psi_m^2,$$

or covariance term,

(3b) $$E\{Y_{j*}, Y_k^{*\prime}\} = \sigma_{jk} = \lambda_j \phi^2 \lambda'_k.$$

It follows that by adding the constraint that $\phi^2 = 1$, we have simplified model variances of

(4a) $$E\{Y_{m*}, Y'_{m*}\} = \sigma_m^2 = \lambda_m 1 \lambda'_m + \psi_m^2 = \lambda_m^2 + \psi_m^2,$$

and covariances,

(4b) $$E\{Y_j, Y'_{k*}\} = \sigma_{jk} = \lambda_j 1 \lambda'_k = \lambda_j \lambda'_k.$$

Note. From *Contemporary Issues in Exploratory Data Mining in the Behavioral Sciences* (pp. 40–41), by J. J. McArdle and G. Ritschard (Eds.), 2013, New York, NY: Taylor & Francis. Copyright 2013 by Taylor & Francis. Adapted with permission.

---

unique factors and with the common factor as well. So, although we have many measured variables (Y_m), we only have one unobserved common factor score (F). As in traditional regression analysis, we presume there is a score for each person and that is multiplied by a group weight (λ_m). So the reason we observe variation in any outcome score is partly due to its common factor component ($\lambda_m F_n$) and partly due to the uncorrelated unique component ($u_{m,n}$).

This set of assumptions implies that the expectation we have for the covariance terms among measures includes only common factor variance, whereas the expected variance terms include both common and specific variance. That is, if this model were true, then each variance and covariance would have the very simple structure as defined in Exhibit 16.1.

The expected parameters of this factor model all include the factor variance term (ϕ^2), so at least one additional restriction will be needed to make the parameters uniquely identified. This is typically done by either restricting the unknown factor variance (ϕ^2 = a positive value, such as 1) or by restricting one of the factor loadings (λ_1 = a positive value, such as 1). The specific choice of the identification constraint (also referred to as "setting the metric") should not really alter the estimation, fit, or interpretation of the result. That is, because the predictor variable is unobserved, the only parameters that are uniquely identified are the ratios of the loadings (e.g., λ_j/λ_k). These need to remain the same under any scaling of the metric of the unobserved variable. But, of course, this is all true only if the model is largely correct and not if it is largely incorrect. So, after adding an appropriate identification constraint ($\phi^2 = 1$), the new covariance expectations are now more "restricted" and can be written in the much simpler form. As it turns out, this provides exactly enough information for us to estimate all factor loadings, and this is used to tell which measured variables are most closely aligned with the unobserved common factor and which are not; that is, the ratio of the loadings is also used to provide a label for the unobserved common factor. This also means the covariance expressions can be examined for fit by comparison to real data (using SEM software), and when this model does not seem to fit, we usually assume the score model of observable variables is not based on a single common factor.

We typically examine whether or not the one-factor model fits the data by comparing the observed variances and covariance (**S**) to the model expected variances and covariance ($\mathbf{\Sigma}$). It is probably important to restate that the observed means are not fitted here. Incidentally, our choice of using M = 4 indicators per common factor should not be considered arbitrary; this is the smallest number of indicators that offers positive degrees of freedom (df) for model evaluation (i.e., $df = 1$) by itself. Of course, with only three indicators we could look at the resulting factor loadings to make sure they are all large and positive, but this is not often done. Instead, many researchers seem to treat this "extraction" as if it were based on the same technical procedures used to form the indicators. Unfortunately, although it is possible to fit a one-factor model with only three indicators, this model always fits the observed data perfectly (because there are as many unknowns as there are knowns), so we have no way to tell if it is incorrect. Perfect fit is generally not possible with four indicators, so we can examine the model fit.

In factor model testing, as a very general alternative, we could simply say there is no common factor at all, so all covariances and correlations are

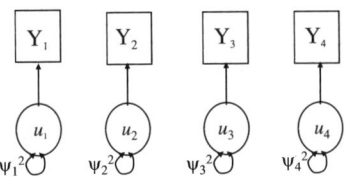

Figure 16.2. A path diagram of a restricted zero common factor model.

collectively zero. This is a typical "baseline" model that, without any doubt, we really must be able to say does not fit our data. This starting or baseline model is drawn in Figure 16.2, and this simpler model could be examined for goodness-of-fit. Of course, we know that if this model fits our data, we are effectively finished. That is, we really must have enough statistical power to reject this kind of no-common-factor hypothesis. If the null baseline model does fit, we might as well stop here because this forms a very simple set of relationships (e.g., the expected correlations are all zero). In any case, the null factors baseline is a simpler and testable alternatives to the one common factor idea.

If the factor model expectations seem to match the observed data, there are many ways to restrict this model even further (see Exhibit 16.2). For example, we could say that all the factor loadings are equal (as typically done in a Rasch-type model; see McDonald, 1999; McArdle, Grimm, Hamagami, Bowles, & Meredith, 2009), and this is done in Figure 16.3 (and Exhibit 16.2), and this simpler model could be examined for goodness-of-fit. If this fits, we can say the common factor has a lot of simple properties (e.g., factor scores can be estimated by summing up the items). Of course, we can always question why we do this at all (MacCallum & Tucker, 1991).

If the simple one common factor model does not seem to provide a good fit, we can go the other direction and perhaps relax some of the model constraints (see Exhibit 16.3). For example, we can posit the existence of a second common factor (F_2), and one simple version of this model is drawn as Figure 16.4. In this simple model, we posit that each common factor is related to a specific set of observed variables. Perhaps it is not clear that this two-factor model is decidedly more complicated than the single factor model. The only difference between this two-factor model and the one-factor model is the covariance among the common factors (ϕ_{12}). That is, if this value turns out to be the same as the variance terms (or the factor intercorrelation $\rho_{12} = 1$), then this model reduces to become the one-factor model. This holds true even when we have more variables measured, as in Figure 16.5. This subtle difference could be important in the model fit, where there is now 1 *df* difference between these models, and we can evaluate the gain in fit (and see McArdle, 2013).

EXHIBIT 16.2
Defining Simpler Common Factor Alternatives
in Structural Equation Modeling

In a different kind of simplification we might require that all loadings be zero, yielding

(1a) $$Y_{m,n} = u_{m,n}$$

for m = 1 to M, and with the associated variance expectations,

(1b) $$E\{Y_{m*}, Y'_{m*}\} = \sigma^2_m = \psi^2_m$$

and the associated covariance expectations,

(1c) $$E\{Y_{j*}, Y'_{k*}\} = \sigma_{jk} = 0,$$

so all covariances (and correlations) are expected to be zero. This is typically termed the *null model*, and it is used as a baseline against which to judge the other more interesting models.

In another type of simplification we might require that all loadings be identical (McDonald, 1999), and this would result in

(2a) $$Y_{m,n} = \lambda F_n + u_{m,n}$$

for m = 1 to M, and with associated variance expectations,

(2b) $$E\{Y_{m*}, Y'_{m*}\} = \sigma^2_m = \lambda^2 + \psi^2_m$$

and with associated covariance expectations

(2c) $$E\{Y_{j*}, Y'_{k*}\} = \sigma_{jk} = \lambda^2,$$

are expected to be the same.

Note. From *Contemporary Issues in Exploratory Data Mining in the Behavioral Sciences* (pp. 43–47), by J. J. McArdle and G. Ritschard (Eds.), 2013, New York, NY: Taylor & Francis. Copyright 2013 by Taylor & Francis. Adapted with permission.

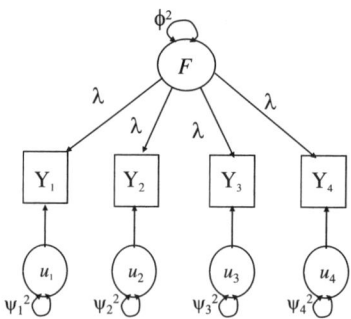

Figure 16.3. A path diagram of a one factor Rasch-type model.

EXHIBIT 16.3
Defining More Complex Common Factor Alternatives in Structural Equation Modeling

Alternatively, more complex models can be fit as well, including several different kinds of two-factor models. This model can generally be written in the form of

(1) $$Y_{m,n} = \lambda_{1,m} F1_n + \lambda_{2,m} F2_n + u_{m,n}.$$

Now, since each common factor is unobserved, we need to identify the model by either fixing the common factor variances (e.g., $\phi_1^2 = 1$ and $\phi_2^2 = 1$) or by restricting a factor loading on each (e.g., $\lambda_1 = 1$ and $\lambda_6 = 1$). In this case, we can write variance expectations as

(2a) $$\sigma_m^2 = \lambda_{1,m}\lambda'_{1,m} + \lambda_{2,m}\lambda'_{2,m} + 2*\{\lambda_{1,m}\rho_{12}\lambda'_{2,m}\} + \psi_m^2$$

and cross-variable covariance expectations as

(2b) $$\sigma_{j,k} = 2*\{\lambda_{1,m}\rho_{12}\lambda'_{2,m}\}.$$

We can consider several restrictions of these parameters. For example, we can assume that there are two common factors and each common factor is indicated by three measured variables. This is written as a factor pattern with columns

(3a) $$\Lambda_{1,m} = [\lambda_{1,1}\,\lambda_{1,2}\,\lambda_{1,3}\ 0\ 0\ 0],$$

and

(3b) $$\Lambda_{2,m} = [0\ 0\ 0\ \lambda_{2,4}\,\lambda_{2,5}\,\lambda_{2,6}],$$

so the zeros are fixed in specific locations to designate no possible influence, but the ρ_{12} and ψ_m^2 are all estimated.

We can also summarize this multiple factor model in a general way by writing

(4a) $$\Sigma = \Lambda\Phi\Lambda' + \Psi^2,$$

where we place all elements of the factor loadings into one matrix

(4b) $$\Lambda = [\Lambda'_{1,m}, \Lambda'_{2,m}]$$

and add the diagonal matrix of uniquenesses,

(4c) $$\Psi^2 = diag\{\psi_m^2\}$$

and this means that all prior single factor principles apply in the multiple factor case.

Note. From *Contemporary Issues in Exploratory Data Mining in the Behavioral Sciences* (pp. 43–47), by J. J. McArdle and G. Ritschard (Eds.), 2013, New York, NY: Taylor & Francis. Copyright 2013 by Taylor & Francis. Adapted with permission.

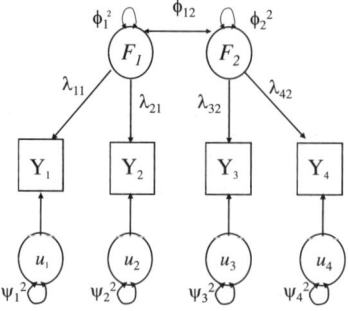

Figure 16.4. A path diagram of a restricted two common factor model.

KNOWN LIMITATIONS ON FACTORIAL IDENTIFICATION

The factor analysis approach is not without its own problems. For example, it seems that only simple kinds of SEMs are the only ones that can be fitted, and this is not true. We can start with the simple two-factor model of Figure 16.5 and add one additional factor loading, where the first factor is indicated by Variable 4, and the second factor is not. This is drawn as a path diagram in Figure 16.6, and it could be a correct representation of the data, even though Variable 4 now loads on Factor 1 and not Factor 2. We would fit both models as alternative, but we would

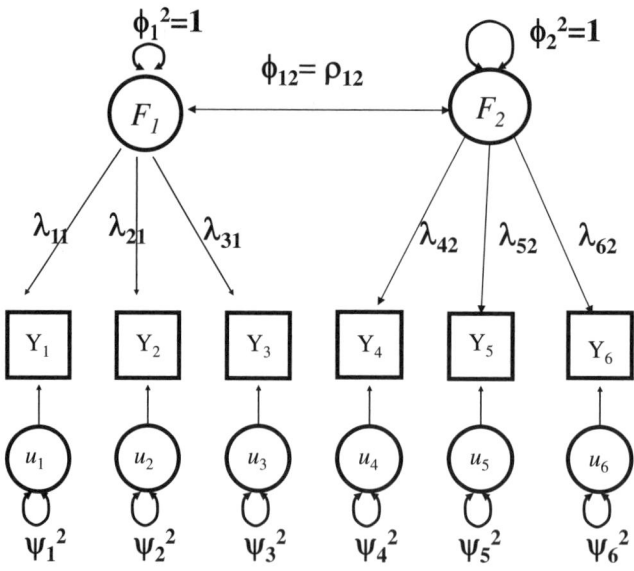

Figure 16.5. A two common factor model with ID constraints.

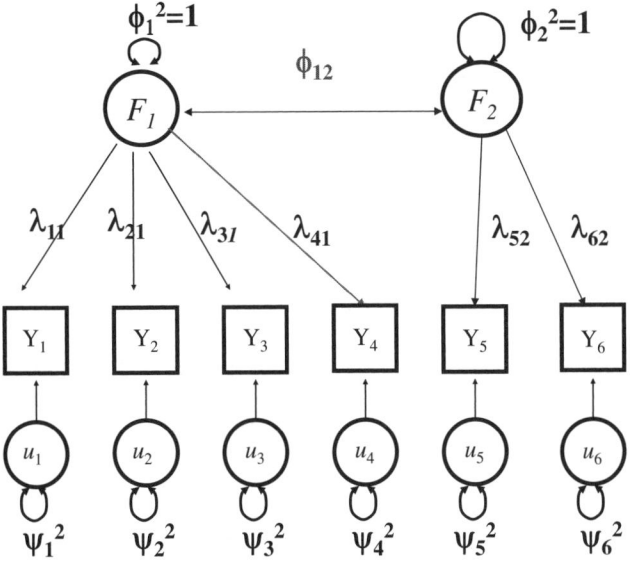

Figure 16.6. A nonnested two common factor model with unbalanced constraints.

quickly see they cannot be compared using our standard logic because they have the same number of parameters and are not proper subsets of one another.

In another example, we can start with the simple two-factor model (of Figure 16.5) and add two additional factor loadings, where common factor 1 is indicated by Variables 4 and 5, and two additional factor loadings, where common factor 2 is indicated by Variables 2 and 3. This is drawn as a path diagram in Figure 16.7. These additional parameters reduce the number of *df* (by 4), but the overall two-factor model loadings can still be identified, and unique estimates can be found for all parameters. We know if we fit this kind of a model, we could trim out the nonsalient loadings and, hope to have a reasonable fitting model. So here our data analysis strategy is put to an important test. Do we use our a priori logic and fit the hypothesized model (i.e., Figure 16.3) so we can use all listed probability calculations? Or do we fit the exactly identified solution to help us to understand our data and gain a good fitting model? Because we typically do not define everything we could do here, we cannot correctly use all SEM probability calculations. In practice, we often find both approaches are used in the same study!

It quickly becomes evident that these are not the only restrictions that can be allowed in the context of factor analysis. In this specific model used here, we have six variables and two common factors, so at least 10 factor

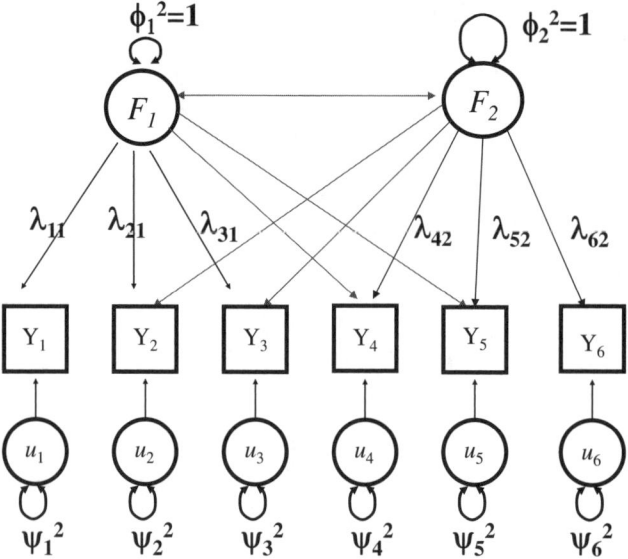

Figure 16.7. A two common factor exploratory model with oblique constraints where Y_1 and Y_6 are the reference variables.

loadings can be placed in different locations. This specific issue is discussed in Exhibit 16.3. Because the overall two-factor model can be represented with different diagrams (i.e., "rotated" into a different position) without any change in fit, this means that we possibly have different parameter values and factorial interpretations (see Figures 16.8 and 16.9).

So, and in general, it is well-known that a comparison of alternative factor models cannot be judged by goodness-of-fit alone (Kaiser, 1976; McArdle & Cattell, 1994). Perhaps more importantly, this also illustrates that the highly restricted two-factor model (of Figure 16.3) is a specific factorial hypothesis that can have a "unique solution" and "cannot be rotated" any further. This is the essential benefit of what is usually termed confirmatory factor analysis (CFA; Jöreskog, 1970b; Lawley & Maxwell, 1963; McDonald, 1985b; Tucker & Lewis, 1973). Just as a clarifying note, in our view, if the factor loading values were all specified in advance, then this would really be a "confirmatory" approach to model evaluation. Of course, this would mean the entire set of covariances was expected rather than just the model pattern. In sum, this later approach is a very rigid form of CFA that is hardly ever used.

What is used is EFA and the introduction of common latent variables limits what we can estimate and test with common factors. Once again, it is possible to fit a one-factor model with only three indicators, but this model always fits the observed data perfectly (it has $df = 0$), and we have no way to

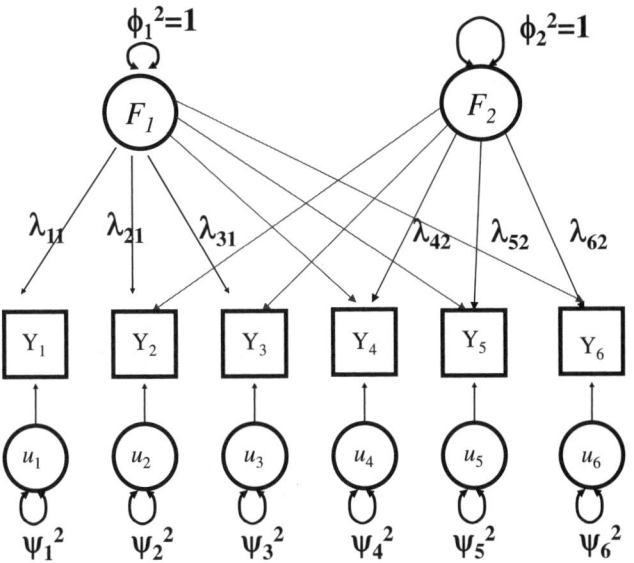

Figure 16.8. A two common factor exploratory model with orthogonality constraints where Y_1 is the reference variable.

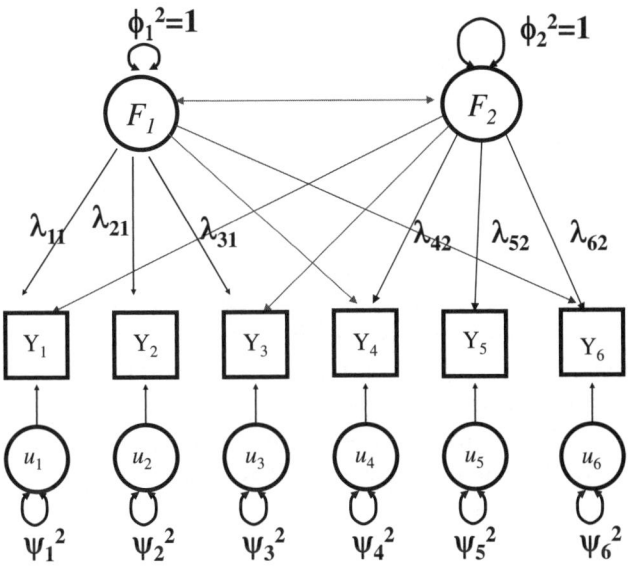

Figure 16.9. Alternative two common factor exploratory model with oblique constraints so Y_2 and Y_5 are the reference variables. Goodness-of-fit remains the same as above.

tell if this is incorrect. However, perfect fit is generally not possible with four indicators ($df = 1$), so we can examine the misfit here.

In the typical unrestricted factor model, we initially estimate a multiple factor orthogonal solution using some "convenient restrictions" (e.g., see Figure 16.8; Jöreskog, 1971, p. 23; Lawley & Maxwell, 1963). In this model the parameters are "exactly-identified" and require further rotation for interpretation. Exactly the same solution can also be obtained from a restricted SEM when we place the minimal constraints necessary for a unique solution. These constraints were previously described by Jöreskog (1971) and are repeated in Exhibit 16.3.

There are many other ways to make these same points (see Exhibit 16.4), but the minimum requirement to uniquely identify a multiple (K) factor model is to place K^2 fixed constraints among the factor loadings (Λ) and the factor covariances (Φ). Typically K constraints are placed as the factor variances (e.g., the diag(Φ) = I) and the other ($K*(K-1)$) constraints are placed on the tables of the factors (via the columns of loadings, Λ; see Jöreskog, 1969). Thus, by imposing exactly these K^2 constraints, we achieve an exactly identified rotation with the same fit.

But these generic statements imply that even more factor loadings can be estimated than we typically think. Most specifically, if we want to estimate two common factors from eight observed variables, we requires only four constraints, and this leaves a combination of 12 free elements in the factor loading (Λ) and the factor covariance (Φ) matrices. One common way to do this in SEM would be to define a fixed unity for each factor (e.g., $\lambda(m,k) = 1$) for scaling purposes, and this largely defines what the factor "is, or should be named." To this we add a fixed zero (e.g., $\lambda(m,k) = 0$) in a different location for each factor, to separate the first and second factor and to designate what the factor "is not, or should not be." This approach allows the estimation of the six other loadings for each factor as well as the correlation between the factors. This is termed an exactly identified two-factor solution, which means it can be rotated. Of course, many alternative K^2 constraints would yield the same goodness-of-fit. That is, we can never be sure we have the correct common factors, just K common factors that work the best for these restrictions.

Interestingly, the mean of the common factors is hardly ever discussed (see Exhibit 16.3). The means are not usually considered in a single occasion factor analysis. It is enough to say that standard factor analysis without reference to the means is equivalent to allowing all intercepts to be freely estimated and fixing the factor means at zero. If we want more, we would need to place additional restrictions on the variable intercepts to estimate the factor means (Cattell, 1971).

EXHIBIT 16.4
General Common Factor Identification in Structural Equation Modeling

If we have measured a set of M variables, we can now write a structural equation model with K common factors as

(1a) $$Y_m = \Lambda_{m,k} F_{k,n} + u_{m,n},$$

so that we have

(1b) $$\Sigma = \Lambda \Phi \Lambda' + \Psi^2,$$

where, for individual n, Y is the M-dimensional vector of observed scores, F is the K-dimensional vector of common factor scores, and u_m is the M-dimensional vector of unique factor scores. We further assume Λ is the $(M \times K)$ matrix of common factor loadings, Φ is the $(K \times K)$ symmetric matrix of common factor covariances, and Ψ^2 is the $(M \times M)$ diagonal matrix of unique variances. Following standard structural equation modeling (SEM) terminology (e.g., Jöreskog & Sörbom, 1985; Lawley & Maxwell, 1963; McDonald, 1985b), we can pattern the elements of matrices Λ, Φ, and Ψ^2 to be fixed, free, or equal as specified by some a priori hypothesis. We will deal with patterning of the mean vector in a later section of this chapter.

The estimation of K common factors from a set of M variables requires specific constraints in the factor loadings Λ. In the typical unrestricted factor model we initially estimate a K-factor orthogonal solution using some "convenient restrictions," e.g., requiring the initial factor intercorrelations to be zero ($\Phi = I$) or to have specific matrix products ($\Lambda \Psi^2 \Lambda'$) to be diagonal (Lawley & Maxwell, 1963; see also Jöreskog, 1971, p. 23). In these models the parameters are "exactly identified" and require further rotation for interpretation. The same solution can also be obtained from SEM when we place the minimal constraints necessary for a unique solution.

To be precise, we can follow the basic rules:

> Two simple sufficient conditions, as given by Howe [1955], are as follows. In the orthogonal case [sic, uncorrelated factors], let $\Phi = I$ and let the columns of Λ be arranged so that, for s = 1,2,..., K, columns contains at least s – 1 fixed elements. In the oblique case, let diag{F} = I, and let each column of Λ have at least K – 1 fixed elements. It should be noted that in the orthogonal case there are ½ K(K + 1) conditions on Φ and a minimum of K(K – 1) conditions on Λ. In the oblique case [sic, correlated factors] there are K normalizations in F and a minimum of K(K – 1) conditions on Λ. Thus, in both cases, there is a minimum of K(K + 1) specified elements in Λ and Φ ... (Jöreskog, 1971, p. 24; see McArdle & Cattell, 1994, p. 73).

It is well-known that we can define a $(K \times K)$ transformation matrix **T**, and then redefine

(2a) $$\Lambda^* = \Lambda \mathbf{T}^{-1},$$

with

(2b) $$\Phi^* = \mathbf{T} \Phi \mathbf{T}'$$

(continues)

EXHIBIT 16.4
General Common Factor Identification in Structural
Equation Modeling   *(Continued)*

so

(2c) $$\Sigma = \Lambda^* \Phi^* \Lambda^{*\prime} + \Psi^2$$

and the common factor model is reparameterized by a new set of rotated factor loadings (Λ^*), and a new set of rotated factor covariances (Φ^*), with the same fit to the data. The minimum requirement to uniquely identify a K-factor factor model is to place K^2 (the number of elements of **T**) fixed constraints in Λ and Φ. Typically K constraints are placed on $diag(\Phi) = \mathbf{I}$ and $K(K-1)$ are placed on the columns of Λ (Jöreskog, 1969). Thus, using this logic, if we impose exactly these K^2 constraints we achieve an exactly identified rotation with same index of fit.

From "Structural Equation Models of Factorial Invariance in Parallel Proportional Profiles and Oblique Confactor Problems," by J. J. McArdle and R. B. Cattell, 1994, *Multivariate Behavioral Research, 29* (1), p. 73. Copyright 1994 by Taylor & Francis. Adapted with permission.

RECONSIDERING FACTORIAL STRUCTURES

The range of possibilities for factorial structures for multiple variables is so vast that it is rare to consider all possible alternatives. Instead we consider the goodness-of-fit of the models to be an indicator of whether a specific model does not fit the data, and we never explicitly know if any specific model is the best one to fit. As with most models, using the classical arguments of Popper (1970), "[W]e can reject models with data, but we can never know we have the best model for any set of data." Another way to say this is that we can use the data to tell us which models are "false," but we cannot use the data to tell us which models are "true."

One of the classical problems in factor analysis with multiple factors is the definition of the position of the factors with respect to the variables. In one of the most important developments in factor analysis, Thurstone (1947) proposed a novel solution:

> One of the turning-points in the solution of the multiple factor problem is the concept of "simple structure." When a factor matrix reveals one or more zeroes in each row, we can infer that each of the tests does not involve all the common factors that are required to account for the intercorrelations of the battery as a whole. This is the principle characteristic of a simple structure (p. 181). . . . The factorial description of a test must remain invariant when the test is moved from one battery to another which involves the same common factors. . . . The factorial composition of a set of primary factors that have been found in a complete and over-determined simple structure remains invariant when the test is moved to another battery involving the same common factors and in which there are enough tests to make the simple structure complete and over-determined. (p. 365)

This concept of simple structure as a goal of exploratory factor rotation has been very influential in factor analysis because it suggested both rules for selecting an optimal test battery (i.e., selection the edges of the conic structure) and a clear set of scientific and technical restrictions on the loadings and the transformations needed (e.g., as in Promax; Browne, 2001). For these reasons, "simple structure" of the loading matrix was the goal used in a lot of studies.

As we have seen earlier, in contemporary SEM we can impose more than K^2 constraints and obtain an overidentified and, therefore, unrotatable solution, but the resulting set of expectations (Σ) might not fit the observed covariances (S) so well. In SFA, the choice of these constraints is used to test the critical hypotheses, and the cost due to these restrictions is judged in the same way as described before (i.e., using L^2, df, and ε_a). Often these hypotheses are based on simple factor patterns, especially those where each measured variable loads on one and only one factor. Although this simple pattern is not a necessary requirement for a good SFA, most current SFA applications try to achieve this level of "very simple structure" (after Revelle & Rocklin, 1979), but this idea probably should be questioned more rigorously.

THE ESTIMATION OF COMMON FACTOR SCORES

The careful reader will notice that we have not mentioned the problem of the calculation of the unobserved common factor scores; this is because factor scores for individuals can be calculated in many alternative ways, so they are usually "indeterminant" (for elaboration, see McDonald, 1985a).

Now the principal components (PCs) of any set of variables is a weighted linear combination of the observed scores, so we can start here. We can always calculate the optimal PC by asking for a first PC with the largest variance. The largest variance is chosen as the criterion because this is the new variable that will capture the most correlation among the variables; hence, it is the most reliable variable of all others we could consider. The second PC can then be extracted as an orthogonal projection to this first PC by calculating the linear combination with the largest variance of what remains after the first PC has been removed, and so on. In this sense the PCs are not really LVs so weighted linear composite scores can be created for them. In general, the PC approach seems very much like the common factor approach, and this is the good news. This is indeed good news, and it should be considered. The bad news is that it is not really possible to test the concept of a PC as a formal hypothesis, and the PC estimated loadings seem to be biased upward (i.e., the values are too large) when we have a small number of indicators per construct (McArdle, 1991b). Thus, we can calculate as many PCs as we like, but we do not have any reliable statistical tests of their utility or potential bias. The PCs can reflect good calculations of the common factors, but they do not test any model.

So factor score calculation is not a problem for the PC approach, because PC scores are in fact linear combinations of observables. This is the good news again. But one simple way to understand this problem is to consider that a Pearson correlation coefficient (r_{yx}) can be uniquely calculated from observed data on two variables (Y and X), but if we simply know the size of the correlation (e.g., $r_{yx} = 0.6$), we cannot recreate the distribution of the observed data (on Y and X) that produced this correlation: there are an unlimited set of scores that could lead to this specific correlation. This can be a considerable problem in working with correlations or with common factors, because in SEM we do not usually obtain a plot of the unobserved common factor scores. It is typical for some to say the SEM evaluation "does not require factor score estimates" rather than they "cannot uniquely estimate factor scores," but this limitation should be understood better. This implies that all the information about the factor scores must come from the model assumptions (i.e., normality of unique factors) rather than the empirical evidence from the score distribution.

Prior research has demonstrated the sequential nature of building a LV path model from cross-sectional data gathered at a single occasion *without* any estimation of factor scores. In one such analyses, McArdle and Prescott (1992) used data on $n > 1,600$ adults from the national sample of data on the Wechsler Adult Intelligence Scale–Revised (Wechsler, 1981). Amidst much discussion of the merits of different formal models, the final model depicted in this article included two common factors (termed Gfv and Gc) and two key predictors: Age and High School (HS) Graduation status. Attempts were made to consider many different kinds of SEMs, including polynomial forms of Age and interactions with HS Graduation. This was all done without creating any factor score estimates. In this research, successive models with a sequence of restrictions suggested that common factor scores were not needed. This work also suggested that that nonlinearity and interactions were not needed when the outcomes were the two most reliable common factors.

But we should not overlook the practical utility of the creation of factor score estimates, or even simple composites, in longitudinal analysis. Indeed, this seems this to be done all the time, and the results can be useful. Rather than work directly with observed raw data and a complex factor pattern, score estimates can be created for each factor in the same way at all times and then be used in subsequent analysis. Basically, we can say a lot about how this actually works. This use of unweighted composites is very practical because it allows us to simplify and summarize the main features of our longitudinal

EXHIBIT 16.5
Calculating Composite Scores (Over Time and Over Measures)

One very simple estimate (F) of a single factor score (F) can be obtained by calculating the unweighted sum of standard scores at any time as

(1) $$F[t]_n = \sum (m = 1 \text{ to } M)\{Y_m[t] - \mu_m[1]/\sigma_m[1]\}/M$$

where we use the vectors of means ($\mu_m[1]$) and deviations ($\sigma_m[1]$) from Time 1 only to create T new composite scores.

We can carry out the same kind of process by averaging all measures scores over all times

(2) $$F_{m,n} = \sum (t = 1 \text{ to } T)\{Y_m[t] - \mu_m[1]/\sigma_m[1]\}/T$$

so the resulting scores are unweighted averages, or grand means, of the same M scores over all times.

Of course, any composite score above could be "weighted" (W_m) by some estimate derived from the data (i.e., maybe based on the variable scaling or the factor loadings), but the Table of these weights should not vary over time.

The basic problems with the singular use of composite scores in longitudinal (or other situations) is that they still carry any unique or error components as part of their construction. This means that any changes in the composites can be seen as a complex combination of changes in the common factor scores, specific factor scores, and errors of measurement.

---

analysis. This is especially true when the scoring systems are relatively simple, such as the proportion correct of the maximum (POM) scores, but it also applies to more complex calculations, such as using the inverse weight of the factor loadings (for more elaboration, see Exhibit 16.5; T. W. Anderson & Rubin, 1956; McArdle, 1991b).

Whenever we do create composite scores, we certainly need to use the same constants in the formulas for the creation of factor scores at each occasion. This simply implies that the changes and difference we observe are among the people based on the variables and not due to the scoring system. The same is true of standardization, but we must apply the same constants to everyone before splitting up the data. This can be simply accomplished by using the same constant subtracted (i.e., e.g., the mean at Occasion 1) and the same divisor (e.g., the deviation at Occasion 1). Using this approach, we can create a very simple estimate of a single factor scores and calculate the simple sum of standard scores at any time where we use the vectors of means ($\mu_m[1]$) and deviations ($\sigma_m[1]$) from Time 1 only. The use of the equivalent formulas for scaling over time is essential if we are ever going to compare repeated scores over time. These scores will be averaged (summed up and divided by their number), but have a mean of zero and can be scaled to unit variance at Time 1, but will then have values "relative to Time 1" (for those with t > 1).

Indeed, because so much is presumably known about their derivation these POM scores would be fairly good scores to use in a subsequent longitudinal analysis. We can apply the same kind of strategy by averaging all measures scores over all time so the resulting scores are unweighted averages, or grand means, of the same M scores over all times (see Exhibit 16.5).

Of course, the main benefit of any composite score formed in this way is that it rules out the spurious variation in the other scores or other occasions. Similarly, any factor score or composite estimate formed in this way retain some of the measurement error, so they typically have larger deviations and lower correlations than would be estimated with true scores (see Burr & Nesselroade, 1990). In essence, we can use SEM to avoid this indeterminant factor scoring step and retain error-free measurements (as in McArdle & Prescott, 1992). However, another key caution, implied above, is that we can always create some kind of composites, but we might not start from the appropriate factor model, and if so we will not have the appropriate factor score estimates, or PCs, for that matter. This implies that the factor analysis model, with special (MFIT) invariance constraints to be described, is an essential ingredient in any longitudinal analysis.

17

CONSIDERING FACTORIAL INVARIANCE IN LONGITUDINAL STRUCTURAL EQUATION MODELING

Let us first point out that longitudinal structural equation modeling (LSEM) was initially expanded in an important way with the addition of common factor models (e.g., Horn & McArdle, 1980; Jöreskog, 1977a; Jöreskog & Sörbom, 1979). Most of this work was designed to ask and test the idea that we have the same constructs over time, and this idea has not really changed. Research on covariance-based LSEMs were extended using concepts derived from autoregressive models identifiable with longer time series. In important theoretical and practical work, Engle and Watson (1981) and Molenaar (1985) used multivariate linear structural equations models of individual time series (McArdle & Nesselroade, 2003). In ecomometrics, Griliches and Hausman (1986) promoted similar ideas for "error in variables" in panel data. But this task seems not to have been fully completed (see McArdle, 2007b).

The case of repeated measures is an important one in modern data analysis, especially because of the importance placed on repeated measures

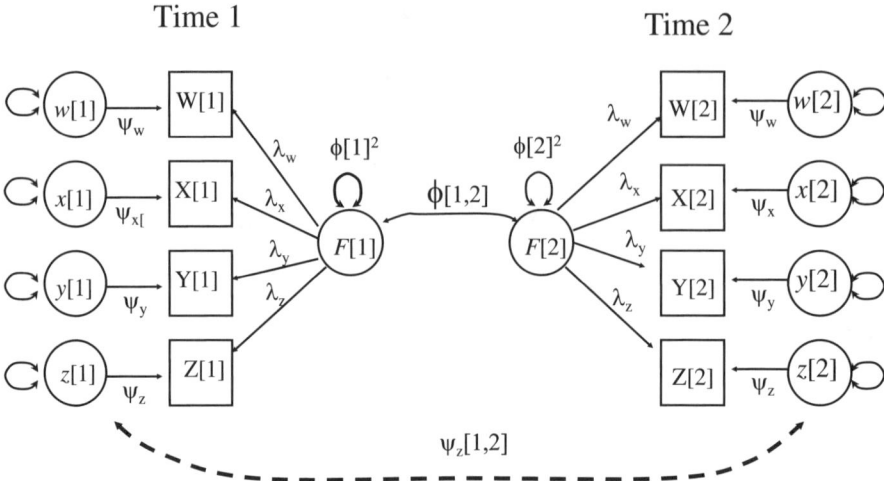

Figure 17.1. A two-occasion metric factor invariance over time covariance model. Subscripts of time are in brackets. From *Life-Span Developmental Psychology: Methodological Innovations* (p. 237), by S. H. Cohen and H. W. Reese (Eds.), 1994, Hillsdale, NJ: Erlbaum. Copyright 1994 by Erlbaum. Adapted with permission.

analysis of variance (RANOVA; as in Bock, 1975). One very simple model was described and used in McArdle and Nesselroade (1994) with only two occasions and four outcome variables, and this general idea is presented here as Figure 17.1.

THE KEY ROLE OF COMMON FACTOR MEANS

The common factor is an unobserved latent variable whose scale is determined by the analyst. Its variance is somewhat artificially set by the user, except it is usually positive, so the mean of this variable seems inexplicable as well. To some degree this is true. Unless some extraordinary circumstances of measurement are created (as in Cattell, 1971), there is no way we will be able to interpret the "absolute values" of factor scores or their means and variances, even if we would like to. However, it is almost always useful to compare "relative changes over time" or "relative differences between groups" in the means of factors. The common factor means are mainly used when we are interested in summarizing the average changes for the group and average differences for the group, and that is what we will do here.

A relatively simple model for common factor means appears in Exhibit 17.1. This standard approach requires the factor means to be estimated from the means of the observed data basically because we have no

EXHIBIT 17.1
Incorporating Common Factor Means Into the Factor Model

In this notation we might write the observed scores as ($m = 1$ to M)

(1a) $$Y_{m,n} = \iota_m + \lambda_{m,k} F_{k,n} + u_{m,n}$$

where the variable intercepts (ι_m) are added. We further assume that the common factor has a mean

(1b) $$E\{F_{k,},1'\} = v_k$$

but the unique score does not

(1c) $$E\{u_{m,},1'\} = 0.$$

This implies the mean vector expectations are

(2) $$E\{Y_m,1'\} = \mu_m = \iota_m + \lambda_{m,k} v_k$$

where the variable intercepts (ι_m) and the common factor means (v_k) are used to produce expectations of the observed variable means (μ_m).

---

idea about the scale of the latent variable. This will generally not be possible without a reference time or reference group, and we will use both ideas here (as in Sörbom, 1974). In a cross-sectional type of analysis, we will assume the common factors are invariant (i.e., same loadings, see below), we will select a "reference group" and will set the factor variance in this group to unity (e.g., $\phi^{2(1)} = 1$) and factor means to zero (e.g., $v^{(1)} = 0$), and we will estimate the other factor deviations and factor means as changes or differences from this reference group. In a longitudinal type of analysis (see Exhibit 17.2), we will assume the common factors are invariant (i.e., same loadings), select the reference time as Time 1, set the factor deviations to unity (e.g., $\phi[1]^2 = 1$) and the factor means to zero (e.g., $v[1] = 0$), and we will estimate the other factor deviations and factor means as changes or differences from this reference point. In a longitudinal multiple group type of analysis, we will assume the common factors are invariant (i.e., same loadings), we will pick one group as the reference group at Time 1 and will set the factor variance at Time 1 to unity in this group (e.g., $\phi[1]^{2(1)} = 1$) and factor means to zero at the first occasion of measurement in this same group (e.g., $v[1] = 0^{(1)}$), and we will estimate the other factor deviations and factor means as changes or differences from this reference group at this point. This will be restricted by design so the required choice of the reference group does not affect the goodness-of-fit of the specific common factor model.

EXHIBIT 17.2
The Application of Multiple Factorial Invariance Over Groups to Multiple Occasions

---

We can start out by assuming that the common factor loadings (λ_m) are invariant over time by writing

(1a) $$Y_m[1]_n = \lambda_m F[1]_n + u_m[1]_n,$$

and

(1b) $$Y_m[2]_n = \lambda_m F[2]_n + u_m[2]_n$$

so the common factor ($F[t]$) is assumed to have the same set of factor loadings within each time (λ_m). Although the observed variables ($Y_m[t]$) indicate the common factor score ($Ft]$) in the same way at any time, the factor score itself can be changing.

Here we only use a simple regression function of the prior ($t = 1$) factor score. If this concept is correct, then some key structural expectations are

(2a) $$\sigma_m[1]^2 = \lambda_m \lambda_m + \psi_m[1]^2,$$

(2b) $$\sigma_m[2]^2 = \lambda_m \phi[2]^2 \lambda_m + \psi_m[2]^2 \text{ and}$$

(2c) $$\phi[1]^2 = 1, \text{ by definition, and}$$

(2d) $$\phi[2]^2 = \beta_f^2 + \zeta^2, \text{ and,}$$

(2e) $$\phi[1,2] = \beta_f,$$

among many other possible covariance restrictions.

THEOREMS ON PARAMETER INVARIANCE OVER GROUPS

In SEM, an important question has previously been raised: "Is exactly the same common factor measured within each group?" This was the topic of multiple factorial invariance over groups (MFIG) raised by Meredith (1964b, 1993) and put into practice by Sörbom (1974; see Jöreskog & Sörbom, 1979). In this context, a model-fitting approach to MFIG has been applied to data by many others (e.g., see Horn & McArdle, 1992; McArdle & Cattell, 1994). Basically, a lot of analyses can follow if we can find some form of MFIG, so we return to this issue in the models of another part here. The important question raised is what type of selection of people would allow use to retain an invariant longitudinal factor pattern.

Meredith (1964b) also provided two rotational methods for taking separate factor solutions from each population and finding an invariant pattern matrix that is best-fitting. One of the most elementary solutions (by Meredith, 1965) was to simply take the grand mean of the covariances and apply a factor model to it. Cattell (1944) had earlier developed the rotational principle of "parallel proportional profiles," which argued for rotating factor solutions so that the pattern matrices are columnwise proportional (McArdle & Cattell, 1994). Jöreskog (1971) then presented a confirmatory factor analytic (CFA) approach to studying factorial invariance in multiple populations (McGaw & Jöreskog, 1971). The method permitted a direct test of fit for an invariant factor pattern, and an estimation algorithm for finding this best-fitting pattern. Other aspects of the factor structure could be evaluated for invariance (e.g., unique factor variances). In subsequent work, Sörbom (1974) extended Jöreskog's approach to include mean structures, adding latent intercept parameters as an essential part of the invariance question.

As just mentioned, these kinds of multiple group models (MGMs) were used in the theoretical and practical analyses of McArdle and Cattell (1994), but these researchers went one step further. They suggested that if an MGM-SEM was used to assert that the model of factorial invariance did not hold over groups, then we needed to relax some of the major simple structure restrictions on the factor pattern to achieved the invariance constraints (as in Exhibit 17.2). This was largely against the prevailing SEM wisdom (as in Horn & McArdle, 1992), where invariance constraints were clear being added to simple structures. But this approach was largely consistent with the work of Meredith (1993). That is, when doing comparative factor analyses of real data, we may need many common factors (K) before we achieve factorial invariance, and we should not expect the resulting invariant factor pattern to also be simple. This research also showed how rotation of the final multifactor invariant pattern over different groups may be needed for substantive understanding. Of course, the common factors could still have different meaning over groups.

THE STRUCTURE OF INVARIANT COMMON FACTORS OVER TIME

The question we now face is what should be done with knowledge of these group differences theorems (to be described in detail in the models at a later point) when we have one group of repeated measures data. The first and most obvious question about longitudinal repeated measures data, of course, is "Do the means change over time?" This informative question can be answered using a number of different analysis of variance (ANOVA) techniques discussed earlier (Hertzog & Rovine, 1985; McCall & Appelbaum, 1984; O'Brien & Kaiser, 1978). Now the first SEM question raised is slightly different: "Is exactly the same common factor measured at each occasion?" Here the topic of metric factorial invariance over groups (Meredith, 1964a, 1964b, 1993) is raised, and now it is applied to a set of observations over time.

In our prior work (McArdle & Nesselroade, 1994) we determined that a generic invariance LSEM approach gave us a substantially different result than either the repeated measures ANOVA (RANOVA) or the multivariate ANOVA (MANOVA), each of which created components that established maximum linear composites for the differences over time but said little about measurement issues. In addition, we added several different features, including the possibility of specific factor covariances over time (Meredith & Horn, 2001). In our analyses, or any others we have done, the correlation of the specific factors over time proved far less important than the issue of factor invariance. But they could be!

As a byproduct of this two-time invariance analysis, McArdle and Nesselroade (1994) then showed that the factors of the averages (or sums) of variables over time would yield the same statistical test as the equivalence of the common factors of the changes over time. This was not completely novel (Nesselroade & Bartsch, 1977) but we used it to show several variations on the way means and covariances could be used, including the initial creation of a latent change score (LCS). In addition, this approach was shown to lead to a more general expression and a test of the general assumption of factorial invariance in multilevel data (as used in McArdle, 2007b; McArdle, Fisher, & Kadlec, 2007; also see the last parts of Exhibit 17.3).

One of the best features of SEM is that the fundamental ideas are broad and general and can be used to consider many different problems. For example, an alternative type of LSEM naturally arises when we have common factors at both occasions, and this permits some important additions. This was depicted in the path diagram of Figure 17.1, which is a model that can be used with multivariate longitudinal data (McArdle, 2005, 2007a, 2010, 2011a; McArdle & Nesselroade, 1994). In these cases, we assume some of the same variables have been measured on both occasions. (We term these M measured variables using the notation of $Y_m[1]$ and $Y_m[2]$). Given a basic array of two-occasion data, we first consider the key SEM issue about the invariance of the common factors over occasions.

This organization of the two-factor longitudinal model permits a few key questions to be examined using specific model restrictions. The first question we can evaluate is whether or not the same number of factors are present at both occasions: "Is the number of common factors the same at both occasions (i.e., is $K[1] = K[2]$)?" Based on this evaluation, we can also ask questions about the invariance of the factor loadings ($\lambda[t]$) over time: "Does the factor loading pattern remain the same over time (i.e., $\lambda[1] = \lambda[2]$)?" Another set of questions can be asked about the invariance of the factor score $F[t]$ over

EXHIBIT 17.3
Latent Change Score From the Multiple Factorial Invariance
Over Time Definitions for Multiple Occasions

We can rewrite a factor model with a simple set of latent change scores as

(1a) $\quad \Delta Y_n = Y[2]_n - Y[1]_n \quad$ or $\quad Y[2]_n = Y[1]_n + \Delta Y_n$

and

(1b) $\quad \Delta F_n = F[2]_n - F[1]_n \quad$ or $\quad F[2]_n = F[1]_n + \Delta F_n$

with

(1c) $\quad \Delta u_n = u[2]_n - u[1]_n \quad$ or $\quad u[2]_n = u[1]_n + \Delta u_n$

where the Δ operator is used to represent vectors of first-level changes among manifest or latent scores. Assuming the invariant common factor model holds, we can write

(2a) $\quad Y[2]_n - Y[1]_n = \{\lambda[2]F[2]_n + u[2]_n\} - \{\lambda[1]F[1]_n + u[1]_n\}$

$\qquad\qquad = \{\lambda[2](F[1]_n + \Delta F_n) + (u[1]_n + \Delta u_n)\} - \{\lambda[1]F[1]_n + u[1]_n\},$

or

(2b) $\quad \Delta Y_n = (\lambda[2] - \lambda[1])F[1]_n + \lambda[2]\Delta F_n + \Delta u_n.$

This final model suggests the changes in the observed scores can be assessed in three parts: (a) the differences in the loadings over time ($\lambda[2] - \lambda[1]$) multiplied by the initial common factor score ($F[1]$), (b) the loadings at Time 2 multiplied by the differences in the factor scores (ΔF), and (c) the differences in the unique factor scores (Δu). Of course, this could not be done in a meaningful way without identical factor loadings.

---

time: "For all persons N, is the common factor score identical over time (i.e., $F[1] = F[2]$)?" This last question is often examined through the correlations over time, that is, "Does $\rho[1,2] = 1$?"

As many researchers have noted, these questions about the stability of the factor pattern and the stability of the factor scores raise both methodological and substantive issues (Heise, 1969; Jöreskog, 1970a; Wiley & Wiley, 1970). This use of multiple indicators allows us to clearly separate the stability due to (a) the internal consistency reliability of the factors and (b) the test–retest correlation of the factor scores. This is not always considered in data analysis, certainly not in using RANOVA. Each set of model restrictions of factor invariance deals with a different question about construct equivalence over time (Nesselroade, 1983). But using LSEM we can examine the evidence for these questions using the standard goodness-of-fit techniques.

In one version of LSEM we can first hypothesize a structural equation that could be applied at both occasions. Within this set of restrictions is the basic requirement of invariance over two occasions. This is defined in Exhibit 17.3. Here we assume that the common factor ($F[t]$) has the same set of factor loadings within each time (λ_m). Although the observed variables ($Y_m[t]$) indicate the common factor score ($F[t]$) in the same way at any time, the factor score itself can be changing. Here we only use a simple regression of the prior ($t = 1$) factor score.

This latent path model is interesting because it is not necessarily true, and it can be tested using all observed variable expectations between Time 1 and Time 2. These expectations require the pattern of the correlations to be exactly proportional (via the variance proportionality $\phi[2]^2$); thus, all correlations can become higher or lower, but they must do this together as a group, and since the loadings are required to be the same within each time, the relative ratios (e.g., λ_j/λ_k) and factorial interpretation must remain the same as well.

The first consideration is fairly unique to LSEM, but it can be useful. Since we have measured the same observed variables over time, we might just assume we have measured the same unobserved factors over time. In principle, this should be an easy idea to follow, especially since we have asserted that we have measured the same persons on the same observed variables over two times (see Exhibits 16.5 and 17.2). Indeed, this is one basic form of factorial equivalence, and it is almost always assumed when using standard procedures such as MANOVA or canonical regression (Tabachnick & Fidell, 2007a, 2007b), even prior to the calculation of optimal weights. This approach allows us to move directly to other analysis, perhaps using aggregated scores.

But when we think about it a bit more, we come to realize that many things could change over time, including the people's responses to the same stimuli. Thus, if we had already made the mistake of mislabeling the key factors at this initial level, our mistakes are likely to become compounded in any subsequent analysis (McArdle, 2007a). So LSEM is useful because it can help us avoid a major mistake at this initial level, and this is probably a mistake from which we could not recover from in data analysis. As many others have suggested, the equivalence of the common factors in multiple factorial invariance over time (MFIT) is a testable hypothesis. That is, LSEM allows us to examine this concept of MFIT using a statistical test. In fact, this a fundamental test and is often considered necessary (McArdle & Nesselroade, 1994) to go on and calculate changes. This is done because if the people are not responding from the same latent sources, this model should not fit the longitudinal data. As an alternative, we may need more than one common factor with a complex pattern of loadings for invariance to hold (McArdle, 2007a). Indeed, it is surprising that so few researchers have done this.

ALTERNATIVES BASED ON LONGITUDINAL CHANGE SCORES

The model of Figure 17.1 is probably the most typical structural factor model examined with longitudinal data, but it is not the only useful organization of these data. One of the main purposes of collecting longitudinal data is to examine changes over time, so it is useful to reconsider the model with change as a primary goal. In this context we can rewrite a factor model with a simple set of LCSs as in Exhibit 17.4.

Assuming the invariant common factor model holds, we can then write that the changes in the observed scores can be assessed in three parts: (a) the differences in the loadings over time ($\lambda[2] - \lambda[1]$) multiplied by the initial common factor score $F[1]$), (b) the loadings at the second occasion multiplied by the differences in the factor scores (ΔF), and (c) the differences in the unique factor scores (Δu) (to this we can always add "model discrepancy"; see MacCallum & Tucker, 1991).

It is most interesting that this change score form does not alter the interpretation or statistical testing of factor invariance over time. If the factor loadings are invariant over time ($\lambda[2] = \lambda[1]$), then the first term in the model drops out and the overall result is clear ($\Delta Y = \Delta F + \Delta u$). This result is practically useful: If the loadings are invariant over time, the factor pattern between occasions is proportional to the factor pattern within occasions (Nesselroade & Bartsch, 1977). This is not a necessary result (because it may not fit well), and the differences in the between- and within-factor loadings may be meaningful (see the final chapters in this volume).

EXHIBIT 17.4
Latent Change Score Means From the Multiple Factorial Invariance Over Time Definitions for Multiple Occasions

We can first rewrite a factor model with a simple set of latent change scores as

(1a) $\Delta F_n = F[2]_n - F[1]_n$

or

(1b) $F[2]_n = F[1]_n + \Delta F_n$

or as

(1c) $F[2]_n = 1F[1]_n + 1\Delta F_n$

If this table of the common factors is correct, it is clear that the latent changes have no measurement error. If we now have the common factors, we can provide means of the common factors and the latent changes. Once again, this could not be done in a meaningful way without identical factor loadings.

This basic result for change scores is consistent with previous multivariate work on this topic, especially by Nesselroade (e.g., 1970, 1983; Nesselroade & Cable, 1974). In this work a clear distinction was made between factors representing "traits" ($F[1]$) and factors representing "states" (ΔF). As stated earlier, several authors raised issues about the problems of measurement error in the observed difference scores (e.g., Cronbach & Furby, 1970). To illuminate solutions to these problems, McArdle and Nesselroade (1994) were among the first researchers to write the change scores as part of the model rather than as a part of the data. That is, instead of creating the Δy by direct calculation in the data (i.e., $Y[2] - Y[1]$), the differences Δy were implied as latent variables by using fixed unit weights (i.e., $Y[2]_n = 1 * Y[1]_n + 1 * \Delta y_n$), and these new LV scores were allowed to be correlated with the unique starting points.

A path diagram illustrating an LSEM where are variables are represented by their changes is presented in Figure 17.2, where the simple restriction of pairs of fixed unit values (one pair per variable) across time allows us to model differences at the level of the observations (Δy) and at the level of the common factors (ΔF). McArdle and Nesselroade (1994) showed how this set of structural equations can be fitted simultaneously and how all implications about model testing and goodness-of-fit can be accomplished without the need to calculate change scores. As it turns out, all results for the factor of change scores in Figure 17.2 are identical to the results of the previous models; that is, the invariance of the loadings of the starting points and the loadings of LCSs are the same. Perhaps most important, if multiple factorial

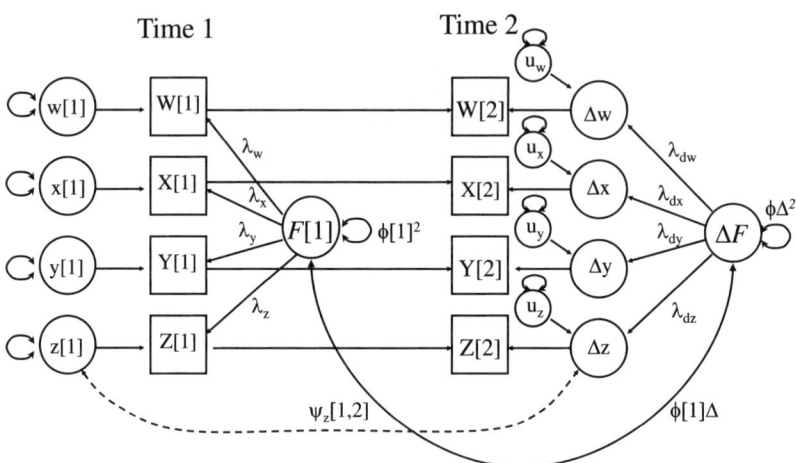

Figure 17.2. A two-occasion factor of changes model. From *Life-Span Developmental Psychology: Methodological Innovations* (p. 254), by S. H. Cohen and H. W. Reese (Eds.), 1994, Hillsdale, NJ: Erlbaum. Copyright 1994 by Erlbaum. Adapted with permission.

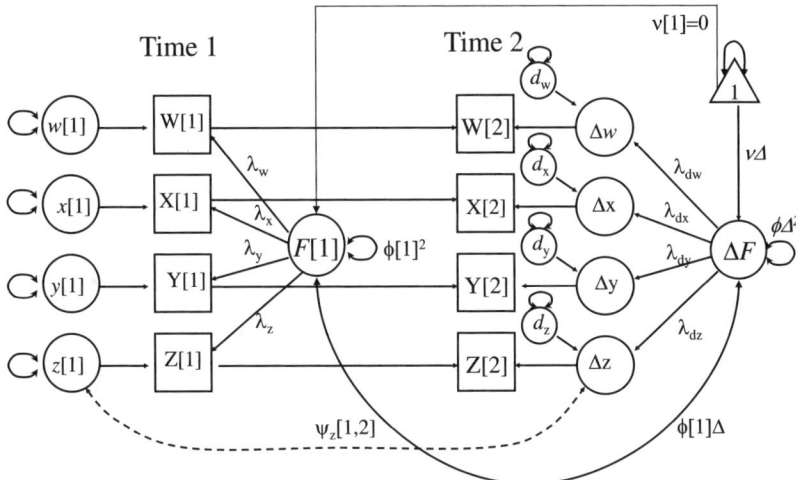

Figure 17.3. A two-occasion factor of changes model with factor means. From *Life-Span Developmental Psychology: Methodological Innovations* (p. 254), by S. H. Cohen and H. W. Reese (Eds.), 1994, Hillsdale, NJ: Erlbaum. Copyright 1994 by Erlbaum. Adapted with permission.

invariance does not fit both the starting point factors and difference factors, then the factorial interpretation of the changes could be interpreted from these loadings.

The model of Figure 17.3 next adds factor means (v[t]) to this change score concept. In all previous diagrams, regression parameters emerge from the constant (1) and go toward a variable representing either the intercepts or the mean of that variable, and this interpretation is the same here. To do this, we can first rewrite a factor model with a simple set of LCSs as in Exhibit 17.4, and we now we have the common factors where we can provide means of the common factors. These parameters from the constant represent the mean of scores, so at Time 1, we often set the factor mean to zero (v[1] = 0) and allow a mean of the change in the factor (vΔ). If the factors patterns are invariant over time (Λ), if the uniquenesses (ψ_m^2) are invariant over time, and if the variable intercepts (ι_m) are also invariant, and they may not be, then this special kind of common factors accounts for all the changes in both the means and covariances completely. Although most researchers do not try to do so, if this LSEM fits the longitudinal data, we have a very simple result.

The final model of Figure 17.4 adds on even more restrictive concepts that can be useful. Assuming we have an invariant set of loadings, we can estimate the same common factor at each time (as described earlier). By assuming that the intercepts of all pairs of the same variables (λ_m) are identical (drawn here as zero) and by assuming that the factor mean at Time 1 is zero (v[1] = 0), we

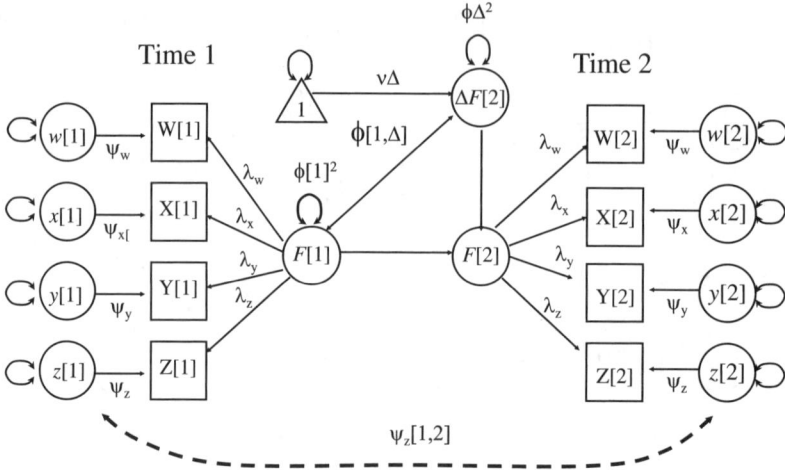

Figure 17.4. A two-occasion multiple factorial invariance over time with latent means model. From *Life-Span Developmental Psychology: Methodological Innovations* (p. 257), by S. H. Cohen and H. W. Reese (Eds.), 1994, Hillsdale, NJ: Erlbaum. Copyright 1994 by Erlbaum. Adapted with permission.

can estimate the mean change in the factor scores directly (ν∆). This is not necessarily the same as the description provided by the prior model (of Figure 17.3) because here all the changes in the variables must show up in the only change allowed (e.g., the factor means). This common factor must account for both the changes in the covariance and the changes in the means. This model description, although atypical, could be considered as an SEM alternative to the "optimal" linear composite used to account for all changes in RANOVA.

TESTS WITH TWO OCCASIONS OF LONGITUDINAL DATA

We often start with the primary hypothesis that there are the same numbers of common factors within each occasion (i.e., $K[1] = K[2]$?). This seems like a fundamental starting point in any traditional longitudinal factor analysis because if this does not fit, neither will the models with more restrictions. We have used the common factor loadings ($\lambda[t]$) as latent variable regression coefficients for the common factor score regressed on the observed scores. These factor loadings are used to define the meaning and the name we assign to the common factor and hopefully this is based on the pattern of relationships with the observed variables. It follows that questions about whether or not we have measured the same factor over time are based solely on answering, "Does $\lambda[1] = \lambda[2]$?" However, as Rozeboom (1975) pointed out, using structural factor analysis (SFA) or other techniques, we can always consider any common factor solution to include factors with zero variance (i.e., as nodes). This unusual logic often makes moot the question about the same number of factors and essentially restates this problem as a broader evaluation of equality of the factor loadings. That is, we want the same factors over time so we can examine their dynamics.

As mentioned earlier, earlier work on this problem suggested a focus on the stability of the factor scores. For example, the canonical solution suggested by Corballis and Traub (1970) essentially maximized the stability of each set of factor scores by requiring the multiple factors to be uncorrelated within time and across time. These restrictions are not used now primarily because they seem to be inconsistent with Meredith's selection theorem. Of course, many other numerical solutions are possible if orthogonal factors are allowed. In this case the common factor scores $F[t]$ are not directly observed (or uniquely identified), but their variances ($\phi[t]^2$) and covariances ($\phi[t,t+1]$) define the relative position of each individual on the factor scores. Thus, we can question the relative size of the variances over time by asking, "Is $\phi[t]^2 = \phi[t+1]^2$?" And we can question the size of the correlation of the factor scores over time by asking, "Is $\rho[t,t+1] = \phi[t,t+1]/(\phi[t]\phi[t+1])^{1/2} = 0$?" But the SFA logic suggests that whether or not we have the same factor over time is not based on the factor score parameters! To be clear on this point, if we want to conclude we have measured the same underlying factors at each time, then the factor loading invariance must provide a reasonable fit to multiple-occasion data, somehow. Then, assuming we have achieved metric loading invariance, we can further examine changes in the common factor scores as if they have the unique properties of repeated measures (see later parts here).

The unique factor parameters allowed the examination of additional forms of invariance. As stated earlier, it is possible to examine the equality of the unique variances over time (i.e., $\psi[1]^2 = \psi[2]^2$), and these restrictions could be useful if the same factor scores are to be used. If some or all of the unique variances are deemed equal we have a simplification of the factorial descriptions: All covariation over time can be captured among the common factor scores. It also seems reasonable to estimate the covariance over time among the parallel unique factors ($\text{diag}(\psi_m^2)$). One of these parameters is depicted as the dashed line in Figure 17.1 (e.g., $\psi_z[1,2]$). But, as suggested by Meredith and Horn (2001), these parameters are termed "covariance of parallel specific factors" over time (avoiding the oxymoron "correlated errors"; see Brown, 2006). Because the inclusion of such parameters is entirely consistent with the common factor model and can simplify the interpretation of the other model parameters, these parallel specific covariances should be routinely included in longitudinal factor analyses just so the common factors can capture the changes. This is not to suggest the specific correlations are important parameters, but they are needed ones if we want to obtain the proper common factors.

18

ALTERNATIVE COMMON FACTORS WITH MULTIPLE LONGITUDINAL OBSERVATIONS

In a broad sense, the typical scientific ideal is to examine whether or not the common factors are invariant over time (Nesselroade, 1993). That is, we want to know what aspects of the same measurements can be compared at each time point. This is important because we definitely want to work with these invariant constructs. But the driving concept of seeking out common factors that are invariant over whatever conditions or groupings we consider, rather than just trying to see if the common factors we consider are invariant, is an unusual approach that also has a number of important merits. First, this allows us to be fairly honest in our approach to data analysis, and this could be critical (McArdle, 2011d). Second, it allows us to recognize that odd sayings, such as "a factor is apparent at some occasion, but it has no variability," is not actually incorrect, but is a very flexible way to think. Indeed, this was exactly the kind of flexible thinking expressed by Rozeboom (1975) when he considered "transient" factors (i.e., strictly defined as "factors with no variance at a particular time"). If we further follow the suggestion of McArdle and Cattell

(1994), we may need to allow for many additional loadings or extra common factors, to achieve multiple factorial invariance over time (MFIT) in this way.

MFIT

This MFIT may not be easy to find on an empirical basis, but we know it is an extremely desirable property to have because it implies we have found a set of common factors that provide a useful template for broad changes. Of course, we may find more than one common factor (as in Figure 17.1 or 17.2), possibly with some unusually complex combination of loadings is what we need, and this can simply be due to an artificial selection of measured variables (McArdle, 2007a; McArdle & Cattell, 1994). Once we define the complete MFIT expressions (see Exhibit 18.1), we can concentrate on the sequential changes in the factor scores (see the models of a later part here).

EXHIBIT 18.1
Extending Meredith's (1993) Tables of Multiple Factorial Invariance Over Groups to Multiple Factorial Invariance Over Time

The general multiple group model principle starts with (m = 1 to M, t = 1 to T)

(1) $\quad Y_m[t]_n = \iota_m[t] + \lambda_{m,k}[t] F_k[t]_n + u_m[t]_n$

which can be seen to lead to an expected mean vector expectations over time as

(2a) $\quad \mu_m[t] = \iota_m[t] + \lambda_{m,k}[t] v_k[t]$

and an expected covariance expectations over time as

(2b) $\quad \Sigma[t] = \Lambda[t]\Phi[t]\Lambda[t]' + \Psi[t]^2.$

These principles can also be defined in terms of levels of multiple factorial invariance over time (MFIT):

MFIT cases (with Meredith, 1993, labels)	Factor loadings	Unique variable variances	Unique variable intercepts	Common factor inter-covariances	Common factor means
I. Configural (or measurement)	$\Lambda[t]$	$\Psi[t]^2$	$\iota_m[t]$	$P[t]$	0
II. Metric (or weak)	Λ	$\Psi[t]^2$	$\iota_m[t]$	$P[1]'\,\Phi[t>1]$	0
III. Strong invariance	Λ	Ψ^2	$\iota_m[t]$	$P[1]'\,\Phi[t>1]$	0
IV. Strict invariance	Λ	Ψ^2	ι_m	$P[1]'\,\Phi[t>1]$	$v_k[t]^{(g)}$

Note. From "Measurement Invariance, Factor Analysis and Factorial Invariance," by W. Meredith, 1993, Psychometrika, 58, pp. 541–542. Copyright 1993 by the Psychometric Society. Adapted with permission.

The MFIT criteria can be expressed using the specific terminology of Meredith (1993) here extended to a longitudinal setting, by writing the following (see Exhibit 18.1):

Case I. Configural (or Measurement) Invariance: Different factor patterns over time ($\Lambda[t]$) with the same pattern of nonzero values, different variable intercepts ($\iota_m[t]$), and different unique variances ($\psi_m^2[t]$) over time. This covariance model can be identified by requiring the factor model constraints required at any time, as well as allowing fixed factor variances (e.g., $\phi[t]^2 = 1$) and fixed factor means ($\nu[t] = 0$).

Case II. Metric (or Weak) Invariance: Invariant factor patterns with exactly the same numerical values of the nonzero parameters (Λ), different variable intercepts ($\iota_m[t]$), and different unique variances ($\psi_m^2[t]$) over time. This metric covariance can be identified by requiring the factor model constraints required at any time, as well as fixed factor variances (e.g., $\phi[t]^2 = 1$) and fixed factor means ($\nu[t] = 0$) over time.

Case III. Strong Invariance: Invariant factor patterns (Λ), different variable intercepts ($\iota_m[t]$) but invariant unique variances (ψ_m^2) over time. This mean and covariance model can be identified by requiring the factor model constraints required at any time, as well as fixing factor variances at Time 1 (e.g., $\phi[1]^2 = 1$) and fixing all factor means (e.g., $\nu[t] = 0$).

Case IV. Strict Invariance: Invariant factor patterns (Λ), invariant variable intercepts (ι_m), and invariant unique variances (ψ_m^2) over all times. This restrictive mean and covariance model allows all changes in the common factors, and it can be identified by requiring the factor model constraints required at one time, as well as fixing factor variances at Time 1 (e.g., $\phi[1]^2 = 1$), and fixing the Time 1 factor means (e.g., $\nu[1] = 0$).

FORMALIZING THE MULTIPLE FACTORIAL INVARIANCE OVER GROUP (MFIG) TO MULTIPLE FACTORIAL INVARIANCE OVER TIME (MFIT)

Using exactly the same multiple factorial invariance over group (MFIG) logic just presented above, we can agree that if there is any form of selection of the people on the predictors, the basic factor loadings of some factors should still remain exactly the same values. This logic can be extended to multiple time points ($t = 1$ to T), and this is also considered in Exhibit 18.2. So in this form of MFIT, the model means are expected to be a function of the invariant manifest variable intercepts (ι_m) and the possibly changing factor means ($\nu_k[t]$), and the model variances within any time point are expected to be a function of the changing common factor variance and covariances ($\phi_k^2[t]$) and unchanging unique factor variances (ψ_m^2). By now it should be clear that what we really want in using MFIT is strong invariance applied to

EXHIBIT 18.2
Strict Versions of Multiple Factorial Invariance Over Time

The general multiple group model principles of Meredith's last form (IV. Strict Invariance Over Time) lead to

(1a) $$Y_m[t]_n = \iota_m + \lambda_{m,k} F_k[t]_n + u_m[t]_n$$

which can then be seen to lead to an expected mean vector expectations over groups of

(1b) $$\upsilon_m[t] = \iota_m + \lambda_{m,k} \nu_k[t]$$

and an expected covariance expectations over groups of

(1c) $$\Sigma[t,t] = \Lambda \phi[t,t] \Lambda' + \Psi^2.$$

Another way to express this is to write

(2a) $$\sigma_m[t]^2 = \lambda_{m,k}^2 \phi_k[t]^2 + 2\sum\{\lambda_{m,k}\phi_{k,j}[t]\lambda_{m,j}\} + y_m^2$$

so the model covariances over time within a variable are expected to be a function of common factor variances only,

(2b) $$\sigma_m[t, t+1] = \lambda_{m,k}^2 \phi_k[t, t+1] + 2\sum\{\lambda_{m,k}\phi_{k,j}[t, t+1]\lambda_{m,j}\}$$

and the model cross-variable covariances over time are expected to be

(2c) $$\sigma_{i,j}[t, t+1] = \lambda_{i,k}^2 \phi_j[t, t+1] + \lambda_{i,k}^2 \phi_k[t, t+1] + 2\sum\{\lambda_{i,j}\phi_{k,j}[t, t+1]\lambda_{i,j}\}.$$

In matrix notation the cross-occasion covariances in this restrictive model could be relaxed some by introducing time-specific specific covariances ($\psi[t, t+1]$) as well.

---

all occasions of measurement. This implies that only a few changes can exist, but all these changes have to be carried through the common factors, so they can be broad in their influence. Of course, this simple idea may not fit the observed data very well.

This leads to an important caveat: Because we know (1) if the common factors do not take some form of MFIT, then (2) the common factors are not the same, and (3) more complex longitudinal models of the factor score changes are not possible. In any new data set, we do not consider the notion of what has been termed *partial invariance* (as in Byrne, Shavelson, & Muthén, 1989; Reise, Widaman, & Pugh, 1993). Instead, we think we should be honest and say that we really want common factors that do allow for strict MFIT so we can look at changes in these factors! If we do so, we could basically (4) design the factor structures to define simplicity, (5) have a high tolerance for misfit (and this is often the case), or we could say (6) we are searching for common factors that are invariant and we will not stop until we find these. In this sense, we just use the misfit as a guide toward finding MFIT. We think the latter argument is compelling and worth pursuing in more detail (McArdle, 2007a).

This longitudinal structural equation modeling (LSEM) question of MFIT can be initially answered by fitting a model to the invariance of the factor pattern over time in a set of scores. Once the best number of factors is determined within each time point, a model of MFIT (same values of factor loadings) can be fitted over time, and the loss of fit can be examined. Now there is no doubt that we want to find invariant factors, so some loss of fit is usually deemed acceptable. Once the common factors are considered invariant, we can examine the mean changes in the common factor scores, and the examination of means of error-free factors become the focus of our analyses. That is, the assertion of MFIT allows us to go much further with statistical comparisons.

The basic concepts of MFIT can be used in any longitudinal repeated measures data set. In every such data set we would want to have the same common factors at each time. This is not to say that the means of these factors ($v_k[t]$) and the covariances of these factors ($\phi_{k,j}[t, t + 1]$) are the same at all time points, just the factor loadings (Λ), variable intercepts (ι_m), and unique variances (ψ_m^2). However, without some factor patterns that are required to equal over repeated observations, we are likely to be stuck analyzing the observed data as separate entities. But, once again, there are a lot of reasons to think MFIT is a useful starting point for longitudinal analysis. That is, assuming we have the same people measured over time, we can think of the time-to-time variation as the effect of person selection alone. We think MFIT is essential to multivariate longitudinal analyses.

MFIT MODEL-FITTING STRATEGIES

What we definitely desire in almost any longitudinal investigation is the smallest number of common factors that meet MFIT criteria, but this goal may require some complexity of loadings and complexity of subsequent interpretations. But because the factor loadings are required to be the same at all occasions, we may not have added many parameters to the overall model, and we may be able to retain a lot of degrees of freedom. This bold requirement for MFIT in multivariate longitudinal data analysis is not a typical argument, but it could be a very useful approach in a practical investigation.

One practical strategy to find the MFIT factor pattern would be to follow Meredith (1965) and fit a model to the grand mean of the data. This still seems like a good idea. In the case of multiple occasion data, we would take the sum scores (or the average scores) and carry out a factor analysis on these scores (as discussed in Chapter 16). Of course, this kind of analysis is only good if the sums have the same factor pattern as the changes (i.e., the change scores). Of course, this is true if we seek MFIT as a goal, so this is certainly acceptable here.

It is also possible that the common factor is identical over time, but the indices used to measure this common factor change. This seems especially true of longitudinal analyses dealing with different kinds of transitions, such as the progression from childhood to adulthood. Constructs such as violent behavior, for example, would be likely to be measured using different variables at different ages (i.e., school year fights in childhood and armed robbery in adulthood). This would just be called "age appropriate," and correlations over time would be used. Nevertheless, if we wanted to deal with these issues in an empirical fashion using any form of change scores, then we would need to measure enough markers of each common factor at each occasion to evaluate this progression (McArdle, Grimm, Hamagami, Bowles, & Meredith, 2009). That is, any changes are assumed to take time, and we would need to have MFIT to be able to separate what is invariant from what changes.

We note that in practice this LSEM approach may be most easily fitted in the reverse order. That is, rather than start with concepts of configural invariance, we will suggest a start with strict invariance and then relax the invariance of parameters as needed. We will also introduce more common factors that retain invariance rather than have less common factors, even simple one, that do not. In sum, if we fit Case IV first, then Case III, then Case II, then Case I, then we will increase the number of free model parameters each time. We are not sure if LSEM researchers already do so, but a model with fewer parameters is generally easier to fit, even if it is incorrect.

In general, the MFIT approach used here is the same strategy we would use for any MFIG analysis (e.g., Horn & McArdle, 1992; Horn, McArdle, & Mason, 1983). One of the most important principles in the MFIT approach is the use of nested tests of effects (Meredith, 1993). So it seems most reasonable to fit models in a specific order:

1. All parameters are invariant over time (to test for random differences).
2. The factor covariances and means are free over time (Meredith's Case IV).
3. Given fixed factor means, the variable intercepts are free over time (Case III).

4. In addition, given fixed factor variances, the uniquenesses are free over time (Case III).
5. In addition, the factor loadings are free over time, but hold the same pattern (Case I).
6. In addition, the placement (or pattern) of all of the factor loadings is allowed to be free over time (allowing all occasions to differ completely).

The previous six steps can be applied to virtually any time-to-time comparison, but we generally suggest starting with everything fixed to be invariant (i.e., the minimal number of parameters) and then allow the specific parameters to be free in this sequence, and we will start with the two most disparate occasions. This is now done in different ways by different researchers depending on the available data.

There is no doubt that these LSEM can be fitted using the generally available SEM programs in other ways, but we do question why some are fitted. This seems like another of the many unfortunate things that can be done with SEM programs that we might think is useful. Other typical examples include the calculation of modification indices, or allowing the uniqueness to vary across a repeated measure, or allowing spurious correlated errors. Although all of these exploratory devices should yield better fitting models (by design), we also know that only models with a priori representations of theory can be compared with data with a known probability basis.

RECONSIDERING THE REPEATED MEASURES ANALYSIS OF VARIANCE APPROACH

Before going further, we must remind ourselves that most researchers in the behavioral sciences do not use anything like the SEM approach we are suggesting. Most often they are told to use the repeated measures or multivariate analysis of variance (RANOVA or MANOVA, respectively) approach. The case of repeated measures (from Fisher, 1925; Winer, 1971) is an important one in modern data analysis, especially because of the importance placed on repeated measures in ANOVA (Bock, 1975). So, in this context, let use examine this approach more carefully.

The techniques of RANOVA are procedures others frequently use. That is, we start analyses by comparing the mean vectors over time without paying much attention to the covariance structures. If we do something special (e.g., MANOVA), we may assume that no prespecified covariance structure is required (O'Brien & Kaiser, 1978), but RANOVA does not explicitly test MFIT, so we just typically assume the answer to MFIT is yes.

That is, we do not test MFIT, but we could. The standard RANOVA approach could be reasonable, after all, because we have measured the same people using the same instruments. So in some substantive problems it is fairly hard to understand how MFIT could be incorrect. But although MFIT may seem like an easy question to answer in the affirmative, it is actually not. That is, just because we can measure the same variables at each time does not mean the persons respond to the same features on the tests at both times. There are many real-life situations where we might think the people have changed in a qualitative way, and the common factors have changed, so the comparison of means, even for the same observed variables, would be unfortunate. We would end up comparing latent apples to latent oranges.

In the RANOVA or MANOVA approach, when multiple variables are measured over two occasions, a new description of these data is provided by calculating three linear composite of the measured scores ($C_n = X_n + \beta Y_n$). This composite is calculated in three distinct ways: (1) the largest possible sum that defines group differences; (2) the largest possible change over time, and (3) the largest possible change over time that defines group differences. These composites are not required to represent the same construct (i.e., the same β-weight). This kind of calculation can make good sense, has a well-developed probability interpretation, and is now a relatively routine calculation (Bock, 1975). At the same time, it is exploratory because no latent loadings are a priori defined, and it requires a large number of parameters to calculate.

The RANOVA model necessarily assumes the MFIT criterion is met, both over time and over group, and does not really allow us to test the initial hypothesis of the same construct over time. We can only be sure that the three composites maximize the changes or the differences. The RANOVA model has colorful names, such as doubly repeated measures, but it could not be said to include any a priori construct. So, although we can routinely fit RANOVA as an alternative model of the data, this is often an impoverished use of the available data.

MULTIPLE COMMON FACTORS WITH MULTIPLE LONGITUDINAL OBSERVATIONS

So now let's assume we have a longitudinal sequence of repeated observations (Y[t], where $T > 2$). In the past, these kinds of data would also typically be analyzed using the ANOVA models for repeated measures, perhaps adding the popular polynomials, and this is probably OK now too. The LSEM point just made here is that the standard general linear model tests are only about the group differences in mean changes over repetitions and do not deal with hypotheses about covariances.

One way to use all the available longitudinal data is to form a composite score for key concepts and use these scores instead of the common factors. This is not a bad idea on several counts. First, it is very practical, and may even give a good representation about what will happen later. However, in the best-case scenario, the composite will simply mimic the result of the common factor (but have more random noise). Of course, we must remember that if the composite behaves differently than the common factors, than we certainly have the wrong composites, or factors, or both. Perhaps we should not be surprised if we obtain different answers from more complex model fitting, because we might have the wrong number of composites, in which case will have the wrong form of LSEM as well.

The use of multiple factor models is now quite common in the longitudinal literature (e.g., McDonald, 1985b; Swaminathan & Gifford, 1985; see also McArdle, Fisher, & Kadlec, 2007). Perhaps we should always analyze just two occasions of measurement: the first and second time points alone or the first and last occasions of measurement alone. Actually, we have found that a good way to start is (1) to deal with the number and nature of the common factors in the grand means or pretest data (as in Exhibit 16.5). After all, this problem is hard enough, and there is no need to add other potential longitudinal complexities yet. After this is completed, we can then (2) combine these with the longest-stretch-of-time variable, to see if we can model the simple linear changes in two-occasion data (as in McArdle & Nesselroade, 1994). Only after all this is done do we consider (3) fitting a model to all available time points. The complexity of the LSEMs may increase quite a bit, but this could be used to get started. Perhaps the optimal strategy would be to do all of this as a multilevel analysis where the factors between times are equivalent to the factors within times (McArdle, 2007a; McArdle et al., 2007; see also Chapter 16, this volume). Of course, we are left to wonder if any of these are an optimal strategy, because maybe they are not.

19

MORE ALTERNATIVE FACTORIAL SOLUTIONS FOR LONGITUDINAL DATA

The longitudinal structural equation models (LSEM) we now consider attempt to elaborate on the factor analysis concepts.

CURVE OF FACTOR SCORES MODELS

The next latent curve model (LCM) is based on multivariate work first suggested by McArdle (1988) and fit to the Wechsler Intelligence Scale for Children, Fourth Edition (Wechsler, 2004) data (McArdle & Epstein, 1987); this is drawn in Figure 19.1. In this view, one natural model for multivariate longitudinal data is to examine the LCM of a common factor score. But this was the first time LCM constraints had been applied to the parameters of a common factor with multiple factorial invariance over time (MFIT) constraints. Basically, each observed variable is thought to be an indicator of one (or more) latent variable that carries the information over time. The key

---

http://dx.doi.org/10.1037/14440-020
Longitudinal Data Analysis Using Structural Equation Models, by J. J. McArdle and J. R. Nesselroade
Copyright © 2014 by the American Psychological Association. All rights reserved.

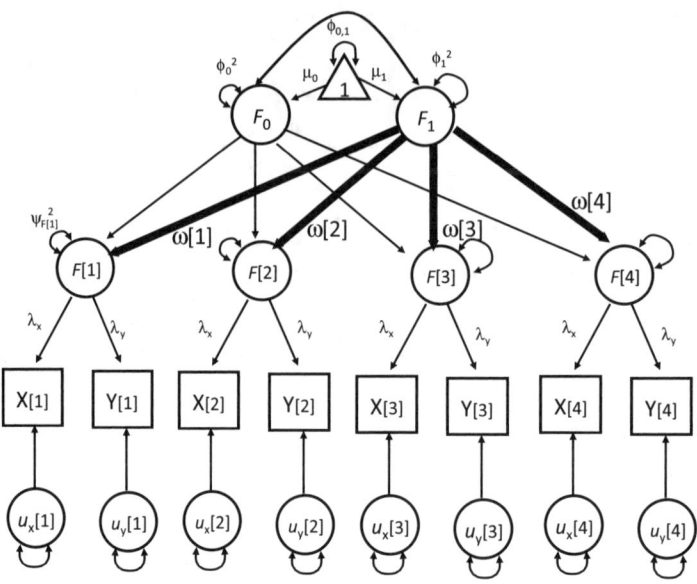

Figure 19.1. A simplified form of a curve-of-factor-scores model. Only two variables, Y[t] and X[t], are depicted here.

requirement here is that the factor pattern for the common factor relationships is invariant over time (McArdle, 1988, 2007a). If MFIT invariance can be established, the LCM can then be applied to the invariant factor score (F[t]) for examination of the common intercepts and slopes. In this model, the unique variance at the second level does not have any measurement error, so we have a clear indication of within-time variability that is not correlated over time (termed state variance by Cattell, 1957, and McArdle & Woodcock, 1997). This model was initially termed a *curve of factor scores* (CUFFS in McArdle, 1988). That is, we assumed a combined model where M = 8, and the structural restrictions of Exhibit 19.1 were used. This CUFFS model still seems useful to others (T. E. Duncan, Duncan, & Strycker, 2013; Ferrer, Belluerka, & Widaman, 2008; Sayer & Cusmile, 2001).

No doubt, there are many other models for multivariate longitudinal data that can answer the kinds of questions we are discussing now. However, most of these do not deal with specific timings, which were a direct focus of the earlier autoregressive starting point. The bivariate and multivariate illustrations presented here dealt with the critical problem of interrelationships among different growth variables. In previous work, McArdle (1988, 1989, 1991b) has outlined some of these issues and fit a model in which the levels and slopes of one series was correlated with, or regressed upon, the levels and slopes of a different series. Multiple variable SEM analysis has been used and

EXHIBIT 19.1
Using Multiple Factorial Invariance Over Time With a Factor
of Curve Scores Model

Let us assume a combined model (from McArdle, 1988), where m = 1 to M and

(1) $$Y_m[t]_n = \iota_m + \lambda_m F[t]_n + u_m[t]_n$$

follows a multiple factorial invariance over time (MFIT) structure, and we can add a latent curve model (LCM) to the common factor scores as

(2) $$F[t]_n = Q\{0\}_n + Q\{1\}_n \omega[t] + z[t]_n$$

Most importantly, these are LCM restrictions of the common factors and not the original variables. As long as strict MFIT restrictions are used to create invariant loadings, this common factor model will be identified if we fix the Time 1 factor variances ($\phi[1]^2 = 1$) and the Time 1 factor means ($v[1] = 0$).

Instead of doing an LCM, we can now include a latent change score model of the common factor scores

(3) $$\Delta F[t]_n = \alpha Q\{1\}_n + \beta F[t-1]_n + z_n$$

Note. From *The Handbook of Multivariate Experimental Psychology, Volume 2* (p. 591), by J. R. Nesselroade and R. B. Cattell (Eds.), 1988, New York, NY: Plenum Press. Copyright 1988 by Springer. Adapted with permission.

reported by others (e.g., Raykov, 1997a, 1997b; Walker, Acock, Bowman, & Li, 1996). These analyses formalize the idea that the correlation among the slopes of two different variables may reflect "common changes" (Griffiths & Sandland, 1984; McArdle & Nesselroade, 1994). We illustrate some results at the end of this chapter.

FACTOR OF CURVE SCORES MODELS

A slightly different model for these same data is presented in Figure 19.2 following the expressions of Exhibit 19.2. This approach involves creating separate LCMs for each measured variable at the first levels, at which point we could establish any similarity of the curves; for example, we can first test the equality of the group slope parameters (e.g., $\omega_i[t] = \omega_j[t]$, over observed variables i and j). Although equality or invariance of this process is not required, it can be studied. Most important, we can join these models at the individual level by correlating the latent intercepts and the slopes (McArdle, 1989). Rather than correlating the variables at the same times, the components of the curves can be correlated. The correlation of two or more latent

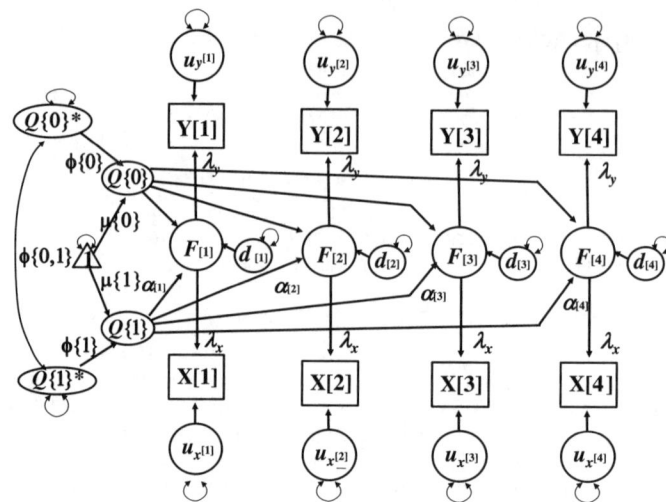

Figure 19.2. A common factor model with dual latent changes.

EXHIBIT 19.2
Using a Factor of Curve Scores (FOCUS) Model Without Multiple Factorial Invariance Over Time

Again, we assume a combined model, where m = 1 to *M* and

(1) $$Y_m[t]_n = Q\{0\}_{m,n} + Q\{1\}_{m,n}\omega_m[t] + u_m[t]_n$$

The factor of curve scores model can be written where, because it is clear that the levels are all correlated and the slopes can all be correlated, we can have "common factors of levels" as

(2a) $$F\{0\}_{m,n} = v\{0\}_m + \gamma\{0\}_m Q\{0\}_{m,n} + u\{0\}_{m,n}$$

and "common factors of slopes":

(2b) $$F\{1\}_{m,n} = v\{1\}_m + \gamma\{1\}_m Q\{1\}_{m,n} + u\{1\}_{m,n}'$$

and these are obviously not the only way to consider these longitudinal relationships.
As a general alternative we can now write a latent change score model at the first level

(3) $$\Delta y[t]_{m,n} = \alpha_m Q\{1\}_{m,n} + \beta_m F[t-1]_n + z_{m,n}$$

before we consider the common factors of these levels and slopes.

Note. From *The Handbook of Multivariate Experimental Psychology, Volume 2* (pp. 590–596), by J. R. Nesselroade and R. B. Cattell (Eds.), 1988, New York, NY: Plenum Press. Copyright 1988 by Springer. Adapted with permission.

slopes offers a broad indication about whether one variable is changing in the same people as another variable.

Testing the similarity of individual changes using the slope scores has proven to be a bit tricky because the variance and covariances of the slopes need to be considered, and one is left wondering what to do about the intercept term. Basically, these are not separable concepts in most observational studies because the intercepts and slopes should be thought to occur at the same times. This LSEM could be a useful beginning when investigating "correlated changes." If the correlation of components of change is our goal, we need not measure the variables at exactly the same occasions, or even with exactly the same frequency.

One obvious extension of the prior logic is to examine common factors of the multiple intercepts and multiple slopes. This approach was initially suggested by McArdle (1988) as a multivariate alternative. A persistent problem with this model is the rather artificial separation of intercepts from slopes, because they are conceptually part of the same process. Nevertheless, such a model was initially termed a *factor of curve scores* (FOCUS; McArdle, 1988), and it is still used by a few researchers (e.g., T. E. Duncan, Duncan, & Stryker, 2013).

The basic FOCUS concept is that each longitudinal outcome variable has a latent level and a latent slope, and it is these common factors that are correlated over time. This was the beginnings of what has been popularized as "parallel growth curves" (by Muthén & Muthén, 2002b), but here we consider many more than just two measured variables. This could be an economic way to parameterize the multivariate longitudinal data, and it certainly does not require MFIT constraints to hold. The FOCUS model requires very few measurement constraints at all.

It should also not come as a surprise that we are now fitting LCS models to the observed variables first. This combination is the variation of Figure 19.3 that can be written as an alteration of first-order model so that each observed variable has a LCS, and the latent factors of this LCS can subsequently be factored into factors of levels and factors of slopes again. The following citation from McArdle (1988), although somewhat outdated, still remains instructive:

> In a mathematical sense the CUFFS and FOCUS models are reversed but are used to account for the same observations. In a statistical sense, however, these two models are alternatives which do not fit the observations to the same degree. Unfortunately, the traditional dLRT model comparison logic seems doomed to failure now because the CUFFS and FOCUS type models are not statistically nested. This is no great surprise, however, because nested statistical hypotheses are not generally possible in most structural applications. . . . In this spirit, I now offer empirical evidence that bears on the primary choice between CUFFS and FOCUS models here. (pp. 596–597)

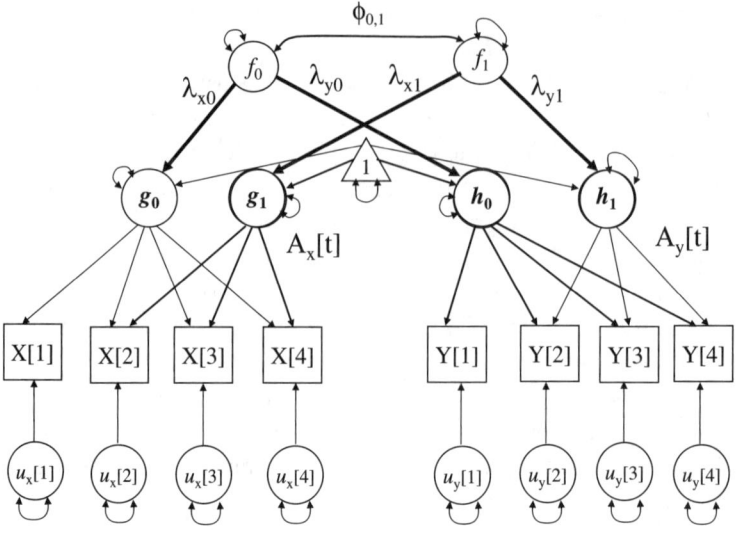

Figure 19.3. A simplified form of a factor-of-curve-scores model. Only two variables, Y[t] and X[t], are depicted here.

THE INCLUSION OF SPECIFIC COVARIANCES

Next we consider the specific covariances of Exhibit 19.3. The prior models mainly assumed the unique variance is unimportant in the analysis of change, and this might not be the case at all. As stated earlier, it was pointed out a long time ago (Jöreskog, 1977a; Nesselroade & Baltes, 1984) that the use of two-occasion data is a special situation in factor analysis where the unique factors could play an important role. We will recall that the factor analysis model allows any unique factor score (u) to be considered in two additive parts: (1) the first is the specific factor score (s), and (2) the second is the error of measurement score (e). This is not trivial because in the assessment of fit, we typically assume the error variables are normally distributed, but now we see these are only one component of the unique score. If the specific variable is probably not normally distributed, then the unique variable will not be normally distributed either. In more recent work, we have investigated data collection designs that can be used to separate specific from error variances (i.e., using split half data; McArdle & Woodcock, 1997).

But if we have repeated measures that are collected over time, this additional definition of unique factors allows us to assume the same specific factor has a covariance for each variable measured. This is commonly termed a *correlated error* (e.g., by Sörbom, 1975; see also Brown, 2006) but

EXHIBIT 19.3
Including Specific Covariances

In symbolic form, the general common factor assumption is written as (see Meredith & Horn, 2001)

(1a) $$u_{m,n} = s_{m,n} + e_{m,n}$$

so

(1b) $$E\{u_m, u_m\} = \psi_m^2 = \phi_{sm}^2 + \psi_{em}^2.$$

This implies that the variance due to the specific score variance (ϕ_{sm}^2) can be added to the independent and identically distributed (IID) error variance (ψ_{em}^2) to form the unique variance (ψ_m^2) for each variable.

But if we have repeated measures that are collected over time, this additional definition of unique factors allows

(2) $$E\{u_m[t], u_m[t+1]\} = \psi_{m[t,t+1]}$$

If there were at least two measurements of each variable at each time ($Y_1[t]$ and $Y_2[t]$), then we might be able to assume the same specific factor, and we could write

(3a) $$u_{mp,n} = s_{p,n} + e_{mp,n}$$

so

(3b) $$E\{u_{mp}, u_{mp}\} = \psi_{mp}^2 = \phi_{sp}^2 + \psi_{emp}^2.$$

Note. Adapted from *New Methods for the Analysis of Change* (p. 206), by L. M. Collins and A. G. Sayer (Eds.), 2001, Washington, DC: American Psychological Association. Copyright 2001 by the American Psychological Association.

---

this monicker should be considered misleading on at least two counts: (1) the errors of measurement are strictly defined to be uncorrelated with each other, and (2) there is no reason for the uniqueness to be correlated except for the presence of a specific factor (Meredith & Horn, 2001). But the reasons these specific covariances over time could be important is that the covariance of the specific factors, besides being misleading within a time, could give us the incorrect picture of the time-to-time determination of the common factors. Essentially, the common factors should not require this level of analysis, but if we find it can be helpful, we will use it. This specific factor covariance may also have a complex structure over time, so we will need to reconsider its importance in the later models here.

The variance of the specific factors could be identified if there were more of them. For example, if there were at least two measurements of each variable (Y_1 and Y_2), then we might be able to assume the same specific factor, and we could write a hierarchical common factor model that separates apart this source of variance. This approach requires multiple indicators of the same common factor within each time, as demonstrated in McArdle and Woodcock (1997), which may require undesirable orthogonal factors, but the idea is a fairly simple separation of the specific variance by assuming it is the same over both measures, whereas the error variance is not. The two realizations of the same scores could even be the separate scores from odd items and even items of the same scale. More indicators can come from more time points, and then it may be possible to examine their correlated changes over time. In any case, specific factors can change over time, and this should not be ignored.

20

EXTENSIONS TO LONGITUDINAL CATEGORICAL FACTORS

The evaluation of models for change over time is conceptually based on longitudinal analyses of multiple trajectories (e.g., McArdle, 2009). Although this approach is not indicated here, there is actually a rather long and detailed history of embedding categorical concepts within repeated measures longitudinal data (e.g., Hamagami, 1998; Koch, Landis, Freeman, Freeman, & Lehnen, 1977; Muthén, 1984). We have found that these approaches can clarify the results if we have either (a) categorical outcomes that are not ordinal, or (b) if the order categories are not equal in the interval between scale points.

A general statement of various techniques can be found in Exhibit 20.1. This shows there are many techniques that can be used to deal with non-normally distributed inputs or outcomes, and we will not be exhaustive here. Up to now, we have only dealt with the upper left-hand quadrant, labeled common factor analysis. The principles we have just stated are very general and can be applied to the other quadrants. For example, we will deal with the quadrant, categorical factor analysis, right below this one, by applying the same

http://dx.doi.org/10.1037/14440-021
Longitudinal Data Analysis Using Structural Equation Models, by J. J. McArdle and J. R. Nesselroade
Copyright © 2014 by the American Psychological Association. All rights reserved.

EXHIBIT 20.1
A Cross-Classification of Some Well-Known Multivariate Models
for Continuous and Categorical Data

Data distribution	Latent = continuous	Latent = categorical
Manifest = continuous	Common factor analysis	Latent transition analysis
Manifest = categorical	Categorical factor analysis	Latent class analysis

common factor identification conditions and also adding extra constraints for the categorical measurement. The upper right-hand quadrant, latent transition analysis (e.g., Bartholomew, 1985; Collins & Lanza, 2010; McDonald, 1999), assumes that the common factors of interest are themselves categories whose membership may be changing over time. Thus, the MFIT criteria appear here too. Finally, in what Lazarsfeld (1955) termed *latent class analysis*, both manifest and latent variables are thought of as categories. We realize this term is being used for *mixture modeling* (Muthén & Muthén, 2006), but this is the classical definition. Of most importance to use, the MFIT criteria apply here as well.

A great deal of the recent structural equation modeling (SEM) literature has been focused on the analysis of variables that are not normally distributed (e.g., Muthén, 1989a, 1989b, 1989c, 1989d). This seems appropriate because, for whatever reason, we often measure outcome variables that are not normally, or even symmetrically, distributed. In some sense, if we did rely on good measurement techniques, we would probably never end up with normally distributed outcome variables (Horn, 2005). Sometimes, the outcomes are even simply events that happen at a specific time and do not continue (P. D. Allison, 1994). In early work on this topic, deviations from normality were not considered to be a very big deal because it was thought this violation did not lead to very much bias in estimation or testing (see, e.g., Boneau, 1960). On the other hand, in more recent work, these assumptions of normality have been considered to be much more important than previously thought (Wilcox, 1998), so we consider some new model-based options here.

In SEM, for example, an accumulation of recent simulation findings (see Prindle & McArdle, 2012; Wang, Fan, & Wilson, 1996) seem to indicate that (1) normal theory maximum likelihood estimates (MLEs) and generalized least squares (GLS) estimators are fairly consistent; (2) standard errors tend to underestimate the true variation of the estimators; (3) the problems are not as serious for very large samples ($N \sim 1,000$) with somewhat conservative (99%) confidence intervals; and (4) the chi-square testing procedure is suspect, but (5) the adjusted chi-square tests seem to be able to give acceptable results (with larger samples). For the most part, then, assuming normality for outcome variables when it is not in fact present can (a) reduce the size of the correlations, (b) reduce the size of the available signal, and (c) reduce the ability of the test indicators to tell the difference.

In this part of the book, we will try to show that, even if some of the variables are measured as ordered categories with nonnormal distributions, including binary responses, some newer approaches allow us to retain all the basic longitudinal concepts presented earlier. We will not alter the basic data as it seems in the solution preferred by many statisticians (i.e., the "trimmed" solutions; Wilcox, 1998). Although this does add one more layer of complexity to the longitudinal SEM (LSEM), because we need to examine the model of the measurement system a bit more closely, it certainly seems worth doing whenever we have any concerns. In any case, we can always do analyses with and without specific persons, or with weighted persons. In the general case, although this may cost us some parameters, outcome nonnormality should not be allowed to distort the basic results.

COMMON FACTORS AS CONTINUOUS AND MEASURED VARIABLES AS CATEGORIES

It seems reasonable to assume that a latent variable that itself has a full range of measurement might be represented in terms of observables that do not fully reflect these systematic individual scores. For example, we might have the simple case of using a single item, scored as *correct* or *incorrect* to represent a broader concept of ability. If so, the model first proposed by Rasch (1960) could be instructive (McDonald, 1999). In a general way, we assume that a factor analytic model exists for the nonzero responses and a model applies to the binary outcomes (Y_m) after the response reaches a threshold (τ_m) for each variable.

This common factor model is written as the combination of the binary outcome variables (Y_m) and a first level of latent variables (Y_m^*) that is assumed to be normally distributed (see Exhibit 20.2). We further assume the threshold (τ_m) is a normal deviate. This means that the observations (Y_m) may not be normally distributed, but the latent variables (LVs) at this first level (Y_m^*) are defined to be so. Next a common factor model applies to this first layer of LVs. We typically assume the first layer of LVs has latent variable means and covariance expectations. We also typically assume the original layer of manifest variables has zero intercepts so the latent variable mean expectations (for variables of any complexity) can be written as a typical common factor mean and covariance expression (see Exhibit 20.2).

Within each variable, we need to estimate both the threshold and the unique means and variances, and this becomes rather complex with binary or categorical data. This kind of a model is depicted in the path diagram of

EXHIBIT 20.2
A Common Factor Model for Categorical Data

This general model is written as the combination of the binary outcome variables (Y_m) and a first level of latent variables ($\mathbf{Y}_m$) written as (see Muthén, 1984)

(1a) $\qquad Prob\{Y_{m,n} = 1 | \mathbf{Y}_{m,n} > \tau_m\} = \mathbf{N}\{\tau_m\}$

where the probability follows a normal distribution (N) so the threshold (τ_m) is a normal deviate. This means that the observations (Y_m) may not be normally distributed, but the latent variables at this first level ($\mathbf{Y}_m$) are defined to be.

Next a common factor model applies to this first layer of latent variables

(1b) $\qquad \mathbf{Y}_{m,n} = \lambda_m F_n + u_{m,n}$

We typically assume the second layer of latent variables has mean expectations

(2a) $\qquad E\{F, 1'\} = v$

and latent variable covariance expectations

(2b) $\qquad E\{F^*, F^{*'}\} = \phi$

and

(2c) $\qquad E\{u, u'\} = \psi^2$

Note. From "A General Structural Equation Model With Dichotomous, Ordered Categorical, and Continuous Latent Variable Indicators," by B. Muthén, 1984, *Psychometrika, 49*(1), pp. 116–117. Copyright 1984 by the Psychometric Society. Adapted with permission.

Figure 20.1. In order to represent the transformation by the threshold in the context of a path model, we have used a special symbol from electrical engineering (i.e., the filled in arrowhead with a line, a diode, or rectifier, the electrical analog to a check-valve; Hamagami, 1998). This symbol is intended to imply that the threshold parameter is like gatekeeper that continues to collect information until enough has been built up to change its state (i.e., 0 turns to 1 on the basis of the probability; sometimes termed a *firing*).

Because the only measurement we have is a binary response (0 or 1), then the observed mean of each outcome variable is simply a proportion ($m_m = p_m$). But the value of this proportion also forms its observed variance ($s_m^2 = p_m 1 - p_m$). Even the correlation of multiple binary scores can be represented as a cross-tabulation, with these values as the marginal proportions. This implies that the measurement of the binary (or categorical) variable is limited: The observed mean (p_m) and the observed variance (s_m^2) are entirely dependent on one another and cannot be easily separated. So we now have a modeling choice: We can either (a) use the concept of thresholds (possibly

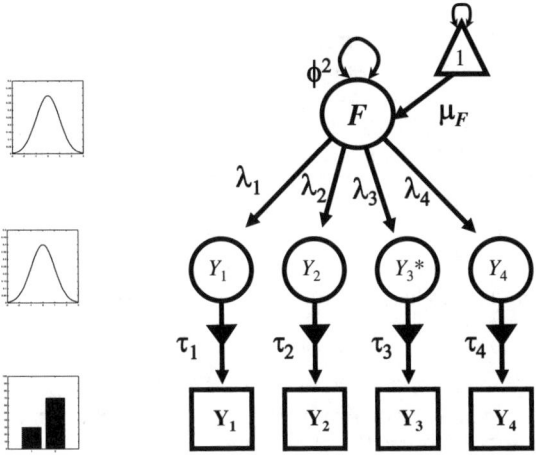

Figure 20.1. Extended path diagram (including theoretical distributions) of a binary factor measurement model.

scaled as a normal deviate above) or (b) consider the concept of a compound uniqueness (with mean and variance). One popular solution has been to use the threshold and implicitly scale the expected variance at unity (termed THETA in MPLUS). This implies that the uniqueness for any variable can be derived as from the other model parameters when the variable intercepts (i.e., means of unique variables) are all forced to zero (see Exhibit 20.2).

Essentially what we can do when we have ordered categories is to divide the observed outcome data into ordered segments (as in Exhibit 20.3). Then we would use the data from multiple scale points (s) to estimate multiple thresholds ($\tau_{w, s-1}$) for each observed variable (Y_m) so that each interval of observation is summarized into a standardized LV ($\mathbf{Y}_m$) with a normal distribution. No alteration is needed if the resulting categories are not ordered, because we can always reorder them later.

Some of the technical background of this approach to the specific categorical problem may be useful. Among many others studying these problems, Burt (1919) proposed we basically ignore these technical problems and simply factor analyze the matrix of Phi coefficients (i.e., Pearson product moment correlations for binary data). Much later, Rasch (1960) introduced the probabilistic model required to meet basic measurement principles for items. McDonald (1982, 1999) introduced an idea of difficulty factor and fitted it using a nonlinear factor model. Christofferson (as cited in Fraser & McDonald, 1988) introduced mathematical models of factor analysis for the dichotomous variables. Muthén (1978) showed a way to construct SEM and factor analysis of the dichotomous dependent variables. Muthén and Christoffersson (1981) extended the item response factor model to analyze

EXHIBIT 20.3
Observed Variable Expectations for a Common Factor
Model for Categorical Data

Expanding on the tables of Exhibit 20.2 (see Muthén, 1984), we typically assume the original layer of manifest variables has zero intercepts (by table, see below) so the LV mean expectations (for variables of any complexity) is written as

(1a) $$E\{Y_m, 1'\} = \lambda_m \nu$$

and the LV covariance expectations are a typical factor expression

(1b) $$E\{Y^*, Y^*\} = \Lambda \Phi \Lambda' + \Psi^2$$

The typical identification solution has been to use the threshold and implicitly scale the expected variance of the first level of latent variables at

(2a) $$\phi_m^2 = 1,$$

and this implies that the uniqueness for any variable is not a free parameter but can be derived from the others as

(2b) $$\psi_m^2 = 1 - \lambda_m \phi \lambda_m$$

when the variable intercepts (i.e., means of unique variables) are all forced to zero. As an alternative, the unique means do not need to be forced to zero, but they can be reconstructed in the form of w thresholds as normal z-scores indicating the required shifts (s) between $w + 1$ categories within each variable. This can basically be defined as

(2c) $$\tau(w) = N\{s(w) - s(w - 1)\}$$

where $s(w)$ is a scale point, N is a normality constraint, and all thresholds ($\tau(w)$) create a zero sum. The basic idea is that these shifts can take the place of the unique means and variances, and they can be interpreted as generalized distributions that are transformed into normality.

Note. From "A General Structural Equation Model With Dichotomous, Ordered Categorical, and Continuous Latent Variable Indicators," by B. Muthén, 1984, *Psychometrika, 49*(1), pp. 116–117. Copyright 1984 by the Psychometric Society. Adapted with permission.

---

the multiple group context. Muthén (1984) generalized the SEM method incorporating dichotomous, ordered categorical, and continuous variables. This last approach has now seems to have taken off and is being used by several SEM programs (e.g., LISCOMP, Mplus). We can find this same model in book-length treatments of item response theory models, including Embretson and Reise (2000); Hambleton, Swaminathan, and Rogers (1991); Lord and Novick (1968); and McDonald (1999). The factor analytic approach presented here is described in more detail in McDonald (1999), but it is easy to

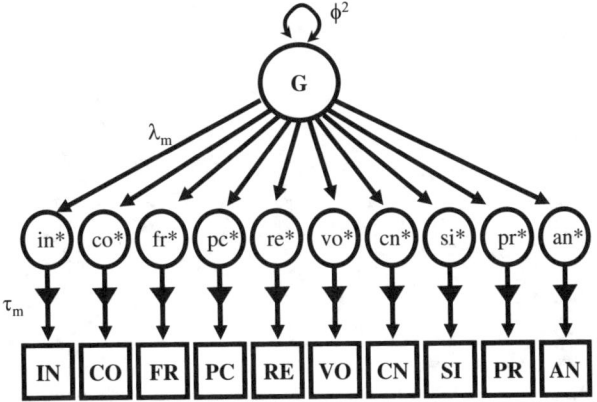

Figure 20.2. Path diagram for a single factor model with item-level data. From *Human Cognitive Abilities in Theory and Practice* (p. 237), by J. J. McArdle and R. W. Woodcock (Eds.), 1998, Mahwah, NJ: Erlbaum. Copyright 1998 by Erlbaum. Adapted with permission.

represent binary data with one common factor (Figure 20.2) or two common factors (Figure 20.3) in path diagrams.

LONGITUDINAL MODELS OF BINARY RESPONSES

In principle, it is not a problem to put these concepts into longitudinal terms although, curiously, this does not seem to have been done very much before (but see Hamagami, 1998). First, we assume that we have repeated

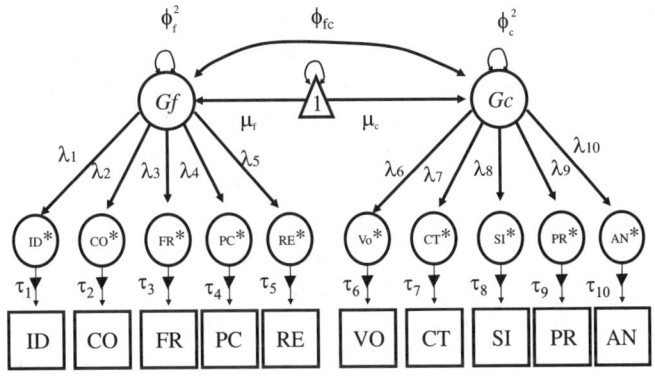

Figure 20.3. Path diagram of a two common factor hypothesis of the Stanford–Binet items. From *Human Cognitive Abilities in Theory and Practice* (p. 237), by J. J. McArdle and R. W. Woodcock (Eds.), 1998, Mahwah, NJ: Erlbaum. Copyright 1998 by Erlbaum. Adapted with permission.

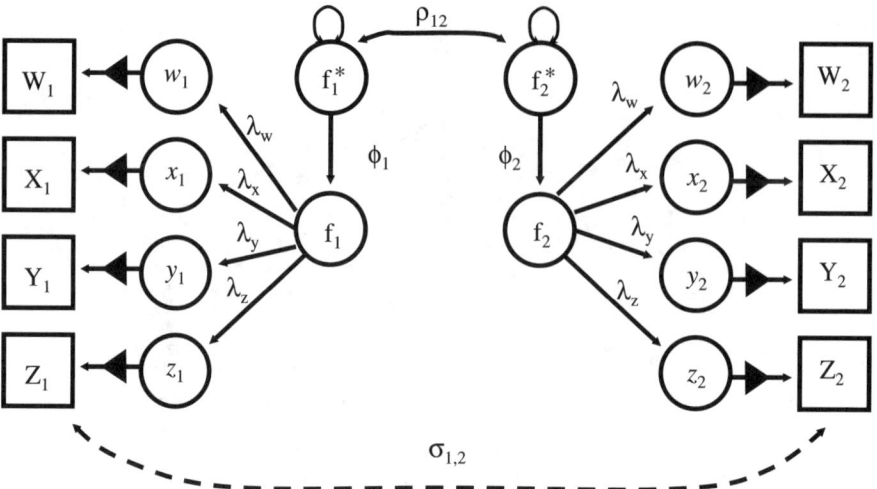

Figure 20.4. A standard factor invariance over time model applied to item-level data. From *Human Cognitive Abilities in Theory and Practice* (p. 238), by J. J. McArdle and R. W. Woodcock (Eds.), 1998, Mahwah, NJ: Erlbaum. Copyright 1998 by Erlbaum. Adapted with permission.

observations of the multiple outcomes ($Y_m[t]$) in the same units. This can be done in terms of the prior two-occasion path model as in Figure 20.4, now with the same thresholds for each variable over time, or in terms of the dual change score (DCS), or in Figure 20.5, where we have multiple measurements and multiple thresholds at each time, but only one set over time (as in Hishinuma, Chang, McArdle, & Hamagami, 2012; and McArdle, Hamagami, Chang, & Hishinuma, in press).

Following the earlier logic, we can now write a longitudinal common factor model in the same way (see Exhibit 20.4). To calculate this discrete measurement model for longitudinal data, we will only estimate only one set of thresholds (τ_m) over all occasions, and we do so to mimic the actions of multiple factorial invariance over time (MFIT) with unique variables. To identify the factor model, we also fix the variance of every Time 1 LV ($\phi[1]^2 = 1$) and the mean of the Time 1 factors ($\nu[1] = 0$). A reasonable question remains about whether or not we should scale each variable's unique variances (ψ^2) differently at each time, and here we do not. Once we write these specific constraints, we can fit the data using a discrete approximation to a common factor model. There is no way to separate the unique means and unique variances from the binary data because all we have is the marginal proportions and the cross-tabulation, but we assume invariant threshold parameters ($\tau_{m,s}$) representing both the unique means and unique variances over all occasions. Again, the minimal constraints would not require us to make these thresholds the same, but for simplicity at the start, we do.

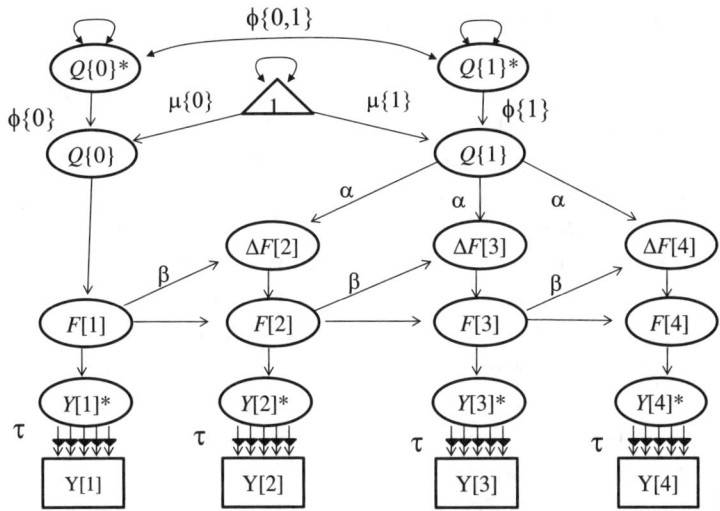

Figure 20.5. A latent change score model of a common factor with multicategorical outcomes at multiple occasions. From "Testing the Idea of General Intelligence", by J. J. McArdle, 2013, *F&M Scientist, 1*, p. 1335. Copyright 2013 by Franklin and Marshall College. Reprinted with permission.

EXHIBIT 20.4
A Longitudinal Common Factor Model for Categorical Data

Following the earlier multiple factorial invariance over time logic (Hamagami, 1998), we can now write

(1a) $$Prob\{Y[t]_{m,n} = 1 | Y[t]_{m,n} > \tau_m\} = \mathbf{N}\{\tau_m\}$$

where the probability follows a normal distribution (N), and so the invariant threshold (τ_m) is itself a normal deviate. Next a common factor model applies to this first layer of latent variables

(1b) $$Y[t]_{m,n} = \lambda_m F[t]_n + u[t]_{m,n}$$

We assume the first layer of latent variables has zero intercepts but also has mean changes

(2a) $$E\{Y[t], 1'\} = E\{F[t]\} = \nu[t]$$

with latent variable covariance expectations

(2b) $$E\{F[t]*, F[t]*\} = \phi[t]^2$$

and

(2c) $$E\{u[t], u[t]\} = \psi^2$$

and so the latent variable covariance expectations can be written as a standard factor model expression

(2d) $$E\{Y[t]*, Y[t]*\} = \Lambda\Phi[t]^2\Lambda' + \Psi^2$$

Note. From *Human Cognitive Abilities in Theory and Practice* (p. 238), by J. J. McArdle and R. W. Woodcock (Eds.), 1998, Mahwah, NJ: Erlbaum. Copyright 1998 by Erlbaum. Adapted with permission.

Following the strict MFIT criteria, we would force the scale points to be invariant over all occasions (or $\tau_{m,s}$; see Figure 20.5). This is equivalent to saying that we want the unique variances and the unique means to be equal over time. In this case we could require the threshold values for a scale, where the specific movement over the scale at any time has the same meaning. And we basically do this so all changes over time are conveyed through the common factors. In our recent work, we ran into an example with high school grades (McArdle, Hamagami, Chang, & Hishinuma, in press). This invariance of measurement would be equivalent to common thoughts in the English languages, like (a) a grade of C will be termed passing no matter at what grade or at what age we measure it, or (b) a person has a disease and will be termed sick no matter what situation we find ourselves in, or (c) a temperature over 100 is high no matter at what age we measure it. Although the first two seem like realistic longitudinal scenarios we can abide by, the third analogy does not always work well. That is, we would probably treat the temperature of infants different from what we do when faced with an elderly person (i.e., the temperature of infants can be high). In this case, what we are not saying is that there is more or less frequency of these events at various occasions, but we are saying that the way we measure these events will not change its basic definition over this period of time. So we can try to add threshold constraints to each occasion, recognizing that constraints are obviously open to required changes.

MULTIPLE THRESHOLD CALCULATIONS

To carry out calculations for the ordinal approach, we can rely on the approach created and programmed by Muthén (1989c), originally using LISCOMP software (Muthén & Satorra, 1995). In this approach, the first step is to use maximum likelihood estimates–missing at random (MLE-MAR) to estimate the empirical distance between each entry of a categorical variable. If we have s possible ratings of a score at each occasion, we can estimate s–1 thresholds describing the estimated difference between these categories. In the second step, we assume that a first layer of latent variables are normally distributed (with mean 0 and variance 1), and we estimate the correlations among LVs using what are termed polychoric procedures. Finally, in a third step, a consistent estimator of the asymptotic covariance matrix of the latent correlations is typically based on a weighted least squares mean adjusted estimator.

Additional model assumptions in longitudinal data can be based on the structure of the thresholds (i.e., invariant over time) or the model correlations (following a latent curve model [LCM] or DCS hypothesis) are added, and the comparative goodness of fit is obtained. If needed, formal tests of the difference between models are made more accurate by using kurtosis adjustments (scaling correction factors; Browne, 1984; Satorra & Bentler, 1994). In any case, each of these steps is now easy to implement with contemporary software (e.g., Mplus; Muthén & Muthén, 2006; Muthén & Satorra, 1995).

An initial description of some relevant summary statistics could be presented here, but we simply refer to those of McArdle, Hamagami, Chang, and Hishinuma (in press). In this longitudinal analysis we include estimated thresholds, means, deviations, and correlations estimated using the most typical incomplete data algorithms (MLE-MAR in Mplus 6.0; Muthén & Muthén, 2006; program scripts available). We noted that the interval score estimates presented do not have any correction for nonnormality, whereas the ordinal score estimates have been corrected.

The estimated thresholds for each measured variable (τ_m) can be obtained using the SEM software (at least Mplus 6.0; Muthén & Satorra, 1995) under the constraint that these thresholds represented differences among the response categories and were the same (i.e., invariant MLE) at each of the longitudinal occasions. We note that this simplification of parameters is not a necessary feature of the data, and the scale could change from one occasion to the next, but this is a prerequisite for all models to follow, and therefore, we present it first.

As an example from our own work on this topic, we estimated thresholds of high school grade point averages (GPAs) for Y_1 from some low category D to a higher category C– (i.e., 1.0 to 1.7), so the threshold had a value of $\tau_1 = -2.14$. Because this was estimated in a normal probability, or probit metric, this value indicates the location on a normal curve for people above and below this Y_1 point (i.e., approximately 2% below and 98% above). The next estimated value of $\tau_2 = -1.60$ suggests that a slightly larger number of people are likely to respond between 1.7 and 2.0. The vector of eight thresholds T = [–2.1, –1.6, –0.9, –.00, +0.0, +0.7, +1.3, +2.0] is seen to increase in order, even though this was not actually restricted (i.e., it was simply categorical). The nonlinear nature of these differences in responses can be seen from the difficulty of shifting between responses formed here as a ratio of the estimated differences to the observed differences (as in McArdle & Epstein, 1987). These differences would be constant if the scaling was equal interval, but these turn out to be $\Delta\tau$ = [= 0, 1.8, 2.5, 2.1, 0.1, 2.3, 1.5, 3.4], and this indicates the apparent difficulty of moving between the response categories not being equal to the stated distance. Linear relations within and among GPA variables are likely to be better represented by an ordinal scale.

In general, we expect higher linear relations when estimated using the polychoric correlation. The polychoric correlation is a technique for estimating the correlation between two theoretical normally distributed continuous latent variables. The tetrachoric correlation is a special case of the polychoric correlation applicable when both observed variables are dichotomous.

(These names seem to derive from the series of mathematical expansions once used for estimation of correlations.) Both correlations within time and over time are likely to be much better represented by this kind of an ordinal scale. When comparing Pearson correlations and polychoric correlations for non-normal data, we find clear attenuation of the Pearson correlations but acceptable polychorics (as in Hamagami, 1998). We also note that outliers in the measured variables are no longer critical, unless they represent values that are out of line (i.e., and probably should be incomplete). Incidentally, the same concepts of fit indices can be used as well.

SHOULD WE USE CATEGORICAL MEASUREMENT CONCEPTS?

We will not provide any illustrations on this topic here, but our prior work has convinced us that this categorical measurement approach works very well when needed (McArdle, Hamagami, Chang, & Hishinuma, in press; Parry & McArdle, 1991). Of most importance here, the basic idea of using invariant thresholds for multiple occasions of many items (see Figure 20.4) or in a latent change score (LCS) with multiple occasions (as in Figure 20.5), just as they were in the common factor model (see Figures 20.1, 20.2, or 20.3), is a good one. Because the scaling of the measured variables can make a difference in the dynamic interpretation over time or between variables, and we know this limits the inferences that can be made using standard interval score models, we should use these models and pay attention to these results whenever we can.

To the degree a variable is highly skewed, this new technology is probably useful. In addition, the categories of any scale used here do not need to be equal. It is not so surprising that when we examined alternative latent change models for either variable, we found that both the form and size of the changes were related to the measurement or scaling of the variables used in the change model. Big differences can arise when we try to link the repeated measures data from one grade level to the next over multiple variables. Any true dynamic expression, no matter how large, could have been masked by an impoverished measurement. Perhaps the fact that we cannot fit a good dynamic expression of change without good measurement of the construct should not be a great surprise either.

The simple models presented here point out a few problems that can be overcome by using contemporary modeling procedures. This LSEM approach can be used to turn important developmental questions about temporal sequences into statistically powerful hypotheses. The fact that this can be done in the presence of ordinal level measurement and large amounts of incomplete data can be demonstrated, and this is probably a necessity for most practical situations. We hope this approach can be useful for many other studies where multivariate longitudinal data have been collected to gain some insight into an ongoing developmental process so there is scientific and applied value.

One classic way to deal with nonnormal outcomes is to use score transformations (i.e., logarithms or square roots), but these will not be helpful when we observe extreme limits of some of our outcomes. Instead, and this probably should be done first, we should use the standard SEM approaches for estimating growth and change under the assumption of an interval scaling of the outcomes without corrections (as in McArdle, 2009). This is not often based on MLE-MAR assumptions, but it is possible to do so. Then, in a subsequent set of analyses, we then can consider the same longitudinal data, but we expand the model to include a set of ordinal thresholds (τ; Hamagami, 1998), and we can highlight any differences in the substantive results for the same data (as done in McArdle, Hamagami, Chang, & Hishinuma, in press).

Of practical importance is that this transformation to ordinal scale points, while potentially costly in terms of parameters to estimate, is relatively inexpensive when so many parameters are equated over time, as in MFIT. This appropriately puts the burden on the computer program to find measurement scale points for each variable, but these are required to remain invariant over time, so this seems like a reasonable task.

V

LONGITUDINAL SEM FOR CAUSES (DETERMINANTS) OF INTRAINDIVIDUAL CHANGES

21

ANALYSES BASED ON CROSS-LAGGED REGRESSION AND CHANGES

Now we arrive at what is possibly the most challenging part of our theory for many readers. Many people collect longitudinal data because they think there is a prima facie reason to believe that some information about the leading and lagging aspects of the sequence of data will emerge. These people are not far from being correct, because if, in fact, they had a specific sequence among the variables they measured, such a result could emerge this way. Unfortunately, in general this is not really easy to see, partly because (a) there could easily be another measured (Z[t]) or unmeasured variable (*Z[t]*, notice the italics) that was creating all the dynamic influences in both outcomes, and (b) we need to measure the changes with enough lag in time (Hamagami & McArdle, 2000). These additional variables have been termed *lurking* variables by others (Shrout, 2011).

Of course, many researchers would like to find "causal relations" with observational data, and this can even be a goal (McArdle, 2011c). This approach is probably needed because we want to be clear about changing or

http://dx.doi.org/10.1037/14440-022
Longitudinal Data Analysis Using Structural Equation Models, by J. J. McArdle and J. R. Nesselroade
Copyright © 2014 by the American Psychological Association. All rights reserved.

controlling our worst outcomes, and we know this is difficult to do on an ethical basis. So this goal can probably never be achieved because of the common problems of incomplete predictors which are not normally distributed. Nevertheless, we can certainly look for earlier predictors of later outcomes and see if we can control these. That is, we may not know the systemic causes, but we can certainly examine the dynamics of the system to try to see how it operates. Even if the collection of observational longitudinal data were enough to define a sequence, the approach to longitudinal data analyses that people seem to carry out now (e.g., repeated measures analysis of variance [RANOVA]) seems rather inconsistent with this fundamental point of view.

What we will do here is start with simple topics and end on more complex topics. We will start with basic models for two variables measured at only two occasions. The issues that have been raised by others are insightful and interesting, and most remain unsolved. Nevertheless, we will start by showing how the current longitudinal structural equation models (LSEMs) do start to approach the problem of causal attribution, but we will raise a set of practical problems. We will show that the standard models of cross-lagged regression do have a simple interpretation in terms of multiple changes that can be helpful in interpretation of any result. We will not try to assert the direction of causation, but we will attempt to understand the system dynamics.

We will then move to cross-lagged models with common factors, and we will show how this could help remove some unwanted changes due to errors of measurement. But then we will move to models with more occasions (and more variables), and we will try to bring together the entire dynamic picture. We will try not to shy away from dynamic arguments, but instead we will embrace these as a reasonable way to deal with nonmanipulative longitudinal data. Finally, we will discuss options for multivariate analysis of real data and will fit some of these LSEMs to the available data using available programs.

The regression model for "crossed-and-lagged" data is probably the most popular structural equation model (SEM; Bohrnstedt, 1969; O. D. Duncan, 1975; Heise, 1975), so we will examine it in some detail here. This model is typically run when we have measured at least two different variables repeatedly over time: the lagging of X[1] and X[2], the lagging of Y[1] and Y[2], the crossing of X[1] to Y[2], and the crossing of Y[1] to Y[2]. As it stands now, this model has a lot of potential when we have repeated assessment of multiple constructs over time, but it still has a lot of problems (e.g., O. D. Duncan, 1969; Greenberg & Kessler, 1982). When we have measured multiple variables we can just assume the multiple factorial invariance over time (MFIT) expressions, or we can just assume that the metric of each variables is the same, so the labels can be repeated with further evaluation. When we do this, we can concentrate on the sequence of changes in the factor scores. But even when we raise this model to the common factor level, most problems of inference do not seem to go away. In fact, a few new problems seem to emerge.

CROSS-LAGGED REGRESSION MODEL

Assuming we have two measured variables (X[t] and Y[t]) within each time, we can next consider a score model that comes from crossed-and-lagged panel analysis (Hsiao, 2005; Jöreskog & Sörbom, 1979; see Exhibit 21.1). This type of model is usually written in mean deviation form, and we use it so we can broadly assert that the "past leads to the future," that is, scores at Time 1 lead to and affect scores at Time 2. It is easy to add intercepts to this model and write it in raw score form, but this is hardly ever done (we will return to this later). A path diagram of this complete model is presented in Figure 21.1. Most important here, we suggest that the each measured variable at the first occasion has both a lagged effect (termed β_{xx} and β_{yy}) on the same variable and a crossed effect (termed γ_{xy} and γ_{yx}) on the other variable. Even so, if the LSEM above were true, then there are actually two separate but possibly correlated disturbance terms (z_x and z_y).

EXHIBIT 21.1
The Crossed-Lagged Regression Model

Assuming we have at least two observed variables repeatedly measured at two specific occasions of time, we can create mean deviated forms (using the asterisk to signify the removal of the mean) and write

(1a) $$X[2]_n^* = \beta_{xx}X[1]_n^* + \gamma_{xy}Y[1]_n^* + z_{x,n}$$

and

(1b) $$Y[2]_n^* = \beta_{yy}Y[1]_n^* + \gamma_{yx}X[1]_n^* + z_{y,n}$$

where, as in typical time-series fashion, we again broadly assert that the "past leads to the future," that is, scores at Time 1 lead to and affect scores at Time 2. It is easy to add intercepts to this model and write it in raw score form as

(2a) $$X[2]_n = \beta_{1x}1_n + \beta_{xx}X[1]_n + \gamma_{xy}Y[1]_n + z_{x,n}$$

and

(2b) $$Y[2]_n = \beta_{1y}1_n + \beta_{yy}Y[1]_n + \gamma_{yx}X[1]_n + z_{y,n}.$$

Most important here, we suggest that the each measured variable at the first occasion has both a lagged effect (termed β_{xx} and β_{yy}) on the same variable and a crossed effect (termed γ_{xy} and γ_{yx}) on the other variable. Even so, if the LSEM above is true, then there are always two separate but possibly correlated disturbance terms (z_x and z_y).

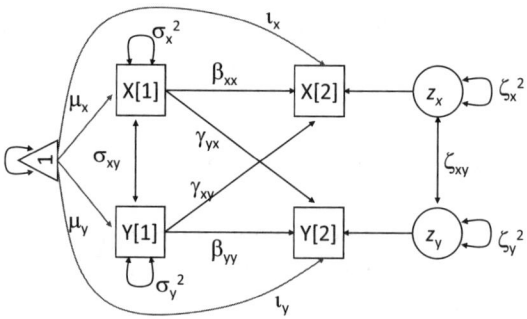

Figure 21.1. A fully saturated two time-point cross-lagged regression (CLR-FS).

Now we can write simple covariance expectations for Time 1 and for Time 2 as well as the covariance expectations between Time 1 scores and Time 2 scores (see Exhibit 21.2). Of course, these are often written in a simple lower triangular matrix format (see O. D. Duncan, 1975). As it turns out, this initial model will fit the data perfectly, because all we have done is turn the covariances into regressions. But in this "fully saturated" format, it is clear that each covariance is seen to be composed of both cross and lagged effects (and other covariance terms).

These kinds of regressions are typically used in these SEMs to overcome the special problems created by correlations. Thus, when we calculate the usual regression formulas, we obtain the separate regression parameters (for X[t], β_{xx}, γ_{xy} and for Y[t], β_{yy}, γ_{yx}), as in Figure 21.2. Of course, one or more of these coefficients could turn out to be zero, and we could then eliminate this path from the diagram, which is done in Figure 21.3. As another alternative, we can imply assume that measured variable X[1] is correlated with the same measurement X[2] over time; then this repeated measures correlation is interpreted as a *reliability* or *stability* over time. But if the structural equation model above is true (Figure 21.3), then there are actually two separate but possibly correlated disturbance terms (z_x and z_y), as highlighted in Figure 21.4. Besides working with measured scores that could have substantial measurement error, we are also trying to understand their independent stability over time (β_{xx} and β_{yy}) and their independent impact on each other (γ_{xy} and γ_{yx}). Another way to say this is that we are looking for is the effect of earlier X[t − 1] on later Y[t] when the prior values of Y[t − 1] have been taken into account.

In the LSEM approach, we can force one or more of the coefficients to be zero, even if this is not the best estimate. These ideas mimic the path tracing of Figure 21.4. Here, in part, the correlation of the variable X with itself is now equivalent to its regression over time (top left in Figure 21.4),

EXHIBIT 21.2
Expectations in the Crossed-Lagged Regression Model

We can write the covariance expectations for Time 1 as

(1) $$E\{X[1]^*, X[1]^{*\prime}\} = \sigma_x^2$$
$$E\{Y[1]^*, Y[1]^{*\prime}\} = \sigma_y^2$$
$$E\{X[1]^*, Y[1]^{*\prime}\} = \sigma_{xy} = \sigma_{yx}$$

and for Time 2 as

(2) $$E\{X[2]^*, X[2]^{*\prime}\} = \sigma_{x[2]}^2 = \beta_{xx}^2 \sigma_x^2 + \gamma_{xy}^2 \sigma_y^2 + 2\beta_{xx}\gamma_{xy}\sigma_{xy} + \psi_x^2$$
$$E\{Y[2]^*, Y[2]^{*\prime}\} = \sigma_{y[2]}^2 = \beta_{yy}^2 \sigma_y^2 + \gamma_{yx}^2 \sigma_x^2 + 2\beta_{yy}\gamma_{yy}\sigma_{xy} + \psi_y^2$$
$$E\{X[2]^*, X[2]^{*\prime}\} = \sigma_{x[2],y[2]} = 2\beta_{xx}\sigma_{xy}\beta_{yy} + 2\beta_{xy}\sigma_{xy}\gamma_{yx} + \psi_{xy}$$

and the covariance expectations between Time 1 scores and Time 2 scores as

(3) $$E\{X[1]^*, X[2]^{*\prime}\} = \sigma_{x[1,2]} = \beta_{xx}\sigma_x^2 + \gamma_{xy}\sigma_{y,x}$$
$$E\{Y[1]^*, Y[2]^{*\prime}\} = \sigma_{y[1,2]} = \beta_{yy}\sigma_y^2 + \gamma_{yx}\sigma_{x,y}$$
$$E\{X[1]^*, Y[2]^{*\prime}\} = \sigma_{x[1],y[2]} = \beta_{yx}\sigma_x^2 + \gamma_{xx}\sigma_{x,y}$$
$$E\{X[2]^*, Y[1]^{*\prime}\} = \sigma_{x[2],y[1]} = \beta_{xy}\sigma_y^2 + \gamma_{yy}\sigma_{y,x}$$

If we force one of the cross-lagged coefficients to zero (say $\gamma_\xi = 0$) as in Figure 4.0c we are asserting that "Y does not affect X but X does affect Y" (assuming $|\gamma_\psi| > 0$), then we have a new and far less complex set of covariance expectations for

(4) $$E\{X[1]^*, X[2]^*\} = \sigma_{x[1,2]} = \beta_{xx}\sigma_x^2$$
$$E\{X[2]^*, Y[1]^*\} = \sigma_{x[2],y[1]} = \beta_{yy}\sigma_{\psi,\xi}$$
$$E\{X[2]^*, Y[2]^*\} = \sigma_{x[2],y[2]} = 2\beta_{xx}\sigma_{x,y}\beta_{yy} + \psi_{xy}.$$

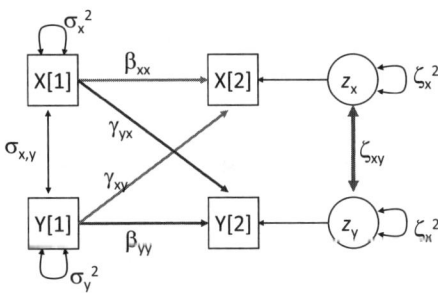

Figure 21.2. A standard covariance-based two time-point crossed and lagged regression path model fit to mean deviated scores.

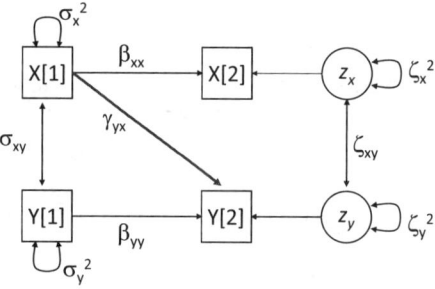

Figure 21.3. A restricted crossed and lagged regression path model; $\gamma_x = 0$. To answer the question "why are y[2] and y[1] supposedly correlated?"

but in addition there exists a correlation over time between all variables, including the X[1] and Y[1] and Y[2]. This, of course, is a very specific reason for the famous dictum "Correlation does not imply causality." If we are incorrect about this multiplicative constraint (e.g., $|\beta_x| > 0$), then this model will not generally fit the observed data as well as the prior fully saturated model. We might try to remove the opposite coefficient, as is done in Figure 21.5, or we might also remove both crossed coefficients as in Figure 21.6, mainly to see what happens. Interestingly enough in this case, both variables are expected to be correlated over time, but neither is thought to cause the other. We again recall the point of the previous saying. Another logical model in this SEM sequence to fit is to force the lagged coefficients to zero, as in Figure 21.7, and this implies the variables are not correlated over time.

In the LSEM logic used here, we will fit several variations of this model in an effort to see if one variable is the "leader" and the other is a "lagger." Of course, with observational data we must keep a big caveat in mind: Both measurements could just be the outcome of an unmeasured variable (e.g., Z[t]), and the whole approach used may be biased and incorrect. Also the model we do not fit is one where both crossed coefficients are forced to be equal to

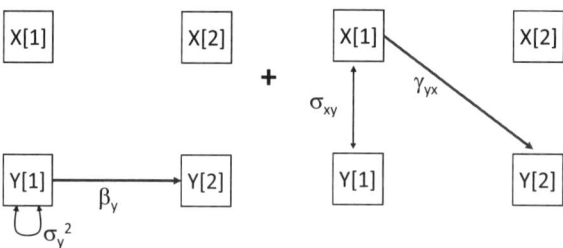

Figure 21.4. Restricted expectations for the covariance $E\{Y[2]^*, Y[1]^*\}$ from crossed and lagged regression.

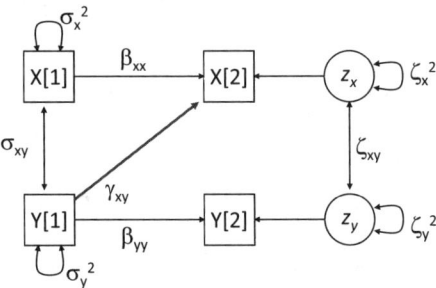

Figure 21.5. An alternative simplified crossed and lagged regression path model; $\gamma_y = 0$, CLR-X0.

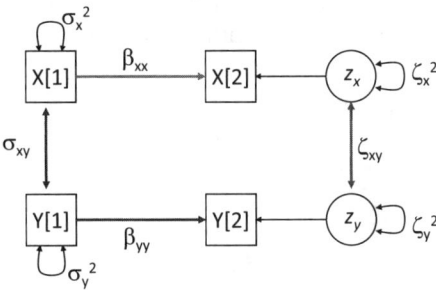

Figure 21.6. An alternative simplified crossed and lagged regression path model (CLR-X0Y0).

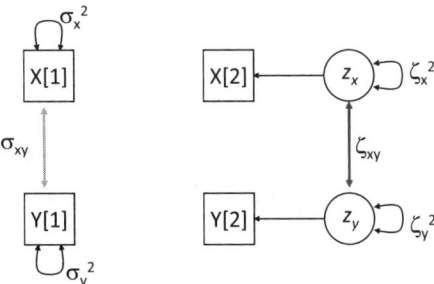

Figure 21.7. A two time-point exogeneous baseline for the regression path model (CLR-B0).

each other. Although this certainly could be done with existing LSEM technology, this was not included because it is not usually warranted when the background variables are based on different scoring systems.

LIMITS IN CROSS-LAGGED REGRESSION INTERPRETATION

Although it is often not mentioned, we can start with a cross-lagged model and write the expected means at Time 1 and Time 2 by adding intercepts (see Exhibit 21.3). Because an intercept (ι_i) is added to each equation at the second time, the observed mean that we estimate can always fit this model exactly, and the Time 1 mean can be said to equal to the Time 2 mean. This is not really necessary, because the Time 1 mean can differ from the Time 2 mean. But this really implies that when using the crossed lag model, there is no attempt made to test mean changes over time. This is a covariance-based model as was the model of common factor analysis. We do not typically test this assumption, but that does not imply that the means are the same, only that they could be. In using this model, the means are not considered important. So the means are typically removed, the model is fitted only to covariances, and we typically use these models to examine variation around the averages (Cattell, in Berieter, 1963).

EXHIBIT 21.3
Stationarity Assumptions in the Crossed-Lagged Regression Model

Symbolically, we can state some simple variance assumptions here as

(1a) $\qquad E\{X[1]^*, X[1]^{*\prime}\} = E\{X[2]^*, X[2]^{*\prime}\} = \sigma_x^2$,

and

(1b) $\qquad E\{Y[1]^*, Y[1]^{*\prime}\} = E\{Y[2]^*, Y[2]^{*\prime}\} = \sigma_y^2$,

and some cross-covariance assumptions as

(1c) $\qquad E\{X[1]^*, Y[1]^{*\prime}\} = E\{X[2]^*, Y[2]^{*\prime}\} = \sigma_{xy}$.

If useful, we could even put these in as required constraints into the structural equation model above.

We could also describe some expectation for the equality of the means in another set of expressions

(2a) $\qquad E\{X[t], 1'\} = \mu_x$,

and

(2b) $\qquad E\{Y[t], 1'\} = \mu_y$.

Another aspect of these models that we usually assume is that the process we are examining has reached a state of equilibrium so it is *stationary* (O. D. Duncan, 1969, 1975; Greenberg & Kessler, 1982). That is, the implied variances at each time are the same within each variable, and the covariances within each time across variables are also the same. Symbolically, we can state these simple assumptions (also in Exhibit 21.3). We often do not put these into the structural equation model because it is somewhat complicated, but we also do not do so because we know it would probably not fit. This simplified assumption implies we can analyze correlations instead of covariances. That is, a zero parameter is zero in either covariance or correlational metric, and so mainly constraints require covariances. Unfortunately, the equality assumption of stationarity is hardly ever tested but is hardly ever true. An alternative way to make this easy to carry out is to assume there is some dynamic information in in the correlations over time as we do later here. Of course, this test of stationarity is not usually done, so mainly we just ignore these key assumptions now.

Now we can ask, "How likely is it that these kinds of conditions (equal means and equal variances over time, equal correlations within times) do in fact exist in any observational data?" The answer seems to be precisely zero. Well, to be fair, there may be some processes that have accumulated all their changes and everyone changes in the same way and all that remains is a steady state where very little movement is going on within or between individuals. Also even more assumptions are made when the data are collected over more than two occasions (to be discussed). Even with these seemingly outrageous assumptions as part of the model estimation, these basic cross-lagged models of causal inference are still widely used.

We can simply look at the values (and possibly the standard errors and presumed significance) of the crossed coefficients to get some idea of the importance of sequential effects (i.e., does X→Y or does Y→X) in light of the time-lagged features. Also, the parameters of interest are themselves likely to be correlated, so they will change together, and this is not typically taken into account in the usual standard errors of the fully saturated regression model. But since crossed coefficients often represent critical issues of inference, we can use the general SEM approach in a more sophisticated fashion. To further specify and fit an alternative model where X[1] does not impact Y[2] (i.e., $\gamma_{yx} = 0$), we simply alter the expectations. If this model still fits the data as well as the previous and less-restricted model, we conclude that we have no evidence for an effect of X →Y. To deal with the bigger questions, we can also fit alternative models where Y[1] does not impact X[2] (i.e., $\gamma_{xy} = 0$) or where neither factor affects the other (i.e., $\gamma_{xy} = 0$ and $\gamma_{yx} = 0$), and possibly other models too.

Incidentally, we hardly ever fit models where the effects are considered equal (i.e., $\gamma_{xy} = \gamma_{yx}$), even though this would be a most interesting test strategy.

Unfortunately, the effects of interest (γ_{jk}) are regression terms so the meaning of any equality constraint would require a nonarbitrary equal scaling of the Time 1 variables as well (i.e., $\varphi_x^2 = \varphi_y^2$). These kinds of equality constraints and tests should probably be avoided when the scale of measurement differs, but they should be emphasized when the scale of measurement is equal.

This basic use of cross-lagged logic is one classical way to examine causality in observational data (see Cochran & Cox, 1950; O. D. Duncan, 1975; Granger, 1969; Pearl, 2000; Sobel, 1982), although there are clear limits to the modeling possibilities. A critical feature of observational data is that perhaps some other variables that could be measured (Z[t]) that actually cause both of the ones we have measured (X[t] and Y[t]). This is an idea that can be directly examined in this framework, and it certainly does not require that all relevant variables be measured. We can test these basic ideas with variables that are assumed to have no measurement error, or we can test these ideas with common factors that are assumed to have no measurement errors. But the only way to evaluate the systematic bias due to missing a variables or missing common factor is to measure them or their surrogates and to use them in the model. These kinds of SEMs are hopefully useful to create a basic understanding of the sequential inferences. Of course, recent work termed *mediation modeling* has often been done in the absence of common factors, and this can be quite misleading (for some good examples, see Cole & Maxwell, 2003).

Some other limits of cross-lagged models have dealt with the time lags required. For example, the early and important critique of O. D. Duncan (1969) pointed out that other alternative models for the same data could exist, but have different patterns of influences. This serious limitation is depicted in Figure 21.8. Here we assume that X[1] impacts Y[2] over time, but we also think that X[2] impacts Y[2] within time. This shorter time scale is often the

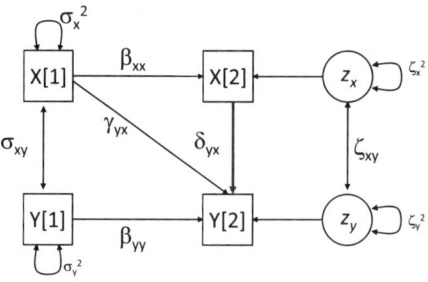

Figure 21.8. Duncan's second alternative crossed and lagged regression path; $\gamma_x = 0$ but $\delta_y > 0$. From "Some Linear Models for Two-Wave, Two-Variable Panel Analysis," by O. D. Duncan, 1969, *Psychological Bulletin, 72*, pp. 171–182. Copyright 1969 by the American Psychological Association.

beginning of a model of *reciprocal causation*, and this is a rather key potential problem (see Greenberg & Kessler, 1982). Figure 21.8 is not a representation that many people use, but it certainly could happen, especially if the time lag between X and Y is very long so the shorter time-lagged influences appear to be *concurrent*. What Duncan showed is that this instantaneous model of influence fit the cross-lagged data as well as a fully saturated model. This was a rather devastating critique because we never know if the change we want to model is occurring over shorter periods of time. This critique is not going to be easy to resolve, but this was only one of several examples of alternative time-dependencies created by O. D. Duncan (1969; see also Greenberg & Kessler, 1982). What Duncan basically suggested is that we may never know that our measured time lags are most appropriate. He also proved that no two-occasion data analysis will ever tell us about the most appropriate models for causation.

A different critique of cross-lagged analysis was made by Gollob and Reichardt (1987), who said we may come to believe that things are happening over longer periods of time when in fact they are happening over shorter periods of time, and vice versa (see their alternative model of Figure 21.9). In our view, the basic conclusion of both previous articles is that time lags chosen can lead to differences in results, and we may not be able to find these out from data analysis alone. The continuous time solution is one possibility here, but we need to make a great number of assumptions (e.g., ergodicity) for this to work. This implies that the solution to these kinds of questions about the most appropriate time lags is not a dilemma that is easily fixed. The optimal time lag can be investigated, and it should be, but this takes a lot of extra effort (see McArdle & Woodcock, 1997). Otherwise, we are simply assuming that what we have done with longitudinal time lags is good for the changes we seek.

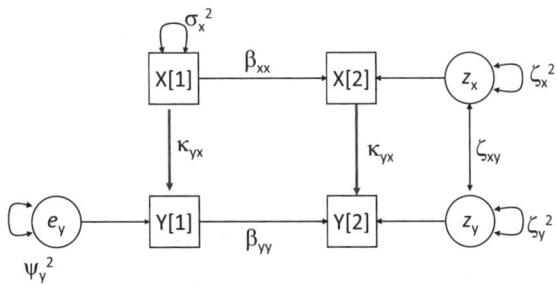

Figure 21.9. Gollob and Reichardt's alternative regression path model; $\gamma_x = \gamma_y = 0$ but $\kappa > 0$. Gollob and Reichardt concluded this is an "impoverished" use of longitudinal data because "effects take time" (cf. Bachman et al., 2002). From "Taking Account of Time Lags in Causal Models," by H. F. Gollob and C. S. Reichardt, 1987, *Child Development, 58*, pp. 80–92. Copyright 1987 by the Society for Research in Child Development. Reprinted with permission.

CHANGE REPRESENTATIONS OF CROSS-LAGGED REGRESSION

The prior cross-lagged regression models seem to have some basic change components, but it is somewhat difficult to tell where change is actually located. This issue can be clarified using models with two change scores, as in Exhibit 21.4. A path diagram of this model is included as Figure 21.10. In this diagram we have also included the means at Time 1 (μ_m) and the intercepts of the changes (α_m) as regression projections from the constant.

By a simple algebraic derivation, it is relatively easy to see some key relationships among these models. That is, we can easily see that the cross-lagged

---

EXHIBIT 21.4
The Crossed-Lagged Regression Model Expressed as a Latent Change Score

Let us first write both scores as observed changes:

(1) $\quad X[2]_n = X[1]_n + \Delta X[2]_n \quad \text{or} \quad \Delta X[2]_n = X[2]_n - X[1]_n$ and
$\quad Y[2]_n = Y[1]_n + \Delta Y[2]_n \quad \text{or} \quad \Delta Y[2]_n = Y[2]_n - Y[1]_n$.

Then suppose we write the basic cross-lagged model with these new changes as the outcomes. Because we are altering basic notation, we can now move to single subscripts and write

(2) $\quad \Delta X[2]_n = \alpha_x + \beta_x X[1]_n + \gamma_x Y[1]_n + z_{x,n}$ and
$\quad \Delta Y[2]_n = \alpha_y + \beta_y Y[1]_n + \gamma_y X[1]_n + z_{y,n}$

Now, we can, for example, add the Time 1 scores to each side of this expression

(3a) $\quad \Delta X[2]_n (+ X[1]_n) = \alpha_x + \beta_x X[1]_n + \gamma_x Y[1]_n + z_{x,n} (+ X[1]_n)$

and

(3b) $\quad \Delta Y[2]_n (+ Y[1]_n) = \alpha_y + \beta_y Y[1]_n + \gamma_y X[1]_n + z_{y,n} (+ Y[1]_n)$,

which is then equivalent to

(4a) $\quad X[2]_n = \alpha_x + \beta_x X[1]_n + X[1]_n + \gamma_x Y[1]_n + z_{x,n}$

and

(4b) $\quad Y[2]_n = \alpha_y + \beta_y Y[1]_n + Y[1]_n + \gamma_y X[1]_n + z_{y,n}$

and which now is seen to be equal to the original cross-lagged equations by writing

(5a) $\quad X[2]_n = \alpha_x + (1 + \beta_{xx}) X[1]_n + \gamma_x Y[1]_n + z_{x,n}$

and

(5b) $\quad Y[2]_n = \alpha_y + (1 + \beta_{yy}) Y[1]_n + \gamma_y X[1]_n + z_{y,n}$.

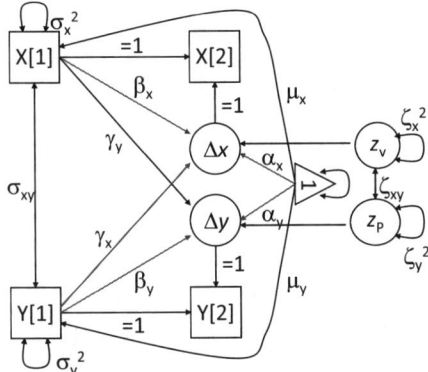

Figure 21.10. A two time-point change score model, including γ cross-regressions of slopes.

regression equations (Exhibit 21.1) have the prediction structure identical to the cross-lagged change equations (Exhibit 21.4). In fact, the intercepts of the score at Time 2 are the same (α_ξ), and the new autoregression is formally identical to one plus the prior lagged terms (the single subscript $\beta_m = 1 + \beta_{mm}$). This means, in using the change expression, we desire to index the *movement* or *instability* in the prior score. However, as we can see, the cross-lagged terms ($\gamma_m = \gamma_{jk}$) are identical to the corresponding change score model parameters. As before, the test statistics obtained by requiring extra constraints remain identical, and so do the limits to inference. We now know where the change is located, but we still have the other assumptions to consider. These are not simply arbitrary results, but when change is the key outcome, these clearly become a necessary feature of the changes. This also implies that the original cross-lagged model was about observed changes as well. Indeed, it is surprising that so few others noticed (but see Greenberg & Kessler, 1982).

CAUSAL INFERENCES FROM LONGITUDINAL DATA

This cross-lagged approach now raises an interesting issue about what has been termed *Granger causality* (see Granger, 1969). The key question raised in this early economic research was, "Can we determine whether one time series was useful in forecasting the other time series?" Crossed-lagged regressions typically reflect movement over specific time points, so they are not precisely the same as a time series, but it still is worthwhile to consider this possibility here. Granger initially suggested that a time series could reflect causal information. In this work, a measured time series X[t] is said to "Granger-cause" another measured variable Y[t] if it can be shown that in a model with lagged values of X and Y, those X values provide statistically significant information about future values of Y. The test for Granger causality starts with a regression of calculated $\Delta Y[t-1]$ on lagged values of calculated $\Delta Y[t]$. In any case, if the lagged values of calculated $\Delta X[t-1]$ add something to this prediction, then we say that X Granger-causes Y. Of course, we would like to have a completely clear story, such as X Granger-causes Y, but not the other way around. In practice, however, it may be found that neither variable Granger-causes the other, or that each of the two variables Granger-causes the other. Of course, the limitations of causal inference without the third variable (Z[t] or Z[t]) are still apparent. This implies that a two-occasion data set is not an optimal choice, and this test of changes predicting changes is not strictly used here because we only have two occasions of measures. In essence, we really want to predict $\Delta Y[t]$ from $Y[t-1]$ and $X[t-1]$ only (but see Figure 21.10).

The basic principle of causal inference remains the same as in time-series models. When we do, we must immediately point out the need in data collections for all relevant predictors. Because we all know that not everything important can be found and measured, formal causal inference is becoming a losing battle. So instead of using the important word *causal* for our results, we can say we are motivated by "causal thinking," but we are basically looking for *dynamic* predictors. These are the predictions of current behaviors based on past behaviors. This seems to be a reasonable choice.

The cross-lagged model also attempts to account for the prior level of the same variable before suggesting that we are able to make a dynamic time-dependent prediction. These kinds of dynamic predictors seem to be necessary in most formal theories of causality (see most any experimental psychology textbook, e.g., Woodworth, 1938, or Holland, 1986). This implies that although we recognize that a dynamic inference is not as good as a causal inference, we also know that a dynamic time-dependent inference is better than nothing at all. In fact, dynamic inferences may be all we will ever be able to have in observational longitudinal data.

As we mention at several points in this book, there seem to be many dissenters to this basic logic. A lot of the ideas we use here come from basic contributions of experimental psychology (see Woodworth, 1938). In statistics, many researchers now seem to follow the lead of Fisher (1925) and use a randomization-to-treatment principle as a condition for causation (for details, see Holland, 1986; Rubin, 1976). There should be no doubt that randomization is a very reasonable approach, and in this sense, we can certainly agree there is "no causation without manipulation" (Holland, 1986). But complete randomization is often very difficult to carry out for both logical and ethical reasons. For example, we can assign adults to a training group arm (as in the Berlin Age Training Study; McArdle, 2009), but we really cannot assign children to have a certain level of "Mother's Education," as in the Wechsler Intelligence Scale for Children, Fourth Edition (Wechsler, 2004) study (see McArdle & Aber, 1990). It is also clear how this cross-lagged logic could be misused in the search for Granger causality, and we must remember that there can be serious problems with almost any randomized manipulations as well (i.e., consider "incomplete assignment to groups" or "leakage of treatments"). About the most productive thing we can say is that the reader should be particularly cautious about making causal inferences from longitudinal data without first considering the extensive literature on this topic (e.g., Blalock, 1971, 1985a, 1985b; Saris & Stronkhorst, 1984; van der Laan & Robins, 2003).

Any numerical results will certainly not overcome the time-lag objections of O. D. Duncan (1969) or Gollob and Reichardt (1987), and we will not argue with either here. The numerical results of any model will be identical to the prior one, including the misfit indices, although the parameters are in a slightly different format. But perhaps now it will become obvious that the parameters are an estimate of changes over some period of time. In fact, because these results are simply reflections (see Exhibit 21.4) of what was learned above in the cross-lagged of latent change score analysis, they will not be presented in further detail.

22

ANALYSES BASED ON CROSS-LAGGED REGRESSION IN CHANGES OF FACTORS

As stated earlier, the regression model for "crossed-and-lagged" data is probably the most popular longitudinal structural equation model (LSEM), or even structural equation model (SEM) for that matter (O. D. Duncan, 1975). This is typically run when we have measured at least two different variables repeatedly over time: the crossing of X[1] and Y[1] and the lagging of X[1] and Y[2] as was demonstrated in Chapter 21. But suppose we have a larger set or vectors of variables measured at each time. For the sake of argument, let us say we have measurements of the same M variables using the same scoring systems and under the same conditions, so we think we now have M repeated measures at each time. In this case, we can try to extend repeated measures analysis of variance (RANOVA) to test for mean differences, and we can assume the multiple factorial invariance over time (MFIT) expressions, or we can just assume that the metric of each variable is the same, so the labels can be repeated as common factor scores, Y[t] and X[t]. The great benefit of doing the latter, assuming we have the correct number

http://dx.doi.org/10.1037/14440-023
Longitudinal Data Analysis Using Structural Equation Models, by J. J. McArdle and J. R. Nesselroade
Copyright © 2014 by the American Psychological Association. All rights reserved.

of factors, is that we now have new variables (i.e., factors) that are allegedly purged of measurement error. As we look back to the early work on observed change score analysis, this was a major problem. If we assume that each common factor is reliably measured, we can focus on the sequence of changes in the factor scores, and this is our main goal.

This basic result for latent change scores is consistent with previous multivariate work on this topic, especially by Nesselroade (e.g., Baltes & Nesselroade, 1973; Nesselroade, 1970, 1983; Nesselroade & Bartsch, 1977). In this work a clear distinction was made between factors representing *traits* ($F[1]$) and factors representing *states* (ΔF). These conclusions were not universally accepted because of confusion surrounding the use of the observed change score:

> Cattell (1966) suggested the more or less straightforward factoring of the intercorrelations of the algebraic difference scores (Occasion-2 minus Occasion-1 scores) as a way to determine patterns of change across multiple measures. The method, labeled differential-R technique (or dR technique) was examined in detail elsewhere (Nesselroade, 1970, 1973) and various modifications, such as using mean cross-products of differences instead of correlations, [were] proposed and tried out on empirical data. In addition to the more parochial objection to this approach—"It involves the unreliable difference score"—Humphreys (1961) and Horn (1963) condemned it on other, more scholarly grounds. Although the matter has not blossomed into an ostentatious debate, at its base lies a compelling point that, on examination, leads naturally into the introduction of a simple model encompassing both traits and states. (Nesselroade & Bartsch, 1977, p. 226)

This result is also consistent with most versions of the models presented by McArdle and Nesselroade (1994). Recall in this work that we first wrote the change scores as part of the model rather than as part of the data (following the model equations in Part II). That is, instead of creating the Δy by direct calculation in the data (i.e., $Y[2]-Y[1]$), the Δy were implied as latent variables by using fixed unit weights (i.e., $Y[2]_n = 1 * Y[1]_n + 1 * \Delta y_n$). Path diagrams illustrating this LSEM was presented in the Figures 17.2 through 17.4. In these figures, the simple restriction of pairs of fixed unit values (one pair per variable) across time allowed us to model differences at the level of the observations (Δy; Figure 17.2) and at the level of the common factors (ΔF; Figure 17.4). Assuming factor loading MFIT, one benefit of this simplification is that we can represent another important multivariate hypothesis: "Are all the mean changes over time in $Y[t]$ accounted for by changes in the common factors ($F[t]$)?" At first, this appears to be the question typically asked in the classical multivariate ANOVA hypothesis (e.g., Bock, 1975). However, it is not what is being asked in RANOVA at all.

In this structural factor analysis, we represent the mean of the latent change factor (μDF), under the restriction that the same factor loadings describing the covariances among variables can also represent the mean changes in the same variables.

CROSS-LAGGED REGRESSION MODEL OF COMMON FACTORS

The basic cross-lagged model of common factor scores was initially advocated and used by Jöreskog and Sörbom (1976), and their original path diagram is represented as Figure 22.1. As can be seen, their original model did have lagged impacts but did not have any crossed impacts. Instead, this model emphasized the possibility of adding correlated specifics, with two-headed arrows from one variable to the same variable at a later time. Of most importance to us, they included invariant common factors as part of their expressions. We emphasize only this last feature here, but we recognize that much more could be included as well.

In Figure 22.1 we assume we have two factor scores ($x[t]$ and $y[t]$) within each time, and we define the MFIT restrictions so each observed score has its own intercept (ι_m), slope (λ_m), and unique variance ($\psi_m[t]^2$). To the degree

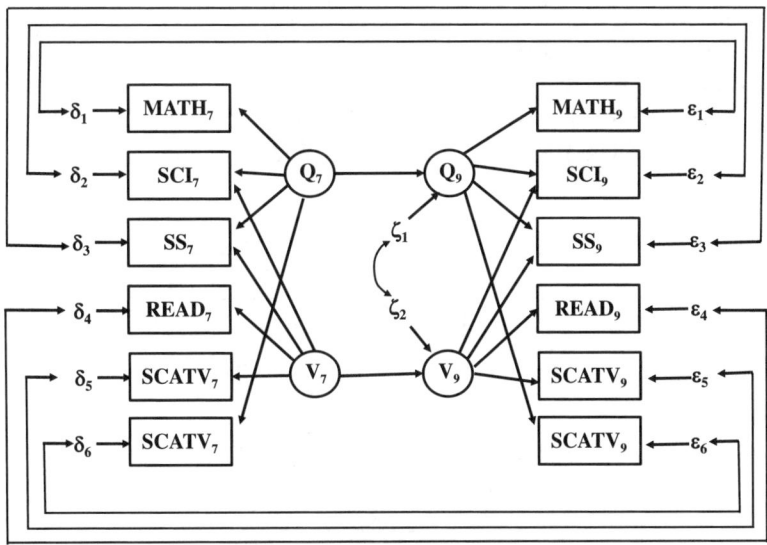

Figure 22.1. A classical bivariate longitudinal factor analysis model. From *Advances in Psychological and Educational Measurement* (pp. 135–157), by D. N. De Gruijter and L. J. T. van der Kamp (Eds.), 1976. London, England: Wiley. Copyright 1976 by John Wiley & Sons, Inc. Adapted with permission.

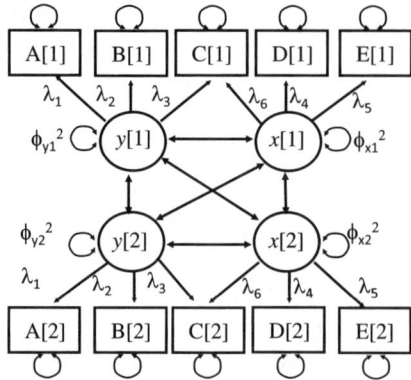

Figure 22.2. A two-occasion measurement model with metric factorial invariance over time.

that this model fits the data (and we realize it might not fit), we can imply that each common factor at Time 1 has the same substantive meaning at Time 2. This representation is the same as the models presented and earlier studies by Jöreskog and Sörbom (1976, 1979).

If the common factors are indeed considered repeated, and they meet MFIT criteria, then we can next consider a score model from crossed-and-lagged panel analysis (Hsiao, 2005; Jöreskog & Sörbom, 1979), but now for the common factors as in Figures 22.2 and 22.3. This type of model can be written here by substituting the factor score labels where we again broadly assert that the "past leads to the future." This basically means that factor scores at Time 1 lead to and affect the factor scores at Time 2; that is the key scores are now common factors devoid of measurement errors. We have

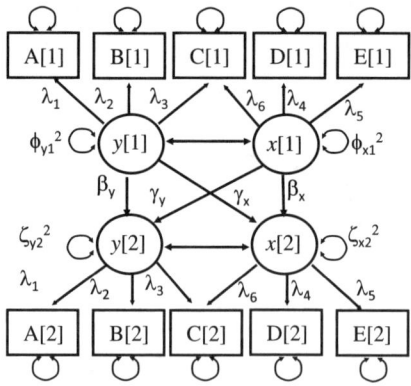

Figure 22.3. A two-occasion measurement model with multiple factorial invariance over time and cross-lagged regressions.

included the required common factor intercept terms as well (i.e., v_k) because these could be associated with either of the measured variables of the common factors. We can now set any parameter to any value, but we usually have the same restrictions as the cross-lagged model. As usual, we hardly ever fit models where the effects are considered equal (i.e., $\gamma_{xy} = \gamma_{yx}$) because these are common factor regression terms and this would require a nonarbitrary equal scaling of the Time 1 factors. Although these factors can be forced to be the same, this is often quite arbitrary, and it does not imply that they actually are the same size at the first time. If each did include the same measures at the first time, invariance could be achieved, and this test could be done.

If MFIT does occur, we can assume the factors at Time 1 have both a lagged effect (βxx and βyy) on the same repeated factor and a crossed effect (γxy and γyx) on the other factor, which is depicted in Figure 22.3. If this LSEM is true, then there are actually two separate but possibly correlated disturbance terms (z_g and z_h). Regressions are typically used in these LSEMs to overcome the special problems created by correlations (as in Figure 22.4). If we can assume MFIT, then all the prior expressions and assumptions of the last section hold. The use of correlated specifics with these common factors (Nesselroade & Baltes, 1984) does not rule out the principles of the cross-lagged regression among the common factors, but it may rule out some of the common factor change models presented next.

The basic rationale for using common factors is that they do not include the unique components, so these common factor scores that we use in the cross-lagged regression do not include error of measurements. This is a fundamental goal of longitudinal change analysis, because we know that the change scores could be affected by the presence of random errors of measurement (see the

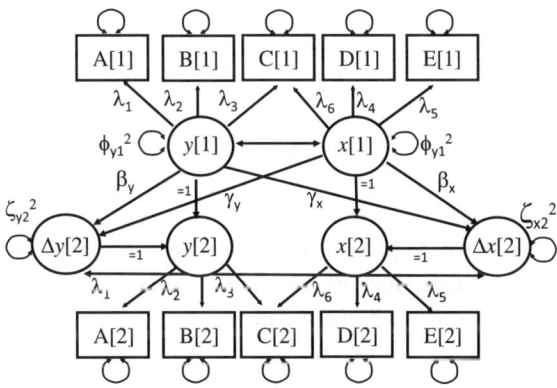

Figure 22.4. A two-occasion measurement model with multiple factorial invariance over time and latent change cross-lagged regressions.

models in Part II of this volume). The alteration of the cross-lagged model from using change scores is trivial at best, and we have included changes in the common factor scores in Figure 22.4. Unfortunately, the common factors have this important property only if we assume the definition of MFIT is correct for the data. Perhaps we should also recognize that these common factor scores do not include any of the specific factors either, so differences in results could exist between the composites (which do include specifics) and the common factors (which do not). These are empirical questions that we think should be consider, and we will consider them in later chapters.

BASIC ISSUES IN CROSS-LAGGED REGRESSION OF COMMON FACTORS

As just mentioned, the issues that arose in cross-lagged regression are basically the same here. The same logic used earlier for measured variables applied to our understanding of the common factors. That is, we can simply look at the values (and possibly the standard errors and significance) of the crossed coefficients to get some idea of the sequential impacts (i.e., do the factor scores $y \to x$ or does $x \to y$) in light of the lagged features. But because crossed coefficients often represent critical issues of inference, we can use this general SEM approach in a more sophisticated fashion. To further specify and fit an alternative model where $y[1]$ does not impact $x[2]$ (i.e., $\gamma xy = 0$), we simply alter the expectations of the common factors. If this model still fits the data as well as the previous and less-restricted model, we conclude that we have no evidence for an effect of $y \to x$. To deal with the bigger questions, we can also fit alternative models, where $x[1]$ does not impact $y[2]$ (i.e., $\gamma yx = 0$) or where neither factor affects the other (i.e., $\gamma xy = 0$, $\gamma yx = 0$) and possibly other models too.

This basic use of cross-lagged common factors is supposedly an improvement on the classical way to examine causality in observational data, largely because we have removed the unique variables before examining the dynamic effects (see Jöreskog & Sörbom, 1979). This could be an improvement, but it certainly requires that we have the correct positioning of the latent factors. In general, there are clear limits to this type of common factor modeling. Let us restate that we may actually have the wrong common factors and the concept of splitting off the unique factors is simply wrong. The critical limit of observational data is not altered by having common factors because some unmeasured factor ($z[t]$) may actually cause both other factors, so this is still relevant. For this reason, we still require that all key variables be measured, but, without any doubt, we hope that these kinds of SEMs are useful to create a basic understanding of the sequential inferences. This has a better chance when multiple indicators are used, but this still does not ensure anything. It has also been shown that recent work on mediation modeling, even when done in the context of common factors, can be quite misleading (see Cole & Maxwell, 2003).

CHANGE REPRESENTATIONS OF CROSS-LAGGED REGRESSION OF COMMON FACTORS

The prior cross-lagged regression models of factor scores seem to have some change components, but it is somewhat difficult to tell where these actually are. This may be further compounded when we move the model up a level, so to speak, to include common factors. This approach can be clarified using models with two change scores (see Exhibits 22.1 and 22.2).

By this simple algebraic derivation, it is relatively easy to see the relationships among these models. A model of this type without intercepts was presented in Figure 22.3. As before, the Time 1 latent intercepts and the cross-lagged terms (γ_{jk}) are completely identical to the corresponding latent change score parameters, whereas the autoregressions are seen as identical to one plus the prior lagged terms ($1 + \beta_{mm}$), and the intercepts of the changes (α_m) is a new parameter. The test statistics obtained by requiring extra constraints are

---

EXHIBIT 22.1
The Crossed-Lagged Regression Model With Latent Factors

Let us now assume that we have two factor scores ($y[t]$ and $x[t]$) within each time, and we define the multiple factorial invariance over time restrictions of

(1a) $\qquad X[t]_n = \iota_x + \lambda_x x[t]_n + u_x[t]_n$

and

(1b) $\qquad Y[t]_n = \iota_y + \lambda_y y[t]_n + u_y[t]_n$

so each observed score has its own intercept (ι_m), slope (λ_m), and unique score ($u_m[t]$). This type of model can be written here as

(2a) $\qquad y[2]_n = \alpha_g + \beta_{yy} y[1]_n + \gamma_{yx} x[1]_n + z_{g,n}$

and

(2b) $\qquad x[2]_n = \alpha_h + \beta_{xx} x[1]_n + \gamma_{xy} y[1]_n + z_{h,n}$

where we again broadly assert that the "past leads to the future," that is, factor scores at Time 1 lead to and affect factor scores at Time 2, and the key scores are now common factors devoid of measurement errors.

EXHIBIT 22.2
The Crossed-Lagged Change Score Model With Latent Factors

Although there is really no alteration required, let us next write both common factor scores as latent changes

(1a) $$y[2]_n = y[1]_n + \Delta y[2]_n \quad \text{or} \quad \Delta y[2]_n = y[2]_n - y[1]_n$$

and

(1b) $$x[2]_n = x[1]_n + \Delta x[2]_n \quad \text{or} \quad \Delta x[2]_{y,n} = x[2]_n - x[1]_n.$$

Then suppose we write the basic cross-lagged model with these changes as the outcomes

(2a) $$\Delta y[2]_n = \alpha_y Q\{1\}_n + \beta_y y[1]_n + \gamma_y x[1]_n + z_{y,n}$$

and

(2b) $$\Delta x[2]_n = \alpha_x P\{1\}_n + \beta_x x[1]_n + \gamma_x y[1]_n + z_{x,n}.$$

To examine the assumptions about of change in the cross-lagged context we can, for example, do as before and simply rewrite this model as

(3a) $$y[2]_n = \alpha_y Q\{1\}_n + (1+\beta_y)y[1]_n + \gamma_y x[1]_n + z_{y,n}$$

and

(3b) $$x[2]_n = \alpha_x P\{1\}_n + (1+\beta_x)x[1]_n + \gamma_x y[1]_n + z_{x,n}.$$

and we can easily see that the models will have the identical prediction structure.

---

the same, as are the limits to inference. These results, when latent changes in the common factors are the key outcomes, remain a key feature of changes.

Of course, the major caution we assert is that if MFIT does not exist, we have no real reason to treat these scores as if they were "repeated." This implies that if only a few of the variables hold MFIT (i.e., what has been termed *partial invariance*), then only those variables can be used in the ways described here. This is not completely devastating, and it could be meaningful, but it is not exactly what we propose here. In sum, we suggest we should deal with complexity of factor patterns rather than with factor scores. A rather complex version of this two-occasion invariant factors model is seen in Figures 22.3 and 22.4. This special type of model was used in a recent analysis by McArdle and Prindle (2008), and one diagram of these results is presented in Figure 22.5, which includes a nonoverlapping and invariant factor pattern over two occasion, and the numerical results are displayed (for independent groups) for the entire change structure.

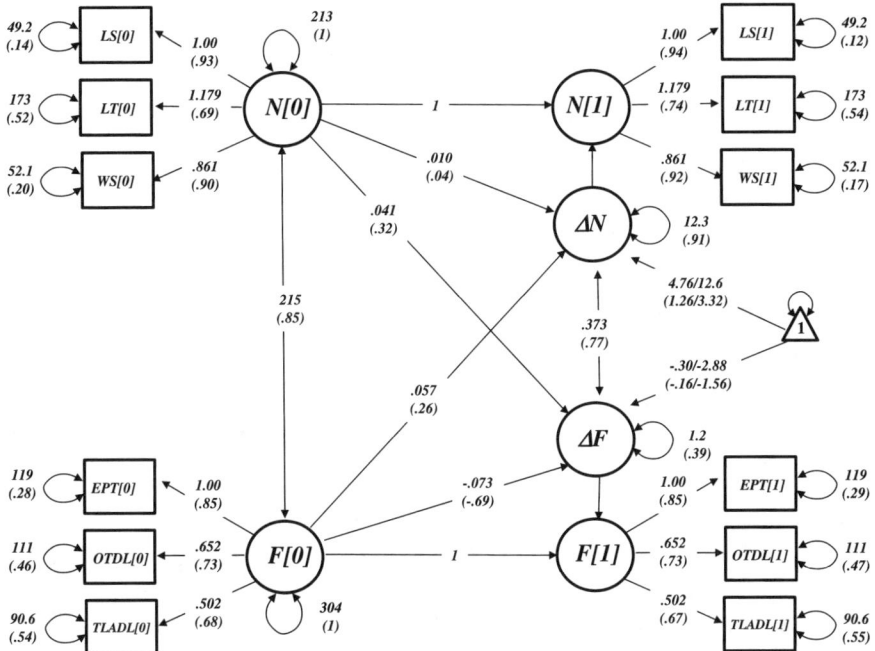

Figure 22.5. A latent change score model for common factors with multiple groups. Adapted from "A Latent Change Score Analysis of a Randomized Clinical Trial in Reasoning Training," by J. J. McArdle and J. J. Prindle, 2008, *Psychology and Aging, 23,* p. 710. Copyright 2008 by the American Psychological Association.

23

CURRENT MODELS FOR MULTIPLE LONGITUDINAL OUTCOME SCORES

What are the alternative longitudinal structural equation models for change with multiple occasions? That is, suppose $T > 2$? As it turns out, assuming we do not count all possible variations of repeated measures analysis of variance (RANOVA), there are only a very few alternatives to standard multivariate analysis. Our models here are limited by the need to have a theory of changes. For example, we need to know that the parameters for one time period might not be the same as for any other time period, and we can start with these simplifying assumptions. Do we need to add multiple outcome variables to this problem? No, but we will do so by using multiple factorial invariance over time (MFIT) common factors, and this will simplify many concerns as well.

Obviously, there are many statistical models we could use, but four special types of models seem popular so they are selected and presented in further detail here. We notice that all such models allow the use of composites or common factors, so we will reconsider this issue here.

---

http://dx.doi.org/10.1037/14440-024
Longitudinal Data Analysis Using Structural Equation Models, by J. J. McArdle and J. R. Nesselroade
Copyright © 2014 by the American Psychological Association. All rights reserved.

DOUBLY REPEATED MEASURES MODELS

By far and away, the most popular model for multiple repeated measures is a variation on RANOVA that deal with multiple outcomes. This model can be written in the same way as before but with two outcomes (see Exhibit 23.1). Here each measured time series (Y[t], X[t]) variable has an initial level (Q{0}, P{0}) with means, variances, and covariances, and each variable has a specific basis function ($\omega_x[t]$, $\omega_y[t]$) allowing these variables to

---

EXHIBIT 23.1
The Model of Doubly Repeated Measures

The repeated measures analysis of variance model can be written for two different variables as

(1a) $$Y[t]_n = Q\{0\}_n + Q\{1\}\omega_y[t] + e_y[t]_n$$

and

(1b) $$X[t]_n = P\{0\}_n + P\{1\}\omega_x[t] + e_x[t]_n$$

so each variable has an initial level (Q{0}, P{0}) with means, variances, and covariances, and each variable has a specific basis function ($\omega_x[t]$, $\omega_y[t]$) allowing these variables to have different shapes over time. The residual terms could be correlated as well.

In addition, we can write group effects on both the levels and slopes, by writing

(2a) $$Q\{0\}_n = v_{0y} + \gamma_{0y}G_n + z_y\{0\}_n, \quad \text{and} \quad Q\{1\} = v_{1y} + \gamma_{1y}G_n$$

and

(2b) $$P\{0\}_n = v_{0x} + \gamma_{0x}G_n + z_x\{0\}_n, \quad \text{and} \quad P\{1\} = v_{1x} + \gamma_{1x}G_n$$

where the slopes have no explicit residuals, but the disturbances from the initial levels could be correlated. Now we can write the canonical score (C1) form of

(3) $$(X[t]_n - \beta_{c1}Y[t]_n) = C1 = Q\{0\}_n + Q\{1\}\omega_{c1}[t] + e_{c1}[t]_n$$

so that we have a linear combination of the observed scores and it has a latent curve model change pattern over time. In addition, we can ask if are there any set of weights (β_{cg}) that maximize a possibly different canonical score (Cg) of the group differences in changes over time, written here as

(3b) $$(X[t]_n - \beta_{cg}Y[t]_n) = Cg = Q\{0\}_n + Q\{1\}\omega_{cg}[t] + e_{cg}[t]_n$$
$$Q\{1\} = v_{1g} + \gamma_{1g}G_n$$

---

have different shapes over time. The residual error terms could be correlated as well. We can also add group effects on both the levels and slopes, and although neither slope allows a residual, the disturbances from the initial levels could be correlated. A seemingly more sophisticated approach is to be to find a set of weights (β_1) that optimize this relationship among scores, so we could even write the canonical score (C1) form of the model, so that we have a linear combination of the observed scores, which has a latent curve model (LCM) change pattern over time. This is designed to answer the question "Are there any set of weights (β_1) that can yield a maximum change over time, and if so, are the changes significant?" In addition, we can ask, "Is there any set of weights (β_g) that maximizes a possibly different canonical score (C_g) of the group differences in changes over time?"

Notice the two big caveats here. First, the canonical scores (C_1 and C_g) are both restricted to be linear contrasts of the original scores by the selection of weights (β_1 and β_g). Second, the canonical scores are not restricted to be of the same structure, so the average change is not necessarily related to the change over groups. This is done as a canonical calculation, which is of closed form, so it is quite naturally very popular (e.g., Cooley & Lohnes, 1971). This approach is undeniably useful when the goal of testing is to see whether or not some linear combination of the original variables could capture change over time and change in groups over time.

As it turns out, these are not models often used by structural equation modeling (SEM) enthusiasts. But in a related standard approach, termed *doubly repeated measures* models, we allow for a test of the mean differences of optimal composite scores that is very flexible in testing hypotheses about the means over time. As always, there is nothing wrong with this type of closed-form analysis, as long as we realize what it is doing (see Bock, 1975; O'Brien & Kaiser, 1978).

CROSS-LAGGED MODELS WITH COMPOSITES OR COMMON FACTORS

The next most popular SEM is probably the crossed-lagged model for many occasions, and it looks very similar. First we assume we have mean deviated measured variables leading to mean deviated common factors at each time point (see Exhibit 23.2). As we also know, if we have enough observed data at multiple time points ($T > 2$), we do not need multiple indicators to estimate the factor loadings (λ_m). Instead, we can assume that they meet MFIT criteria and obtain the uniqueness (ψ_m^2) of the composite scores.

In any case, the rest of the model can be written as the usual first-order form, where t = 1 to $T > 2$. Once again, we know that the parameters for one

EXHIBIT 23.2
Alternative Multivariate Models With Common Factor Scores

Let us assume that we have mean deviated measured variables leading to mean deviated common factors at each time point

(1a) $$Y[t]_n^* = \lambda_y y[t]_n^* + u_y[t]_n$$

and

(1b) $$X[t]_n^* = \lambda_x x[t]_n^* + u_x[t]_n.$$

In this case, the rest of the cross-lagged model can be written as the usual first-order form of

(2a) $$y[t]_n^* = \beta_{yy} y[t-1]_n^* + \gamma_{yx} x[t-1]_n^* + z_{q,n}$$

and

(2b) $$x[t]_n^* = \beta_{xx} x[t-1]_n^* + \gamma_{xy} y[t-1]_n^* + z_{p,n}$$

where $t = 1$ to $T > 2$.

This alternative latent curve model (LCM) can be written in two parts as

(3a) $$Y[t]_n = Q\{0\}_n + \omega[t]_y Q\{1\}_n + u_y[t]_n$$

and

(3b) $$X[t]_n = P\{0\}_n + \omega[t]_x P\{1\}_n + u_x[t]_n$$

so, to start, there can be a LCM for each variable.

---

time period might not be the same as for any other time period, but we can most easily start with these equality assumptions. This popular cross-lagged common factors model is depicted in Figure 23.1.

CONSISTENCY OF CROSS-LAGS

It has been shown that we can examine the model of consistency in panel designs (Greenberg & Kessler, 1982; Greenberg, Kessler, & Logan, 1979). In this general approach, more than two time points are required ($T > 2$), and all first-order regression coefficients representing the same information (i.e., the effects $X[1] \rightarrow X[2] = X[2] \rightarrow X[3]$) are assumed to be of

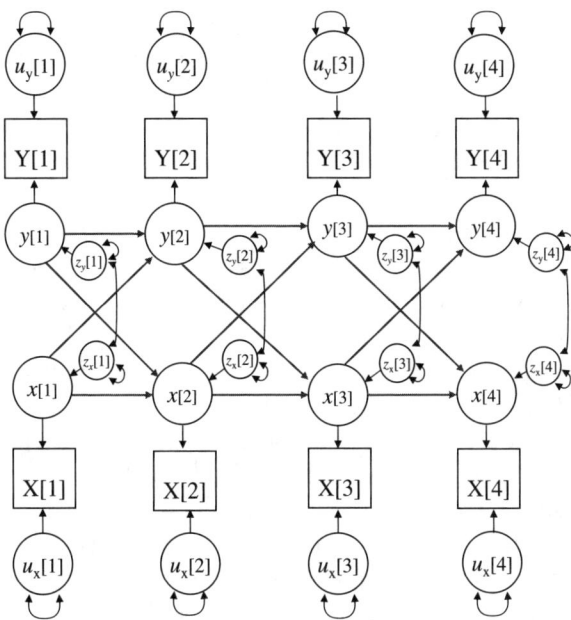

Figure 23.1. Cross-lagged latent regression model with invariant factor patterns.

identical size. This restriction is placed on the coefficients to help identify the within-time effects (both feedbacks of Y[t] → X[t] and X[t] → Y[t]). These restrictions seem very reasonable if (a) the assumptions of stationarity and equilibrium exist, (2) the process is measured over equivalent gaps in time (i.e., $\Delta t = 1$), (3) there are no higher order effects (i.e., all X[1] → X[3] = 0), and also, (4) the model has no lurking inputs (z[t]). However, the author(s) point out at several junctures that they are fitting this model of consistency mainly to let the "data speak up" and presumably tell us where these restrictions were incorrect. This overall modeling idea has a lot of merit.

The basic questions we can ask of this cross-lagged model of multiple times are straightforward: (a) "Are the common factors invariant over all occasions?" (b) "Is the influence of all measured variables carried only by the common factors?" (c) "Are the parameters of influence always the same at all time periods (i.e., consistency)?" (d) "Are the common factor covariances always the same (i.e., stationarity)?" and (e) "What happens to the means over time (equilibrium)?"

This cross-lagged model has been used by many contemporary researchers (e.g., Hawkley, Thisted, Masi, & Cacioppo, 2010), often examining the covariances over time just after running a multivariate ANOVA model for doubly repeated observations (see above). Now we can ask, "Does this two-part approach, first analyzing means and then analyzing covariances, represent a good longitudinal SEM (LSEM) analysis of the changes in the scores?" This can be a substantive choice, but it may not be the best option.

LCMs WITH COMPOSITES OR COMMON FACTORS

Another alternative model for the same data is presented in Figure 23.2. In this case the model could rely on the same kind of common factors, but instead we write out the LCM for each variable and then correlate the slopes. This model is written in two parts: (1) first as an LCM for each variable and then (2) as a model of the covariances of these latent variables (P{0}, P{1}, Q{0}, Q{1}). Putting two measured longitudinal variables (X[t] and Y[t]) together in the model allows many testable hypotheses, including whether the slopes are correlated ("Does $\rho[P\{1\}, Q\{1\}] = 0$?") and also whether the loadings (i.e., shapes) of the changes are parallel ("Does $\Omega[P\{1\}] = \Omega[Q\{1\}]$?").

This type of mean and covariance model now seems to be popular under the name *parallel growth curve* model (Muthén & Muthén, 2002b), and this approach was once even advocated by one of us (McArdle, 1989). The reasons for this are clear. It surely seems that the correlations in the way people change could be answered in this model, and any hypothesis of parallel shapes could be answered as well. In any case, this model does allow all of these tests without the intrusion of measurement errors (i.e., ψ_x^2, ψ_y^2). Indeed, as of this date, the virtues of this multivariate model seem be useful to many substantive researchers (e.g., Walker, Acock, Bowman, & Li, 1996).

But this interesting set of alternative models can also be seen as misleading in a number of ways. First, the correlation of the slopes does not

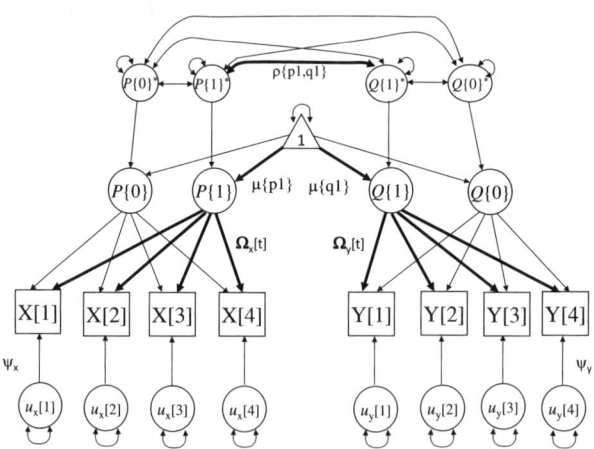

Figure 23.2. Alternative bivariate latent growth curves with correlated slopes.

fully represent the connection of the common factors of changes over time, and this is usually what we are after (Hertzog, Lindenberger, Ghisletta, & Oertzen, 2006). That is, if we want to know if the two slopes have any connection at all, we need to eliminate all model parameters dealing with their connection, and this would need to include at least two other model parameters. To form a hypothesis of "no connection," we need to place constraints in three parameters, all of which connect the common latent variables. If these constraints fit the data, it would imply that the two variables are likely to be unconnected. In this case, the difference in misfit could then be used as an index of connectedness. We could also add that connectedness hypotheses are about all time points used here, so they are not specifically about any pre–post predictions. Second, if we want to test hypotheses about true parallel changes, we might need to consider additional model parameters, such as the equality of the latent slope means over variables (i.e., $\mu(Q\{1\}) = \mu(P\{1\})$; McArdle, 1989).

Another alteration of this model that could be considered from this initial dual LCM starting point is one where the two latent slopes ($Q\{1\}$, $P\{1\}$) are considered a function of the two latent levels ($Q\{0\}$, $P\{0\}$ (see Snyder et al., 2003). Presumably this is an effort to mimic the dynamic interpretations of the cross-lagged model of influences over time, by writing a model where there is an LCM-based cross-lagged change model of latent factors (as in Chapter 22).

If this model is used, we must also assume that the latent levels emerged before (in time) the latent slopes. Unfortunately, this is usually not a feasible or testable assumption in observational data. Most often in observational data we simply assume both latent influences emerge at the same time, and we give no time-order precedence to the latent levels and latent slopes, and if we stop to think about it, this strict timing assumption is true of many models of data analysis. This specific LCM allows for flexible model-fitting procedures where we can alter the position of the latent level as needed. If there is a natural zero point in the data (i.e., everyone starts the series on the day after an operation), then this bivariate approach might be useful, but in most cases the model parameters that emerge for a parallel analysis of this kind can be confusing (e.g., Snyder et al., 2003).

TIME-VARYING COVARIATE MODELS

This seems like the best term possible for a model, and it was developed in a rigorous fashion by Cox (1972) and is now depicted in Figure 23.3 and Exhibit 23.3. As with the other SEMs, there is really nothing wrong with this model; it can be very useful in terms of treatment effects (McCoach &

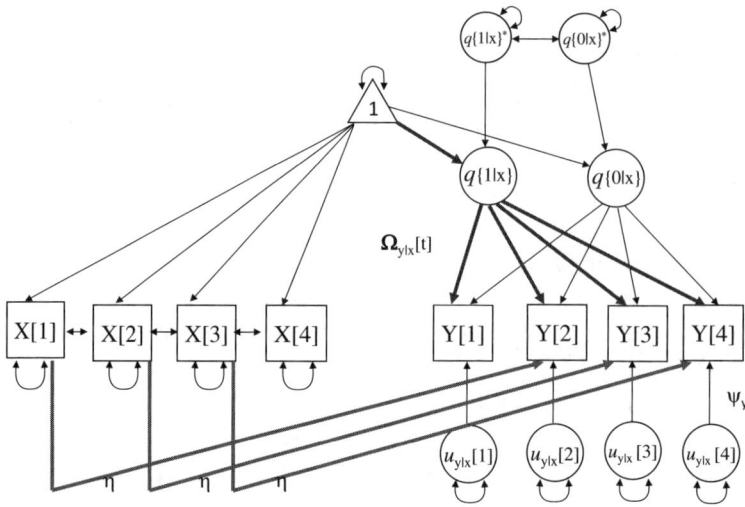

Figure 23.3. A time-varying lagged covariate X[t − 1] in a latent growth curve for Y[t].

Kaniskan, 2010) and is often expected to pick up on other dynamic influences, but does not seem to do so. In this model we assume that we have at least two measured time series (X[t] and Y[t]), where both variables can change over time and one influences to other.

At the outset we should point out that the original model (Cox, 1972) was based on variables that had a categorical origin, and multiple survival concepts were evident, but now these concepts are used for variables that are quantitative (or continuous) in origin. To consider this quantitative model, we can write one of the variables as an outcome so we basically have a multilevel change process (see Exhibit 23.2 and Chapter 11). This is usually considered as an LCM form after the effect of X[t] is removed, and the coefficient of the effect (γ_{yx}) of earlier X[t−1] on later Y[t] is itself presumed to be the invariant over all occasions. Perhaps one reason this model is so popular is that is can easily be fitted using virtually any multilevel software program (see Snijders & Bosker, 1999).

This interpretation of dynamic inferences based on a partialling out procedure should not be understated. This time-varying covariate (TVC) model basically takes away variation due to one influence (X[t]) so we can look at the residual LCM components. Presumably, if anything was removed (in Y[t]), it was due to the presence of the covariate (X[t]). Thus, the more complete linear impact of X[t] on Y[t] is obtained indirectly. If the covariate was not manipulated, it may be useful to examine the model the other ways too. That is, maybe the alternative is true: "Does Y[t] impact X[t]?" If this additional relationship were of interest to us, we would also need to write the

EXHIBIT 23.3
Alternative LCM Multivariate Models With Common Factor Scores

Fitting two variables together in a model allows many testable hypotheses, including

(1a) $$E\{Q\{1\}^*, P\{1\}^{*'}\} = 0,$$

and

(1b) $$\omega[t]_y = \omega[t]_x.$$

The hypothesis of "no connection" can be fitted by placing constraints on any of three parameters,

(2a) $$E\{Q\{0\}, P\{1\}\} = 0,$$

and

(2b) $$E\{P\{0\}, Q\{1\}\} = 0,$$

and

(2c) $$E\{Q\{1\}, P\{0\}\} = 0.$$

We can try to mimic the dynamic interpretations of the cross-lagged model of influences over time, by writing

(3a) $$Q\{1\}_n = \beta_{q0} Q\{0\}_n + \gamma_{q0} P\{0\}_n + z_{q,n}$$

and

(3b) $$P\{1\}_n = \beta_{p0} P\{0\}_n + \gamma_{p0} Q\{0\}_n + z_{p,n}$$

but this only applied to situations where the level temporally is ahead of the slope.

To consider the time-varying covariate model, we can pick one outcome series (Y[t]) and one input series (X[t]) and write

(4a) $$Y[t]_n = Q\{0|x\}_n + Q\{1|x\}_n \omega_y[t]|x + \beta_y X[t-1]_n + u_y[t]_n.$$

After fitting this model, we may also write the reverse model, where

(4b) $$X[t]_n = P\{0|y\}_n + P\{1|y\}_n \omega_x[t]|y + \beta_y Y[t-1]_n + u_x[t]_n.$$

additional expression for X[t] so the Y[t − 1] could impact the X[t] as well. If this is what is desired, then this is a good model of choice. Another unresolved issue is about what appropriate time lag is best (t − 1 is typically used here) and whether or not the effect coefficients are constant over all occasions. Although this is seen here as a relatively simple model of multivariate partialling, without any doubt, this approach clearly has the best moniker (i.e., TVC) of all models presented here.

Additional graphic illustrations will show only a sampling of the family of curves that can be generated from the few model parameters. Tests for these kinds of bivariate models are well-known in the SEM literature. A more challenging set of models consists of those based on *dynamical systems models*, which are often not fully specified in SEM terms. However, let us now consider a bivariate model of change where we write the prior change equation for more than one dynamic variable.

24

THE BIVARIATE LATENT CHANGE SCORE MODEL FOR MULTIPLE OCCASIONS

Each of the multiple outcome models just presented has strengths and weaknesses in real-life data analysis. We will now move back to the real data with these formal issues in mind. Of course, there are many alternative longitudinal structural equation models (LSEMs) that can be fitted to most any kind of longitudinal data. Some of these models even take into account the ordering of responses. But these technical and substantive issues are hard to organize and understand in the way they are usually presented. What we would like to have is a single model that combines the best of all the ideas just presented. We also do not want to lose anything useful in the translation, and we do not want to make assumptions that are unreasonable. To do all of this, we will define an alternative approach, created for this purpose (McArdle, 2009), termed a *bivariate latent change score* model (BLCS).

BIVARIATE CHANGE MODELS DEFINED

Following the previous work on common factor analysis and cross-lagged regression (Horn & McArdle, 1980; Jöreskog & Sörbom, 1979), we can assume that, for the measured variable X[t], the observed raw score can be decomposed into the sum of a common factor score ($x[t]$ or $F[t]$) and a unique factor score ($u[t]$). The same will be true for the measured Y[t]. In this way we can illustrate a latent variable without having multiple indicators. The prior work by Jöreskog (1971) and Heise (1974) showed alternative ways these parameters can be identified. This type of algebraic form is depicted in the path diagram of Figure 24.1 with latent scores and unique scores summing to each other (i.e., with unit weights) to form the observed variables. Of course, other factor analysis models could be used as well. The restrictive assumptions about random errors imply that the true scores include any common factors as well as any specific factors.

We next represent the changes within a person over time (see Exhibit 24.1). We define a latent change score (LCS) between any two latent scores as the part

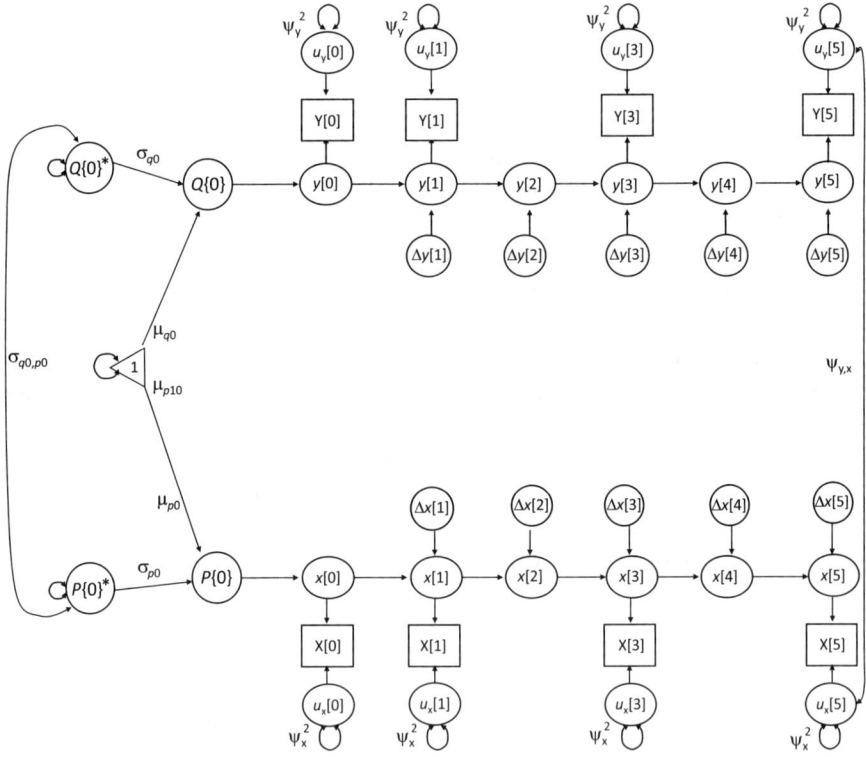

Figure 24.1. A bivariate baseline model for correlated levels and no changes.

EXHIBIT 24.1
A Bivariate Latent Change Score Model

Let us now assume that we have two common factor scores ($F1[t]$ and $F2[t]$) within each time and we define the usual multiple factorial invariance over time restrictions of

(1a) $$Y[t]_{mn} = \iota_{ym} + \lambda_{ym} F1[t]_n + u_{ym}[t]_n$$

and

(1b) $$X[t]_{mn} = \iota_{xm} + \lambda_{xm} F2[t]_n + u_{xm}[t]_n$$

so each observed score has an intercept (ι_m), a slope (λ_m), and a uniqueness ($u_m[t]$), possibly broken up into $F1[t]$ and $F2[t]$ common factor scores over time.
Let us next write both scores as latent changes

(2a) $$F1[t]_n = F1[t-1]_n + \Delta F1[t]_n \text{ or } \Delta F1[t]_n = F1[t]_n - F1[t-1]_n$$

and

(2b) $$F2[t]_n = F2[t-1]_n + \Delta F2[t]_n \text{ or } \Delta F2[t]_n = F2[t]_n - F2[t-1]_n.$$

This automatically leads to a set of mean and covariance expectations that can be summarized by writing

(3a) $$F1[t]_{mn} = Q\{0\}_n + \sum (j=1 \text{ to } t)\{\Delta F1[j]_n\} + u_{ym}[t]_n,$$

and

(3b) $$F2[t]_{mn} = P\{0\}_n + \sum (j=1 \text{ to } t)\{\Delta F2[j]_n\} + u_{xm}[t]_n.$$

The implied changes can be written symbolically as

(4a) $$\Delta F1[t]_n = fun\{\alpha_1, \beta_1, \gamma_1, F1[t-1]_n, F2[t-1]_n, z_{1,n}\}$$

and

(4b) $$\Delta F2[t]_n = fun\{\alpha_2, \beta_2, \gamma_2, F2[t-1]_n, F1[t-1]_n, z_{2,n}\}.$$

Note. Adapted from *New Methods for the Analysis of Change* (pp. 139–176), by L. M. Collins and A. G. Sayer (Eds.), 2001, Washington, DC: American Psychological Association. Copyright 2001 by the American Psychological Association.

---

of a later latent score at one time that is not part of it at the earlier time. That is, let us now assume that we have two factor scores ($F1[t]$ and $F2[t]$ or simply $x[t]$ and $y[t]$) within each time (as in Figure 24.1), and that we define the usual multiple factorial invariance over time (MFIT) restrictions so each observed score has an intercept (ι_m), a slope (λ_m), and a uniqueness ($\psi_m[t]^2$) possibly broken up into $x[t]$ and $y[t]$ common factor scores over time. We have found we do not need to measure everyone at all occasions, and here we assume no one is measured at Time 2 or Time 4 (following McArdle & Aber, 1990). Once again, we will simplify the required algebra by always assuming that the interval of time between latent variables is the same, even if this is not true of the measured observations (McArdle & Woodcock, 1997). Of course, this data description can be altered as needed.

These issues can be clarified using models with two change scores. We can first consider the full cross-lagged model with the same coefficients over all times but with these new changes as the outcomes. This implies that the trajectory of any measured score is now a function of the latent initial level, an accumulation of latent changes, and a unique latent variable. This is the same as the LCS model, but now the explicit changes can be function of anything we have in the model. This can be written using anything that could be used to describe the simultaneous changes that accumulate over time (see Exhibit 24.1). Of course, this is just a small sampling of the kinds of models we can accumulate now.

This also implies that different variations of our basic change models could lead to different model expectations (see Exhibit 24.2). For example, we could have a model where we write that the changes are not a function of anything else, so the model expectations suggest that nothing changes, and we would have a model like the path diagram of Figure 24.1, which will be commonly used as a baseline model in our analyses.

In a model where the changes are both additive and correlated, we might write a different model so the bivariate model expectations lead to a parallel change score model, as drawn as Figure 24.2. If we then force all the coefficients to be unity (i.e., $\lambda_x = 1$), it is the same as having two linear slopes for two variables, and we could fit such a model easily. In an alternative model where the changes are both additive and proportional, but also correlated, we might write a model where the bivariate expectations lead to a new kind of dual change score (DCS), drawn as Figure 24.3.

Alternatively, in a model where the changes are both additive and proportional, but correlated, and the $x[t]$ variable also creates variation in the $y[t]$ score, we might write a SEM so the bivariate model expectations lead to a new kind of DCS model drawn as Figure 24.4. In a model where the changes are both additive and proportional and also correlated and the $x[t]$ and the $y[t]$ score are both "coupled," we might write a model so the bivariate model expectations lead to a new kind of DCS model drawn as Figure 24.5. The full generalization of this concept might be the same as before but include correlated innovations as well, and, if so, the model expectations would be created automatically, but in a more complex fashion (see Grimm & McArdle, 2005).

The careful reader will note that we have not done very much with the flexible latent basis coefficients of the triple change score (TCS) models here. This is not because these parameters might not lead to better fit; however, because they often do, it is largely because we do not want to complicate matters

EXHIBIT 24.2
Variations on the Bivariate Latent Change Score Model

This prior model implies that different variations of our basic change models could lead to different model expectations. For example, we could have a model where we write

(1) $\quad \Delta F1[t]_n = 0_n$ and $\Delta F2[t]_n = 0_n$,

or in a model where the changes are both additive and correlated, we might write

(2) $\quad \Delta F1[t]_n = \alpha_1 Q\{1\}_n$ and $\Delta F2[t]_n = \alpha_2 P\{1\}_n$

so the bivariate model expectations lead to a parallel change score model.

In a model where the changes are additive and proportional, but also correlated, we write

(3) $\quad \Delta F1[t]_n = \alpha_1 Q\{1\}_n + \beta_1 F1[t-1]_n$ and $\Delta F2[t]_n = \alpha_2 P\{1\}_n + \beta_2 F2[t-1]_n$

so the bivariate model expectations lead to a new kind of dual change score (DCS) model.

In a model where the changes are both additive and proportional, but correlated, and the $F2[t]$ variable also creates variation in the $F1[t]$ score, we might write

(4a) $\quad \Delta F1[t]_n = \alpha_1 Q\{1\}_n + \beta_1 F1[t-1]_n + \gamma_1 F2[t-1]_n$,

and

(4b) $\quad \Delta F2[t]_n = \alpha_2 P\{1\}_n + \beta_2 F2[t-1]_n$

so the bivariate model expectations lead to another new kind of DCS model.

In a model where the changes are both additive and proportional, correlated, and the common factor scores $F1[t]$ and the $F2[t]$ are considered "coupled," we might write

(5a) $\quad \Delta F1[t]_n = \alpha_1 Q\{1\}_n + \beta_1 F1[t-1]_n + \gamma_1 F2[t-1]_n$,

and

(5b) $\quad \Delta F2[t]_n = \alpha_2 P\{1\}_n + \beta_2 F2[t-1]_n + \gamma_2 F1[t-1]_n$,

so the bivariate model expectations lead to yet another new kind of DCS model.

The full linear generalization of this concept could include correlated innovations as well,

(6a) $\quad \Delta F1[t]_n = \alpha_1 Q\{1\}_n + \beta_1 F1[t-1]_n + \gamma_1 F2[t-1]_n + z_{1,n}$,

and

(6b) $\quad \Delta F2[t]_n = \alpha_1 P\{1\}_n + \beta_2 F2[t-1]_n + \gamma_2 F1[t-1]_n + z_{2,n}$.

Note. Adapted from *New Methods for the Analysis of Change* (pp. 139–176), by L. M. Collins and A. G. Sayer (Eds.), 2001, Washington, DC: American Psychological Association. Copyright 2001 by the American Psychological Association.

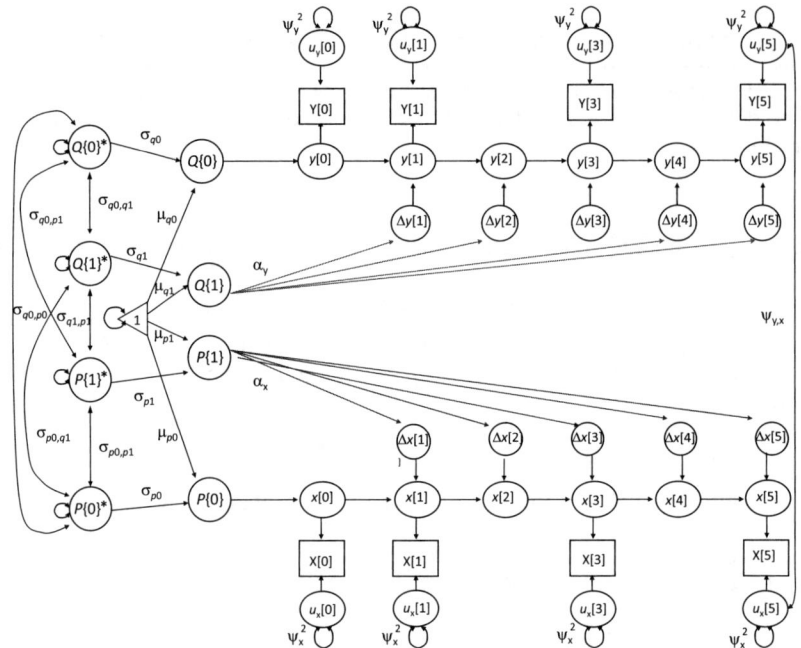

Figure 24.2. A bivariate change model for correlated curves.

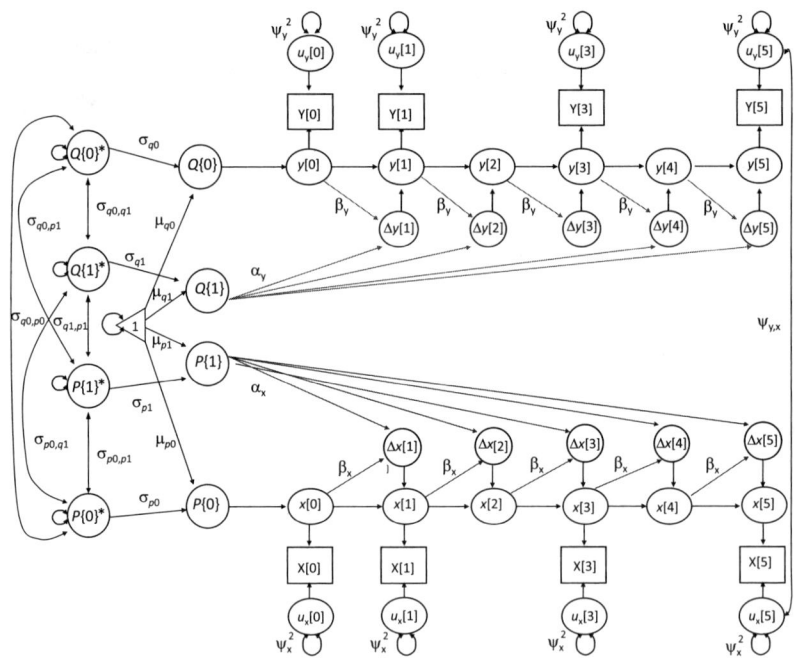

Figure 24.3. A bivariate dual change score model.

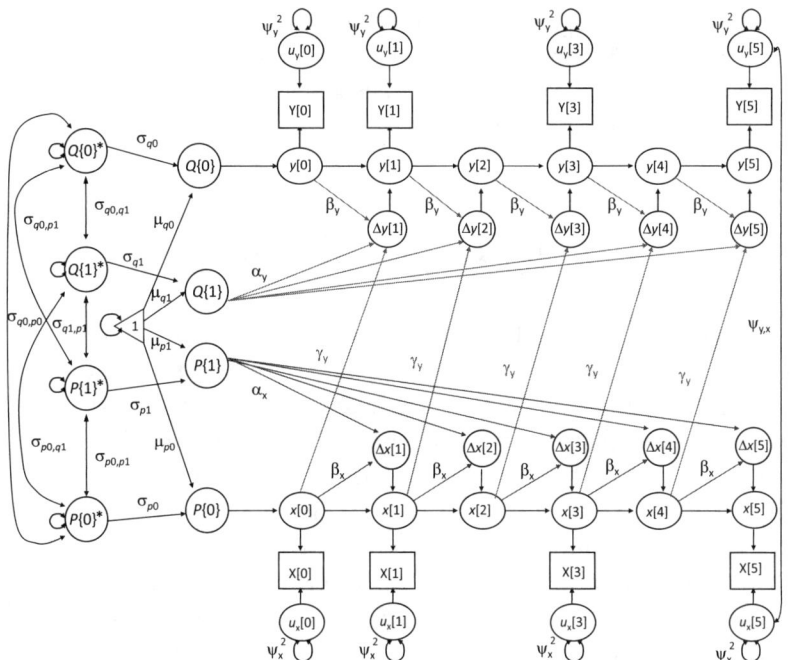

Figure 24.4. A coupling in which X → Y as a bivariate dual change score model.

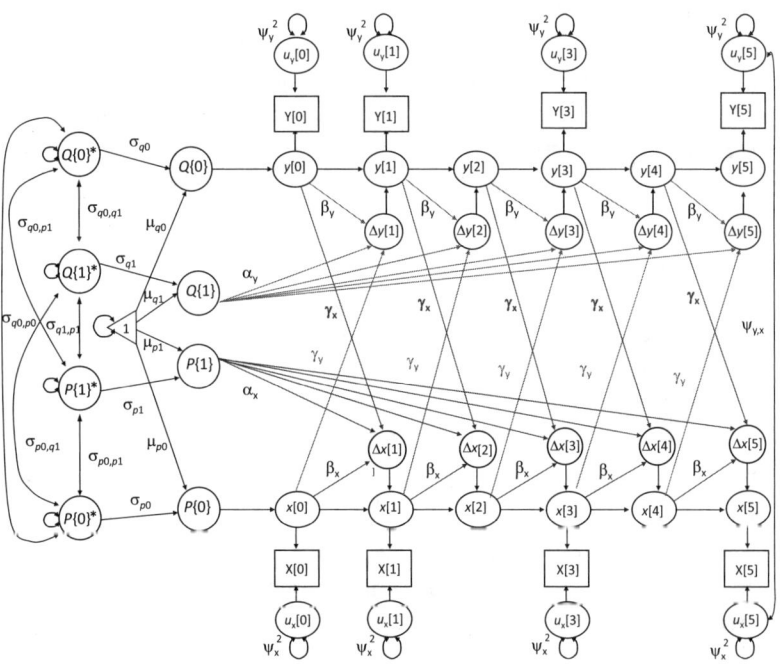

Figure 24.5. A complete bivariate dual change score model.

THE BIVARIATE LATENT CHANGE SCORE MODEL   297

any further now. These parameters, of course, could easily be part of the dynamics required, and the same timing adjustments would not be needed for each variable. The equality of latent basis coefficients within and between variables could be a key testable hypothesis.

A NOTE ON FEEDBACK LOOPS IN LONGITUDINAL STRUCTURAL EQUATION MODELING

One cannot help but be impressed by all the serious modeling attention given to the estimation of feedback or *nonrecursive* loops in structural equation modeling (SEM; see J. G. Anderson & Evans, 1974; O. D. Duncan, Haller, & Portes, 1968; Goldberger, 1973; Greenberg & Kessler, 1982; Hayduk, 1996; Strotz & Wold, 1960). Nonrecursive parameters for feedback loops are supposedly estimates of concurrent ($\Delta t = 0$) impacts of both $X[t] \to Y[t]$ together with $Y[t] \to X[t]$. The emphasis for estimation of both concurrent effects seems to comes from work on both cybernetics and philosophy (see Ashby, 1957; Ramaprasad, 1983; Salmon, 1980). But this kind of thinking was also considered to be important in the area of econometrics as a way to identify all nonrecursive mathematical elements (Strotz & Wold, 1960). Of course, this was alternatively done by introducing instrumental variables where additional measured variables $W[t]$ and $Z[t]$ were assumed not to create variation in the outcomes (see Angrist & Kreuger, 2001; Bound, Jaeger, & Baker, 1995).

Incidentally, the feedback estimation was taken seriously by Sewell Wright (1960), the inventor of path analysis, when he suggested feedback coefficients could be estimated in path analysis terms (and he gives several examples). But most important for us, feedback was not actually a part of what he termed his theoretical reciprocal interaction (see his Figure 1, p. 424). In this specific sense, Wright suggested,

> For the most accurate results, the interval between observations should equal or be an aliquot [sic., denoting an exact divisor or factor of an integer] part of the lag. As there is not likely to be exact correspondence, representation is in general most adequate if the observational intervals are much shorter that the lags. (p. 424)

The question for us in doing real data analysis will be "Have we picked the proper observational time?" or "Have we picked the half-way point of the maximum effects?" The answer to both questions will be a resounding no, and we will need to experiment with the times chosen (as in the random time lags of McArdle & Woodcock, 1997). That is, if we really want to learn if one variable influences another, we cannot simply stick to the convenient time lags of 1 day, 1 week, 1 month, or 1 year.

In another elegant and efficient approach, Greenberg and Kessler (1982) showed how to identify each part of the feedback by treating the concurrent coefficients as identical (equal) and the long-run coefficients as identical (equal). This kind of consistency was only done within a lag-one model, but the other lags presumably could be added. Another way to deal with the estimation of variable feedback is to (a) add latent variables and (b) estimate the unstandardized coefficients of influence as equal (O. D. Duncan, Haller, & Portes, 1968). These are relatively well-known examples in SEM, and these kinds of models are routinely considered among the best examples in the field.

No doubt, nonrecursive or feedback parameters are most interesting from a mathematical and statistical point of view (i.e., they can certainly be identified), as are many other kinds of problems, but it is also clear that the longitudinal coefficients we seek are related to time and these feedback coefficients are not. We realize that this is a somewhat radical position, but we suggest that in longitudinal data the nonrecursive coefficients should not be estimated at all. This is not to say that they could not be estimated or are not true representation of the data; it is just to say they should not be estimated because it will cost us unnecessary confusion. If any coefficient reflects an index of time (i.e., β^t) and the time between observations is longer than these, constant coefficients should get smaller. Thus, leaving this form of feedback out of the model, without any real effort to identify the within-time components, should not really lead to unreplicable results.

Perhaps what we are saying here is just that it takes time for causes to emerge (as in Gollob & Reichardt, 1987; Shrout, 2011). We basically think that longitudinal data collection is an attempt to overcome these kinds of concurrent influences and get more directly at the timing necessary to understand the influences. If we analyze a data set where the time interval is too short, then the models we advocate should show higher coefficients, and maybe these would need some feedback loops. Alternatively, if the data are collected at an interval that is too long, we should have lower coefficients and probably no feedback. In any case, these time intervals should be investigated. If the feedback is not a big part of the process, we still can have the wrong timing, but the proportionality of all effects can still be evaluated (by the TCS model).

The estimation of a feedback loop does not seem needed if the continuous time (CT) translation of some discrete time (DT) results is used. This approach can give us an estimate of the CT *instantaneous result* (where $dt = 0$), including the parameter standard errors, from the DT intervals that we actually measure, so there is little need to estimate feedback parameters directly from the data in the usual way. Of course, some basic form of parameter consistency is required, but it still can work.

Another reason we do this is that the estimation of feedback could be misleading. One form of what would appear to be feedback could be the overaggregation of people, for some of whom ($G = 1$) where $X[t-1] \rightarrow Y[t]$ and for another group of people ($G = 2$), where $Y[t-1] \rightarrow X[t]$. Although we basically assume this does not happen in any model, it could, and we hardly ever test for this form of unobserved heterogeneity (although we could). As stated, this could affect any regression parameter in the model so this is not specific to feedbacks, but it is still a concern here.

Just in case our somewhat radical suggestion is not clear, in longitudinal research we should (1) openly admit we have a potentially serious problem in determining the optimal timing and (2) consider, but not count on (or even estimate), the concurrent (feedback) expressions. Anything that tells us very little about the phenomena of interest, the ones we can later control, could take away from our time-lagged expressions.

# 25

PLOTTING BIVARIATE LATENT CHANGE SCORE RESULTS

The interpretation of all the resulting dynamic coefficients can be tested for salience using the likelihood-based procedures of longitudinal structural equation modeling (LSEM). But if more than a few model parameters are needed, the interpretation can be a daunting task. So we will do the same thing we typically do whenever we have complex algebraic expressions: We will basically try to create a Cartesian plot of the expectations. In almost any case, the specific lag of time used in the data collection could be arbitrary, so we desire a plotting procedure that is immune to this scaling, and the plot of the scores over time serves this purpose. At this point, it also seems quite natural to plot each of the pairs of latent responses ($x[t]$ and $y[t]$) over time using a trajectory plot. After this, we can combine both scores into a bivariate plot that has the same features as the single trajectory. The complexity comes when we try to plot more than one variable in the same one-dimensional space.

http://dx.doi.org/10.1037/14440-026
Longitudinal Data Analysis Using Structural Equation Models, by J. J. McArdle and J. R. Nesselroade
Copyright © 2014 by the American Psychological Association. All rights reserved.

The first thing we can do is to plot the expected mean trajectory for each measured variable over time. The expected mean at each time is easy to plot, and this can be done for several model alternatives (as in the typical latent curve of Chapter 7). Then we can plot the expected individual latent scores ($x[t]$, $y[t]$); we can then estimate random levels ($Q\{0\}$, $P\{0\}$) and random slopes ($Q\{1\}$, $P\{1\}$) using the parameters within each variable. This could lead us to a better understanding of the initial size of the variation around the mean and the size and shape of the changes that come about afterward.

Plotting the expected values at each time together is a bit more challenging because we probably have to do this for both variables at the same time, and they can influence one another. As a first approach to this problem, we will take the expected latent scores ($x[t]$, $y[t]$) and plot these as pairs, basically assuming they are measuring the same factor at an equal interval of time. This type of plot is often called a *phase diagram* because it is a discrete geometric representation of the trajectories of a dynamical system in the phase plane and will use the pairs of expected values to highlight movements of the pairs from one time to the next. This will be done by averaging into a simple pattern of which way are the scores moving at a particular scale for both the $x[t]$ and $y[t]$ coordinates. This joint expression of *directional derivatives* will be used to describe all model parameters. Although we could certainly just stop here, we will take one further step and produce a *vector field* (Boker & McArdle, 1995) to illustrate the statistical integrity of the changes:

> In vector calculus, a vector field is an assignment of a vector to each point in a subset of Euclidean space. A vector field in the plane . . . can be visualized as a collection of arrows with a given magnitude and direction each attached to a point in the plane. Vector fields are often used to model, for example, the speed and direction of a moving fluid throughout space, or the strength and direction of some force, such as the magnetic or gravitational force, as it changes from point to point. . . . Vector fields can usefully be thought of as representing the velocity of a moving flow in space, and this physical intuition leads to notions such as the divergence (which represents the rate of change of volume of a flow) and curl (which represents the rotation of a flow) . . . Vector fields are often discussed on open subsets of Euclidean space, but also make sense on other subsets such as surfaces, where they associate an arrow tangent to the surface at each point (a tangent vector). (Wikipedia, 02/13)

These kinds of plots have already been used and described by both Coleman (1968) and Hannan and Tuma (1979) in their uses of continuous time models.

The theoretical vector field plots of Figure 25.1 can be used to help interpret bivariate latent change score model results. In these cases the intercepts ($\alpha_x = \alpha_y = 1$) and the autoregression coefficients are assumed to be small ($\beta_x = \beta_y = -.01$). The first plot (Figure 25.1, top left) describes a system where neither variable has much influence on the other ($\gamma_x = \gamma_y = .01$). If this is true, then the plot shows little activity. The second plot (Figure 25.1, top right) describes a system where the first variable (X[t]) has a lot of influence on the other variable ($\gamma_x = .50, \gamma_y = .01$). The result is a vector field where X[t–1] → Y[t] at all levels, but this has its largest directional arrows at the higher levels of X[t], and these produce bigger changes in Y[t]. The third plot (Figure 25.1, bottom left) describes a system where the second variable (Y[t]) has a lot influence on the other variable ($\gamma_x = .01, \gamma_y = .50$). The result is a vector field where Y[t–1] → X[t] at all levels, but this has its largest directional arrows at the higher levels of Y[t], and these produce bigger changes in X[t]. The fourth plot (Figure 25.1, bottom right) describes a system where both variables (X[t], Y[t]) have a lot influence on each other ($\gamma_x = .50, \gamma_y = .50$). The result is a vector field where X[t–1] → Y[t] and Y[t–1] → X[t] at all levels, but this has its largest directional arrows

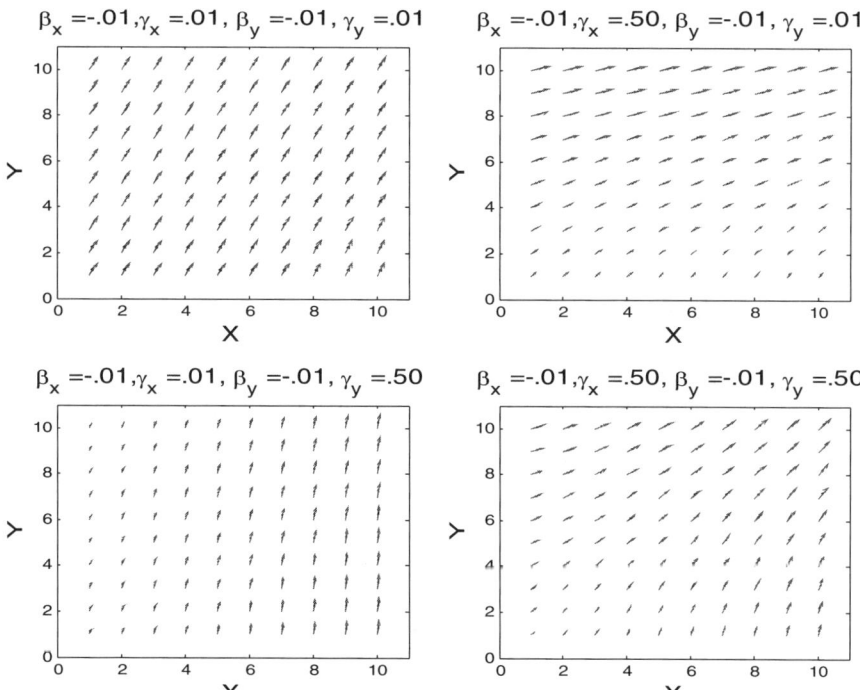

Figure 25.1. Theoretical vector field plots based on β_x, γ_x, β_y, γ_y.

at the higher levels of both X[t] and Y[t], and there is a clear "pulling" across both scores.

More can be added to this plot, including some fixed idea about where the people actually are at any point in time (F[t]). Because the overall plot of actions can be misleading if no one is observed at that specific juncture, we will routinely add a 95% confidence ellipsoid to this plot representing an estimate of the initial stating point (F[0]). We realize this is only one way to create a statistical vector field (SVF; see Boker & McArdle, 1995; McArdle et al., 2004), but we use it to help us interpret the BLCS results more easily.

VI

LONGITUDINAL SEM FOR INTERINDIVIDUAL DIFFERENCES IN CAUSES (DETERMINANTS) OF INTRAINDIVIDUAL CHANGES

26
DYNAMIC PROCESSES OVER GROUPS

Our final goal is to combine the concepts of the previous dynamic models with solutions for some separate group issues. Groups here will only be defined by persons separated on observed variables. In this logic, one person can only belong to one group, and we can define that group in advance, or as a part of the longitudinal data collection. This is not the only way this can be done.

Obviously, there are many more complex concepts that could be introduced at this point. For example, we could use continuous variables and introduce multiple grouping variables, including interactions or fully realized "networks." Or we could introduce "latent classes" or "regime switches" of persons into groups, where the grouping variable is not directly observed but is defined by the behaviors themselves; these are fairly advanced concepts compared with what we have in mind now.

In the previous latent change score (LCS) models, it is also important to recognize that models of individual differences relationships among dynamic variables were expected to reflect dynamic processes for the group. Perhaps the latter interpretation requires a focus on time-based parameters in the models rather than the time-independent correlation of the time-based scores (e.g., Gollob & Reichardt, 1987). Or perhaps the dynamic influences really differ over groups. The problem we consider now is, "How can we tell if the dynamic influences are the same or if they differ over measured groups?" As it turns out, there are many ways to do this.

The simplest way to deal with this problem is to consider that the previous coefficients of our models could be altered by group information. If we can say that this is primarily a function of the change in the means, then we can use the multilevel modeling (MLM)–structural equation modeling (SEM) approach defined earlier (see Chapter 11). In this approach we use the group information as an additional predictor in the dynamic model, and we try to explain how and why the dynamics operate with and without this variable. Of course, we can also add more complex interactions to such a model and allow for many kinds of group differences in otherwise aggregated model parameters. We can, of course, restrict the solutions by forcing the effects to zero and examining the resulting misfit. If we go as far as having the dynamic coefficients change due to group membership (an interaction), we could then say that each group requires a different dynamic process. This can even be done in MLM-SEM fashion with models of common factor scores (McArdle & Prescott, 1992, 2010).

A slightly different way to approach this problem comes from the MGM-SEM techniques. Here we split the data into subgroups for further analysis. If the only group differences are in the means or regressions, we can do everything that was considered in the MLM approach. But now we can also suggest that the random parameters differ over groups. In the case of any model just defined, we could have each variable's variance or covariance terms, or corresponding disturbance terms, and these might differ over groups. Yes, this implies that both the size of the effect and the prediction of the changes might differ over groups as well. If we go as far as having the dynamic coefficients change over groups and the disturbance variance change over groups, we could again say that each group requires a different dynamic process.

One way to consider this situation is as a MGM-SEM that begins with the bivariate change model in Figure 24.5 (initially presented in McArdle, 2007a). Without adding further details to the figure, we can imagine this path diagram for multiple groups (as in McArdle & Prindle, 2008). Many forms of between-group analysis are of obvious importance in the study of dynamics. For example, manifest variables that are measured at one time (static) can be added into the dynamic model, and this could change the coupling parameters. The use of the MGM-SEM approach allows a wider variety of options, including allowing the dynamic influences to be completely different across different manifest groups. The idea that incomplete data modeling by MGM-SEM or other approaches also seems fundamental in dynamic analysis (Hamagami & McArdle, 2000). The determination of unobserved latent classes of persons who are following the same dynamic process may be an essential ingredient in good dynamic analyses (McArdle & Prindle, 2008). Variations on multiple group modeling-SEM can be used to examine different combinations of variables or latent mixtures (Muthén & Muthén, 2002b; Muthén & Satorra, 1995; Nagin, 1999). There is a difference—and the difference is usually exploratory!

In most cases we would probably start with the simpler MLM-SEM approach and use these results to get started. Here we would simply be writing a model where the group variable is used as a partial coefficient, but we would not stop there. We would go on to the MGM-SEM approach and see if any parameter is changed in the dynamic system and if the series of inferences made would differ over groups.

A reasonable researcher will always ask, "What should be the same and what should be different over groups?" One answer to this particularly puzzling question was initially provided in the multiple factorial invariance over groups (MFIG) criteria of Meredith (1993), and we use these again now.

THEOREMS ON PARAMETER INVARIANCE OVER GROUPS

In SEM, a question has previously been raised: "Is exactly the same common factor measured within each group?" This was actually the topic of MFIG raised by Meredith (1964a, 1993) and put into practice by Sörbom (1974; see Jöreskog & Sörbom, 1979). A model-fitted approach to MFIG has been applied to data by many others (e.g., Horn & McArdle, 1992; McArdle & Cattell, 1994; McGaw & Jöreskog, 1971). Basically, a lot can be done if we can find some form of MFIG, so the question was raised as to what type of selection of people would allow use to retain an invariant factor pattern. According to a recent discussion by Millsap and Meredith (2007), we should understand that Aitken (1935), building on Pearson (1902, as cited in Millsap & Meredith, 2007), and assuming multivariate normality, described how the alteration of a portion of a covariance matrix through direct selection would affect the rest of the covariance matrix indirectly. In subsequent work, Lawley (1943) showed that Aitken's results hold under weaker conditions of linearity and homoskedasticity of regressions. Thomson and Ledermann (1939) used the Aitken results to show the implications of selection for the factor structure in the selected groups. The key here was that direct selection operates on a subset of the measured variables. Ahmvaara (1954) derived an expression for the factor pattern matrix after selection. He confirmed Thurstone's (1947) claim regarding simple structure invariance (under certain conditions).

This early work led to several important theorems on factor analysis by Meredith (1964a, 1964b). Meredith showed that under Lawley's selection theorem, we would have MFIG in the factor pattern matrix provided that (1) measures are expressed in common units across populations, (2) the factor solution is not required to be orthogonal in all subpopulations, and (3) the regressions of the common factors on the selection variables are linear and homoskedastic. In Meredith's approach, the selection variables are external and need not be measured, or even known. This latter point is important, although it is often unclear or understated.

Meredith (1964a) suggested that if selection were to occur on the common factors, and not the unique factors, then the factor loadings would remain invariant over any groups selected in such ways. The general MGM principle (see Exhibit 18.1) started with a common factor model whose elements were free to vary over groups, and this can be seen to lead to separate mean vector expectations over groups as well as separate covariance expectations over groups.

Meredith (1964b) also provided two rotational methods for taking separate factor solutions from each population and finding an invariant pattern matrix that is best-fitting. One of the most elementary solutions (by Meredith, 1965) was to simply take the grand mean of the covariances and apply a factor model to it. Earlier, Cattell (1944) had developed the rotational principle of *parallel proportional profiles*, which argued for rotating factor solutions so that the pattern matrices are columnwise proportional (see McArdle & Cattell, 1994). Jöreskog (1971) then presented a confirmatory factor analytic (CFA) approach to studying factorial invariance in multiple populations. The method permitted a direct test of fit for an invariant factor pattern and an estimation algorithm for finding this best-fitting pattern. Other aspects of the factor structure could be evaluated for invariance (e.g., unique factor variances). In subsequent work, Sörbom (1974) extended Jöreskog's approach to include mean structures, adding latent intercept parameters as an essential part of the invariance question. For a clear discussion, we encourage the reader to see Dolan and Molenaar (1994).

The early MGM–SEM concepts were put into path diagram form in the analysis of McArdle, Johnson, Hishinuma, Myamoto, and Andrade, (2001b), where data from the Hawaii High School (HHS) study was used to examine multiple group modeling factor analytic hypotheses using the depression symptom index from the Center for Epidemiological Studies (CES-D). In the models from the HHS study, persons who were ethnically different (Hawaiian vs. non-Hawaiian) were split into separate groups to see if the factor patterns were the same across groups.

Meredith (1993) made it clear that unique parameters (i.e., intercepts, variances, etc.) could also remain invariant, but might not, and because the original selection of persons was unknown, he suggested this this was an empirical endeavor. He created various MFIG criteria by isolating four specific cases with group differences:

- *Case I. Configural* (or *measurement*) *Invariance:* Different factor patterns ($\Lambda[t]^{(g)}$) with the same pattern of non-zero loadings, different variable intercepts ($\iota_m^{(g)}$), and different unique factors ($\Psi_m^{2(g)}$) over groups. This configural covariance model can be identified by requiring the factor model constraints required within any group, as well as fixed factor variances (e.g., $\varphi_k^{2(g)} = 1$) and factor means ($\nu_k^{(g)} = 0$) over groups.
- *Case II. Metric* (or *weak*) *Invariance:* Invariant factor patterns (Λ), with exactly the same numerical values, but different variable intercepts ($\iota_m^{(g)}$) and different unique factors ($\psi_m^{2(g)}$) over groups. This metric covariance can be identified by requiring the factor model constraints required by any group, as well as fixed factor variances in the first group (e.g., $\varphi_k^{2(1)} = 1$) and fixed factor means ($\nu_k^{(g)} = 0$) in all groups. [Presumably this is termed "weak" by Meredith because it does not involve any means.]
- *Case III. Strong Invariance:* Invariant factor patterns (Λ), different variable intercepts ($\iota_m^{(g)}$) but invariant unique factors (Ψ_m^2) over time. This strong invariance mean and covariance model can be identified by requiring the factor model constraints required in any group, as well as fixing factor variances in Group 1 (e.g., $\varphi_k^{2(1)} = 1$), and then fixing all factor means (e.g., $\nu_k^{(g)} = 0$).
- *Case IV. Strict Invariance:* Invariant factor patterns (Λ), invariant variable intercepts (ι_m), and invariant unique factors (Ψ_m^2) over time. This strict invariance mean and covariance model can be identified by requiring the common factor model constraints required in any group, as well as fixing factor variances in Group 1 (e.g., $\varphi_k^{2(1)} = 1$) and fixing the Group 1 factor means (e.g., $\nu_k^{(1)} = 0$).

RECONSIDERING PARAMETER INVARIANCE OVER GROUPS

The general multiple group modeling principles of the last form (Case IV. Strict Invariance) can be seen to lead to the simplest set of mean vector expectations over groups and simple covariance expectations over groups (see Exhibit 26.1). Perhaps now we can see this is identical to the prior multiple group modeling concepts on regression analysis (as in the models of Part III, except here the latent common factors (F_k) are the predictors, and they are unobserved. But this research demonstrates the factor loading coefficients (Λ) are invariant over groups if the groups have been selected in any way (i.e., randomly or nonrandomly) on the predictor but not on the outcome.

EXHIBIT 26.1
Meredith's (1993) Tables of Multiple Factorial Invariance Over Groups

The general multiple group model (MGM) principle started with (m = 1 to M; and g = 1 to G)

(1a) $\quad Y_{m,n}^{(g)} = \iota_m^{(g)} + \lambda_{m,k}^{(g)} F_{k,n}^{(g)} + u_{m,n}^{(g)}$

which can be seen to lead to an expected mean vector expectations over groups of

(2a) $\quad \mu_m^{(g)} = \iota_m^{(g)} + \lambda_{m,k}^{(g)} v_k^{(g)}$

and an expected covariance expectations over groups of

(2b) $\quad \Sigma^{(g)} = \Lambda^{(g)} \Phi^{(g)} \Lambda^{(g)\prime} + \Psi^{2(g)}$.

These principles can be defined in terms of levels of multiple factorial invariance over groups (MFIG):

MFIG cases (with Meredith, 1993, labels)	Factor loadings	Unique variable variances	Unique variable intercepts	Common factor inter-covariances	Common factor means
I. Configural (or measurement)	$\Lambda^{(g)}$	$\Psi^{2\,(g)}$	$\iota_m^{(g)}$	$P^{(g)}$	0
II. Metric (or weak)	Λ	$\Psi^{2\,(g)}$	$\iota_m^{(g)}$	$P^{(1)}$, $\Phi^{(g)}$	0
III. Strong invariance	Λ	Ψ^2	$\iota_m^{(g)}$	$P^{(1)}$, $\Phi^{(g)}$	0
IV. Strict invariance	Λ	Ψ^2	ι_m	$P^{(1)}$, $\Phi^{(g)}$	$v_k^{(g)}$

And the general MGM principles of the last form (Case IV. Strict Invariance) lead to

(3a) $\quad Y_{m,n}^{(g)} = \iota_m + \lambda_{m,k} F_{k,n}^{(g)} + u_{m,n}^{(g)}$

which can then be seen to lead to an expected mean vector expectations over groups of

(3b) $\quad \mu_m^{(g)} = \iota_m + \lambda_{m,k} v_k^{(g)}$

and an expected covariance expectations over groups of

(3c) $\quad \Sigma^{(g)} = \Lambda \Phi^{(g)} \Lambda' + \Psi^2$.

Note. From "Measurement Invariance, Factor Analysis and Factorial Invariance," by W. Meredith, 1993, *Psychometrika, 58,* p. 524. Copyright 1993 by the Psychometric Society. Adapted with permission.

Meredith (1993) thought these were important considerations:

> It should be obvious that measurement invariance, weak measurement invariance, strong and strict factorial invariance are idealizations. They are, however, enormously useful idealizations in their application to psychological theory building and evaluation. Their validity and existence in the real world of psychological measurement and research can never be finally established in practice.... The results of simultaneous model fitting are clearly informative no matter which case holds. Now distinguish the scientific from the practical use of simultaneous factoring. From the point of view of the scientist all four cases [from Bloxom's (1972)] are meaningful and acceptable if the results fit into a substantive theoretical framework. For Case I we would surely want configural invariance to hold. For Case II we would want simple structure, or some other form of theoretical driven structure to hold, and the mean differences of the unique factors to fall in some pattern consistent with psychological theory. We argue, however, that invariance of Λ should take primacy over simple structure in this case and in Cases III and IV as well. This means, in our view, that simply identified invariant models should be fit first and simple structure specifications introduced subsequently (see McArdle & Cattell, 1994). It can be shown that underrepresentation of "primary" factors, that is, fewer than three "markers," can lead to Case II. Adding manifest variables can turn unique factors into common factors with Cases III or IV resulting.... From the point of view of the scientist either Cases III or IV are the most desirable outcomes. The fact that so many of our samples are samples of convenience adds intuitive weight to this argument. (pp. 541–542)

THEORY AND PRACTICE OF ESTABLISHING FACTORIAL INVARIANCE OVER GROUPS

As just mentioned, these kinds of MGMs were used in the theoretical and practical analyses of McArdle and Cattell (1994), but these researchers went one step further. They suggested that if a MGM-SEM was used to assert that the model of factorial invariance did not hold over groups, then we probably needed to relax some of the major simple structure restrictions on the factor pattern to achieved the invariance constraints. This was largely against the prevailing SEM wisdom, where invariance constraints were clear being added to simple structures. But this approach was largely consistent with Meredith (1993; see prior quote). That is, when doing comparative factor analyses of real data, we may need many common factors (K) before we achieve factorial invariance, and we should not expect the resulting invariant factor pattern to also be simple. This research also showed how rotation of the final multifactor invariant pattern over different groups may be needed for substantive understanding.

In more recent discussions, we can find Meredith suggesting:

> Establishing factorial invariance involves a hierarchy of levels that include tests of weak, strong, and strict invariance. Pattern (metric or weak) factorial invariance implies that the regression slopes are invariant across groups. Pattern invariance requires only invariant factor loadings. Strong factorial invariance implies that the conditional expectation of the response, given the common and specific factors, is invariant across groups. Strong factorial invariance requires that specific factor means (represented as invariant intercepts) also be identical across groups. Strict factorial invariance implies that, in addition, the conditional variance of the response, given the common and specific factors, is invariant across groups. Strict factorial invariance requires that, in addition to equal factor loadings and intercepts, the residual (specific factor plus error variable) variances are equivalent across groups. The concept of measurement invariance that is most closely aligned to that of item response theory considers the latent variable as a common factor measured by manifest variables; the specific factors can be characterized as nuisance variables. (Meredith & Teresi, 2006, p. S69)

27
DYNAMIC INFLUENCES OVER GROUPS

In this longitudinal structural equation modeling (LSEM) approach, we have created a new set of principles for what we now term *dynamic invariance over groups* (DIOG; see Exhibit 27.1). Here we present DIOG as a sequence of alternative models in multiple group modeling (MGM)–structural equation modeling (SEM). As will be clear from the following discussion, these DIOG criteria are all based on the prior principles of person selection to groups (as in multiple factorial invariance over groups [MFIG]).

CONSIDERING DYNAMIC PARAMETER INVARIANCE OVER GROUPS

The next set of parameters that might actually vary over groups are the dynamic coefficients. It is possible to isolate some of these coefficients from the others, especially the coupling coefficients, so we present this

EXHIBIT 27.1
Suggested Sequential Criteria for Dynamic Invariance Over Groups Using a Multiple Group Modeling–Structural Equation Modeling Approach (and Assuming G Independent Groups Are Measured Over Times T)

0. Start any group dynamic analysis with *all* parameters invariant over all groups G.
1. Allow the factor (or composite) means ($\mu\{k\}$) at Time 1 to vary (but this is not needed if groups are randomly assigned at Time 0 before a treatment at Time 1).
2. Allow the factor (or composite) variances ($\sigma\{k\}^2$) and covariances ($\varphi\{k, j\}$) at Time 1 to vary (again, this is not needed if groups are randomly assigned before treatment).
3. Allow the dynamic variances ($\zeta\{k\}^2$) and covariances ($\zeta\{k, j\}$) to vary over groups.
4. Allow the dynamic coupling coefficients (γ) to vary over groups.
5. Allow the dynamic proportions (β) to vary as needed over groups.
6. Allow the dynamic additions (α) to vary as needed over groups.

Assuming common factors are present, and we use a MGM-SEM, we rely on the typical MFIG criteria:

7. Allow the unique means (ι) to vary over groups (Case III).
8. Allow the unique variances (ψ^2) to vary over groups (Case II).
9. Allow the factor loadings (Λ) to vary over groups (Case I).
10. Allow the number of common factors (K) to vary over groups (this is possible).
11. Allow all model parameters to vary over groups (possible) or analyze the groups separately.

---

in DIOG as three steps (γs then βs then αs). This is done in a sequence that reflects the order of interpretation and allows for different dynamic displays. It is not hard to envision a real-time process where the dynamics might differ from one group to the next and what we thought we isolated was a set of coefficients that described the average or aggregate person within a group. The next set of parameters that we expect to differ over groups deals with the variance of the dynamic process; these parameters might be related to the latent changes or the disturbances in the process and may differ slightly over different models. Because a strict version of multiple factorial invariance over time (MFIT) will typically be assumed, the very last thing we expect to change over groups are the measurement features, and no unique means, unique variances, or factor loadings will be altered here. We could then go on to examine unique means and unique variances, but we will focus on a model with strict factorial invariance over both time (as before) and groups.

We could now focus on substantive examples to carry our main message. In using such a strategy, we could first use observational data and only consider one grouping variable. But instead we will end this part of the book on selected models, including randomized groups, and on repeated measures analysis of variance (RANOVA) as a popular alternative.

CONCLUSIONS ABOUT DIOG

In DIOG, the first thing that we should expect to see in variation over groups is in the means of the initial predictors. This is true whether or not the means are based on common factors or composites. If these differences are large, we might have evidence for nonrandom selection. This could even occur if the groups are randomly assigned, but we would not let this prior difference affect our other estimates. In general, the groups may differ at this point, and we would want to know this fact.

The next things that might vary over groups are the variances and covariances of the initial predictors. There could be group differences here if the people were self-selected into groups. Incidentally, this kind of model is not usually considered in multilevel modeling–SEM, but it is a natural part of DIOG using MGM–SEM.

28

APPLYING A BIVARIATE CHANGE MODEL WITH MULTIPLE GROUPS

This longitudinal structural equation modeling (LSEM) approach allows us to consider four key cases of group differences: (1) in the standard cross-lagged change score model, (2) in the nonstandard bivariate latent change score (BLCS) model, (3) in the BLCS model with common factors, and (4) in the BLCS model with incomplete data. Within each problem, we can try to fit models based on both the multilevel modeling–SEM ideas and models based on multiple group modeling–SEM ideas. Our main hope is that these discussions will go some way toward understanding the possibilities for LSEM analyses of group dynamics.

DYNAMIC INVARIANCE OVER GROUPS IN STANDARD CROSS-LAGGED MODELS

In the standard cross-lagged change score model, we can consider group differences. It is potentially obvious, but the cross-lagged influences that operate in one group might not be the same across every measured group. In one group X[t–1] may cause Y[t], and in another group Y[t–1] may cause X[t]. In still other groups there may be combined patterns of influence (both) or no influences at all (none). To get a better look at these patterns, we could try to fit a model of the multilevel modeling (MLM)-SEM type, and all this would allow is mean differences over groups. Anytime we are dealing with a pattern of changes we may need something more like the multiple group modeling-SEM setup. This is not really hard to do because we can simply start by (1) separating the data into groups and (2) asserting that everything is invariant over the groups, and then (3) we can postulate some differences. The key differences may be in the means of the scores (and this can be stated) or in the pattern of the influences. The goodness-of-fit applies directly.

DIOG IN NONSTANDARD BLCS MODELS

In the nonstandard BLCS model, we can also have group differences, and we would treat this in the same way as we did above. We could see if the statistical vector field was the same by drawing the patterns in a comparative plot, and we could get a statistical indication of equality of dynamics by forcing all parameters to be equal and then relaxing these constraints. Having more time points allows us the estimate the measurement errors, and having more groups allow us an opportunity to see if the measurement error is the same size in each group . . . and it may not be. This is acceptable, because the measurement error does not need to be the same size for valid group comparisons, but it should be noted.

In the nonstandard BLCS with common factors we can have group differences. The fact is that we now have an opportunity to use measurement constraints both over time and over groups. If all this seems to fit, especially strict forms of multiple factorial invariance over time (MFIT) and multiple factorial invariance over groups (MFIG), we can go on and consider the BLCS in the same way we did before. We may require more than two factors, and a third or fourth common factor may be indicated. If these are invariant over time and groups, we have no real problems, but we need to consider extending the dynamic model past the bivariate case (McArdle, Hamagami, Meredith, & Bradway, 2001a). However, if we find a lack of metric factorial measurement invariance either over time or over groups, we need to recognize that this can completely alter the interpretation of the dynamic results. It can easily change the interpretations. Indeed, MFIT and MFIG are key concerns here.

In the nonstandard BLCS with incomplete data, we can have group differences among those that complete the longitudinal data collection and those that do not. Among the many new ways to deal with this problem, we can either (a) just use the complete cases or (b) include all the data and assume the data are missing completely at random (MCAR). As an alternative, we can also test if the data are MCAR by fitting multiple group models (based in incomplete patterns) and seeing if the models of MCAR fit. If not, we can always assume a missing at random pattern and get the best BLCS estimates under this condition. Of course, if the data are not missing at random and the incomplete selection is unobserved in the data we have, we will run the danger of estimating the incorrect dynamic. So we need to treat these assumptions with appropriate caution.

29

NOTES ON THE INCLUSION OF RANDOMIZATION IN LONGITUDINAL STUDIES

Randomization is a very useful principle, mainly because it can lead to clear inferences. Research on group differences in dynamics have not yet been used much with any longitudinal data, but we have tried to do this here with observational data. The inferences that can be made from this approach are noteworthy. Our prior comparisons in the Wechsler Intelligence Scale for Children, Fourth Edition (Wechsler, 2004), were based on the selection of groups of children whose mothers were observed to have different levels of formal education (see McArdle & Epstein, 1987). The comparisons in other studies (see McArdle, 2006; McArdle & Prindle, 2008) were between groups of adults who were randomized to different levels of training. As we have illustrated here, these comparisons use the same variety of analytic methods. But, as we have also illustrated here, the use of randomization to groups allows much stronger inferences about group differences.

http://dx.doi.org/10.1037/14440-030
Longitudinal Data Analysis Using Structural Equation Models, by J. J. McArdle and J. R. Nesselroade
Copyright © 2014 by the American Psychological Association. All rights reserved.

THE PURPOSES OF RANDOMIZATION TO GROUPS

Thus, as any well-trained experimental psychologist knows, randomization to groups is an essential ingredient in making a clear causal interpretation (see Holland, 1986). Indeed, the separation of *observational* studies from *controlled-manipulative* studies is a key division in all data collections (Cattell, 1966c; Cochran & Cox, 1950). Since the introduction of randomization of persons into groups by Sir R. A. Fisher (1925), it has been thought that, in the long run (i.e., with large enough sample sizes), the use of randomization of persons to treatments ensures that all unmeasured causes are equally balanced, and therefore any observed group difference cannot be attributed to other causes (see Holland, 1986). We think there is simply no way around this design issue, so we embrace it.

The very clever introduction of *instrumental variables* in economic research (e.g., Angrist & Krueger, 2001) provides a special way to capture the natural experiments going on all around us. The approach searches for conditions that, although naturally occurring, allow us to estimate parameters as if there were a random selection of people. To show how such issues can be included in our treatment of longitudinal data, we have tried to demonstrate how the longitudinal structural equation modeling (LSEM) analyses of data can be carried out in the context of a randomized trial when one does not actually exist (McArdle & Prescott, 2010).

RANDOMIZATION IN LONGITUDINAL CONTEXTS

This basic reasoning seems appropriate in carefully measured longitudinal studies, where self-selection effects are usually present and inferences become difficult if not impossible. It is often said that a third variable could be responsible for the actions of two others (see Kenny, 1979), and this may be true. Of course, there are many sciences in which observational studies are the only kind of experiments that can be done (e.g., astronomy, geology), and some of these have to do with ethical issues in manipulations (e.g., in psychology, we do not routinely manipulate depression). And it is also true that any understanding of causes (e.g., Pearl, 2000) will probably to some degree rely on observations beyond the scope of routine randomization, which implies that observational study has important benefits too, but does not deny the importance of randomization where possible.

These experimental design features are also well-known to researchers using SEM (see references in McArdle, 2007a). That is, when group assignment can be assumed to be uncorrelated with all residual terms (in large samples), then this leads to unambiguous attribution of the treatment effects in size and direction (e.g., Fisher, 1925). The SEM approach can be used to consider more general possibilities for experimental effects and for evaluating nonrandom confounds and subsequent causal inference. The seminal works of Blalock (1985a, 1985b), Miller (1985, as cited in Blalock, 1985b), Costner (1985, as cited in Blalock, 1985b), and Alwin and Tessler (1985, as cited in Blalock, 1985b) provide classic examples of how SEM can help deal with potential confounds to allow appropriate causal inference.

The key message in these historical articles is that SEM should be used to clarify the relationship between model assumptions and related causal inferences. Clarity of design leads to clarity of inference. This is not surprising because these ideas are a reflection of the long history of creating powerful experimental designs in the behavioral sciences (e.g., Fisher, 1925; Healy, Proctor, & Weiner, 2003; Woodworth & Schlosberg, 1938, 1954). It is also not surprising that models with strong causal inference have become a key feature of contemporary statistical modeling (e.g., Holland, 1986; Pearl, 1995, 2000; Rubin, 1997). It seems to us that any good LSEM researcher should appreciate the benefits of randomization, and we try to keep this in mind.

LSEM analyses could be presented here to describe contemporary longitudinal alternatives for the standard mean comparisons so prevalent in analyses of randomized experiments. Indeed, one main point implied here is that the effect of experiments may not always be found in the mean changes between groups (i.e., there may be differences in the dynamic parameters). This point of view seems to be understood in longitudinal studies where randomization to groups is not possible (i.e., quasi-experiments) and dynamic concepts are heralded (Cook & Campbell, 1979). Nevertheless, the issues of group differences in dynamic parameters seem to be overlooked in much of the important literature on randomized clinical trials (Cnaan, Laird, & Slasor, 1997).

RANDOMIZATION IN LONGITUDINAL MULTIPLE GROUP CONTEXTS

We can now use the general treatment of the multiple group modeling (MGM)–SEM issue using concepts derived from multiple group factor models (e.g., Horn & McArdle, 1992; Jöreskog & Sörbom, 1999; McArdle & Cattell, 1994). The multiple group change model (as in Figure 29.1) permits the examination of the presumed invariance of the latent basis functions and the rejection of these constraints (possibly based on some form of L^2/df) implies that some independent groups have a different basic shape of their trajectory. MGMs can be a useful way to express problems of incomplete data.

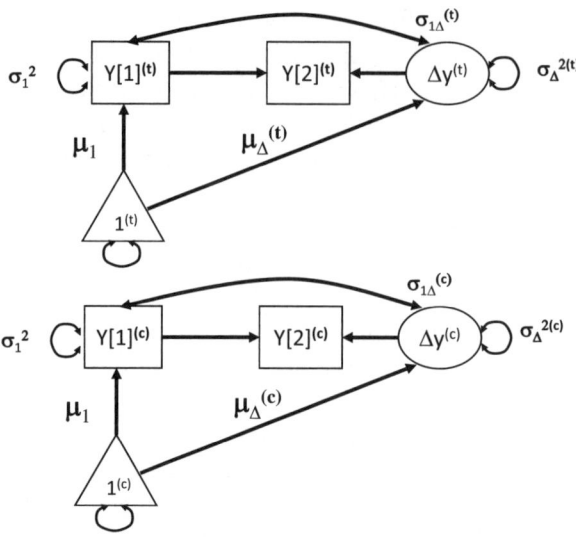

Figure 29.1. A multiple group latent change score model with selected group differences; T = trained group; C = control group.

Longitudinal data collections often include different numbers of data points for different people and different variables, and one good way to deal with these kinds of statistical problems is to include MGMs, which permit different numbers of data points on each person (e.g., McArdle, 1994; McArdle & Bell, 2000).

The careful reader will notice that we have not emphasized the examination of the invariance of the groups at the initial time of measurement (i.e., the pretest). In these examples, comparisons at baseline can be provided, but here we take an unusually dogmatic perspective: In randomized experiments, the parameters of the pretest scores should not routinely be allowed to vary over groups. That is, even if there was some lack of randomization to groups—and there were differences at the pretest, the inferences about change require invariance at baseline, and it seems more appropriate to allow misfit and have a proper interpretation of the changes from a common set of baseline parameters. This SEM principle of an invariant statistical starting point can be used to statistically adjust any "cross-over" controversy (e.g., Lord, 1969) and can be seen as an extension of the missing-completely-at-random assumption used with incomplete data (as in McArdle & Hamagami, 1992).

On the other hand, there may be many additional variables that are randomly related to the group membership that can have an effect on the results within groups and between groups (i.e., the measured demographics here). Initial group differences within groups may have contributed to the high initial level variance and level-slope correlations. In this experiment, the selection of persons was designed to examine older ages with different educational levels, and previous experiments have found age and education effects can impact outcomes of learning new tasks. To examine these possibilities, we can next fit a few additional models including age as a variable or represented in terms of age groups. In the first model, we could include group invariant regressions of latent levels and slopes on the measured age variable. Additional degrees of freedom will come from the model restriction that all age effects can be accounted for at the latent variable level.

If we fit these kinds of models, we can describe differences in the dynamic features of the models using a comparison of multiple statistical vector fields, which is done in Figure 29.2.

We should not allow the demographic (Age plus Education) level regressions to vary over groups, to retain our inferential (i.e., randomized) baseline, but we can still examine group differences in the demographic (Age plus Education) slope relationships; that is, they could have changed in different ways. In further models, we can also examine direct Age plus Education change relationships, and we certainly can allow these to vary over groups. Some of these models are not a typical of the current literature, but they are fairly easy to fit and may have direct consequences on the other predictions within the dynamic model.

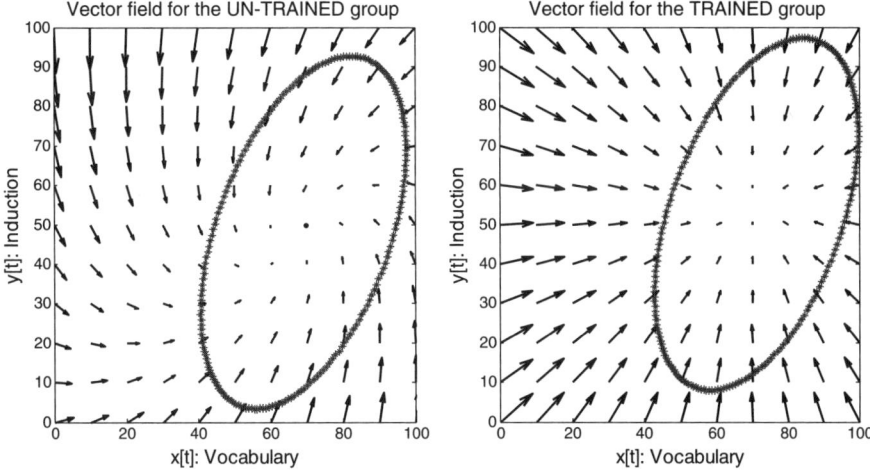

Figure 29.2. Vector field plots for common factor results from McArdle (2007b) for the untrained and trained groups from the Berlin Aging Training Study. Ellipse is 95% confidence boundary around actual stating points, and arrows represent direction of changes; see text for details. From *Longitudinal Models in the Behavioral and Related Sciences* (pp. 159–188), by K. Montfort, H. Oud, and A. Satorra (Eds.), 2007, Mahwah, NJ: Erlbaum. Copyright 2007 by Taylor & Francis. Reprinted with permission.

30

THE POPULAR REPEATED MEASURES ANALYSIS OF VARIANCE

Clearly, we should be able to run a repeated measures analysis of variance (RANOVA; Bock, 1975; Fisher, 1925; McCall & Applebaum, 1984; O'Brien & Kaiser, 1978; Winer, 1971) just like everyone else. This is what is ordinarily done to assert group differences, and we should certainly be able to do it here. We also need to face the fact that the model we are advocating in latent change score (LCS) modeling is very similar to the RANOVA model: the bivariate LCS model seems to go a bit further. Although it is true that RANOVA does not have a simple way to deal with incomplete data, any versions of RANOVA can be fitted using mixed-effects software (McArdle, 2006; McArdle & Hamagami, 2014b). So this is not really the key issue; the key issue is the RANOVA model itself.

FITTING RANOVA MODELS

As we have expressed it here, RANOVA, even with its many flexible analysis of covariance options (see Bock, 1975; Muller & Stewart, 2006; O'Brien & Kaiser, 1978), has a fundamental limitation that probably should be considered a flaw in longitudinal research. That is, all correlations of measures do not realistically have the same values. Although it can be corrected when testing for significance (Greenhouse & Geisser, 1962; Hertzog & Rovine, 1985), this is not true of estimation. These RANOVA models all assume that there is only one source of common variance due to individuals: The level variance is separated from the residual variance. This is primarily because the fixed effects (group means) are the primary objective in most longitudinal analysis. Thus, the misfits are first determined by evaluating the initial covariances and means, but then all subsequent models rely on alternatives based on a better accounting for fixed effects.

RANOVA IS VERY POPULAR

We must deal with the fact that behavioral science researchers seem to like to like the RANOVA, possibly because it is so widespread and so easy to carry out. Our suggestion is to carry out the RANOVA first, because this is a very simple model, and subsequently treat this as one of the most important models in longitudinal research—because it is. If these models are merely simplifications of what we are doing, these models should be fitted first, and perhaps ruled out in the usual way, before going on to more complicated explanations.

VII
SUMMARY AND DISCUSSION

IV

31

CONTEMPORARY DATA ANALYSES BASED ON PLANNED INCOMPLETENESS

We have now come a fairly long way down the road in this survey of developmental longitudinal structural equation models (LSEMs), and perhaps some of these concepts are already being used by the reader or other persons. We have tried to illustrate the many alternatives that are available, and we have made a few suggestions about which of these can be most useful in practice. With these possibilities in mind, we now look a bit further ahead and try to suggest other extensions of these basic ideas.

We want to recognize that there are several other variations of this basic latent change score (LCS) approach that can be used to create an alternative set of model expectations (Hamagami & McArdle, 2001, 2007). We have presented only a few reasonable-seeming alternatives here, primarily to show how they can be considered, and we will leave these more-advanced models to other presentations (Hamagami & McArdle, 2007; McArdle & Hamagami, 2014b).

---

http://dx.doi.org/10.1037/14440-032
Longitudinal Data Analysis Using Structural Equation Models, by J. J. McArdle and J. R. Nesselroade
Copyright © 2014 by the American Psychological Association. All rights reserved.

We try to do something simpler in this part of the book. First, we elaborate on the contemporary use of popular techniques in psychological research. It seems that repeated measures analysis of variance (RANOVA) is the most prominent model of data analysis, and we basically wonder why this is so. We then provide some comments about accumulating results and summarizing research data. The careful reader will note that we are not fully enthusiastic about the current uses of "meta-analysis" either, and we try to explain why. We next consider some of the benefits and limitation of randomization of people in longitudinal settings, which we certainly advocate. In fact, we expand this idea and next consider the more complete randomization of occasions and measurements in longitudinal data collections. We then provide some comments about multivariate measurement and suggest how the multiple factorial invariance over time model presented here can be useful in understanding future dynamics. We finish by elaborating on concepts and models for intensively measured repeated measurements, and we leave the reader ready and eager to go on to further longitudinal data collection and analyses.

This is not intended to be a technical discussion, so we do not use definitions or numerical tables anymore. Instead, we will just use words and figures to convey our final messages.

There are now literally thousands of examples of excellent incomplete longitudinal data analysis available, and we will not try to summarize them. We will say that most of these are geared toward the analysis of all the data available, not just the data from the complete cases (see Exhibit 14.1). We will highlight the key features of these models, and we will try to illustrate some consensus in the field.

SELECTING PEOPLE IN LONGITUDINAL STUDIES

One interesting approach to data analysis is not to measure some people all the time. This approach was used by Nesselroade and Baltes (1974), where a subgroup of adolescents was intentionally not measured at some occasions just to see if they would differ in their outcomes. Our first illustration of this basic form of incomplete data is presented in Figure 31.1.

In Figure 31.1, we represent four groups of people who have been so designated by their pattern of incomplete data. In this case, the people were randomly assigned to each group, and each group has a special feature. In Group 1, we think of the people as each having a pretest score (Y[1]) and a posttest score (Y[2]), and we presume something went on in between (i.e., the treatment). This is the standard experimental group. In Group 2, we have the same setup, but we assume these people did not have the treatment. This is the standard control group. We can then fit a simple two-group change model to estimate the differences between the outcomes and, assuming

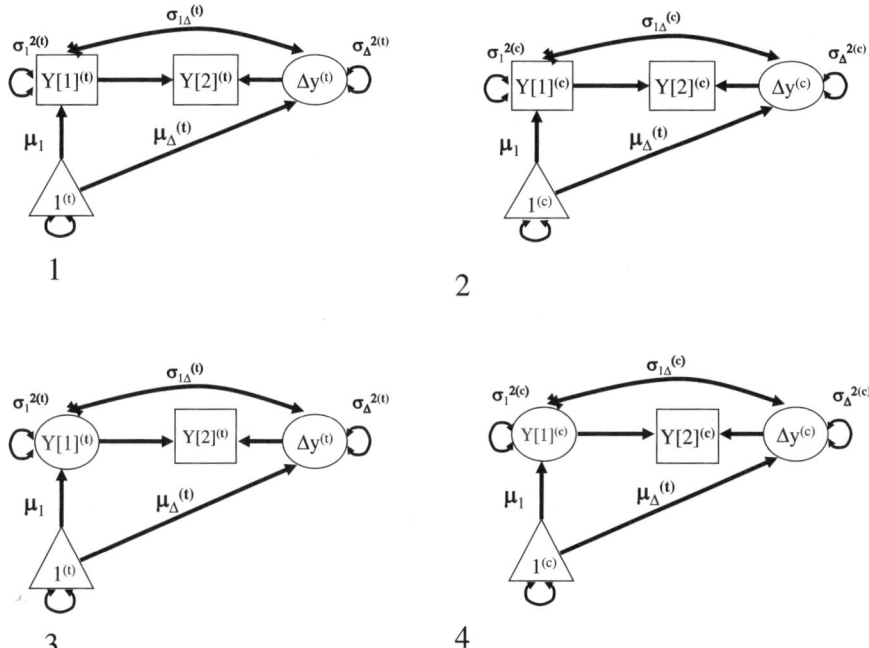

Figure 31.1. A structural equation modeling version of the Solomon four-group design; 1. Pre–post with treatment; 2. Pre–post with no treatment; 3. No pretest with treatment; 4. No pretest with no treatment.

random assignment to groups, we can estimate an expected change on any of the model statistics (e.g., mean of changes, variance of changes, covariance of changes, and initial levels). This is very much what we have already done (in McArdle, 2006), but we used more time points (i.e., $T = 4$).

What makes this figure different, however, is that here a special Subgroup 3 was not intentionally measured at Time 1 and yet received the treatment. Assuming people are randomly assigned to group, any comparisons of statistics between Group 3 and Group 1 would show the effect of the measurement, and it could have affected the treatment in several ways, such as increases in scores due to practice or due to increased confidence in taking the tests. For completion, Group 4 people are randomly selected, measured at Time 2 but not at Time 1, and do not receive the treatment. This design affords lots of opportunities to understand the treatment effects while simultaneously estimating the effect of repeated measurement. This has been termed a *Solomon four-group design* (for details, see Graziano & Raulin, 2000), and it is thought that it is an improvement over the classical design because it controls for the effect of the pretest. In fact, it allows for a rather thorough examination of group differences in both treatment and measurement.

Any variation of this data design can be fit using multiple group modeling (MGM)–structural equation modeling (SEM), including a model where there were no differences between groups at all. But, most important, this is a case in which the people have been randomly assigned to groups, so the inferences about any group differences are due to their random placement in the specific group. This creation and subsequent use of incomplete data is a first case of "planned incompleteness" (as in McArdle, 1994).

In Figure 31.2, we also present four groups of people who have been separated by their patterns of complete and incomplete data. In this common data collection, the people who do not come back for a second measurement, either with or without treatment, do so by their own choice, and this is not typically considered a random process. But, and this is the important issue, as long as we have some measures of why they did not come back and we include these measurements in our models, then the rest of the effects will be preserved. This is essentially the missing at random (MAR) logic, and it can be expressed here by requiring invariance over all the groups needed (i.e., treatment may exist). Of course, to the degree that this behavior is random, we may have a missing completely at random (MCAR) situation. More likely, it is the case that we have not measured the key features of attrition so

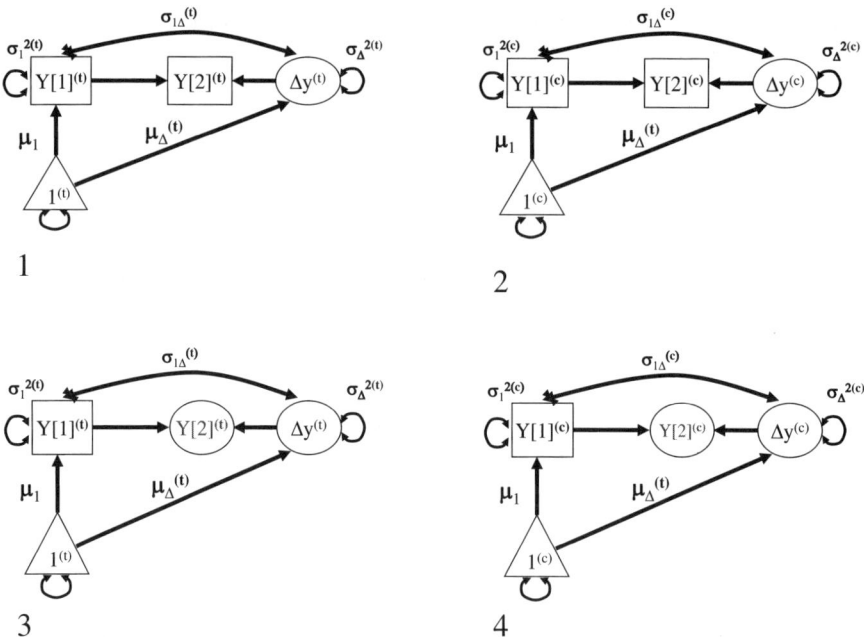

Figure 31.2. A structural equation modeling version of the longitudinal treatment design; 1. Pre–post with treatment; 2. Pre–post with no treatment; 3. Pretest, treatment, and attrition; 4. Pretest, no treatment, and attrition.

we cannot correct for the self-selection. This is clearly a case of "unplanned incompleteness" (as in McArdle, 1994).

MODELING EXISTING DATA WITH LESS THAN COMPLETE OCCASIONS

These simple designs anticipate an issue that emerges all the time: "How much data do we actually need?" In recent work, more complex models of planned incompleteness have been fitted using a raw data approach that does not require blocking the data into simple group patterns (see Hamagami & McArdle, 2001; McArdle & Woodcock, 1997; McArdle et al., 2002). The previous curve of factor scores (CUFFS) model was fitted by McArdle (1988), McArdle and Woodcock (1997), and McArdle et al. (2002). But in this research we wanted to estimate a full latent curve model (LCM) over many occasions, but a premium was placed on people's time (largely because we wanted to administer up to 17 tests). So we used the basic logic of latent variables as incomplete data to design a data collection plan (see Chapter 29). We measured each individual at a first occasion and then at a second occasion that was spaced out in time by our data collection design. The basis of the LCM we fitted is drawn as a path diagram (t = 0) or was a not-measured "circle in the square," indicating the person may or may not have been measured (as in McArdle, 1994), and we did this for up to four follow-up times (t = 1–4). This general data collection design is outlined in Figure 31.3.

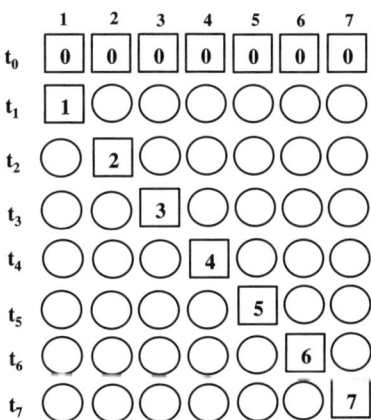

Figure 31.3. Planned incomplete test–retest time lag. Adapted from "Expanding Test–Retest Designs to Include Developmental Time-Lag Components," by J. J. McArdle and R. W. Woodcock, 1997, *Psychological Methods, 2,* p. 408. Copyright 1997 by the American Psychological Association.

In Figure 31.3, we illustrate a data collection plan in which people are measured only twice, and the first occasion is the same for all persons, but the second one is spaced at different distances in time. This kind of time-lag delay was randomly assigned to the participants and was intended to separate out components of changes from practice effects over multiple occasions, in an effort to better understand the timing of the changes (McArdle, Hamagami, Meredith, & Bradway, 2001).

We applied this principle of a random time lag to estimate and test developmental functions where the person was measured only twice but where we could estimate a multiple occasion LCM. We also found we could apply a second slope component that connected the two points in time, and this led to our independent estimate of a nontrivial practice function (with estimates of both μp and ϕp^2). This same approach was applied to multiple indicators of multiple constructs where, by assuming factorial invariance, we could separate the true-score changes from state-dependent changes and from test-specific practice effects (McArdle & Woodcock, 1997). One point of this research was to state that we do not need to measure all the people all the time in order to fit these models as long as there is random assignment to groups.

One of the first practical studies that used and evaluated this extended MGM–SEM logic was Horn and McArdle (1980), where components of simulated data were joined together. In a later substantive example, McArdle and Anderson (1990) used Bell's (1954) model of "acceleration" and "convergence" but estimated the relevant summary statistics using MGM-SEM. In these analyses, four samples of people of different initial ages who had longitudinal data from the Wechsler Adult Intelligence Scale (WAIS; Wechsler, 1955; from Ilene Seigler's Duke University studies) were put together using the MGM–maximum likelihood of estimates (MLE) approach, and various alternative LCMs were tested. Indeed, the MGM-MLE approach seemed to work.

McArdle and Hamagami (1991, 1992) attempted to check this MGM-SEM logic with a simple simulation study. In these studies, we generated data on $n = 100$ persons from a nonlinear-shaped LCM with $T = 4$ (so $d = 400$), and we fit the original LCM to establish the target results. We also fit a linear LCM to this nonlinear LCM data to show that it did not fit. We then eliminated some of the longitudinal data in particular ways. First, we randomly sampled people so they each only had $T = 2$ consecutive time points of data, mimicking what would happen if the investigators had only four groups of people measured twice over 10 years ($n = 25$ in each group but with only $d = 200$). We then refit the nonlinear LCM and the linear LCM, and were still able to choose the correct model.

McArdle and Hamagami (1991, 1992) then took these same longitudinal data and added a small increment to each individual's second score, to mimic second-time practice effects, and we found that we could not estimate the correct LCM unless the retest effect was taken into account. Obviously, having the correct model for the data counted. We next dropped (or masked) the second score of this set from individual's for whom we had generated low initial level scores at Time 1. This was intended to mimic the longitudinal case where people drop out who did not score well the first time. The LCM was refitted using MGM-MAR convergence techniques, using eight groups (i.e., where half of the people had two scores but another half only had one score), and the result was very similar to the original LCM. In a final selection, we dropped (or masked) data from people to whom we had assigned high slope scores in the original model: We reasoned that this type of selection is possible if people drop out are also those who change a lot. Of course, this is not something we would ever actually know about, but this was a statistical simulation so we did have this knowledge. The LCM was refitted using the eight-group MGM-MAR techniques (i.e., where some people had two scores, and some only had one score), and the result was a complete crash of the LCM with very poor results. We assumed that it took at least two occasions for change to be measured, and the LCM behaved accordingly.

In sum, the longitudinal simulation study of McArdle and Hamagami (1991, 1992) demonstrated that the MGM-SEM approach could work if the information about the selected data was either random of part of what was measured. The unfortunate fact is that the original investigators, McArdle and Anderson (1990), had no way of knowing what was true of their selected WAIS data. The limits of the nonrandomized models of incomplete data were beginning to become clear.

Other studies have been carried out where the LCS model was used instead of the LCM. The basic idea has been discussed earlier as unbalanced data in the prior models here. What we can do is to use a latent variable in place of a measured outcome. These specific techniques are illustrated in Figure 31.4 in an application to the Bradway longitudinal data (McArdle & Hamagami, 2006; see also McArdle, Grimm, Hamagami, Bowles, & Meredith, 2009). In these long-term longitudinal studies, the individuals were measured once at about age 5, age 15, age 30, age 40, age 55, and age 65. Of course, not all people were exactly the target ages, but we found that the exact ages did not matter very much. The LCS and bivariate LCS (BLCS) models were fitted to examine the patterns of influence among many different variables, but the assumption of MAR was used throughout. We assumed that the selection of occasions was our choice (not theirs), and if they did drop out at any time, it was indicated by the measurements at the prior time points. Thus, we used assumptions that allowed us to deal with all the longitudinal data: the overall $N = 111$ rather than complete cases where $n = 29$. We assume that most long-term longitudinal studies have these kinds of features.

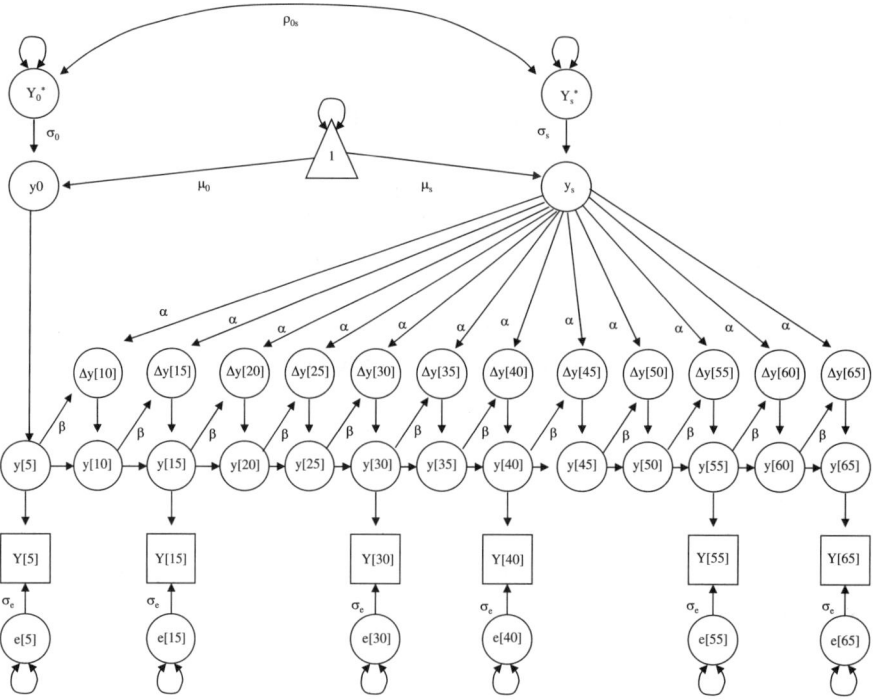

Figure 31.4. A path diagram of a latent change score model with incomplete data. From *Methodological Issues in Aging Research* (p. 61), by C. Bergeman and S. M. Boker (Eds.), 2006, Mahwah, NJ: Erlbaum. Copyright 2006 by Taylor & Francis. Adapted with permission.

RANDOMLY SELECTING MEASURES TO INCLUDE

This MGM-SEM approach also was used in an example of confirmatory factor analysis (CFA) of incomplete data by McArdle (1994). In this study, we first considered what would happen if a one- versus two-common factor model for the WAIS was the key issue, and we obtained an overall result with complete cases from the national sample. We then masked the available data in several different ways, including MCAR, MAR, and not missing at random (NMAR). A random fractional factorial design of measures was chosen as an optimal and quick way to test the specific hypothesis. In this data collection design, a first group of persons was chosen at random, and only half of the WAIS scales (four of eight) were administered.

A second randomly selected group was then administered a different set of half of the WAIS scales (four of eight, but a different four). This process was repeated until eight groups with a different pattern of four WAIS measures were obtained. Various models were fitted using an eight-group structural equation model, all with factorial invariance constraints, and the results were compared for one versus two common factors. In all cases, the resulting misfit suggested that two factors were needed. It was pointed out that such a fractional factorial data collection, if it were actually undertaken (i.e., not just masked), should take only about half of the usual testing time for any person. Thus, we viewed this approach as a trade-off of testing time for statistical power.

The power of the statistical tests for one versus two common factors was compared when there were between $m = 1$ to 8 variables measured in each required subgroup. The resulting power calculations, based on the Satorra and Saris (1985) method, were plotted for different sample sizes, and the results were somewhat surprising. For example, if we used the fractional factorial blocks design based on $m = 4$ variables in each group and we wanted to achieve a power of $(1 - \beta) = 0.95$, we would only need about $n = 80$ persons in each of the eight subgroups. Not surprisingly, as the power requirements grew larger so did the required samples sizes, and as the number of variables measured became smaller, so did the resulting power. But, in general, to retain relatively high power for the test of one versus two common factors, it seemed that relatively few individuals were actually needed in each subgroup (and see McArdle, 2011d; McArdle & Hamagami, 2001).

This research collectively demonstrated that we could recover the model parameters and test statistics with far less data than previously considered (McArdle, 1994). This work seemed to lead to a flurry of articles on "planned incomplete data," where we could easily assume a random component of missing data mechanisms. Of course, this result is entirely model dependent (i.e., we do need to have several assumptions), and the fewer data points involved, the less power we have to detect that our model is wrong. Either way, then, it seems far better to have selected data than not to have data at all.

JOINT GROWTH–SURVIVAL MODELING

This leads us to slightly different and highly technical topic: the use of shared parameter models in terms of growth and change (see Figure 31.5). In these kinds of joint analyses, some kind of time-to-event or "survival" model is considered as well as an LCS or other kind of longitudinal model. In McArdle, Small, Backman, and Fratiglioni (2005), we examined the longitudinal changes in word recall, and the simultaneous event that we examined in time was declared to be demented. We reasoned this was a date that could represent an approximation to an unrecoverable mental death, but the actual date of death could be used instead. The reason these

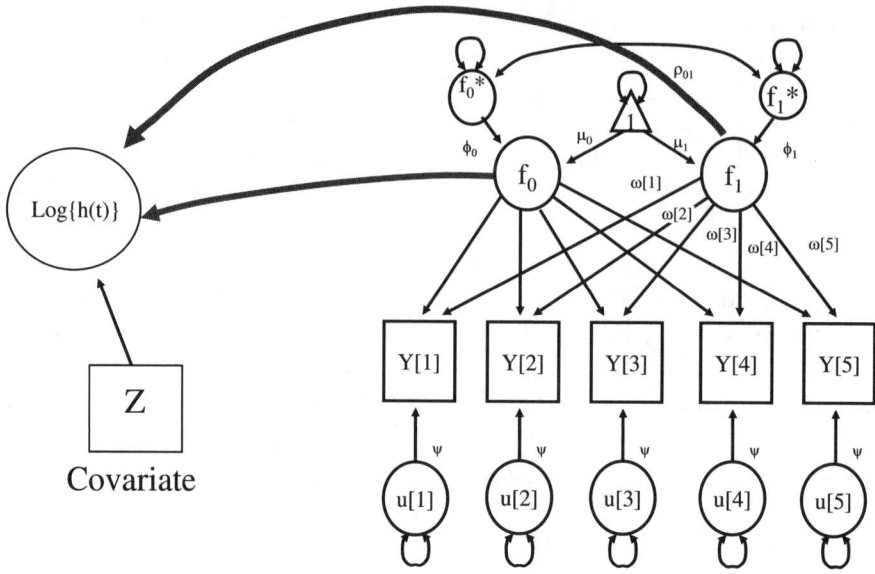

Figure 31.5. A recent model of mixed survival and growth in which level and slope scores are used to predict hazard (survival) scores. From "Longitudinal Models of Growth and Survival Applied to the Early Detection of Alzheimer's Disease," by J. J. McArdle, B. J. Small, L. Backman, & L. Fratiglioni, 2005, *Journal of Geriatric Psychiatry and Neurology, 18*, p. 235. Copyright 2005 by SAGE. Reprinted with permission.

model are joint is that all parameters are estimated simultaneously. The way we considered it, the variables that produced the survival curve were also responsible for some alteration of the levels and slopes of the word recall scores over time.

Although not much new information was actually uncovered in our analysis, it forced us to highlight a slightly different population problem. That is, we might think we are trying to make assumptions about either (1) all the people as if they had stayed alive for testing (i.e., MAR), but by using the joint growth–survival models, we have come to realize that our population of inferences in life-span research is actually a bit more complex, and we need to consider (2) if they survive, how do they change over time? The survival parameters are used to "condition" the other model expectations, no matter what they are. This can produce results that are substantially different from using the MAR assumption (Assumption 1), when these joint results (Assumption 2) are in fact conditional on the measured time-to-event scores. Thus, this joint growth–survival modeling seems like a very reasonable approach that should be used more often, especially to understand data collected where the persons cannot possibly respond (e.g., dementia, death).

MASKING CURRENTLY AVAILABLE DATA

To demonstrate the viability of any incomplete data estimation techniques, we can certainly mask some of our existing longitudinal data. This takes little work, so it is surprising that it is not considered more often. Although the results shown here leave something to be desired, the benefits of considering incomplete group longitudinal data are profound in terms of the results and in terms of the research design as well. For example, one of the corollary between-group issues is the potential for combining cross-sectional and longitudinal data. In one early resolution of these problems, Bell (1953) created a data collection he termed accelerated longitudinal data. To ensure uniformity of the outcomes, Bell suggested a test of convergence of the cross-sectional and longitudinal data, created by joining the shorter spans of data from people who were most similar at the end points. In contemporary work, this same set of assumptions is now fitted with "invariance of the basis coefficients" (McArdle & Anderson, 1990). In his earlier work, Bell (1954) used masking techniques, and he demonstrated that estimates and inferences were basically the same even though the data collection was accelerated. Of course, we now do the same analysis using statistical solutions for incomplete data (Hsiao, 2003; McArdle & Bell, 2000; Miyazaki & Raudenbush, 2000).

CONTEMPORARY LONGITUDINAL ANALYSES

It now seems that all contemporary analyses can be represented as MGM–SEM with different numbers of data points on each person (McArdle & Hamagami, 1992). In this case, a model of longitudinal convergence (after Bell, 1954; McArdle & Bell, 2000) is a reasonable goal of many studies, even if it is not always a hypothesis that can be testable with incomplete patterns (McArdle & Anderson, 1990).

It follows that the MAR assumption is best when viewed as a convenient starting point, allowing us to use all the available information in one analysis, but we need to remember that it could be incorrect for a number of reasons (e.g., Heyting, Tolboom, & Essers, 1992; McArdle, 1994). One key reason seems to be the nonrandom self-selection of persons to testing. Obviously, these key assumptions could alter our results, so they need to be examined in detail. That is, instead of simply stating that MAR is a reasonable assumption, we should investigate methods for evaluating the failure of these assumptions (i.e., the joint growth–survival models). We can examine a model on the data that are already available, as in masking, or we can gather the required information about the person (or variable) selection process (for more detail, see Hedeker & Gibbons, 1997).

So what seemed fairly simple earlier is not actually very simple, especially if we do not know why people drop out of our longitudinal studies. We can assume MCAR, as we have typically done, or we can use any of the MAR corrections, which seem very reasonable today. But we still may be in an NMAR situation and not realize it. Most new SEM computer programs allow for the full information maximum likelihood (FIML) representation, so it is fairly easy to make this kind of MGM-SEM quite practical (i.e., this is now the default of many computer programs).

However, we may actually have longitudinal data that are NMAR, not MAR, and we may be getting the wrong answers. In fact, this danger seems even more likely in the longitudinal design because of the increasing demands placed on all participants. In some extreme cases, the people may drop out of the study because of age-related health failures, and surely this is NMAR-based person selection. There are a few contemporary ways to deal with these NMAR issues, but they are fairly novel (e.g., McArdle, Small, Backman, & Fratiglioni, 2005). So we will try not to obtain biased results, even for the selected longitudinal data presented.

32

FACTOR INVARIANCE IN LONGITUDINAL RESEARCH

We introduced common factors into longitudinal research here to recognize the importance of keeping some things constant (i.e., factor loadings) so we could examine changes in other things (i.e., factor scores). Until now, we have based a lot of our inferences on the multiple factorial invariance over time (MFIT) criteria, and although we know that the models do not fit the multivariate data perfectly, we are satisfied that we have made some progress in the right direction. Other possibilities for checking on the best rotation and the utility of these common factors exist, and we want to mention two additional possibilities now.

BIOMETRIC DESIGN POSSIBILITIES WITH COMMON FACTORS

One area of research that counts heavily on multiple group models (MGMs)–structural equation models (SEMs) is the study of biometric genetics with twins and their families. In this area, we started by demonstrating how

http://dx.doi.org/10.1037/14440-033
Longitudinal Data Analysis Using Structural Equation Models, by J. J. McArdle and J. R. Nesselrode
Copyright © 2014 by the American Psychological Association. All rights reserved.

common factors of change (McArdle, 1986; McArdle & Plassman, 2009) and measurement (McArdle & Goldsmith, 1990) could be a major part of twin research. One unusual aspect of this work is that we assumed that the standard twin model, including groups of monozygotic and dizygotic twins, could be used to determine treasonable psychometric common factors (i.e., the ones that fit best). This approach using twin models as a vehicle to isolate common factors, to our knowledge, has not been used as a formal criterion in factor rotation (see McArdle & Prescott, 1996).

We continued using longitudinal structural equation models (LSEMs) with twins and found out that the latent curve model (LCM) was a good way to analyze longitudinal twin data (see McArdle, 1986), and it could be fitted using many different programs (McArdle & Prescott, 1996), including the standard provisions for incomplete data (McArdle & Plassman, 2009; McArdle, Prescott, Hamagami, & Horn, 1998). We considered the twin design for estimating dynamic parameters as well (Finkel, Reynolds, McArdle, Hamagami, & Pedersen, 2009; McArdle & Hamagami, 2004).

In our most recent work (McArdle & Prescott, 2010), we considered different models for the inclusion of measured genetic information (e.g., apolipoprotein ε groups). Although we did not come to a conclusion about the optimal way to deal with this problem, we did show that the longitudinal repeated measurements, in the context of any model, add reliability to the phenotypic scores. These alternative models were not used to find the best common factors, but they could have been.

LONGITUDINAL ALTERNATIVES TO SIMPLE STRUCTURE ROTATION

In the absence of MFIT, we do not assert that the same factors are measured with the same variables, which is definitely a reason that we advocate the MFIT criteria. Although we might be interested in evidence for a qualitative change, it is difficult to go much further because we do not have analytic tools to "compare apples to oranges." Unfortunately, in many applied cases, the tests in the battery are not chosen by a clear simple structure theory but are packaged together to span a broad range of attributes. In these cases, we might find that some specific variables may be the reason for lack of invariance and rely on a model with partial invariance, but we have not considered this in any detail.

Of course, this means that different numbers of common factors can emerge at each occasion, but we can always consider any common factor solution to include factors with zero variance (i.e., as nodes or phantom variables). This structural expression is usually not meaningful in single occasion data, but in two-occasion data it now plays a role in the evaluation of equal number of factors at each time. That is, we can essentially restate the number of factor problems in terms of "How many factors are needed for the equality of the factor loadings?" or "How many common factors are needed to accept metric invariance?" This type of evaluation strategy sets up an important trade-off between the utility of invariant factors versus the cost of dealing with different factors at different occasions.

In some prior work on this topic, Cattell (1944) proposed an alternative to Thurstone's (1947) simple structure in terms of factorial invariance over multiple groups. In subsequent work on this problem, Meredith (1964a) showed that covariances were required for Cattell's form of "parallel proportional profiles" with multiple groups (G). Following this lead, McArdle and Cattell (1994) provided conditions for structural factor identification of confactor rotation with multiple groups. In multiple group problems, it is possible to identify all rows and columns of the invariant factor loadings (Λ) model by only requiring restrictions on multiple group covariances matrices. The extension of this confactor logic to longitudinal factor problems implies there may be a unique but complex set of loadings that are invariant over all occasions T. We can write the multiple group and corresponding multiple occasion constraints as restrictions on the other model parameters (McArdle, 2007b).

One set of restrictions uses covariance constraints within the occasions ($\Sigma[t,t]$) as if each occasion were a separate group but allows many over-time covariance matrices ($\Phi[t > 2, t > 2]$) to be unrestricted. This result is practically useful because it suggests that the multiple occasion factor constraints can be placed so that an invariant factor pattern can be identified without any restrictions. These invariant factor loadings may then be rotated using any procedure, but the factor pattern Λ used for all occasions will remain invariant over even after any rotation, and thus can lead to parsimony (i.e., when $T > K$).

One basis for this premise of complex but invariant factors is illustrated in Figures 32.1 through 32.4. In the left-hand side of Figure 32.1, we presume the existence of a population model with ten observed variables and two common factors ($F1$ and $F2$). As depicted here, the first three variables load only on the first factor ($F1$), and the last three variables load only on the second factor ($F2$). This is a complex pattern that might not be clear in a single occasion simple structure rotation. Our analysis would be simpler if we selected (or measured) only the first three variables and the last three variables, as in Figure 32.2. But if by some chance, we had only measured the middle four variables, all of which have complex loadings on both factors, we would obtain the complex structural result of Figure 32.3. Of course, there are many other possibilities.

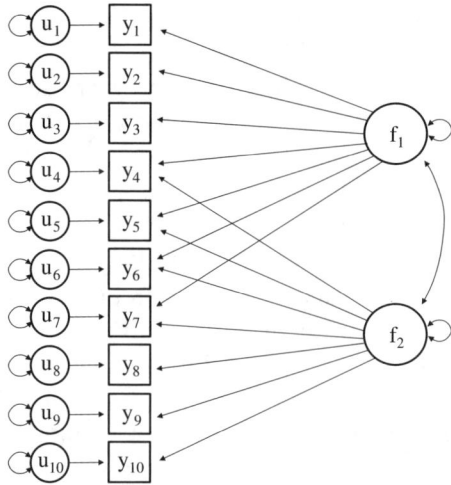

Figure 32.1. A two-factor population model.

LONGITUDINAL ROTATION TO SIMPLE DYNAMICS

Although the latter situation is not desirable, it may be the one we find ourselves in. It is thought that this kind of complexity can be avoided by good test design (i.e., pure markers), but it is a reasonable possibility when we must examine an existing test battery, for example, the Wechsler Adult Intelligence Scale–Revised (Wechsler, 1981). The key opportunity that two-occasion data offers is the possibility that this set of loadings is parsimonious: complex but invariant with no cross-occasion loadings, as depicted in Figure 32.4. Multiple

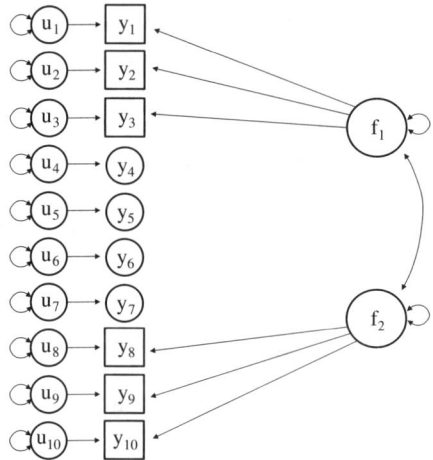

Figure 32.2. A simple selection result.

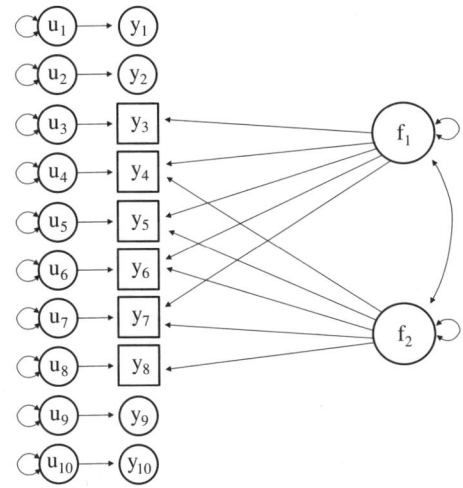

Figure 32.3. A complex selection result.

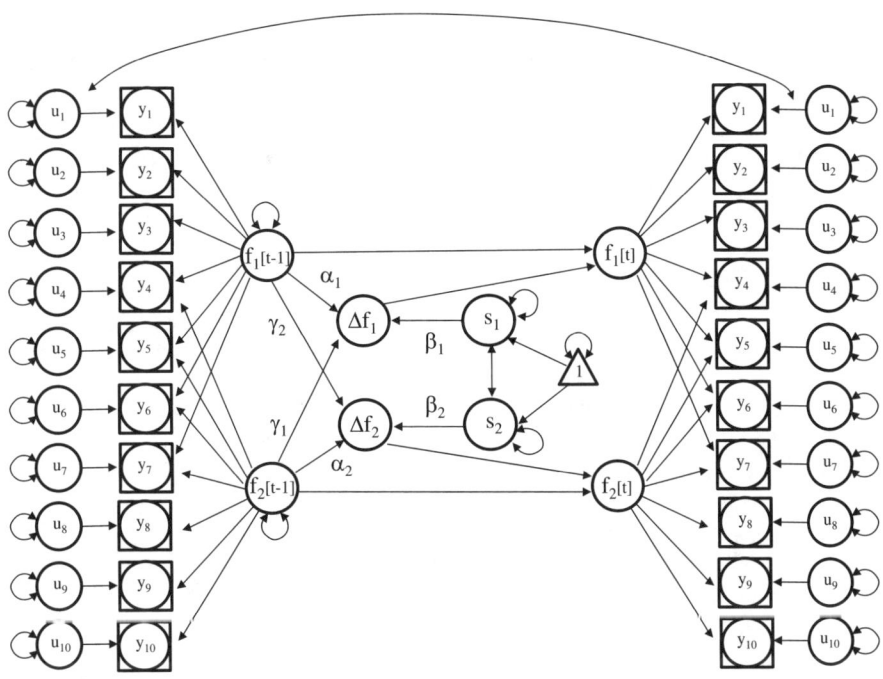

Figure 32.4. A two-factor repeated measures model with confactor invariance at all occasions.

occasion data can be used to help resolve the factorial complexity of a population model, especially when it is considered in the context of a dynamic model. Given a K-factor hypothesis at several occasions, we may identify all elements of the factor loading matrix (Λ) by creating dynamic restrictions over time (McArdle, 2007b). The second set of longitudinal constraints can be formed from restrictions with variables having no cross-correlation over time or be based on specific dynamic structures with zero elements. In the third time we identify all factor loadings by using latent variable regression restrictions where the partial covariances among residual factors are zero. This final set of restrictions can be used to identify the factor model where we propose that "Factor 1 is the leader of Factor 2." In all cases, we can identify these factors with no additional restrictions on the factor loadings.

Using model restrictions over time to identify factor loadings was a main theme of A. Arbuckle and Friendly (1977). The focus on invariant factor loadings and, hence, the invariant factors, was initially described as "rotation to simple dynamics" (McArdle & Nesselroade, 1994, 2003). A contemporary approach to selection of these kinds of restrictions can be evaluated by computational procedures for identification, and further explorations of dynamic forms of confactor rotation in longitudinal multiple occasion data are needed.

This final approach would require some simplicity of the parameters representing the dynamics over time. In essence, this advocates the use of an invariant factor pattern or confactor solution for repeated measures where simple dynamics are used as the rotational criteria (as suggested by McArdle, 2007b). Incidentally, this approach seems entirely consistent with the MFIT principles presented and used here.

33

VARIANCE COMPONENTS FOR LONGITUDINAL FACTOR MODELS

The common collection of multiple occasion longitudinal data has led to a variety of other alternatives. One of the first structural factor models for longitudinal data was presented by Jöreskog (1969) in terms of the structuring of the covariance into different factorial components. If we rewrite the longitudinal factor model so the observed scores at any occasion are decomposed into (1) a factor score ($Fc[t]$) that is common over all measures and times, (2) another factor score (Fs) that is specific to each measured variable, and (3) another factor ($u[t]$) that is unique to ever variable at each time, then this decomposition of the specific covariances of one variable into a specific factor is not possible without multiple manifestations of the same specific factor. But Jöreskog (1969) recognized that this was possible with multiple occasion data of the same measurement. Provisions can also be made for the invariance of the common factors and lack of invariance for the specific factors, allowing a form of the prior model of partial invariance.

http://dx.doi.org/10.1037/14440-034
Longitudinal Data Analysis Using Structural Equation Models, by J. J. McArdle and J. R. Nesselroade
Copyright © 2014 by the American Psychological Association. All rights reserved.

One potential problem with using this model is that the identification constraints needed to separate the common factors and the specific factors are based on an orthogonality restriction typically used in multiple mode models of Kenny and Zautra (1995), McArdle and Woodcock (1997), and Kroonenberg and Oort (2003). All of these models offer a decomposition of factorial influence based on the orthogonality of the common and specific components and between the specific factors as well. These alternatives models have interesting interpretations, but they do not provide the same result as some the other models described here (i.e., latent change score models). Indeed, we could move to a model that looks more like Figure 33.1.

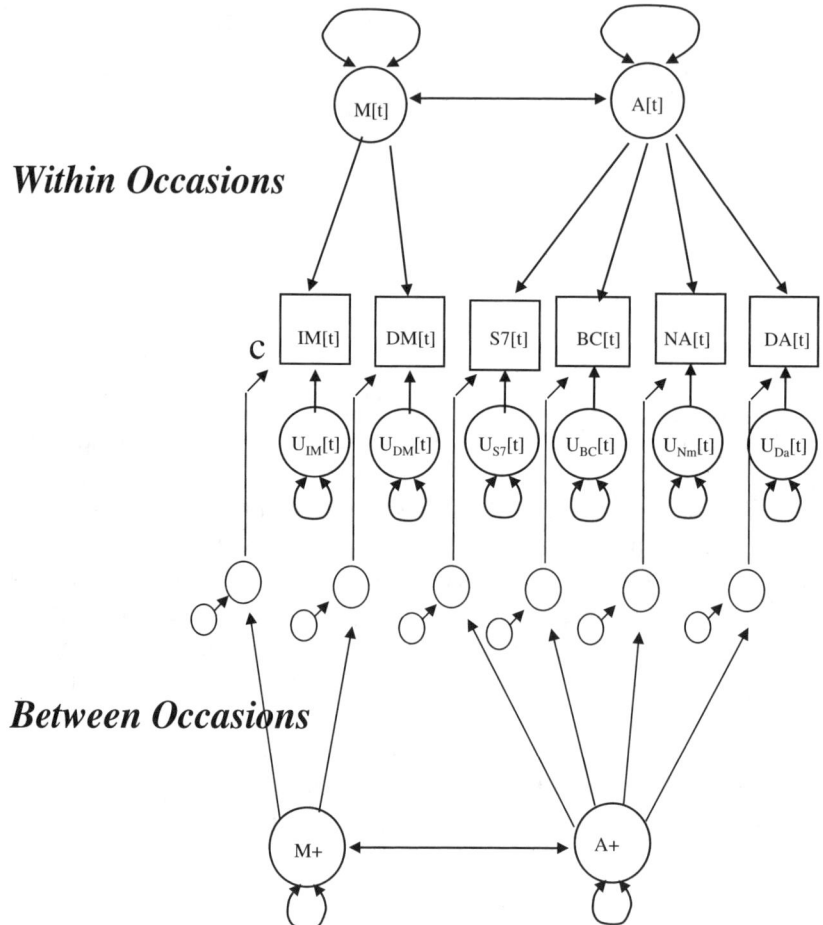

Figure 33.1. The path diagram of a longitudinal multilevel model. From *Factor Analysis at 100 Years* (pp. 115–117), by R. Cudeck and R. MacCallum (Eds.), 2007, Mahwah, NJ: Lawrence Erlbaum Associates, Inc. Copyright 2007 by Taylor & Francis. Reprinted with permission.

The collection of multiple occasion longitudinal data creates opportunities for several other alternatives. One practical solution for the problem of factor loading invariance in multiple occasion data comes in the form of a multiple level factor analysis model (after McArdle & Hamagami, 1996; McDonald & Goldstein, 1989).

We can rewrite the longitudinal factor model for a set of individual average scores over time (Y[+]), perhaps estimated from a common factor model for the between occasions cross-products $\Sigma[+]$. Similarly, we can rewrite the factor model in terms of T sets of individual deviation scores over time (i.e., Y[–] = Y[t] – Y[+]). Using this approach we remove the individual averages over time from the observed scores to obtain deviations for a $(T \times T)$ within occasion covariance matrix $\Sigma[-]$ based on $N*(T-1)$ pieces of information. The person-centering technique used in here resembles other classical approaches: (a) a standard between–within factor analysis of family data (Nagoshi, Phillips, & Johnson, 1987), (b) the multiple situation functional analysis of variance (ANOVA) approach used by Gollob (1968), and (c) the occasion-discriminant approach created by Horn (1972).

Using contemporary structural modeling software (e.g., Mplus, Mx, NLMIXED), we can carry out a precise form of these operations by fitting both concepts directly. In this form of a multilevel model (MLM), we consider both a first-order latent variable model ($\Lambda[-]$) for a person in terms of the deviations around the averages over time and a second-order model ($\Lambda[+]$) of the variation between people over time. By restating the original model in this way, we can now use a structural principle discussed earlier: If the loadings are invariant over time, the factor pattern between occasions $\Lambda[+]$ should equal all the factor pattern within occasions $\Lambda[-]$.

Given this setup, in order to test the broad hypothesis of multiple occasion loading invariance over time, we simply have to test whether or not the same pair of variable loadings between occasions equals the variable loadings within occasions no matter how many time points are available. Using this multiple level approach, we can also effectively consider cases where each person has different amounts of longitudinal data (i.e., incomplete data due to attrition, etc.).

The process of factorial modeling of longitudinal data is now easily extended to include many occasions. First, we can fit a one-factor model to up to T-occasions of data per person with (a) an $(M \times 1)$ vector of loadings (Λ) equal over all times, (b) M unique variances (Ψ^2) equal over all times, (c) a restricted factor variance at Time 1 ($\Phi[1]^2 = 1$), but with (d) no restriction on the later factor variances ($\Phi[t > 1]^2$) or covariances ($\Phi[t > 1, t + j]$). Next we use the same models, but we relax the assumption of strict metric invariance over the loadings between occasions and within occasions and examine the change in fit.

The relaxation of invariant loadings in the same configuration may yield important information about specific occasions of measurement, and virtually any model can fit or fail. Although the constraints on the between and within occasion matrix yields much smaller restrictions (i.e., degrees of freedom) than in other models, the basic result and conclusions are often identical, so the key question remains the same: "Do these data display a reasonable form of invariance over time?" If this test fails, we must conclude that we do not have repeated constructs and other forms of the common factor models might be more useful (e.g., FOCUS).

There are a few caveats about the use of this general approach to multiple occasion data based on multilevel factor analysis. First, in the typical multilevel estimation we require the between and within components to be uncorrelated, and this may not be a reasonable assumption for some constructs. Second, and in contrast to other longitudinal latent variable models, information about the time-based order of occasions is not actually used here. Thus, any representation of the sequence of events over time is not used and is uninformative. Third, the within-group estimation of the factor model also does not depend on a strict time order, so within-person and within-measure specific covariance are now aggregated as a part of the overall within-time variance (i.e., no specific over-time covariances). Fourth, in this multilevel format the missing at random assumptions are used, but they are more difficult to evaluate than in other models (e.g., see Figure 33.1). Thus, this MLM is especially useful at a first stage of multiple occasion analysis to test the key questions of factorial invariance.

Once multiple factorial variance over time can be established, by assuming that the between-factor loadings equal the within-factor loadings, we can move on to other models in a later stage of analysis (e.g., using latent change score models). This use of MLMs is not very popular, but it will be as soon as researchers realize its full potential and practicality. Until then, the MLM seems a bit confusing, and this is too bad, because it is really very important for good longitudinal analyses.

34

MODELS FOR INTENSIVELY REPEATED MEASURES

We are now near the end of our discourse, so we will try not to expand our view of longitudinal research. In their oft-cited comment, "every man is in certain respects like all other men, like some other men, like no other man," Murray and Kluckhohn (1953) succinctly, if broadly, circumscribed the arena in which students of behavior conduct their inquiry. Murray and Kluckhohn's statement provides us a springboard into a somewhat sparsely populated end of the pool, but it is an end where the water is deep and the swimming exciting for those who dare to venture there. Ignoring the epoch-centric sexism of their wording, the bulk of behavioral research is either overtly or tacitly oriented either toward how "every man is in certain respects like all other men" or "like some other men." These two foci are consistent with the nomothetic goals of scientific inquiry and, in fact, lie at the heart of concerns about establishing the generalizability of lawful relations (Nesselroade & Molenaar, 2010b).

---

http://dx.doi.org/10.1037/14440-035
Longitudinal Data Analysis Using Structural Equation Models, by J. J. McArdle and J. R. Nesselroade
Copyright © 2014 by the American Psychological Association. All rights reserved.

The third aspect of the Murray and Kluckhohn account—"every man is in certain respects like no other man"—has tended to be rather inconsequential except for either providing grist for a convenient "error term" against which to evaluate outcomes in the first two categories or a venue into which there are only occasional forays aimed at integrating an idiographic perspective into nomothetic inquiry (e.g., Lamiell, 1981; Nesselroade, Gerstorf, Hardy, & Ram, 2007; Zevon & Tellegen, 1982). For reasons to be discussed subsequently, we believe that the disparity in attention paid to the three categories should be remedied and that it should be done by putting more emphasis on the integration of the third category into empirical inquiry involving the first two. It seems clear to us that there are both measurement and analysis concerns that are highly pertinent to longitudinal modeling to which we must attend if this integration is to be productive. We will examine some of these in what follows.

QUOTABLE QUOTES

To approach how it is that "every man is in certain respects like no other man" can be emphasized and incorporated directly into inquiry requires us to find variation that we can manipulate, dissect, even "torture" as necessary to the extent that it reveals something informative about the individual's behavior. The key role of variation in the subject matter of empirical science cannot be overstated, and it is reinforced from many quarters (Nesselroade & Molenaar, 2010b).

The psychological literature is rife with statements that identify key roles played by variation, variation representing many different time scales. One comes from L. L. Thurstone's writings (Torgerson, 1958):

> Each stimulus when presented to an observer gives rise to a discriminal process. Because of *momentary fluctuations* [italics added] in the organism, a given stimulus does not always excite the same discriminal process, but may excite one at a higher or lower value on the psychological continuum. . . . If we present the stimulus to the observer a large number of times, we can think of a *frequency distribution* [italics added] on the psychological continuum of discriminal processes associated with that stimulus. (p. 156)

In the case of scaling, for example, it was often so that many judges were used once, as opposed to one judge being used many times, in order to scale stimuli. This exemplifies how in our efforts to identify variation that can be studied, we sometimes substitute between-person information for within-person information. One can read in the implication that within-person information is the ideal and the between-person information an approximation of that ideal. It is a topic that we will come back to, at least implicitly, over and over.

Another example comes from Gulliksen's (1950) book on classical test theory in which he identified the lack of "normal daily variability" as a problem in estimating test–retest reliability with immediate test–retest values:

> The major difficulty with reliability obtained by the successive administration of parallel forms is that it is too high. This is because there is no possibility for the variation due to *normal daily variability* [italics added] to lower the correlation between forms. (p. 197)

What Gulliksen was referring to as a problem, that is, normal daily variability, is an example of what we believe is worth studying. At the very least, Gulliksen recognized that it is there.

John Horn (1972), reporting the results of a study of prisoners whom he measured weekly for 10 weeks with a battery of ability tests, wrote:

> The results illustrated how fluid intelligence (as well as other attributes of intellectual test behavior) *varies* [italics added] functionally within persons and also represents a stable pattern of performances that distinguishes one person from another. (p. 47)

Raymond B. Cattell (1966d) made a similar point and also introduced what might be termed a *morality aspect*, by arguing:

> However, if a trait fluctuates at all—and even a man's stature we are told varies slightly from day to day, then the widespread practice of taking a single occasion measurement and calling it a trait measurement is wrong. In practice it may even be morally wrong, as when we measure an individual's IQ on a single occasion and allot or do not allot a scholarship to him on the basis of that result. (p. 357)

These quotes amply illustrate the salience of variation in the quest to understand behavior and behavior change. In this chapter, we focus on measuring and modeling variation at the individual level.

THREE KEY PREMISES

As instructors, we have learned that it is essential to be as open as possible about the premises that underlie one's efforts. Three premises are key to the contents of the present chapter. How they bear on both what we will discuss and the broader scale of inquiry will be evident as we proceed.

First, the individual is the primary unit of analysis for studying behavior—and behavior changes. This old sentiment, which appears repeatedly in the psychological literature, was stated forcefully in a comment by

Horn (personal communication, 2006): "The individual is the fundamental unit of the science of psychology, not individual differences and certainly not aggregates of individuals." It is also at the heart of Molenaar's (2004) discussion of units of analysis for behavioral researchers and underlies the intentions of those who promote a "person-centered" orientation to the study of changes (Magnusson, 2000). In relation to our present aims, it helped to pave the way to dealing with the uniqueness of the individual and its role in identifying and studying the similarities among individuals that are part and parcel of understanding behavior.

Second, latent variables are central to psychological research and theorizing. They populate our research and theory—requiring us to develop valid measurement models. Latent variables have been a salient component of the modeling discussions in this book, beginning with the models of Part II and continuing to the models of Part VI. Historically, their use and the growth of multivariate modeling techniques, especially factor analysis, have been mutually reinforcing and are now widespread. It is our belief that this is a positive and productive development because of the power the concepts lend to the development of theory. As a science, psychology aims to establish lawful relations that have generality across people. Generality is achieved with the use of latent variables. For example, contrast "Frustration produces aggression" with "Cutting off another driver in traffic produces obscene finger gestures." One is a broad, theoretical statement made possible by the use of the latent variables Frustration and Aggression. The other is a much narrower statement, many different variations of which would be needed to capture the range of meaning in "Frustration produces aggression."

Third, determining invariant relations—what attributes of entities remain invariant under which transformations—is a primary objective of scientific inquiry (Keyser, 1956). Invariance, in some form, is used to demonstrate that the "same" latent variable is being measured in different samples of participants at the same time (cross-sectional) or in the same samples of participants at different times (longitudinal). For example, in order for the concept of "change" to be meaningful in studying behavior, the pertinent measurements used to construct a change score are taken to represent the same "dimension."

An important way to establish "sameness" is by applying the criterion of factorial invariance across occasions of measurement. Consider the basic factor specification equation presented earlier (see the first two equations of Exhibit 17.1). Now, consider a second equation in which the *bracket* indicates that an individual has been remeasured at a later time, and the *change* between scores Y[1] and Y[2], which signifies the change in that individual from the first to the second occasion can be written as a factor outcome $F[2] - F[1]$, provided that the factor loadings are invariant over occasions of measurement. Thus, invariant factor loadings make it plausible to argue that it is the behavior of the person rather than what the instrument is measuring that has changed. This is a compelling line of reasoning that has served us for a century or so, but it holds only so long as the factor loadings are invariant over occasions. "Watering down" the invariance notion to achieve a better fit to empirical data (e.g., configural invariance, partial invariance) dilutes this powerful use of factorial invariance concepts.

Given these three premises, we will now probe more deeply into the building of measurement models and their incorporation into structural models involving multiple latent variables.

ESTABLISHING MEASUREMENT MODELS FOR LATENT VARIABLES

Assembling data in a persons (N) × variables (M) data matrix, an initial step in evaluating factorial invariance, implies that a person is the same person across all p variables. However, and this point is seldom made, it also implies that a variable is the same variable across all N persons. As Figure 34.1 indicates, there is an integrity to the matrix as a matrix because of the continuity in the meaning of the entries both across the rows and down the columns.

However, suppose the measured or observed variables that are ostensibly the same do not actually represent the same qualities from one person to another. Harking back to the comment by Murray and Kluckhohn (1953) with which we opened this chapter, suppose each person is like no other person in regard to what a given observed variable represents. Examples of such discontinuities are found in idiosyncratic uses of what is ostensibly a common language, response specificity in autonomic nervous system behavior, and shifting factor loadings of a given test as a function of age, practice, etc. We will examine the implications of such discontinuities when working with empirical data.

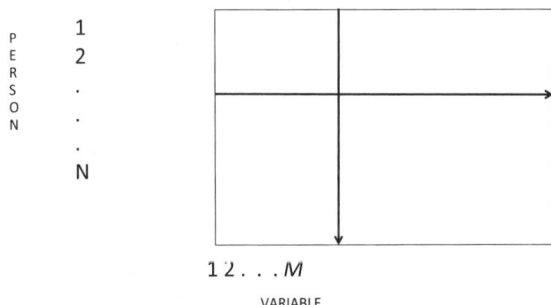

Figure 34.1. A traditional persons-by-variable view of a matrix of data.

The "Data Box"

The *data box* (Cattell, 1957) is probably a familiar heuristic to most readers. The $N \times M$ matrix shown earlier can be turned into the familiar three-dimensional data box by adding an *occasion* axis as shown in Figure 34.2. But if we allow that the variables may not represent the same qualities across persons and disaggregate the data box to show this as has been done on the right side of the figure, one has a group of N "slices" of data, each one signifying one person measured on a battery of M variables repeatedly over T occasions of measurement.

Each one of these slices represents what Cattell (1952) referred to as *P-technique data*. We will look more closely at modeling that kind of data subsequently. To emphasize the point, P-technique data are data that represent a sampling of variables and a sampling of occasions for one person. Thus, they comprise a two-way data matrix (variables × occasions), but it is a data matrix derived from one person. Berieter (1963) argued, "P-technique is the logical technique for studying the interdependencies of measures" (p. 15). In relation to a point made earlier, Bereiter also warned that the typical reliance on variation between persons (individual differences) might or might not be an acceptable substitute for variation within an individual over time. This same sentiment was examined in great detail by Molenaar (2004).

When one has multiple cases of P-technique data, they can be modeled with an eye to ascertaining how the individuals are different from each other just as much as how they are similar. Such designs have been called *MRSRM designs* (multivariate, replicated, single-subject, repeated measurements designs; Nesselroade & Ford, 1985). As will be seen, one can still covary variables in this format, but the variables are covaried across occasions rather than across persons. We will return to that idea subsequently.

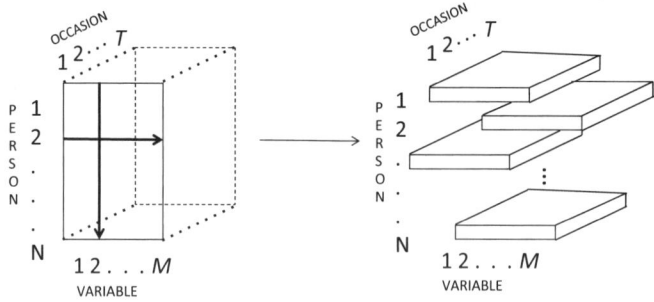

Figure 34.2. The "data box." From the *Handbook of Multivariate Experimental Psychology* (p. 69), by R. B. Cattell (Ed.), 1966, Chicago, IL: Rand-McNally. Copyright 1966 by Raymond B. Cattell.

"... In Certain Respects Like No Other Man"

We have made the points that psychology involves the study of behaving individuals and behaving individuals are somewhat idiosyncratic beings, for example, having different genes and different learning and conditioning experiences. Yet, as a science, psychology aims to establish lawful relations that have generality across people—"... in certain respects like all other men, like some other men..." Here is an inevitable tension that has haunted the study of behavior for more than a century (Lamiell, 1998). Earlier, we alluded to attempts to effect a rapprochement between the idiographic and the nomothetic (Lamiell, 1981; Nesselroade et al., 2007, Zevon & Tellegen, 1982). One of these we are going to discuss in more detail because it aims to resolve matters in part as a basic measurement problem as well as a modeling one.

The approach has been dubbed the *idiographic filter* because it describes a way in which one can think of these latent variables as theoretically sound and common to the collective (nomothetic), with the observable indicators that are used to index them being somewhat different from individual to individual (idiographic). Thus, basic differences among individuals that already exist at the level of variables or that we might elect to measure are not treated as though they are the same across individuals and allowed to "wreck" the search for invariance described earlier. Before we can do this, however, it seems appropriate to present and discuss the basic P-technique factor analysis model and its derivatives.

P-Technique Factor Analysis

P-technique data can be modeled with the basic factor analytic model (Cattell, 1963) and this is done to determine covariation patterns in the individual's behavior over time. Covariation between two variables over time can only be defined in the presence of variation over time in both variables, but that is behavior at the individual level. The essential P-technique factor analysis model can be written in the same way as before, but now for each individual measured on many variables over many occasions: Using the notation already developed, we still use t indexes time (occasion of measurement), Y[t] is a p-variate observed time series for one individual, F(t) is a q-variate latent time series (factor scores over time), Λ is a M × K matrix of factor loadings, and u(t) is a M-variate unique process series with diagonal covariance matrix and is assumed to be uncorrelated with the K-variate latent factor series, F(t). Both the observed and latent time series are assumed to have time-invariant means and covariance structures. A path diagram of the basic P-technique factor model is shown in Figure 34.3.

P-technique factor analysis has been used to model intraindividual variation in a wide variety of content domains (Jones & Nesselroade, 1990; Luborsky & Mintz, 1972). Essentially, the modeling is conducted just as are other factor analyses with decisions regarding the number of factors, rotation, etc., needing to be made. Typically, steps are taken, if necessary, to de-trend the observed time series prior to fitting the factor model.

Dynamic Factor Analysis

Several important extensions of the basic P-technique model have been developed and implemented in the past couple of decades that can generally be called *dynamic factor analysis models* (see, e.g., Browne & Nesselroade, 2005; Molenaar, 1985; Nesselroade, McArdle, Aggen, & Meyers, 2001). The model in Figure 34.3 was implemented to eliminate some of the shortcomings of the basic P-technique factor model that were identified by Cattell (1963), Holtzman (1963), and others. Chief among these were the P-technique factor model's inability to account for lagged relations in the time series, either

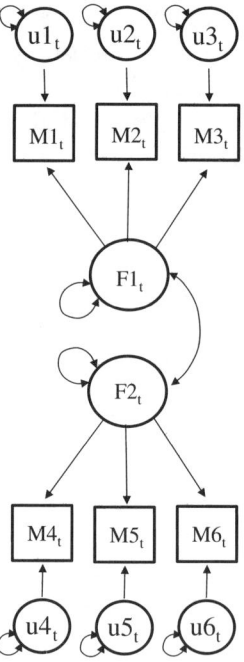

Figure 34.3. A path diagram of a P-technique factor analysis (for any occasion *t*). From *Modeling Individual Variability With Repeated Measures Data: Advances and Techniques* (p. 242), by D. M. Moskowitz and S. L. Hershberger (Eds.), 2001, Mahwah, NJ: Erlbaum. Copyright 2001 by Taylor & Francis. Reprinted with permission.

among factors or between factors and observed variables. An exemplary dynamic factor analytic model can be written as a common factor model for multiple time lags (see Nesselroade & Molenaar, 2003, 2010c; see the models of Part IV). As described by Molenaar and Nesselroade (2012), the process noise is assumed to be white noise (lacking sequential dependence), so the full covariance matrix acknowledges that the process noise can have contemporaneous (time lag = 0) correlations among its (q) component time series. A path diagram for this full dynamic factor model (with s = 2) is shown in Figure 34.4.

More information on fitting these models can be found in Browne and Nesselroade (2005) and Nesselroade et al. (2001). For additional model estimation options, please consult Browne and Zhang (2005).

The Idiographic Filter

Armed with the P-technique and dynamic factor analysis models, we return to the recurring theme of "in certain respects like no other man." Let us first consider some measurement matters in this light. As we noted

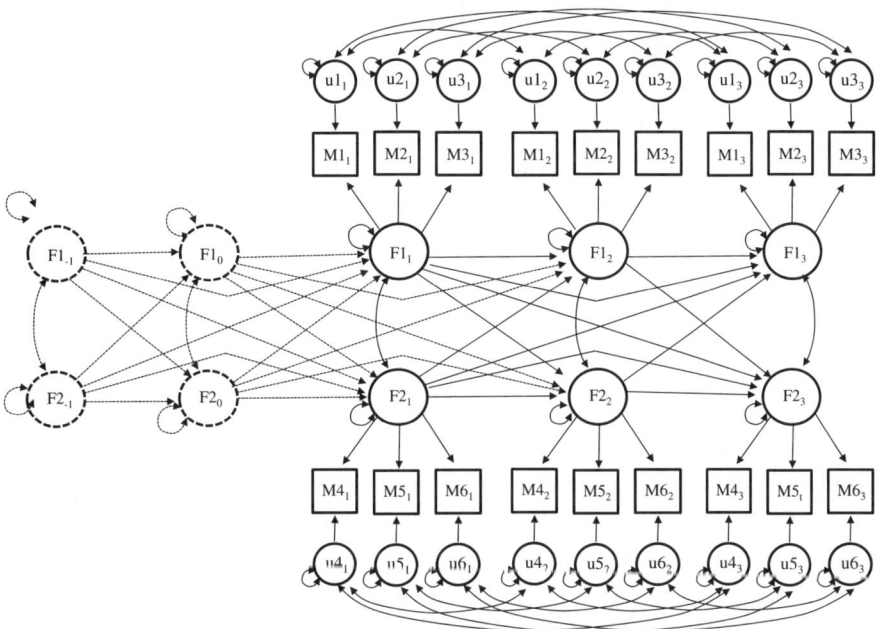

Figure 34.4. A path diagram of a dynamic factor analysis. From *Modeling Individual Variability With Repeated Measures Data: Advances and Techniques* (p. 242), by D. M. Moskowitz and S. L. Hershberger (Eds.), 2001, Mahwah, NJ: Erlbaum. Copyright 2001 by Taylor & Francis. Reprinted with permission.

earlier, we believe that there is considerable promise in loosening some of the highly restrictive bonds that have forced behavioral scientists to treat observed variables as though they are the same qualities, but with different quantities from one individual to another. Recognizing the possibility that observed variables did not necessarily have the same meaning from one individual to another, Nesselroade, Gerstorf, Hardy, and Ram (2007) sought a method for measuring latent variables (e.g., depression, anxiety, life-satisfaction, expertise) that were different, if appropriate, for different individuals but that held constant the meaning of those latent variables from one individual to another.

Nesselroade et al. (2007) argued that good theory rests on latent variables and their interrelations, but measurement operations were needed that allowed for idiosyncrasy in the measurement of the latent variables (LVs) while also allowing for relations among those LVs to be testable and falsifiable. They sought alternative measurement operations that permitted the maintenance of rigorous mathematical concepts of invariance while accommodating idiosyncratic features of individuals.

The person as unit-of-analysis as embodied in P-technique factor analysis provided a way to approach this matter. Using the MRSRM design described earlier, multiple P-technique data sets were simultaneously modeled (each data set was regarded as a group in the multiple group structural equation modeling [MGM-SEM] sense). But instead of constraining the factor loadings to be invariant across groups, Nesselroade et al. (2007) constrained the factor intercorrelations to be invariant across groups and allowed the factor loadings to manifest idiosyncrasy. To the extent that this model fit the data, one had uniquely patterned first-order factors but invariant second-order factors. Hence, the term *higher order invariance* is sometimes used to describe the approach. The key feature of the approach is the tailoring of the loading patterns to the individual while at the same time preserving the invariance of the loadings at the second order.

Nomothetic relations can be defined and studied at the level of interrelations among LVs (constructs) but that these can be measured idiographically. Thus, an individual can be like either "all or some other men" at the abstract level and like "no other man" at the observable level. Although any figure can portray a generalized S-R model (context-behavior), it can also represents theories involving multiple constructs.

In their initial attempt to fit the idiographic filter, Nesselroade et al. (2007) glossed over many concerns, but they tried to do so in a conservative fashion, such as restricting the amount of idiosyncrasy permitted in the loading patterns. Zhang, Browne, and Nesselroade (2011) dealt with these issues formally, and tests to falsify the higher order invariance model can now be conducted in a straightforward way. It should be noted that there may be loci other than the factor intercorrelations at which to define invariance while maintaining the idiographic filter rationale. We strongly encourage efforts to do so. The merit of the idiographic filter approach is the disentangling of the ways in which one person is like no other person so that we can more clearly see the ways in which persons are similar to each other.

The Idiographic Filter and Dynamic Factor Analysis for Modeling Process

Molenaar and Nesselroade (2012) extended the idiographic filter approach to dynamic factor analysis as a technique for modeling process. The idea is to define, in a rigorous fashion, latent mechanisms (processes) that are the same for different individuals but can manifest in different patterns of observables for those individuals. For example, in two single-parent families (a mother–child and a father–child configuration) the process of socialization will appear to be somewhat different in terms of the observables—but it is still socialization.

Harking back to the dynamic factor model path diagram, constraining the factor correlations and autoregressions and cross-regressions to be invariant across multiple individuals is sufficient to identify the solution, leaving the factor loadings generally free (need minimal constraints on loadings to identify an oblique solution) to vary from individual to individual. Model fit is testable. This seems to us to be an important step in the direction of modeling important longitudinal information that goes well beyond the classical individual differences approach focused more on static attributes. Of course, dynamic factor analysis is not the only way to model process. Others should be tried.

Molenaar has applied the idiographic filter logic to behavior genetics modeling to develop individual-level heritability coefficients (Nesselroade & Molenaar, 2010a). He combined the idiographic filter (iF) and the behavior genetics ACE models to form the iFACE model with which he has analyzed intensive measurement systems (e.g., EEG records).

35

CODA: THE FUTURE IS YOURS!

So now we are at the end of this book, and we wish you all good luck in dealing with your own set of longitudinal questions. Remember that if you can use a latent change model to help guide you, go ahead and do it. Don't hesitate to see if it can be fitted to your data. Maybe it does not work very well, and you will be better off if you move to some other formal conception. But maybe it will work, and maybe you will make some progress, or even be finished. But, either way, to quote Kaiser (1976), "... delight in its elegance ... but for God's sake, don't take it seriously!" (p. 587).

STUDYING LONGITUDINAL DATA WITH CONTEMPORARY STRUCTURAL EQUATION MODELING

In addition to its scientific value, this analysis of longitudinal trajectories can be a great deal of fun for the eager analyst. In our work we have experienced an overwhelming sense that something useful, even special,

http://dx.doi.org/10.1037/14440-036
Longitudinal Data Analysis Using Structural Equation Models, by J. J. McArdle and J. R. Nesselroade
Copyright © 2014 by the American Psychological Association. All rights reserved.

could emerge from analyzing longitudinal data. After all, almost any longitudinal data collection takes a lot more time and effort than the more typical cross-sectional data collection. So, whether or not it is deserved, longitudinal analyses often take on a special importance.

But for very similar reasons, these analyses can be very difficult. Longitudinal analyses can be difficult to organize, difficult to work with to do something simple and useful (like plotting the data), and unclear about when to choose more advanced analyses. To organize and discuss these issues, we have placed structural equation modeling (SEM) in the context of five goals of longitudinal research suggested by Baltes and Nesselroade (1979). We suggest that you consider analyses you or others have done using the five steps outlined above as a template. It is not necessary to carry them out in this order, but we have tried to present it as a logical approach: Each step can build on the results from the prior steps.

Once again, the choice of a discrete dynamic model is intimately tied to the substantive theory and available data. Perhaps this is represented in Figure 35.1, but the choice between using an autoregressive approach, a linear latent basis, or a polynomial, or other nonlinear model can be substantively important. A fundamental idea from Wishart (1938) was that the basic shape of each individual curve could be captured with a small number of fixed parameters and random variance components. In some cases, a fixed basis polynomial model is more parsimonious than a free basis model (McArdle & Bell, 2000). But many recent textbooks overlook the latent basis model (e.g., S. C. Duncan, Duncan, & Strycker, 2000; J. Singer & Willett, 2003), an option that we believe remains a most useful empirical choice. But this is up to you.

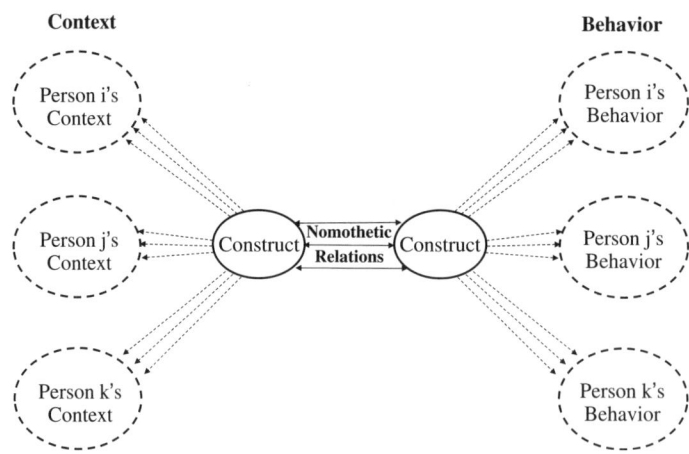

Figure 35.1. A general nomothetic model involving latent variables.

One way to combine recent ideas about dynamics and retain all the statistical and practical benefits of SEM is to use a model based on the latent change score (LCS; Hamagami & McArdle, 2001; McArdle, 2001; McArdle & Hamagami, 2001). Indeed, the introduction of individual differences in change analyses has led to a great deal of statistical controversy in model fitting (e.g., Nesselroade & Bartsch, 1977; Sullivan, Pfefferbaum, Adalsteinsson, Swan, & Carmelli, 2002). These kinds of *difference* or *gain* score calculations are relatively simple and theoretically meaningful, but the potential confounds due to the accumulation of random errors has been a key concern in previous studies using observed change scores or rate of change scores (e.g., Berieter, 1963; Burr & Nesselroade, 1990; Cronbach & Furby, 1970; Nesselroade & Boker, 1994; Rogosa & Willett, 1985; Willett, 1989). This recently available SEM approach allows us to write expectations in terms of the first-, or second-, or higher order latent differences, and we can have the SEM program automatically generate the required nonlinear expectations of the scores.

Along this way, we also found out that the flexibility of a discrete model could lead us directly to a representation of differential equations (continuous time) models of change (as in Nesselroade & Boker, 1994). Aspects of these models are illustrated in Figure 35.2. What we have learned in this respect is

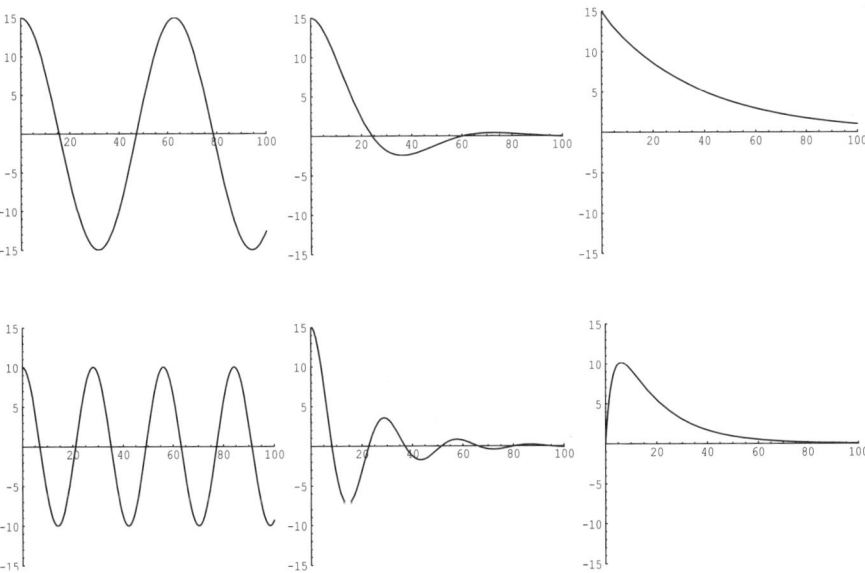

Figure 35.2. Difference equations versus differential equations. Adapted from *Can Personality Change?* (pp. 121–147), by T. F. Heatherton and J. L. Weinberger (Eds.), 1994, Washington, DC: American Psychological Association. Copyright 1994 by the American Psychological Association.

that any discrete model that we have presented here can be reinterpreted in differential terms, and this could be useful. The differential equation is used to describe *instantaneous* changes (at $t = 0$), and here we plot some variations of the size of the parameters of a second-order model from Nesselroade and Boker (1994). This approach certainly could be useful for dynamic parameters that are non-zero or nonequal, because these could take on substantively different estimates. But what will not differ is the overall dynamic approach, the model fit statistics, or the sign of the coefficients. Because of these strong similarities, we have simply decided to phrase all of our models in terms of discrete terms and not differential terms. But possibly we will learn more in the future!

BENEFITS AND LIMITATIONS

Finally, we want the reader to recognize that there are many benefits and limitations of the longitudinal structural equation models presented here. The possibilities for a thorough longitudinal measurement analysis were limited here by the data collections (Horn & McArdle, 1992; McArdle & Cattell, 1994; McArdle & Nesselroade, 1994; McArdle, Prescott, Hamagami, & Horn, 1998). As just stated, the discrete LCS approach used here is not identical to the differential equations considered by others (e.g., Arminger, 1987; Coleman, 1968); nor is it the same as the differential structural equation models proposed by others (e.g., Oud & Jansen, 2000) or the models of Boker (2001).

However, the general themes presented here can be used with most of these alternative approaches. This LCS approach offers a practical approximation with dynamic interpretations for traditional experimental data with repeated measures. One key advantage of this approach is that this dynamic model is a natural extension of current standards of repeated measures analyses. Another advantage is that these types of models can be fitted using standard SEM software. The structural path diagrams illustrate how fundamental change score concepts can be directly represented using standard longitudinal structural equation models. As in other latent change models, the numerical values of the parameters (α, β, and γ) can now be combined to form many different kinds of individual and group trajectories over age or time, including the addition of covariates. All these features are apparent without directly specifying an integral equation for the trajectory over time. Variations on any of these models can be considered by adding more factors or adding structure to the specific factors, but we did not investigate these possibilities here (e.g., Cnaan, Laird, & Slasor, 1997; Littell, Milliken, Stroup, & Wolfinger, 1996).

Another important issue that we did not pursue is the discrimination of (a) models of multiple curves for a single group of subjects from (b) models of multiple groups of subjects with different curves. These substantive issues set the stage for models that test hypotheses about trajectories between latent groups, and others have gone much further with this approach. Many recent LV analyses provide a test of the invariance of longitudinal model parameters without knowing exactly the group membership of each individual. By combining some aspects of the previous sections, we can consider a group difference dynamic change score model in different ways. In one model, we add the group contrasts as a covariate in the difference model. In another model, we add a multiple level prediction structure of the dynamic slopes. In general, we can always consider that a model where multiple groups are independent or probabilistic, and where the group dynamics are different.

In summary, the dynamic analyses presented here represent only one subset of a much larger family of dynamic possibilities. To reflect true effects (e.g., of cognitive training on longitudinal sequences) we surely need to expand this to include more variables. In recent research, we have examined four variables in a dynamic system over the adult part of the life span and concluded that the network of cognitive dynamic relationships is far more complex than the one portrayed herein (McArdle, Hamagami, Meredith, & Bradway, 2001a). We hope that the current models point the way toward representing dynamic changes and differences that can be used to better understand the complex cognitive trajectories we are traveling on and that they may be reasonably accurate even with small samples—maybe even for the perplexing cognitive dynamic network of a single individual (see Nesselroade, 2004).

FINAL REMARKS

This book represents our explicit attempt to recognize the importance of a fundamental matter that is often downplayed, if not ignored altogether, in the conduct of behavioral research programs, including those aimed at the study of changes. It is a matter that we believe is currently waxing in terms of the recognition of its salience for theorists and researchers. Simply put, the individual is the fundamental unit of analysis for studying behavior. Many of us whose intellectual rearing was dominated by the "individual differences" approach believe that the individual is our unit of analysis but in practice, the study of individual differences places much more emphasis on the differences than it does on the individuals.

But our unease with the individual differences approach is driven by more than the proper unit of analysis question. It has to do with the very nature of empirical inquiry. We believe that an honest examination of some of the premises underlying the dominant approaches to studying behavior and behavior change raises questions that for too long have gone unasked and that need to be asked—now and with enthusiasm! We have all heard assertions to the effect that psychology—the study of human behavior—is a difficult science. Why?

Whereas we cannot pretend to know the answer to the question "Why is the study of human behavior so difficult?" we can dare to speculate a bit. We think it is so difficult in part because of a reason discussed earlier: Variables that are taken to represent the same quality from one person to another do not actually do so. Yet, we act as though they do, and we formulate our data and draw up our analysis procedures as though they do. And we never question the matter again.

Science is all about formulating general lawful relations. In the face of idiosyncrasy, this is a difficult task, unless the idiosyncrasy can be isolated and rendered harmless. The "certain respects in which every man is like no other man" cannot merely be averaged away if one is trying to formulate strong relations. Nor is it satisfying to take refuge behind a series of probabilistic statements such as, "We don't know where a given leaf will fall but we can specify how the distribution of fallen leaves will look." There is even less comfort in the thought that "there will be 243 homicides in City A this year, but we can't predict just who the perpetrators and the victims will be." Yet this is probably all we can do right now. We hope the future will be better.

REFERENCES

Ahmvaara, Y. (1954). The mathematical theory of factorial invariance under selection. *Psychometrika, 19*, 27–38. doi:10.1007/BF02288991

Aitken, A. C. (1935). Note on selection from a multivariate normal population. *Proceedings of the Edinburgh Mathematical Society, 4*, 106–110. doi:10.1017/S0013091500008063

Allison, D. B., Allison, R. L., Faith, M. S., Paultre, F., & Pi-Sunyer, F. X. (1997). Power and money: Designing statistically powerful studies while minimizing financial costs. *Psychological Methods, 2*, 20–33. doi:10.1037/1082-989X.2.1.20

Allison, P. D. (1987). Estimation of linear models with incomplete data. In C. C. Clogg (Ed.), *Sociological methodology, 1987* (pp. 71–103). Washington, DC: American Sociological Association. doi:10.2307/271029

Allison, P. D. (1990). Change scores as dependent variables in regression analysis. In C. C. Clogg (Ed.), *Sociological methodology 1990* (pp. 93–114). San Francisco, CA: Jossey-Bass. doi:10.2307/271083

Allison, P. D. (1994). Using panel data to estimate effects of events. *Sociological Methods and Research, 23*, 174–199. doi:10.1177/0049124194023002002

Alwin, D. F. (2007). *Margins of error: A study of reliability in survey measurement.* New York, NY: Wiley.

Anderson, J. G., & Evans, F. B. (1974). Causal models in educational research: Recursive models. *American Educational Research Journal, 11*, 29–39. doi:10.3102/00028312011001029

Anderson, J. G., & Gerbing, D. W. (1988). Structural equation modeling in practice: A review and recommended two-step approach. *Psychological Bulletin, 103*, 411–423.

Anderson, T. W. (1957). Maximum likelihood estimates for a multivariate normal distribution when some observations are missing. *Journal of the American Statistical Association, 52*, 200–203. doi:10.1080/01621459.1957.10501379

Anderson, T. W., & Rubin, H. (1956). Statistical inference in factor analysis. In J. Neyman (Ed.), *Proceedings on the Third Berkeley Symposium on Mathematical Statistics and Probability.* Berkeley: University of California Press.

Angrist, J. D., & Krueger, A. B. (2001). Instrumental variables and the search for identification: From supply and demand to natural experiments. *Journal of Economic Perspectives, 15*, 69–85. doi:10.1257/jep.15.4.69

Arbuckle, A., & Friendly, M. L. (1977). Rotation to smooth functions. *Psychometrika, 42*, 127–140.

Arbuckle, J. L., & Wotke, W. (2004). *AMOS 5.0 user's guide.* Chicago, IL: Smallwaters.

Arminger, G. (1986). Linear stochastic differential equation models for panel data with unobserved variables. In N. Tuma (Ed.), *Sociological methodology 1986* (pp. 187–212). San Francisco, CA: Jossey-Bass. doi:10.2307/270923

Arminger, G. (1987). Misspecification, asymptotic stability, and ordinal variables in the analysis of panel data. *Sociological Methods and Research, 15*, 336–348.

Ashby, W. R. (1957). *An introduction to cybernetics.* London, England: Chapman & Hall.

Bachman, J. G., O'Malley, P. M., & Johnston, J. (1978). *Adolescence to adulthood: Change and stability in the lives of young men.* Ann Arbor, MI: Institute for Social Research.

Baguley, T. (2009). Standardized or simple effect size: What should be reported? *British Journal of Psychology, 100*, 603–617.

Baltagi, B. (2009). *The econometric analysis of panel data.* New York, NY: Wiley.

Baltagi, B. H. (2010). Spatial panels. In A. Ullah & D. E. A. Giles (Eds.), *Handbook of empirical economics and finance* (pp. 435–454). Boca Raton, FL: Chapman & Hall/CRC.

Baltes, P. B., & Nesselroade, J. R. (1973). The developmental analysis of individual differences on multiple measures. In J. R. Nesselroade & H. W. Reese (Eds.), *Lifespan developmental psychology: Methodological issues* (pp. 219–251). New York, NY: Academic Press.

Baltes, P. B., & Nesselroade, J. R. (1979). History and rationale of longitudinal research. In J. R. Nesselroade & P. B. Baltes (Eds.), *Longitudinal research in the study of behavior and development* (pp. 1–39). New York, NY: Academic Press.

Baltes, P. B., Reese, H. W., & Nesselroade, J. R. (1977). *Life-span developmental psychology: Introduction to research methods.* Monterey, CA: Brooks/Cole.

Bartholomew, D. J. (1985). Foundations of factor analysis: Some practical implications. *British Journal of Mathematical and Statistical Psychology, 38*, 1–10.

Bartlett, M. S. (1946). On the theoretical specification and sampling properties of autocorrelated time series. *Supplement to the Journal of the Royal Statistical Society, 8*, 27–41.

Bell, R. Q. (1953). Convergence: An accelerated longitudinal approach. *Child Development, 24*, 145–152. doi:10.2307/1126345

Bell, R. Q. (1954). An experimental test of the accelerated longitudinal approach. *Child Development, 25*, 281–286. doi:10.2307/1126058

Berieter, C. (1963). Some persistent problems in measuring change. In C. W. Harris (Ed.), *Problems in measuring change: Proceedings of a conference sponsored by the Committee on Personality Development in Youth of the Social Science Research Council, 1962* (pp. 3–21). Madison: University of Wisconsin Press.

Blalock, H. M. (1971). Causal models involving unmeasured variables in stimulus–response situations. In H. M. Blalock (Ed.), *Causal models in the social sciences* (pp. 335–347). New York, NY: Aldine-Atherton.

Blalock, H. M. (Ed.). (1985a). *Causal models in panel and experimental designs.* New York, NY: Aldine.

Blalock, H. M. (Ed.). (1985b). *Causal models in the social sciences.* Hawthorne, NY: Aldine de Gruyter.

Bloxom, B. (1972). Alternative approaches to factorial invariance. *Psychometrika, 37,* 425–440.

Bock, R. D. (1975). *Multivariate statistical methods in behavioral research.* New York, NY: McGraw-Hill.

Bohrnstedt, G. W. (1969). Observations on the measurement of change. In E. F. Borgotta & G. W. Bohrnstedt (Eds.), *Sociological methodology 1969* (pp. 113–133). San Francisco, CA: Jossey-Bass.

Boker, S. M. (2001). Differential structural equation models. In L. Collings & A. Sayer (Eds.), *Methods for the analysis of change* (pp. 3–28). Washington, DC: American Psychological Association.

Boker, S. M., & McArdle, J. J. (1995). Statistical vector field analysis applied to mixed cross-sectional and longitudinal data. *Experimental Aging Research, 21,* 77–93. doi:10.1080/03610739508254269

Boker, S. M., & Nesselroade, J. R. (2002). A method for modeling the intrinsic dynamics of intraindividual variability: Recovering the parameters of simulated oscillators in multi-wave panel data. *Multivariate Behavioral Research, 37*(1), 127–160. doi:10.1207/S15327906MBR3701_06

Bollen, K. A., & Curran, P. J. (2004). Autoregressive latent trajectory (ALT) models: A synthesis of two traditions. *Sociological Methods and Research, 32,* 336–383. doi:10.1177/0049124103260222

Bollen, K. A., & Curran, P. J. (2006). *Latent curve models: A structural equation perspective.* New York, NY: Wiley.

Boneau, C. A. (1960). The effects of violations of assumptions underlying the *t* test. *Psychological Bulletin, 57,* 49–64.

Boomsma, D. I., & Molenaar, P. C. M. (1987). Constrained maximum likelihood analysis of familial resemblance of twins and their parents. *Acta Geneticae Medicae et Gemellologiae, 36,* 29–39.

Bound, J., Jaeger, D. A., & Baker, R. M. (1995). Problems with instrumental variables estimation when the correlation between the instruments and the endogenous explanatory variable is weak. *Journal of the American Statistical Association, 90,* 443–450.

Box, G. E. P., & Jenkins, G. M. (1970). *Time series analysis, forecasting and control.* San Francisco, CA: Holden-Day.

Brown, T. A. (2006). *Confirmatory factor analysis for applied research.* New York, NY: Guilford Press.

Browne, M., & du Toit, S. H. C. (1991). Models for learning data. In L. Collins & J. L. Horn (Eds.), *Best methods for the analysis of change* (pp. 47–68). Washington, DC: American Psychological Association.

Browne, M. W. (1984). Asymptotically distribution-free methods for the analysis of covariance structures. *British Journal of Mathematical and Statistical Psychology, 37,* 62–83. doi:10.1111/j.2044-8317.1984.tb00789.x

Browne, M. W. (2001). An overview of analytic rotation in exploratory factor analysis. *Multivariate Behavioral Research, 36,* 111–150. doi:10.1207/S15327906MBR3601_05

Browne, M. W., & Cudeck, R. (1993). Alternative ways of assessing model fit. In K. A. Bollen & J. S. Long (Eds.), *Testing structural equation models* (pp. 136–162). Beverly Hills, CA: Sage Publications.

Browne, M. W., & Nesselroade, J. R. (2005). Representing psychological processes with dynamic factor models: Some promising uses and extensions of ARMA time series models. In A. Maydeu-Olivares & J. J. McArdle (Eds.), *Psychometrics: A festschrift to Roderick P. McDonald* (pp. 415–452). Mahwah, NJ: Erlbaum.

Browne, M. W., & Zhang, G. (2005). *User's guide: DyFA—Dynamic factor analysis of lagged correlation matrices.* Columbus: Psychology Department, Ohio State University.

Bryk, A. S., & Raudenbush, S. W. (1987). Application of the hierarchical linear models to assessing change. *Psychological Bulletin, 101,* 147–158. doi:10.1037/0033-2909.101.1.147

Bryk, A. S., & Raudenbush, S. W. (1992). *Hierarchical linear models in social and behavioral research: Applications and data analysis methods.* Newbury Park, CA: Sage.

Burnham, K. P., & Anderson, D. R. (1998). *Model selection and inference: A practical-theoretic approach.* New York, NY: Springer-Verlag.

Burr, J. A., & Nesselroade, J. R. (1990). Change measurement. In A. Von Eye & M. Rovine (Eds.), *Statistical methods in longitudinal research* (pp. 3–34). New York, NY: Academic Press.

Burt, C. (1919). The development of reasoning in school children. *Journal of Experimental Pedagogy, 5,* 68–77.

Byrne, B. M., Shavelson, R. J., & Muthén, B. (1989). Testing for the equivalence of factor covariance and mean structures: The issue of partial measurement invariance. *Psychological Bulletin, 105,* 456.

Campbell, D., & Stanley, J. (1963). *Experimental and quasi-experimental designs for research.* Chicago, IL: Rand-McNally.

Cattell, R. B. (1944). A note on correlation clusters and cluster search methods. *Psychometrika, 9,* 169–184. doi:10.1007/BF02288721

Cattell, R. B. (1952). The three basic factor-analytic research designs—Their interrelations and derivatives. *Psychological Bulletin, 49,* 499–520.

Cattell, R. B. (1957). *Personality and motivation structure and measurement.* Yonkers, NY: World Book.

Cattell, R. B. (1963). The structuring of change by P-technique and incremental R-technique. In C. Harris (Ed.), *Problems in measuring change* (pp. 167–198). Madison: University of Wisconsin Press.

Cattell, R. B. (1966a). Higher-order factor structures and reticular versus hierarchical formula for their interpretation. In C. Banks & P. L. Broadhurst (Eds.), *Studies in psychology* (pp. 223–266). London, England: University of London Press.

Cattell, R. B. (1966b). Multivariate behavioral research and the integrative challenge. *Multivariate Behavioral Research, 1*, 4–23. doi:10.1207/s15327906mbr0101_1

Cattell, R. B. (1966c). The data box: Its ordering of total resources in terms of possible relational systems. In R. B. Cattell (Ed.), *Handbook of multivariate experimental psychology* (pp. 67–78). Chicago, IL: Rand-McNally.

Cattell, R. B. (1966d). *The handbook of multivariate experimental psychology*. New York, NY: Rand-McNally.

Cattell, R. B. (1971). *Abilities: Their structure, growth, and action*. Boston, MA: Houghton Mifflin.

Chou, C.-P., & Bentler, P. M. (2002). Model modification in structural equation modeling by imposing constraints. *Computational Statistics and Data Analysis, 41*, 271–287. doi:10.1016/S0167-9473(02)00097-X

Church, C. K., & Schwenke, J. R. (1986). Autoregressive errors with a repeated measures design in clinical trials. *Controlled Clinical Trials, 7*, 149–164.

Claeskens, G., & Hjort, N. L. (2008). *Model selection and model averaging*. Cambridge, England: Cambridge University Press.

Cnaan, A., Laird, N. M., & Slasor, P. (1997). Using the general linear mixed model to analyze unbalanced repeated measures and longitudinal data. *Statistics in Medicine, 16*, 2349–2380. doi:10.1002/(SICI)1097-0258(19971030)16:20<2349::AID-SIM667>3.0.CO;2-E

Cochran, W. G., & Cox, G. M. (1950). *Experimental design* (2nd ed.). New York, NY: Wiley.

Cohen, J. (1988). *Statistical power analysis for the behavioral sciences*. Hillsdale, NJ: Erlbaum.

Cohen, J., & Cohen, P. (1983). *Applied multiple regression/correlation analysis for the behavioral sciences*. Hillsdale, NJ: Erlbaum.

Cohen, J., Cohen, P., West, S., & Aiken, L. (2003). *Applied multiple regression/correlation analysis for the behavior sciences* (3rd ed.). Hillsdale, NJ: Lawrence Erlbaum Associates.

Cole, D. A., & Maxwell, S. E. (2003). Testing meditational models with longitudinal data: Questions and tips in using structural equation models. *Journal of Abnormal Psychology, 112*, 558–577. doi:10.1037/0021-843X.112.4.558

Coleman, J. (1968). The mathematical study of change. In H. M. Blalock & A. B. Blalock (Eds.), *Methodology in social research* (pp. 428–475). New York, NY: McGraw-Hill.

Collins, L. M., & Lanza, S. T. (2010). *Latent class and latent transition analysis: With applications in the social, behavioral, and health sciences*. Hoboken, NJ: Wiley.

Collins, L. M., & Sayer, A. G. (Eds.). (2001). *New methods for the analysis of change*. Washington, DC: American Psychological Association. doi:10.1037/10409-000

Cook, T. D., & Campbell, D. T. (1979). *Quasi-experimentation: Design and analysis issues for field settings*. Boston, MA: Houghton Mifflin.

Cooley, W., & Lohnes, P. R. (1971). *Multivariate data analysis*. New York, NY: J. Wiley and Sons.

Corballis, M. C., & Traub, R. E. (1970). Longitudinal factor analysis. *Psychometrika, 35*, 79–98. doi:10.1007/BF02290595

Cox, D. R. (1972). Regression models and life-tables. *Journal of the Royal Statistical Society. Series B. Methodological, 34*, 187–220.

Cronbach, L. J. (1957). The two disciplines of scientific psychology. *American Psychologist, 12*, 671–684. doi:10.1037/h0043943

Cronbach, L. J., & Furby, L. (1970). How we should measure change—Or should we? *Psychological Bulletin, 74*, 68–80. doi:10.1037/h0029382

Cudeck, R. (2000). An estimate of the covariance between two variables which are not jointly observed. *Psychometrika, 65*, 539–546. doi:10.1007/BF02296344

Cudeck, R., & Browne, M. W. (1983). Cross-validation of covariance structures. *Multivariate Behavioral Research, 18*, 147–167.

Cudeck, R., du Toit, S., & Sörbom, D. (Eds.). (2001). *Structural equation modeling: Present and future*. Lincolnwood, IL: Scientific Software International.

Dempster, A. P., Laird, N. M., & Rubin, D. B. (1977). Maximum likelihood from incomplete data via the EM algorithm. *Journal of the Royal Statistical Society. Series A (General), 39*, 1–38.

Dolan, C. V., & Molenaar, P. C. (1994). Testing specific hypotheses concerning latent group differences in multi-group covariance structure analysis with structured means. *Multivariate Behavioral Research, 29*, 203–222.

Duncan, O. D. (1966). Path analysis: Sociological examples. *American Journal of Sociology, 72*(1), 1–16. doi:10.1086/224256

Duncan, O. D. (1969). Some linear models for two-wave, two-variable panel analysis. *Psychological Bulletin, 72*, 177–182. doi:10.1037/h0027876

Duncan, O. D. (1975). *Introduction to structural equation models*. New York, NY: Academic Press.

Duncan, O. D., Haller, A. O., & Portes, A. (1968). Peer influences on aspirations: A reinterpretation. *American Journal of Sociology, 74*, 119–137. doi:10.1086/224615

Duncan, S. C., Duncan, T. E., & Strycker, L. A. (2000). Risk and protective factors influencing adolescent problem behavior: A multivariate latent growth curve analysis. *Annals of Behavioral Medicine, 22*, 103–109.

Duncan, T. E., Duncan, S. C., & Strycker, L. A. (2013). *An introduction to latent variable growth curve modeling: Concepts, issues, and application*. New York, NY: Routledge Academic.

du Toit, S. H. C., & Browne, M. W. (2001). The covariance structure of a vector time series. In R. Cudeck, S. H. C. du Toit, & D. Sörbom (Eds.), *Structural equation modeling: Present and future* (pp. 279–314). Chicago, IL: Scientific Software International.

Embretson, S. E., & Reise, S. P. (2000). *Item response theory for psychologists*. Mahwah, NJ: Erlbaum.

Engle, R., & Watson, M. (1981). A one-factor multivariate time series model of metropolitan wage rates. *Journal of the American Statistical Association, 76*, 774–781. doi:10.1080/01621459.1981.10477720

Fan, X. (2003). Power of latent growth modeling for detecting group differences in linear growth trajectory parameters. *Structural Equation Modeling, 10*, 380–400. doi:10.1207/S15328007SEM1003_3

Ferrer, E., Balluerka, N., & Widaman, K. F. (2008). Factorial invariance and the specification of second-order latent growth models. *Methodology: European Journal of Research Methods for the Behavioral and Social Sciences, 4*, 22–36.

Ferrer, E., Hamagami, F., & McArdle, J. J. (2004). Modeling latent growth curves with incomplete data using different types of structural equation modeling and multilevel software. *Structural Equation Modeling, 11*, 452–483. doi:10.1207/s15328007sem1103_8

Ferrer-Caja, E., Crawford, J. R., & Bryan, J. (2002). A structural modeling examination of the executive decline hypothesis of cognitive aging through reanalysis. *Neuropsychology, Development, and Cognition. Section B, Aging, Neuropsychology and Cognition, 9*, 231–249. doi:10.1076/anec.9.3.231.9611

Finkel, D., Reynolds, C. A., McArdle, J. J., Hamagami, F., & Pedersen, N. L. (2009). Genetic variance in processing speed drives variation in aging of spatial and memory abilities. *Developmental Psychology, 45*, 820–834.

Fisher, R. A. (1919). The correlation between relatives on the supposition of Mendelian inheritance. *Transactions of the Royal Society of Edinburgh, 52*, 399–433. doi:10.1017/S0080456800012163

Fisher, R. A. (1925). *Statistical methods for research workers*. London, England: Oliver and Boyd.

Fitzmaurice, G. (2001). A conundrum in the analysis of change. *Nutrition (Burbank, Los Angeles County, Calif.), 17*, 360–361. doi:10.1016/S0899-9007(00)00593-1

Fraser, C., & McDonald, R. P. (1988). COSAN: Covariance structure analysis. *Multivariate Behavioral Research, 23*, 263–265. doi:10.1207/s15327906mbr2302_8

Fox, J. (1997). *Applied regression analysis, linear models, and related methods*. Thousand Oaks, CA: Sage.

Goldberger, A. S. (1973). Structural equation models: An overview. In A. S. Goldberger & O. D. Duncan (Eds.), *Structural equation models in the social sciences* (pp. 1–18). New York, NY: Seminar Press.

Goldberger, A. S., & Duncan, O. D. (Eds.). (1973). *Structural equation models in the social sciences*. New York, NY: Seminar Press.

Goldstein, H. (1995). *Multilevel statistical models* (2nd ed.). London, England: Edward Arnold.

Gollob, H. F. (1968). A statistical model which combines features of factor analytic and analysis of variance techniques. *Psychometrika, 33*, 73–115. doi:10.1007/BF02289676

Gollob, H. F., & Reichardt, C. S. (1987). Taking account of time lags in causal models. *Child Development: Special section on structural equation modeling, 58,* 80–92.

Granger, C. W. J. (1969). Investigating causal relations by econometric models and cross-spectral methods. *Econometrica, 37,* 424–438. doi:10.2307/1912791

Graziano, A. M., & Raulin, M. L. (2000). *A process of inquiry: Research methods.* London, England: Allyn & Bacon.

Greenberg, D. F., & Kessler, R. C. (1982). Equilibrium and identification in linear panel models. *Sociological Methods and Research, 10,* 435–451.

Greenberg, D. F., Kessler, R. C., & Logan, C. H. (1979). A panel model of crime rates and arrest rates. *American Sociological Review, 44,* 843–850.

Greenhouse, S. W., & Geisser, S. (1959). On methods in the analysis of profile data. *Psychometrika, 24,* 95–112. doi:10.1007/BF02289823

Griffiths, D. A., & Sandland, R. L. (1984). Fitting generalized allometric model to multivariate growth data. *Biometrics, 40,* 139–150. doi:10.2307/2530752

Griliches, Z., & Hausman, J. A. (1986). Errors in variables in panel data. *Journal of Econometrics, 31,* 93–118. doi:10.1016/0304-4076(86)90058-8

Grimm, K. J. (2012). Intercept centering and time coding in latent difference score models. *Structural Equation Modeling, 19,* 137–151. doi:10.1080/10705511.2012.634734

Grimm, K. J., & McArdle, J. J. (2005). A note on the computer generation of mean and covariance expectations in latent growth curve analysis. In F. Dansereau & F. J. Yammarino (Eds.), *Multi-level issues in strategy and methods* (pp. 335–364). New York, NY: Elsevier. doi:10.1016/S1475-9144(05)04015-4

Gulliksen, H. (1950). *Theory of mental tests.* New York, NY: Wiley.

Hamagami, F. (1998). A developmental-based item factor analysis. In J. J. McArdle & R. W. Woodcock (Eds.), *Human cognitive abilities in theory and practice* (pp. 231–246). Mahwah, NJ: Erlbaum.

Hamagami, F., & McArdle, J. J. (2001). Advanced studies of individual differences linear dynamic models for longitudinal data analysis. In G. Marcoulides & R. Schumacker (Eds.), *New developments and techniques in structural equation modeling* (pp. 203–246). Mahwah, NJ: Erlbaum.

Hamagami, F., & McArdle, J. J. (2007). Dynamic extensions of latent difference score models. In S. M. Boker & M. L. Wegner (Eds.), *Quantitative methods in contemporary psychology* (pp. 47–85). Mahwah, NJ: Erlbaum.

Hambleton, R. K., Swaminathan, H., & Rogers, H. J. (1991). *Fundamentals of item response theory.* Newbury Park, CA: Sage.

Hannan, M. T., & Tuma, N. B. (1979). Methods for temporal analysis. *Annual Review of Sociology, 5,* 303–328.

Hauser, R. M., & Goldberger, A. S. (1971). The treatment of unobservables in path analysis. In H. L. Costner (Ed.), *Sociological methodology 1971* (pp. 81–117). San Francisco, CA: Jossey Bass. doi:10.2307/270819

Hauser, R. M., Tsai, S.-L., & Sewell, W. H. (1983). A model of stratification with response error in social and psychological variables. *Sociology of Education, 56,* 20–46. doi:10.2307/2112301

Hawkley, L. C., Thisted, R. A., Masi, C. M., & Cacioppo, J. T. (2010). Loneliness predicts increased blood pressure: 5-year cross-lagged analyses in middle-aged and older adults. *Psychology and Aging, 25,* 132–141.

Hayduk, L. (1996). *LISREL: Issues, debates and strategies.* Baltimore, MD: Johns Hopkins University Press.

Healy, A., Proctor, R. W., & Weiner, I. B. (2003). *Handbook of psychology: experimental psychology* (Vol. 4). New York, NY: Wiley.

Hedeker, D., & Gibbons, R. (1997). Application of random-effects pattern-mixture models for missing data in longitudinal studies. *Psychological Methods, 2,* 64–78. doi:10.1037/1082-989X.2.1.64

Heise, D. R. (1969). Separating reliability and stability in test–retest correlation. *American Sociological Review, 34,* 93–101. doi:10.2307/2092790

Heise, D. R. (1970). Causal inference from panel data. *Sociological Methodology, 2,* 3–27. doi:10.2307/270780

Heise, D. R. (1974). Some issues in sociological measurement. In H. Costner (Ed.), *Sociological methodology: 1973–1975* (pp. 1–16). San Francisco, CA: Jossey-Bass.

Heise, D. R. (1975). *Causal analysis.* New York, NY: Wiley.

Hertzog, C., Lindenberger, U., Ghisletta, P., & Oertzen, T. (2006). On the power of multivariate latent growth curve models to detect correlated change. *Psychological Methods, 11,* 244–252. doi:10.1037/1082-989X.11.3.244

Hertzog, C., Oertzen, T., Ghisletta, P., & Lindenberger, U. (2008). Evaluating the power of latent growth curve models to detect individual differences in change. *Structural Equation Modeling, 15,* 541–563.

Hertzog, C., & Rovine, M. (1985). Repeated-measures analysis of variance in developmental research: Selected issues. *Child Development, 56,* 787–809.

Heyting, A., Tolboom, J., & Essers, J. (1992). Statistical handling of drop-outs in longitudinal clinical trials. *Statistics in Medicine, 11,* 2043–2061. doi:10.1002/sim.4780111603

Hindley, C. B. (1972). The place of longitudinal methods in the study of development. In F. J. Monks, W. W. Hartup, & J. De Witt (Eds.), *Determinants of behavioral development* (pp. 22–51). New York, NY: Academic Press.

Hishinuma, E. S., Chang, J. Y., McArdle, J. J., & Hamagami, F. (2012). Potential causal relationship between depressive symptoms and academic achievement in the Hawaiian High Schools Health Survey using contemporary longitudinal latent variable change models. *Developmental Psychology, 48,* 1327–1342. doi:10.1037/a0026978

Hoenig, J. M., & Heisey, D. M. (2001). The abuse of power. *American Statistician, 55,* 19–24.

Holland, P. W. (1986). Statistics and causal inference. *Journal of the American Statistical Association, 81,* 945–960. doi:10.1080/01621459.1986.10478354

Holtzman, W. H. (1963). Statistical models for the study of change in the single case. In C. Harris (Ed.), *Problems in measuring change* (pp. 199–211). Madison: University of Wisconsin Press.

Horn, J. L. (1963). Equations representing combinations of components in scoring psychological variables. *Acta Psychologies, 21*, 184–217.

Horn, J. L. (1972). State, trait, and change dimensions of intelligence. *British Journal of Mathematical and Statistical Psychology, 42*, 159–185.

Horn, J. L. (2005). Neglected thinking about measurement in behavioral science research. In A. Maydeau-Olivares & J. J. McArdle (Eds.), *Contemporary psychometrics* (pp. 103–125). Mahwah, NJ: Erlbaum.

Horn, J. L., & McArdle, J. J. (1980). Perspectives on mathematical and statistical model building (MASMOB) in research on aging. In L. Poon (Ed.), *Aging in the 1980s: Psychological issues* (pp. 503–541). Washington, DC: American Psychological Association. doi:10.1037/10050-037

Horn, J. L., & McArdle, J. J. (1992). A practical guide to measurement invariance in aging research. *Experimental Aging Research, 18*, 117–144. doi:10.1080/03610739208253916

Horn, J. L., & McArdle, J. J. (2007). Understanding human intelligence since Spearman. In R. Cudeck & R. MacCallum (Eds.), *Factor analysis at 100: Historical developments and future directions* (pp. 205–247). Mahwah, NJ: Erlbaum.

Horn, J. L., McArdle, J. J., & Mason, R. (1983). When is invariance not invariant: A practical scientist's look at the ethereal concept of factor invariance. *Southern Psychologist, 1*, 179–188.

Hsiao, C. (1981). Autoregressive modeling and money-income causality detection. *Journal of Monetary Economics, 7*, 85–106. doi:10.1016/0304-3932(81)90053-2

Hsiao, C. (2003). *Analysis of panel data* (2nd ed.). New York, NY: Cambridge Press. doi:10.1017/CBO9780511754203

Hsiao, C. (2005). Why panel data? *Singapore Economic Review, 50*, 143–154. doi:10.1142/S0217590805001937

Huynh, H., & Feldt, L. S. (1970). Conditions under which mean square ratios in repeated measurement designs have exact F-distributions. *Journal of the American Statistical Association, 65*, 1582–1589. doi:10.1080/01621459.1970.10481187

Jacob, F. (2011). The birth of the operon [Editorial]. *Science, 332*, 767. doi:10.1126/science.1207943

Jensen, A. R. (1980). Use of sibling data in educational and psychological research. *American Educational Research Journal, 17*, 153–170. doi:10.3102/00028312017002153

Jones, C. J., & Nesselroade, J. R. (1990). Multivariate, replicated, single-subject designs and P-technique factor analysis: A selective review of intraindividual change studies. *Experimental Aging Research, 16*, 171–183.

Jöreskog, K. G. (1969). A general approach to confirmatory maximum likelihood factor analysis. *Psychometrika, 34*, 183–202. doi:10.1007/BF02289343

Jöreskog, K. G. (1970a). Estimation and testing of simplex models. *British Journal of Mathematical and Statistical Psychology, 23,* 121–145. doi:10.1111/j.2044-8317.1970.tb00439.x

Jöreskog, K. G. (1970b). A general model for the analysis of covariance structures. *Biometrika, 57,* 239–251.

Jöreskog, K. G. (1971). Simultaneous factor analysis in several populations. *Psychometrika, 36,* 409–426. doi:10.1007/BF02291366

Jöreskog, K. G. (1973a). Analysis of covariance structures with means. In A. S. Goldberger & O. D. Duncan (Eds.), *Structural equation models in the social sciences.* New York, NY: Seminar Press.

Jöreskog, K. G. (1973b). A general method for estimating a linear structural equation system. In A. S. Goldberger & O. D. Duncan (Eds.), *Structural equation models in the social sciences* (pp. 85–112). New York, NY: Seminar Press.

Jöreskog, K. G. (1974). Analyzing psychological data by structural analysis of covariance matrices. In D. H. Krantz, R. C. Atkinson, R. D. Luce, & P. Suppes (Eds.), *Contemporary developments in mathematical psychology* (Vol. II, pp. 1–56). San Francisco, CA: Freeman.

Jöreskog, K. G. (1977a). Factor analysis by least-squares and maximum-likelihood methods. In K. Enslein, A. Ralston, & H. S. Wilf (Eds.), *Statistical methods for digital computers* (pp. 125–153). New York, NY: Wiley.

Jöreskog, K. G. (1977b). Statistical models and methods for the analysis of longitudinal data. In D. V. Aigner & A. S. Goldberger (Eds.), *Latent variables in socioeconomic models.* Amsterdam, Netherlands: North Holland.

Jöreskog, K. G., & Sörbom, D. (1976). Statistical models and methods for test–retest situations. In D. N. M. De Gruijter & L. J. T. van der Kamp (Eds.), *Advances in psychological and educational measurement* (pp. 135–157). New York, NY: Wiley.

Jöreskog, K. G., & Sörbom, D. (1977). Statistical models and methods for analysis of longitudinal data. In D. Aigner & A. S. Goldberger (Eds.), *Latent variables in socioeconomic models* (pp. 285–325). Amsterdam, Netherlands: North-Holland.

Jöreskog, K. G., & Sörbom, D. (1979). *Advances in factor analysis and structural equation models.* Cambridge, MA: Abt Books.

Jöreskog, K. G., & Sörbom, D. (1985). *LISREL-VI program manual.* Chicago, IL: International Educational Services.

Jöreskog, K. G., & Sörbom, D. (1999). *LISREL 8.30: LISREL 8: Structural equation modeling with the SIMPLIS command language.* Hillsdale, NJ: Scientific Software International.

Kaiser, H. F. (1976). Lawley and Maxwell's factor analysis as a statistical method. *Educational and Psychological Measurement, 36,* 586–589. doi:10.1177/001316447603600256

Kenny, D. A. (1979). *Correlation and causality.* New York, NY: Wiley.

Kenny, D. A., & Zautra, A. (1995). The trait-state-error model for multiwave data. *Journal of Consulting and Clinical Psychology, 63,* 52–59.

Kessler, R. C., & Greenberg, D. F. (1981). *Linear panel analysis: Models of quantitative change*. New York, NY: Academic Press.

Keyser, C. J. (1956). The group concept. In J. R. Newman (Ed.), *The world of mathematics* (Vol. 3, pp. 1538–1557). New York, NY: Simon & Schuster.

King, D. W., King, L. A., & Foy, D. W. (1996). Prewar factors in combat-related posttraumatic stress disorder: Structural equation modeling with a national sample of female and male Vietnam veterans. *Journal of Consulting and Clinical Psychology, 64*, 520–531. doi:10.1037/0022-006X.64.3.520

Kline, R. (2005). *Principles and practices in structural equation modeling*. New York, NY: Guilford Press.

Kline, R. B. (2011). *Principles and practice of structural equation modeling* (3rd ed.). New York, NY: Guilford Press.

Koch, G. G., Landis, J. R., Freeman, J. L., Freeman, D. H., Jr., & Lehnen, R. C. (1977). A general methodology for the analysis of experiments with repeated measurement of categorical data. *Biometrics, 33*, 133–158. doi:10.2307/2529309

Kroonenberg, P. M., & Oort, F. J. (2003). Three-mode analysis of multimode covariance matrices. *British Journal of Mathematical and Statistical Psychology, 56*, 305–335. doi:10.1348/000711003770480066

Lamiell, J. T. (1981). Toward an idiothetic psychology of personality. *American Psychologist, 36*, 276–289.

Lamiell, J. T. (1998). "Nomothetic and idiographic": Contrasting Windelband's understanding with contemporary usage. *Theory and Psychology, 8*, 23–38.

Laursen, B., Little, T. D., & Card, N. A. (Eds.). (2012). *Handbook of developmental research methods*. New York, NY: Guilford Press.

Lawley, D. N. (1943). A note on Karl Pearson's selection formulae. *Proceedings of the Royal Society of Edinburgh, 62*, 28–30.

Lawley, D. N., & Maxwell, A. E. (1963). *Factor analysis as a statistical method*. London, England: Butterworth & Co.

Lawley, D. N., & Maxwell, A. E. (1971). *Factor analysis as a statistical method* (2nd ed.). London, England: Butterworth & Co.

Lazersfeld, P. F. (1948). The use of panels in social research. *Proceedings of the American Philosophical Society, 92*, 405–410.

Lazarsfeld, P. F. (1955). Recent developments in latent structure analysis. *Sociometry, 18*, 391–403.

Lee, S.-Y. (2007). *Structural equation modeling: A Bayesian approach*. New York, NY: Wiley. doi:10.1002/9780470024737

Li, C. C. (1975). *Path analysis: A primer*. Pacific Grove, CA: Boxwood Press.

Linn, R. L., & Slinde, J. A. (1977). The determination of the significance of change between pre- and post-testing periods. *Review of Educational Research, 47*, 121–150. doi:10.3102/00346543047001121

Littell, R. C., Milliken, G. A., Stroup, W. W., & Wolfinger, R. D. (1996). *SAS system for mixed models*. Cary, NC: SAS Institute.

Little, R. J. A., & Rubin, D. J. (1987). *Statistical analysis with missing data*. New York, NY: Wiley.

Little, R. J. A., & Rubin, D. J. (2002). *Statistical analysis with missing data* (2nd ed.). New York, NY: Wiley.

Loehlin, J. C. (1987). *Latent variable models: An introduction to factor, path, and structural analysis*. Hillsdale, NJ: Erlbaum.

Loehlin, J. C. (1998). *Latent variable models: An introduction to factor, path, and structural analysis* (3rd ed.). Mahwah, NJ: Erlbaum.

Loehlin, J. C. (2004). *Latent variable models: An introduction to factor, path, and structural analysis* (4th ed.). Mahwah, NJ: Erlbaum.

Longford, N. T. (1993). *Random coefficient models*. New York, NY: Oxford University Press.

Lord, F. (1952). *A theory of test scores* (Psychometric Monograph No. 7). Richmond, VA: Psychometric Corporation. Retrieved from http://www.psychometrika.org/journal/online/MN07.pdf

Lord, F. M. (1955). Estimation of parameters from incomplete data. *Journal of the American Statistical Association, 50*, 870–876. doi:10.1080/01621459.1955.10501972

Lord, F. M. (1967). A paradox in the interpretation of group comparisons. *Psychological Bulletin, 68*, 304–305. doi:10.1037/h0025105

Lord, F. M. (1969). Statistical adjustments when comparing preexisting groups. *Psychological Bulletin, 72*, 336–337.

Lord, F. M., & Novick, M. R. (1968). *Statistical theories of mental test scores*. Boston, MA: Addison-Wesley Publishing Company.

Luborsky, L., & Mintz, J. (1972). The contribution of P-technique to personality, psychotherapy, and psychosomatic research. In R. M. Dreger (Ed.), *Multivariate personality research: Contributions to the understanding of personality in honor of Raymond B. Cattell* (pp. 387–410). Baton Rouge, LA: Claitor's Publishing Division.

MacCallum, R. C., & Austin, J. T. (2000). Application of structural equation modeling in psychological research. *Annual Review of Psychology, 51*, 201–226.

MacCallum, R. C., Browne, M. W., & Cai, L. (2006). Testing differences between nested covariance structure models: Power analysis and null hypotheses. *Psychological Methods, 11*, 19–35.

MacCallum, R. C., Browne, M. W., & Sugawara, H. M. (1996). Power analysis and determination of sample size for covariance structure modeling. *Psychological Methods, 1*, 130–149. doi:10.1037/1082-989X.1.2.130

MacCallum, R. C., & Tucker, L. R. (1991). Representing sources of error in the common-factor model: Implications for theory and practice. *Psychological Bulletin, 109*, 502–511. doi:10.1037/0033-2909.109.3.502

Magnusson, D. (2000). The individual as the organizing principle in psychological inquiry: A holistic approach. In L. R. Bergman, R. B. Cairns, L.-G. Nilsson, & L. Nystedt (Eds.), *Developmental science and the holistic approach* (pp. 33–47). Mahwah, NJ: Erlbaum.

Mandys, F., Dolan, C. V., & Molenaar, P. C. (1994). Two aspects of the simplex model: Goodness of fit to linear growth curve structures and the analysis of mean trends. *Journal of Educational and Behavioral Statistics, 19,* 201–215.

Marini, M. M., Olsen, A. R., & Rubin, D. B. (1980). Maximum-likelihood estimation in panel studies with missing data. In K. F. Schuessler (Ed.), *Sociological methodology* (pp. 314–357). San Francisco, CA: Jossey-Bass.

Maxwell, S. E. (2004). The persistence of underpowered studies in psychological research: Causes, consequences, and remedies. *Psychological Methods, 9,* 147–163. doi:10.1037/1082-989X.9.2.147

Maxwell, S. E., & Delaney, H. D. (2004). *Designing experiments and analyzing data: A model comparison perspective* (2nd ed.). Mahwah, NJ: Erlbaum.

McArdle, J. J. (1977). The statistical analysis of Monte Carlo simulation data using the techniques of discrete multivariate analysis. In D. Hogbin & D. W. Fife (Eds.), *Proceedings of the tenth annual symposium on the interface of computer science and statistics* (p. 241–246). Washington, DC: National Bureau of Standards.

McArdle, J. J. (1978). A structural view of structural models. Paper presented at the *Winter Workshop on Latent Structure Models Applied to Developmental Data*, University of Denver, COO, December. (Note: Also presented at the 1979 Meetings of *Psychometric Society*, Monterey, Aand the *American Psychological Association*, New York.).

McArdle, J. J. (1979). The development of multivariate software. In J. Hirschbuhl (Ed.), *Proceedings of the Association for the Development of Computer-based Instructional Systems*. Akron, OH: University of Akron Press. (Note: Also presented at the 1979 meeting of the American Statistical Association, San Diego, CA).

McArdle, J. J. (1986). Latent variable growth within behavior genetic models. *Behavior Genetics, 16,* 163–200. doi:10.1007/BF01065485

McArdle, J. J. (1988). Dynamic but structural equation modeling of repeated measures data. In J. R. Nesselroade & R. B. Cattell (Eds.), *The handbook of multivariate experimental psychology* (Vol. 2, pp. 561–614). New York, NY: Plenum Press. doi:10.1007/978-1-4613-0893-5_17

McArdle, J. J. (1989). Structural modeling experiments using multiple growth functions. In P. Ackerman, R. Kanfer, & R. Cudeck (Eds.), *Learning and individual differences: Abilities, motivation, and methodology* (pp. 71–117). Hillsdale, NJ: Erlbaum.

McArdle, J. J. (1991a). Comments on "Latent variable models for studying difference and changes." In L. Collins & J. L. Horn (Eds.), *Best methods for the analysis of change* (pp. 164–169). Washington, DC: American Psychological Association.

McArdle, J. J. (1991b). Principles versus principals of structural factor analysis. *Multivariate Behavioral Research, 25,* 81–87.

McArdle, J. J. (1994). Structural factor analysis experiments with incomplete data. *Multivariate Behavioral Research, 29,* 409–454. doi:10.1207/s15327906mbr2904_5

McArdle, J. J. (1996). Current directions in structural factor analysis. *Current Directions in Psychological Science, 5,* 11–18.

McArdle, J. J. (1997). Modeling longitudinal data by latent growth curve methods. In G. Marcoulides (Ed.), *Modern methods for business research* (pp. 359–406). Mahwah, NJ: Erlbaum.

McArdle, J. J. (1998). Contemporary statistical models for examining test bias. In J. J. McArdle & R. W. Woodcock (Eds.), *Human abilities in theory and practice* (pp. 157–195). Mahwah, NJ: Erlbaum.

McArdle, J. J. (2001). A latent difference score approach to longitudinal dynamic structural analysis. In R. Cudeck, S. du Toit, & D. Sörbom (Eds.), *Structural equation modeling: Present and future* (pp. 342–380). Lincolnwood, IL: Scientific Software International.

McArdle, J. J. (2005). The development of RAM rules for latent variable structural equation modeling. In A. Madeau & J. J. McArdle (Eds.), *Contemporary advances in psychometrics* (pp. 225–273). Mahwah, NJ: Erlbaum.

McArdle, J. J. (2006). Latent curve analyses of longitudinal twin data using a mixed-effects biometric approach. *Twin Research and Human Genetics, 9,* 343–359. doi:10.1375/twin.9.3.343

McArdle, J. J. (2007a). Dynamic structural equation modeling in longitudinal experimental studies. In K. Montfort, H. Oud, & A. Satorra (Eds.), *Longitudinal models in the behavioral and related sciences* (pp. 159–188). Mahwah, NJ: Erlbaum.

McArdle, J. J. (2007b). Five steps in the structural factor analysis of longitudinal data. In R. Cudeck & R. MacCallum (Eds.), *Factor analysis at 100 years* (pp. 99–130). Mahwah, NJ: Erlbaum.

McArdle, J. J. (2009). Latent variable modeling of longitudinal data. *Annual Review of Psychology, 60,* 577–605. doi:10.1146/annurev.psych.60.110707.163612

McArdle, J. J. (2010). Contemporary challenges of longitudinal measurement using HRS data. In G. Walford, E. Tucker, & M. Viswanathan (Eds.), *The Sage handbook of measurement* (pp. 509–536). London, England: Sage.

McArdle, J. J. (2011a). Foundational issues in the contemporary modeling of longitudinal trajectories. In B. Laursen, T. D. Little, & N. A. Card (Eds.), *Handbook of developmental research methods* (pp. 385–410). New York, NY: Guilford Press.

McArdle, J. J. (2011b). Latent curve modeling. In R. Hoyle (Ed.), *Handbook of structural equation modeling* (pp. 547–570). New York, NY: Guilford Press.

McArdle, J. J. (2011c). Longitudinal panel analysis of the HRS cognitive data. *Advances in Statistical Analyses, 95,* 453–480.

McArdle, J. J. (2011d). Some ethical issues in factor analysis. In A. Panter & S. Sterber (Eds.), *Handbook of ethics in quantitative methodology* (pp. 313–339). New York, NY: Routledge.

McArdle, J. J. (2013a). Dealing with longitudinal attrition using logistic regression and decision tree analyses. In J. J. McArdle & G. Ritschard (Eds.), *Contemporary issues in exploratory data mining in the behavioral sciences* (pp. 282–311). New York, NY: Taylor & Francis.

McArdle, J. J. (2013b). Testing the idea of general intelligence. *F&M Scientist, 1*, 27–66.

McArdle, J. J., & Aber, M. S. (1990). Patterns of change within latent variable structural equation models. In A. von Eye (Ed.), *New statistical methods in developmental research* (pp. 151–224). New York, NY: Academic Press.

McArdle, J. J., & Anderson, E. (1990). Latent variable growth models for research on aging. In J. E. Birren & K. W. Schaie (Eds.), *The handbook of the psychology of aging* (pp. 21–44). New York, NY: Plenum Press.

McArdle, J. J., & Bell, R. Q. (2000). An introduction to latent growth curve models for developmental data analysis. In T. D. Little, K. U. Schnabel, & J. Baumert (Eds.), *Modeling longitudinal and multiple-group data: Practical issues, applied approaches, and scientific examples* (pp. 69–107). Mahwah, NJ: Erlbaum.

McArdle, J. J., & Boker, S. M. (1990). *RAMpath: A computer program for automatic path diagrams.* Hillsdale, NJ: Erlbaum.

McArdle, J. J., & Cattell, R. B. (1994). Structural equation models of factorial invariance in parallel proportional profiles and oblique confactor problems. *Multivariate Behavioral Research, 29*, 63–113. doi:10.1207/s15327906mbr2901_3

McArdle, J. J., & Epstein, D. B. (1987). Latent growth curves within developmental structural equation models. *Child Development, 58*, 110–133. doi:10.2307/1130295

McArdle, J. J., Ferrer-Caja, E., Hamagami, F., & Woodcock, R. W. (2002). Comparative longitudinal multilevel structural analyses of the growth and decline of multiple intellectual abilities over the life-span. *Developmental Psychology, 38*, 115–142. doi:10.1037/0012-1649.38.1.115

McArdle, J. J., Fisher, G. G., & Kadlec, K. M. (2007). Latent variable analysis of age trends in tests of cognitive ability in the health and retirement survey, 1992–2004. *Psychology and Aging, 22*, 525–545. doi:10.1037/0882-7974.22.3.525

McArdle, J. J., & Goldsmith, H. H. (1990). Alternative common factor models for multivariate biometric analyses. *Behavior Genetics, 20*, 569–608.

McArdle, J. J., Grimm, K., Hamagami, F., Bowles, R., & Meredith, W. (2002, October). *A dynamic structural equation analysis of vocabulary abilities over the life-span.* Presented at the annual meeting of the Society of Multivariate Experimental Psychologists, Charlottesville, VA.

McArdle, J. J., Grimm, K. J., Hamagami, F., Bowles, R. P., & Meredith, W. (2009). Modeling life-span growth curves of cognition using longitudinal data with multiple samples and changing scales of measurement. *Psychological Methods, 14,* 126–149. doi:10.1037/a0015857

McArdle, J. J., & Hamagami, F. (1989). A review of Hayduk's "Structural Equation Modeling with LISREL: Essentials and Advances." *Applied Psychological Measurement, 13,* 107–112.

McArdle, J. J., & Hamagami, E. (1991). Modeling incomplete longitudinal and cross-sectional data using latent growth structural models. In L. Collins & J. L. Horn (Eds.), *Best methods for the analysis of change* (pp. 276–304). Washington, DC: American Psychological Association. doi:10.1037/10099-017

McArdle, J. J., & Hamagami, E. (1992). Modeling incomplete longitudinal and cross-sectional data using latent growth structural models. *Experimental Aging Research, 18,* 145–166. doi:10.1080/03610739208253917

McArdle, J. J., & Hamagami, F. (1996). Multilevel models from a multiple group structural equation perspective. In G. Marcoulides & R. Schumacker (Eds.), *Advanced structural equation modeling techniques* (pp. 89–124). Hillsdale, NJ: Erlbaum.

McArdle, J. J., & Hamagami, F. (2001). Linear dynamic analyses of incomplete longitudinal data. In L. Collins & A. Sayer (Eds.), *New methods for the analysis of change* (pp. 139–175). Washington, DC: American Psychological Association. doi:10.1037/10409-005

McArdle, J. J., & Hamagami, F. (2003). Structural equation models for evaluating dynamic concepts within longitudinal twin analyses. *Behavior Genetics, 33,* 137–159. doi:10.1023/A:1022553901851

McArdle, J. J., & Hamagami, F. (2004). Longitudinal structural equation modeling methods for dynamic change hypotheses. In K. van Montfort, J. Oud, & A. Satorra (Eds.), *Recent developments in structural equation models* (pp. 295–335). London, England: Kluwer Academic Publishers. doi:10.1007/978-1-4020-1958-6_15

McArdle, J. J. & Hamagami, F. (2006). Longitudinal tests of dynamic hypotheses on intellectual abilities measured over sixty years. In C. Bergeman & S. M. Boker (Eds.), *Methodological issues in aging research* (pp. 43–98). Mahwah, NJ: Erlbaum.

McArdle, J. J., & Hamagami, F. (2014a). *Advanced features of latent change score models*. Unpublished manuscript.

McArdle, J. J., & Hamagami, F. (2014b). *Advanced issues in longitudinal structural equation modeling*. Charlottesville, VA: Longitudinal Research Institute Press.

McArdle, J. J., Hamagami, F., Chang, J., & Hishinuma, E. (in press). Longitudinal dynamic analyses of depression and academic achievement in the Hawaiian High Schools Health Survey using contemporary latent variable change models. *Structural Equation Modeling*.

McArdle, J. J., Hamagami, F., Jones, K., Jolesz, F., Kikinis, R., Spiro, A., & Albert, M. S. (2004). Structural modeling of dynamic changes in memory and brain structure using longitudinal data from the normative aging study. *The Journals of Gerontology. Series B, Psychological Sciences and Social Sciences, 59B,* P294–P304. doi:10.1093/geronb/59.6.P294

McArdle, J. J., Hamagami, F., Meredith, W., & Bradway, K. P. (2001a). Modeling the dynamic hypotheses of Gf-Gc theory using longitudinal life-span data. *Learning and Individual Differences, 12*, 53–79.

McArdle, J. J., Johnson, R. C., Hishinuma, E. S., Myamoto, R. H., & Andrade, N. (2001b). Structural equation modeling of group differences in CES-D ratings of native Hawaiian and non-native Hawaiian high school students. *Journal of Adolescent Research, 16*, 108–149. doi:10.1177/0743558401162002

McArdle, J. J., & Kadlec, K. M. (2013). Structural equation modeling. In T. Little (Ed.), *Oxford handbook of quantitative methods* (pp. 295–337). New York, NY: Oxford University Press.

McArdle, J. J., & McDonald, R. P. (1984). Some algebraic properties of the Reticular Action Model for moment structures. *British Journal of Mathematical and Statistical Psychology, 37*, 234–251. doi:10.1111/j.2044-8317.1984.tb00802.x

McArdle, J. J., & Nesselroade, J. R. (1994). Using multivariate data to structure developmental change. In S. H. Cohen & H. W. Reese (Eds.), *Life-span developmental psychology: Methodological innovations* (pp. 223–267). Hillsdale, NJ: Erlbaum.

McArdle, J. J., & Nesselroade, J. R. (2003). Growth curve analyses in contemporary psychological research. In J. Schinka & W. Velicer (Eds.), *Comprehensive handbook of psychology, Volume 2: Research methods in psychology* (pp. 447–480). New York, NY: Pergamon Press. doi:10.1002/0471264385.wei0218

McArdle, J. J., & Nesselroade, J. R. (2014). *Applications of longitudinal data analysis using structural equation models*. Manuscript in preparation.

McArdle, J. J., & Plassman, B. (2009). A biometric latent curve analysis of memory decline in older men of the NAS-NRC twin registry. *Behavior Genetics, 39*, 472–495.

McArdle, J. J., & Prescott, C. A. (1992). Age-based construct validation using structural equation modeling. *Experimental Aging Research, 18*, 87–115. doi:10.1080/03610739208253915

McArdle, J. J., & Prescott, C. A. (1996). Contemporary models for the biometric genetic analysis of intellectual abilities. In D. P. Flanagan, J. L. Genshaft, & P. L. Harrison (Eds.), *Contemporary intellectual assessment: Theories, tests, and issues* (pp. 403–436). New York, NY: Guilford Press.

McArdle, J. J., & Prescott, C. A. (2010). Contemporary modeling of gene × environment effects in randomized multivariate longitudinal studies. *Perspectives on Psychological Science, 5*, 606–621.

McArdle, J. J., Prescott, C. A., Hamagami, F., & Horn, J. L. (1998). A contemporary method for developmental-genetic analyses of age changes in intellectual abilities. *Developmental Neuropsychology, 14*, 69–114. doi:10.1080/87565649809540701

McArdle, J. J., & Prindle, J. J. (2008). A latent change score analysis of a randomized clinical trial in reasoning training. *Psychology and Aging, 23*, 702–719. doi:10.1037/a0014349

McArdle, J. J., & Ritschard, G. (Eds.) (2013) *Contemporary issues in exploratory data mining in the bahavioral sciences*. New York, NY: Taylor & Francis.

McArdle, J. J., Small, B. J., Backman, L., & Fratiglioni, L. (2005). Longitudinal models of growth and survival applied to the early detection of Alzheimer's disease. *Journal of Geriatric Psychiatry and Neurology, 18*, 234–241. doi:10.1177/ 0891988705281879

McArdle, J. J., & Woodcock, R. W. (1997). Expanding test–rest designs to include developmental time-lag components. *Psychological Methods, 2*, 403–435. doi:10.1037/1082-989X.2.4.403

McCall, R. B., & Applebaum, M. I. (1973). Bias in the analysis of repeated measures designs: Some alternative approaches. *Child Development, 44*, 401–415. doi:10.2307/1127993

McCoach, D. B., & Kaniskan, B. (2010). Using time-varying covariates in multilevel growth models. *Frontiers in Quantitative Psychology and Measurement, 1*(17). doi:10.3389/fpsyg.2010.00017

McDonald, R. P. (1980). A simple comprehensive model for the analysis of covariance structures: Some remarks on application. *British Journal of Mathematical and Statistical Psychology, 33*, 161–183. doi:10.1111/j.2044-8317.1980.tb00606.x

McDonald, R. P. (1982). A note on the investigation of local and global identifiably. *Psychometrika, 47*, 101–103. doi:10.1007/BF02293855

McDonald, R. P. (1985a). Exploratory and confirmatory nonlinear common factor analysis. In H. Wainer & S. Messick (Eds.), *Principles of modern psychological measurement* (pp. 197–213). Hillsdale, NJ: Erlbaum.

McDonald, R. P. (1985b). *Factor analysis and related methods.* Hillsdale, NJ: Erlbaum.

McDonald, R. P. (1999). *Test theory: A unified treatment.* Mahwah, NJ: Erlbaum.

McDonald, R. P., & Goldstein, H. (1989). Balanced versus unbalanced designs for linear structural relations in two-level data. British *Journal of Mathematical and Statistical Psychology, 42*, 215–232.

McGaw, B., & Jöreskog, K. G. (1971). Factorial invariance of ability measures in groups differing in intelligence and socioeconomic status. *British Journal of Mathematical and Statistical Psychology, 24*, 154–168. doi:10.1111/j.2044-8317.1971. tb00463.x

McLuhan, M. (1964). *Understanding media: The extension of man.* New York, NY: McGraw-Hill.

McQuitty, S. (2004). Statistical power and structural equation models in business research. *Journal of Business Research, 57*, 175–183.

Mehta, P. D., & West, S. G. (2000). Putting the individual back into individual growth curves. *Psychological Methods, 5*(1), 23–43. doi:10.1037/1082-989X.5.1.23

Meredith, W. (1964a). Notes on factorial invariance. *Psychometrika, 29*, 177–185. doi:10.1007/BF02289699

Meredith, W. (1964b). Rotation to achieve factorial invariance. *Psychometrika, 29*, 187–206. doi:10.1007/BF02289700

Meredith, W. (1965). A method for studying differences between groups. *Psychometrika, 30*, 15–29. doi:10.1007/BF02289744

Meredith, W. (1993). Measurement invariance, factor analysis and factorial invariance. *Psychometrika, 58*, 525–543. doi:10.1007/BF02294825

Meredith, W., & Horn, J. L. (2001). The role of factorial invariance in modeling growth and change. In A. G. Sayer & L. M. Collins (Eds.), *New methods for the analysis of change* (pp. 203–240). Washington, DC: American Psychological Association. doi:10.1037/10409-007

Meredith, W., & Teresi, J. A. (2006). An essay on measurement and factorial invariance. *Medical Care, 44*, S69–S77. doi:10.1097/01.mlr.0000245438.73837.89

Meredith, W., & Tisak, J. (1990). Latent curve analysis. *Psychometrika, 55*, 107–122. doi:10.1007/BF02294746

Millsap, R. E., & Meredith, W. (2007). Factorial invariance: Historical perspectives and new problems. In R. Cudeck & R. MacCallum (Eds.), *Factor Analysis at 100* (pp. 131–152). Mahwah, NJ: Lawrence Erlbaum.

Miyazaki, Y., & Raudenbush, S. W. (2000). A test for linkage of multiple cohorts from an accelerated longitudinal design. *Psychological Methods, 5*, 44–63. doi:10.1037/1082-989X.5.1.44

Molenaar, P. C. (1985). A dynamic factor model for the analysis of multivariate time series. *Psychometrika, 50*, 181–202. doi:10.1007/BF02294246

Molenaar, P. C. (2004). A manifesto on psychology as idiographic science: Bringing the person back into scientific psychology, this time forever. *Measurement, 2*, 201–218.

Molenaar, P. C. M., & Nesselroade, J. R. (2012). Merging the idiographic filter with dynamic factor analysis to model process. *Applied Developmental Science, 16*, 210–219.

Montfort, K., Oud, H., & Satorra, A. (Eds.). (2007). *Longitudinal models in the behavioral and related sciences*. Mahwah, NJ: Erlbaum

Mulaik, S. (1971). A note on some equations of confirmatory factor analysis. *Psychometrika, 36*, 63–70. doi:10.1007/BF02291423

Muller, K. E., & Stewart, P. W. (2006). *Linear model theory: Univariate, multivariate, and mixed models*. New York, NY: Wiley. doi:10.1002/0470052147

Murray, H. A., & Kluckhohn, C. (1953). *Personality in nature, society, and culture* (2nd ed.). New York, NY: Alfred A. Knopf.

Muthén, B. (1978). Contributions to factor analysis of dichotomous variables. *Psychometrika, 43*, 551–560. doi:10.1007/BF02293813

Muthén, B. (1984). A general structural equation model with dichotomous, ordered categorical, and continuous latent variable indicators. *Psychometrika, 49*, 115–132. doi:10.1007/BF02294210

Muthén, B. (1989a). Dichotomous factor analysis of symptom data. *Sociological Methods and Research, 18*, 19–65.

Muthén, B. (1989b). Latent variable modeling in heterogeneous populations. Presidential address to the Psychometric Society, July, 1989. *Psychometrika, 54*, 557–585.

Muthén, B. (1989c). Tobit factor analysis. *British Journal of Mathematical and Statistical Psychology, 42*, 241–250. doi:10.1111/j.2044-8317.1989.tb00913.x

Muthén, B. (1989d). Using item-specific instructional information in achievement modeling. *Psychometrika, 54*, 385–396. doi:10.1007/BF02294624

Muthén, B., & Christoffersson, A. (1981). Simultaneous factor analysis of dichotomous variables in several groups. *Psychometrika, 46*, 407–419. doi:10.1007/BF02293798

Muthén, B. O., & Curran, P. (1997). General longitudinal modeling of individual differences in experimental designs: A latent variable framework for analysis and power estimation. *Psychological Methods, 2*, 371–402. doi:10.1037/1082-989X.2.4.371

Muthén, B. O., & Satorra, A. (1995). Technical aspects of Muthén's LISCOMP approach to estimation of latent variable relations within a comprehensive measurement model. *Psychometrika, 60*, 489–503. doi:10.1007/BF02294325

Muthén, L. K., & Muthén, B. O. (2002a). How to use a Monte Carlo study to decide on sample size and determine power. *Structural Equation Modeling, 4*, 599–620. doi:10.1207/S15328007SEM0904_8

Muthén, L. K., & Muthén, B. O. (2002b). *Mplus, the comprehensive modeling program for applied researchers user's guide*. Los Angeles, CA: Muthén & Muthén.

Muthén, L. K., & Muthén, B. O. (2006). *Mplus*. Los Angeles, CA: Muthén and Muthén.

Nagin, D. S. (1999). Analyzing developmental trajectories: Semi-parametric, group-based approach. *Psychological Methods, 4*, 139–157. doi:10.1037/1082-989X.4.2.139

Nagoshi, C. T., Phillips, K., & Johnson, R. C. (1987). Between- versus within-family factor analyses of cognitive abilities. *Intelligence, 11*, 305–316.

Neale, M. C. Boker, S. M., Xie, G., & Maes, H. H. (1999). *Mx statistical modeling* (5th ed.). Unpublished program manual. Richmond, VA: Virginia Institute for Psychiatric and Behavioral Genetics, Medical College of Virginia, Virginia Commonwealth University.

Nesselroade, J. R. (1970). Application of multivariate strategies to problems of measuring and structuring long term change. In L. R. Goulet & P. B. Baltes (Eds.), *Life-span developmental psychology: Research and theory* (pp. 193–207). New York, NY: Academic Press.

Nesselroade, J. R. (1972). Note on the "Longitudinal factor analysis model." *Psychometrika, 37*, 187–191. doi:10.1007/BF02306776

Nesselroade, J. R. (1983). Temporal selection and factor invariance in the study of development and change. In P. B. Baltes & O. G. Brim Jr. (Eds.), *Life-span development and behavior* (Vol. 5, pp. 59–87). New York, NY: Academic Press.

Nesselroade, J. R. (1993). Whether we Likert or not, personality measurement and the study of developmental change are demanding activities. *Psychological Inquiry, 4*, 40–42. doi:10.1207/s15327965pli0401_8

Nesselroade, J. R. (2004). Intraindividual variability and short term change [Commentary]. *Gerontology, 50*, 44–47.

Nesselroade, J. R., & Baltes, P. B. (1974). Adolescent personality development and historical change: 1970–1972. *Monographs of the Society for Research in Child Development, 39*, 1–80.

Nesselroade, J. R., & Baltes, P. B. (Eds.) (1979). *Longitudinal research in the study of behavior and development.* New York, NY: Academic Press.

Nesselroade, J. R., & Baltes, P. B. (1984). From traditional factor analysis to structural-causal modeling in developmental research. In V. Sarris & A. Parducci (Eds.), *Perspectives in psychological experimentation* (pp. 267–287). Hillsdale, NJ: Erlbaum.

Nesselroade, J. R., & Bartsch, T. W. (1977). Multivariate experimental perspectives on the construct validity of the trait-state distinction. In R. B. Cattell & R. M. Dreger (Eds.), *Handbook of modern personality theory* (pp. 221–238). Washington, DC: Hemisphere/Halsted.

Nesselroade, J. R., & Boker, S. M. (1994). Assessing constancy and change. In T. F. Heatherton & J. L. Weinberger (Eds.), *Can personality change?* (pp. 121–147). Washington, DC: American Psychological Association. doi:10.1037/10143-006

Nesselroade, J. R., & Cable, D. G. (1974). "Sometimes it's okay to factor difference scores"—The separation of trait and state anxiety. *Multivariate Behavioral Research, 9*, 273–281. doi:10.1207/s15327906mbr0903_3

Nesselroade, J. R., & Ford, D. H. (1985). P-technique comes of age: Multivariate, replicated, single-subject designs for research on older adults. *Research on Aging, 7*, 46–80.

Nesselroade, J. R., & Ford, D. H. (1987). Methodological considerations in modeling living systems. In M. E. Ford & D. H. Ford (Eds.), *Humans as self-constructing living systems: Putting the framework to work* (pp. 47–79). Hillsdale, NJ: Lawrence Erlbaum Associates.

Nesselroade, J. R., Gerstorf, D., Hardy, S. A., & Ram, N. (2007). Idiographic filters for psychological constructs. *Measurement, 5*, 217–235.

Nesselroade, J. R., McArdle, J. J., Aggen, S. H., & Meyers, J. (2001). Dynamic factor analysis models for multivariate time series analysis. In D. M. Moskowitz & S. L. Hershberger (Eds.), *Modeling individual variability with repeated measures data: Advances and techniques* (pp. 233–266). Mahwah, NJ: Erlbaum.

Nesselroade, J. R., & Molenaar, P. C. M. (2003). Quantitative models for developmental processes. In J. Valsiner & K. Connolly (Eds.), *Handbook of developmental psychology* (pp. 622–639). London, England: Sage.

Nesselroade, J. R., & Molenaar, P. C. M. (2010a). Analyzing intra-person variation: Hybridizing the ACE model with P-technique factor analysis and the idiographic filter. *Behavior Genetics, 40*, 776–783. doi:10.1007/s10519-010-9373-x

Nesselroade, J. R., & Molenaar, P. C. M. (2010b). Emphasizing intraindividual variability in the study of development over the lifespan. In R. M. Lerner & W. F. Overton (Eds.), *Cognition, biology, and methods across the lifespan. Handbook of life-span development* (Vol., 1, pp. 30–54). Hoboken, NJ: Wiley.

Nesselroade, J. R., & Molenaar, P. C. M. (2010c). When persons should be few and occasions should be many: Modeling a different kind of longitudinal data. *International Society for the Study of Behavioral Development Bulletin, 57*, 2–4.

Ntzoufras, I. (2009). *Bayesian modeling using WinBUGS*. New York, NY: Wiley. doi:10.1002/9780470434567

Oakes, J. M., & Feldman, H. A. (2001). Statistical power for nonequivalent pretest–posttest designs: The impact of change-score versus ANCOVA models. *Evaluation Review, 25*, 3–28. doi:10.1177/0193841X0102500101

O'Brien, R. G., & Kaiser, M. K. (1985). MANOVA method for analyzing repeated measures designs: An extensive primer. *Psychological Bulletin, 97*, 316–333. doi:10.1037/0033-2909.97.2.316

Oertzen, T. (2010). Power equivalence in structural equation modelling. *British Journal of Mathematical and Statistical Psychology, 63*, 257–272.

Olsson, U., & Bergman, L. F. (1977). A longitudinal factor model for studying change in ability structure. *Multivariate Behavioral Research, 12*, 221–241. doi:10.1207/s15327906mbr1202_8

Oud, J. H. L., & Jansen, R. A. R. G. (2000). Continuous time state space modeling of panel data by means of SEM. *Psychometrika, 65*, 199–215. doi:10.1007/BF02294374

Parry, C., & McArdle, J. J. (1991). An applied comparison of methods for least squares factor analysis of dichotomous variables. *Applied Psychological Measurement, 15*(1), 35–46. doi:10.1177/014662169101500105

Pearl, J. (1995). Causal diagrams for empirical research. *Biometrika, 82*, 669–688.

Pearl, J. (2000). *Causality: Models, reasoning, and inference*. New York, NY: Cambridge University Press.

Pearson, K. (1912). *The groundwork of eugenics*. London, England: Dulau.

Pinheiro, J. C., & Bates, D. M. (2000). *Mixed-effects models in S and S-Plus*. New York, NY: Springer. doi:10.1007/978-1-4419-0318-1

Popper, K. R. (1970). Normal science and its dangers. *Criticism and the Growth of Knowledge, 4*, 51–58.

Pothoff, R. F., & Roy, S. N. (1964). A generalized multivariate analysis of variance model useful especially for growth curve problems. *Biometrika, 51*, 313–326.

Prindle, J. J., & McArdle, J. J. (2012). An examination of statistical power in multigroup dynamic structural equation models. *Structural Equation Modeling, 19*, 351–372.

Rabe-Hesketh, S., Skrondal, A., & Pickles, A. (2004). *GLLAMM manual*.

Ramaprasad, A. (1983). On the definition of feedback. *Behavioral Science, 28*, 4–13. doi:10.1002/bs.3830280103

Rao, C. R. (1958). Some statistical methods for comparison of growth curves. *Biometrics, 14*, 1–17. doi:10.2307/2527726

Rao, C. R. (1965). *Linear statistical inferences and its applications.* New York, NY: Wiley.

Rasch, G. (1960). *Probabilistic models for some intelligence and attainment tests.* Chicago, IL: University of Chicago Press.

Raudenbush, S. W. (2005). Learning from attempts to improve schooling: The contribution of methodological diversity. *Educational Researcher, 34,* 25–31. doi:10.3102/0013189X034005025

Raudenbush, S. W., & Bryk, A. S. (2002). *Hierarchical linear models in social and behavioral research: Applications and data analysis methods* (2nd ed.). Newbury Park, CA: Sage.

Raudenbush, S. W., & Liu, X. (2000). Statistical power and optimal design for multisite randomized trials. *Psychological Methods, 5*(2), 199–213. doi:10.1037/1082-989X.5.2.199

Raykov, T. (1997a). Disentangling intervention and temporal effects in longitudinal designs using latent curve analysis. *Biometrical Journal, 39,* 239–259. doi:10.1002/bimj.4710390211

Raykov, T. (1997b). Growth curve analysis of ability means and variances in measures of fluid intelligence of older adults. *Structural Equation Modeling, 4,* 283–319. doi:10.1080/10705519709540078

Raykov, T., & Marcoulides, G. A. (2006). *A first course in structural equation modeling.* Mahwah, NJ: Erlbaum.

Reinert, T. (1970). Comparative factor analytic studies of intelligence throughout the life span. In L. R. Goulet & P. B. Baltes (Eds.), *Lifespan developmental psychology: Research and theory* (pp. 476–484). New York, NY: Academic Press.

Reise, S. P., Widaman, K. F., & Pugh, R. H. (1993). Confirmatory factor analysis and item response theory: Two approaches for exploring measurement invariance. *Psychological Bulletin, 114,* 552–566. doi:10.1037/0033-2909.114.3.552

Revelle, W., & Rocklin, T. (1979). Very simple structure: Alternative procedure for estimating the optimal number of interpretable factors. *Multivariate Behavioral Research, 14,* 403–414.

Rindskopf, D. (1983). Parameterizing inequality constraints on unique variances in linear structural models. *Psychometrika, 48,* 73–83. doi:10.1007/BF02314677

Rogosa, D., & Willett, J. B. (1985). Satisfying a simplex structure is simpler than it should be. *Journal of Educational Statistics, 10,* 99–107. doi:10.2307/1164837

Rogosa, D. R., & Willett, J. B. (1983). Demonstrating the reliability of the difference score in the measurement of change. *Journal of Educational Measurement, 20,* 335–343. doi:10.1111/j.1745-3984.1983.tb00211.x

Rozeboom, W. W. (1975). *Dynamic multivariate models.* Unpublished manuscript, Department of Psychology, University of Alberta, Edmonton, Canada.

Rubin, D. B. (1976). Inference and missing data. *Biometrika, 63,* 581–592. doi:10.1093/biomet/63.3.581

Rubin, D. B. (1997). Estimating causal effects from large data sets using propensity scores. *Annals of Internal Medicine, 127*, 757–763.

Salmon, W. C. (1980). *Causation*. New York, NY: Oxford University Press.

Saris, W. E., & Satorra, A. (1993). Power evaluations in structural equation models. In K. Bollen & S. Long (Eds.), *Testing Structural Equation Models* (pp. 181–204). Beverly Hills, CA: Sage.

Saris, W. E., & Stronkhorst, L. H. (1984). *Causal modeling in nonexperimental research: An introduction to the LISREL approach*. Amsterdam, the Netherlands: Sociometric Research Foundation.

Satorra, A., & Bentler, P. M. (1994). Correction to test statistics and standard errors in covariance structure analysis. In A. von Eye & C. C. Clogg (Eds.), *Latent variables analysis: Applications to developmental research* (pp. 399–419). Thousand Oaks, CA: Sage Publications.

Satorra, A., & Saris, W. (1985). Power of the likelihood ratio test in covariance structure analysis. *Psychometrika, 50*, 83–90. doi:10.1007/BF02294150

Sayer, A. G., & Cusmile, I. (2001). Second-order growth models. In L. Colins & A. G. Sayer (Eds.), *New methods for the analysis of change* (pp. 179–200). Washington, DC: American Psychological Association.

Schmitz, S., Cherny, S. S., & Fulker, D. W. (1998). Increase in power through multivariate analyses. *Behavior Genetics, 28*, 357–363.

Singer, H. (1993). Continuous-time dynamical systems with sampled data, errors of measurement, and unobserved components. *Journal of Time Series Analysis, 14*, 527–545.

Singer, J. (1998). Using SAS PROC MIXED to fit multilevel models, hierarchical models, and individual growth models. *Journal of Educational and Behavioral Statistics, 23*, 323–355.

Singer, J., & Willett, J. (2003). *Applied longitudinal data analysis*. New York, NY: Oxford University Press. doi:10.1093/acprof:oso/9780195152968.001.0001

Shrout, P. E. (2011). Integrating causal analysis into psychopathology research. In P. E. Shrout, K. Keyes, & K. Ornstein (Eds.), *Causality and psychopathology: Finding the determinants of disorders and their cures* (pp. 3–24). New York, NY: Oxford University Press.

Snijders, T., & Bosker, R. (1999). *Multilevel analysis: An introduction to basic and advanced multilevel modeling*. London, England: Sage.

Snyder, J., Brooker, M., Patrick, M. R., Snyder, A., Schrepferman, L., & Stoolmiller, M. (2003). Observed peer victimization during early elementary school: Continuity, growth, and relation to risk for child antisocial and depressive behavior. *Child Development, 74*, 1881–1898. doi:10.1046/j.1467-8624.2003.00644.x

Sobel, M. E. (1982). Asymptotic intervals for indirect effects in structural equations models. In S. Leinhart (Ed.), *Sociological methodology 1982* (pp. 290–312). San Francisco, CA: Jossey-Bass.

Sörbom, D. (1974). A general method for studying differences and factor means and factor structure between groups. *British Journal of Mathematical and Statistical Psychology, 27,* 229–239. doi:10.1111/j.2044-8317.1974.tb00543.x

Sörbom, D. (1975). Detection of correlated errors in longitudinal data. *British Journal of Mathematical and Statistical Psychology, 28,* 138–151. doi:10.1111/j.2044-8317.1975.tb00558.x

Sörbom, D. (1978). An alternative to the methodology for analysis of covariance. *Psychometrika, 43,* 381–396. doi:10.1007/BF02293647

Spearman, C. E. (1904). "General intelligence," objectively determined and measured. *American Journal of Psychology, 15,* 201–293. doi:10.2307/1412107

Spearman, C. E. (1927). *The abilities of man.* New York, NY: Macmillan.

Stapleton, L. M., & Leite, W. L. (2005). Teacher's corner: A review of syllabi for a sample of structural equation modeling courses. *Structural Equation Modeling, 12,* 642–664. doi:10.1207/s15328007sem1204_7

Steiger, J. H. (1990). Structural model evaluation and modification. *Multivariate Behavioral Research, 25,* 173–180. doi:10.1207/s15327906mbr2502_4

Steiger, J. H., Shapiro, A., & Browne, M. W. (1985). On the multivariate asymptotic distribution of sequential chi-square statistics. *Psychometrika, 50,* 253–263.

Strotz, R. H., & Wold, H. A. O. (1960). Recursive vs non-recursive systems: An Attempt at synthesis. *Econometrica, 28,* 417–427. doi:10.2307/1907731

Sullivan, E. V., Pfefferbaum, A., Adalsteinsson, E., Swan, G. E., & Carmelli, D. (2002). Differential rates of regional brain change in callosal and ventricular size: A 4-year longitudinal MRI study of elderly men. *Cerebral Cortex, 12,* 438–445.

Swaminathan, H., & Gifford, J. A. (1985). Bayesian estimation in the two-parameter logistic model. *Psychometrika, 50,* 349–364.

Tabachnick, B. G., & Fidell, L. S. (2007a). *Experimental designs using ANOVA.* Belmont, CA: Duxbury.

Tabachnick, B. G., & Fidell, L. S. (2007b). *Using multivariate statistics* (5th ed.). Boston, MA: Allyn and Bacon.

Tanaka, J. S. (1987). "How big is big enough?": Sample size and goodness of fit in structural equation models with latent variables. *Child Development, 58,* 134–146.

Thomas, L. (1997). Retrospective power analysis. *Conservation Biology, 11,* 276–280.

Thomson, G. H., & Ledermann, W. (1939). The influence of multivariate selection on the factorial analysis of ability. *British Journal of Psychology, 29,* 288–306.

Thurstone, L. L. (1947). *Multiple-factor analysis.* Chicago, IL: University of Chicago Press.

Torgerson, W. S. (1958). *Theory and methods of scaling.* Oxford, England: Wiley.

Tucker, L. (1958). Determination of parameters of a functional relation by factor analysis. *Psychometrika, 23,* 19–23. doi:10.1007/BF02288975

Tucker, L. R. (1966). Learning theory and multivariate experiment: Illustration by determination of parameters of generalized learning curves. In R. B. Cattell (Ed.), *The handbook of multivariate experimental psychology* (pp. 476–501). Chicago, IL: Rand-McNally.

Tucker, L. R., Damarin, F., & Messick, S. (1966). A base-free measure of change. *Psychometrika, 31*, 457–473.

Tucker, L. R., & Lewis, C. (1973). A reliability coefficient for maximum likelihood factor analysis. *Psychometrika, 38*, 1–10.

Tukey, J. W. (1949). Comparing individual means in the analysis of variance. *Biometrics, 5*, 99–114. doi:10.2307/3001913

van der Laan, M. J., & Robins, J. M. (2003). *Unified methods for censored longitudinal data and causality.* New York, NY: Springer.

Wainer, H. (1991). Adjusting for differential base rates: Lord's paradox again. *Psychological Bulletin, 109*, 147–151. doi:10.1037/0033-2909.109.1.147

Walker, A. J., Acock, A. C., Bowman, S. R., & Li, F. (1996). Amount of care given and caregiving satisfaction: A latent growth curve analysis. *The Journals of Gerontology, Series B: Psychological Sciences and Social Sciences, 51*, 130–142.

Walls, T. A., & Schafer, J. L. (2006). *Models for intensive longitudinal data.* New York, NY: Oxford University Press. doi:10.1093/acprof:oso/9780195173444.001.0001

Wechsler, D. (1955). *The Wechsler adult intelligence scale.* New York, NY: Psychological Corporation.

Wechsler, D. (1981). *The Wechsler adult intelligence scale—revised.* New York, NY: Psychological Corporation.

Werts, C. E., & Linn, R. L. (1970). Path analysis: Psychological examples. *Psychological Bulletin, 74*, 193–212. doi:10.1037/h0029778

Werts, G. E., Pike, L. W., Rock, D. A., & Gandy, J. (1981). Applications of quasi-Markov simplex models across populations. *Educational and Psychological Measurement, 41*(2), 295–307. doi:10.1177/001316448104100207

Widaman, K. F. (1985). Hierarchically nested covariance structure models for multitrait-multimethod data. *Applied Psychological Measurement, 9*, 1–26. doi:10.1177/014662168500900101

Wilcox, R. R. (1998). How many discoveries have been lost by ignoring modern statistical methods? *American Psychologist, 53*, 300–314.

Wiley, D. (1973). The identification problem for structural equation models with unmeasured variables. In A. S. Goldberger & O. D. Duncan (Eds.), *Structural equation models in the social sciences* (pp. 69–83). New York, NY: Seminar Press.

Wiley, D. E., & Wiley, J. A. (1970). The identification of measurement errors in panel data. *American Sociological Review, 35*, 112–117. doi:10.2307/2093858

Willett, J. B. (1989). Some results on reliability for the longitudinal measurement of change: Implications for the design of studies of individual growth. *Educational and Psychological Measurement, 49*, 587–602.

Willett, J. B., & Sayer, A. G. (1994). Using covariance structure analysis to detect correlates and predictors of individual change over time. *Psychological Bulletin, 116*, 363–381. doi:10.1037/0033-2909.116.2.363

Winer, B. J. (1962). *Statistical principles in experimental design.* New York, NY: McGraw-Hill. doi:10.1037/11774-000

Winer, B. J. (1971). *Statistical principles in experimental design* (2nd ed.). New York, NY: McGraw-Hill.

Wishart, J. (1938). Growth rate determinations in nutrition studies with the bacon pig, and their analyses. *Biometrika, 30*, 16–28.

Wohlwill, J. F. (1991). Relations between method and theory in developmental research: A partial-isomorphism view. In P. van Geert & L. P. Mos (Eds.), *Annals of theoretical psychology* (Vol. 7, pp. 91–138). New York, NY: Plenum Press. doi:10.1007/978-1-4615-3842-4_5

Wold, H. O. A. (1980). Soft modelling: Intermediate between traditional model building and data analysis. *Mathematical Statistics, 6*, 333–346.

Woodworth, R. S. (1938). *Experimental psychology.* New York, NY: Holt.

Woodworth, R. S., & Schlosberg, H. (1954). *Experimental psychology.* Oxford, England: Oxford University Press and IBH Publishing.

Wright, S. (1918). On the nature of size factors. *Genetics, 3*, 367–374.

Wright, S. (1921). Correlation and causation. *Journal of Agricultural Research, 20*, 557–585.

Wright, S. (1934). The method of path coefficients. *Annals of Mathematical Statistics, 5*, 161–215. doi:10.1214/aoms/1177732676

Wright, S. (1960). The treatment of reciprocal interaction, with or without lag, in path analysis. *Biometrics, 16*, 423–445. doi:10.2307/2527693

Yuan, K. H., & Hayashi, K. (2003). Bootstrap approach to inference and power analysis based on three test statistics for covariance structure models. *British Journal of Mathematical and Statistical Psychology, 56*, 93–110.

Zazzo, R. (1967). Diversity, reality, and the illusions of the longitudinal method: Introductory report to the Symposium on Longitudinal Studies. *Enfance, 20*, 131–136. doi:10.3406/enfan.1967.2414

Zevon, M. A., & Tellegen, A. (1982). The structure of mood change: An idiographic/nomothetic analysis. *Journal of Personality and Social Psychology, 43*, 111–122.

Zhang, Z., Browne, M. W., & Nesselroade, J. R. (2011). Higher-order factor invariance and idiographic mapping of constructs to observables. *Applied Developmental Science, 15*, 186–200.

Zhang, Z., Hamagami, F., Wang, L., Grimm, K. J., & Nesselroade, J. R. (2007). Bayesian analysis of longitudinal data using growth curve models. *International Journal of Behavioral Development, 31*, 374–383. doi:10.1177/0165025407077764

INDEX

Accumulation, 125
Accuracy, 50
Additive latent change score models
    bivariate, 294, 295
    expected trajectory for, 123
    path diagrams of, 126–128
Additivity assumption, 53
Age, between-persons variability and, 19
Age appropriate indices, 226
Ahmvaara, Y., 309–310
AIC (An Information Criterion), 50
Aitken, A. C., 309
American Psychological Association (APA), x
AMOS, 41
Analysis of covariance (ANCOVA) model, 146, 149–150
Analysis of variance (ANOVA), 5, 7. *See also* Multivariate analysis of variance (MANOVA); Repeated measures analysis of variance (RANOVA)
    for changes in means over time, 211
    for group differences, 144, 151
    and model expectations, 46
    multiple situation functional, 353
    RANOVA vs., 154
ANCOVA (analysis of covariance) model, 146, 149–150
Anderson, E., 338, 339
Andrade, N., 310
ANOVA. *See* Analysis of variance
APA (American Psychological Association), x
Applications of Longitudinal Data Analysis Using Structural Equation Models (McArdle and Nesselroade), x, 11
Arbuckle, A., 350
ARIMA (autoregressive integrated moving average) analysis, 112, 113
Arminger, G., 139
Arrow matrix, 60

Assumptions
    additivity, 53
    common factor, 237
    equal parameters for equal amounts of time, 134
    ergodicity, 123, 265
    linearity, 53
    stationarity, 117, 262–263
    with statistical models, 53
    with time series regressions, 117
Attrition, 71, 178
Autoregression models
    with group differences, 144, 146
    with incomplete data, 180
    multiple group, 168, 180
    time series-based, 29
    Type A, 85–87
Autoregressive integrated moving average (ARIMA) analysis, 112, 113
Autoregressive latent trajectory approach, 120
Autoregressive moving average model, 112, 113
Autoregressive simplex models, 76
Average sums of squares and cross-products (SSCP)
    index for, 49
    model of, 99
    and tracing rules, 84
Average sums of squares and cross-products (SSCP) matrix expectation, 61, 62

Bachman, J. G., 91
Backman, L., 341–342
Baltes, P. B., 3–4, 9–10, 18–23, 143, 151, 368
Baltes, Paul, x
Bartsch, T. W., 272
Baseline models
    bivariate, 292, 294
    common factor, 192–194
    cross-lagged regression, 260, 261
    latent change score, 126, 127
    latent curve, 99–100

Bayesian Information Criteria
    (BIC), 50
Behavior
    difficulty of studying, 372
    multivariate perspective on, 22
Behavioral change, interrelations in, 22
Behavior analysis, individual as unit of,
    357–358
Bell, R. Q., 338, 343
Berieter, C., 360
Best linear unbiased estimates (BLUE),
    31, 52
Between-group differences
    dynamic analysis of, 308–309
    multilevel modeling of, 354
Between groups (term), 151
Between–within factor analysis of family
    data, 353
Biases
    in linear regression, 30, 32–37, 58
    missing predictor variable, 32–34
    systematic, 264
BIC (Bayesian Information Criteria), 50
Binary factor measurement model,
    241–245
Binary outcome variables, 241–242
Binary responses, longitudinal models
    of, 245–248
Binary scores, for latent variables with
    range of responses, 241
Biometric design, 345–346
Bivariate latent change score models,
    291–300
    defined, 292–294
    and dynamic influence over groups,
        308–309
    dynamic invariance in, 320–321
    and feedback loops, 298–300
    with multiple groups, 319–321
    path diagrams of, 292, 296–297
    and RANOVA, 329
    variations on, 294–298
Bivariate latent change scores, 301–304
    Cartesian plots of, 301–302
    phase diagrams of, 302
    vector fields of, 302–304
Bivariate latent growth curves, 286–287
Bivariate longitudinal factor analysis
    model, 273
Blalock, H. M., 188, 325

BLUE (best linear unbiased estimates),
    31, 52
Boker, S. M., 61, 62, 121, 370
Boker, Steven M., 17
Bollen, K. A., 94, 120
Bridges, 62
Browne, M., 94, 103
Browne, M. W., 56, 363–365
Burt, C., 243

Cai, L., 56
CALIS, 41
Campbell, D., 23–24
Canonical scores, 283
Cartesian plots, of bivariate latent
    change scores, 301–302
Case I invariance
    over groups, 311–313
    over time, 222, 223, 226, 227
Case II invariance
    over groups, 311–313
    over time, 222, 223, 226
Case III invariance
    over groups, 311–313
    over time, 222, 223, 226
Case IV invariance
    over groups, 311–313
    over time, 222–224, 226
Categorical data, common factor model
    for, 241–245
Categorical factor analysis, 239–240.
    See also Longitudinal categorical
    factors
Cattell, R. B., 9, 201, 211, 221–222,
    272, 310, 313, 347, 357, 360, 362
Causal inference
    dynamic vs., 268
    from longitudinal data, 267–269
    and randomization, 8–9, 323, 325
Causality, Granger, 267–269
Causal lag, 24–25
Causal relations, in observational data,
    255–256, 264, 276–277
Causation, reciprocal, 264–265
Change(s). See also Intraindividual
    changes
    bivariate latent change score model
        for, 294, 295
    common, 233
    correlated, 235, 294–296

coupled, 294, 295, 297
in cross-lagged regression models, 266–267, 277–279
differential equations models of, 121–122, 139, 369–370
dual latent, 233
and growth, x, 29
instantaneous, 370
interrelations in, 22
multilevel modeling of, 160–161
multiple group modeling of, 167–171
person-centered orientation to, 358
proportional, 294, 295
and stability, 17
within-person, 9, 10
Change analysis, x, 121
Change over time, 5, 19–20
Change regression, 86
Change score models
confusion about, 91
cross-lagged, 278, 319–320
group difference dynamic, 371
observed, 78–80, 85–86, 146–147
parallel, 294, 295
two-occasion, 90–92
Type A, 85–86
Type D, 83–84
Type DR, 86–88
Type Δ and ΔR, 88–90
Change scores. *See also* Latent change scores
critique of, 78–82
defining, 76
dual, 246
in latent curve models, 102–103
observed, 76–78, 81–82
residual, 86, 92
time-to-time prediction of, 85–86
Chi-square testing, 240
X-square value, 56, 57
Christoffersson, A., 243, 244
Classical test theory, 357
Clustering, 71
Coefficients
factor loading, 311–313
feedback, 298
heritability, 365
latent basis, 134–136

reliability, 51
restricted, in cross-lagged regression models, 258, 260, 261
in Type A autoregression model, 85
Cohen, J., 55
Coleman, J., 302
Common changes, 233
Common factor assumption, 237
Common factor models, 120, 239
for categorical data, 241–248
defining, 193–195
in history of SEM, 42
for multiple common factors with multiple observations, 228–229
one-factor, 193, 194, 245
path diagrams of, 190, 193, 194, 196–199
structure of, 190–196, 202–203
two-factor, 193, 195–199, 245
zero-factor, 192–194
Common factors, 187–206. *See also* Factor analysis; Factorial invariance
biometric design with, 345–346
bivariate latent change score model with, 320
covariance among, 193
cross-lagged models with, 271–279, 283–285
defining, 190–191
dynamic invariance over groups with, 316
latent, 311–313
in latent curve model, 100–102
latent curve models with, 286–287
limitations on identification of, 196–202
in LISREL approach, 43, 44
loadings of, 218–219
means of, 208–210
in multilevel modeling, 165
with multiple groups, 279, 280
RANOVA with, 155
simple structure of, 202–203, 313–314, 347
testing hypotheses about, 188–190
in twin research, 345–346
in Type Δ models, 89, 90
variance of, 208

Common factor scores. *See also*
   Composite scores
   (common factor)
 alternative multivariate models with, 284, 289
 cross-lagged regression with, 273–275
 from decomposition of observed scores, 292, 351, 352
 estimation of, 203–206
 and structure of common factor models, 190–191
 of X- and Y-side variables, 44
Composite scores (common factor), 204–206
 cross-lagged models with, 283–285
 latent curve models with, 286–287
 for multiple longitudinal observations, 229
 in RANOVA and MANOVA, 228
Compound symmetry, 153
Computer programs, 40–41, 45
"Conclusion procedures," 5
Concurrent influences, 265
Conditioning, 342
Configural invariance (Case I)
 over groups, 311–313
 over time, 222, 223, 226, 227
Confirmation, exploration vs., 68–69, 72
Confirmatory analysis, 188
 with RANOVA, 157
 with SEM, 41–43
Confirmatory factor analysis
 in history of SEM, 43–45
 with incomplete data, 340–341
 for invariance in groups, 211, 310
 two-factor models for, 198
Connectedness hypotheses, 287
Connections, 62, 98
Consistency, of cross-lagged models, 284–286
Constraints
 equality, 263–264
 exponential, 108
 identification, 192
 oblique, 197–199
 orthogonal, 199
 unbalanced, 196–197

Continuous time (CT) approach
 in cross-lagged regression models, 265
 in estimation of feedback loops, 299
 in latent change score models, 138–140
 in models of change, 121–122, 369–370
Control(s)
 for pretest effect, 335
 statistical, 32
Controlled-manipulative studies, 324
Convergence, model, 71
Cooley, W., 5
Corballis, M. C., 219
"Correct models," 6
Correlated changes, 235, 294–296
Correlated errors, 219, 227, 236, 237
Correlated slopes, 286–287
Correlations
 and cross-lagged regression models, 258, 260
 Pearson, 250
 polychoric, 249–250
 and stationarity assumption, 263
 tetrachoric, 249–250
COSAN (covariance structure analysis), 59, 60
Coupled changes, 294, 295, 297
Covariance(s)
 among common factors, 193
 and cross-lagged model of multiple times, 285–286
 cross-variable, 224
 and incomplete data, 180
 of initial predictors for groups, 317
 in latent curve model, 98
 in linear regression, 32, 33
 and means, 36–37
 in models of change, 76
 in multilevel modeling, 161, 169
 observed, 41
 in RANOVA, 156
 selection and, 309–310
 specific, 236–238
 statistical power and structure of, 56
 in Type D models, 83, 84
 in Type Δ models, 89

Covariance expectations. *See also*
        Expected covariance
    in bivariate latent change score
        model, 293
    in common factor models, 194, 195
    in cross-lagged regression model,
        258–260
    expected, 222, 224, 312
    in latent curve models, 96–98
    latent variable, 244, 247
    in multilevel modeling, 163
    and multiple factorial invariance
        over groups, 312
    and multiple factorial invariance
        over time, 222, 224
    in multiple group modeling, 168
Covariance structure analysis
    (COSAN), 59, 60
Cox, D. R., 287
Cronbach, L. J., 78, 79
Crossed effect, 257
Cross-lagged change score model
    with dynamic invariance in groups,
        319–320
    with latent factors, 278
Cross-lagged latent regression model,
    277, 285
Cross-lagged models
    with composites/common factors,
        283–285
    of multiple times, 284–286
Cross-lagged regression, fully saturated,
    258, 265
Cross-lagged regression model of
        common factors, 271–279
    change representations of, 277–279
    issues with, 276–277
    path diagram for, 273–275, 285
    RANOVA and MFIT vs., 271–273
    rationale for using, 275–276
Cross-lagged regression models, 255–269
    and causal inferences, 267–269
    change representations of, 266–267
    expectations with, 258, 259
    fitting variations of, 258–262
    goal of, 255–256
    interpretation of, 262–265
    latent, 277, 285
    path diagram for, 257–261, 265, 267

problems with, 256–257
    simplified/restricted, 258, 260–261
    two time-point exogenous baseline
        for, 260, 261
Cross-over controversy, 326
Cross-products. *See* Average sums
        of squares and cross-products
        (SSCP)
Cross-sectional data, 7, 343
Cross-series data, 70
Cross-variable covariance, 224
CT approach. *See* Continuous time
        approach
Cudeck, R., 56
Curran, P. J., 94, 120
Curve of factor score (CUFFS) models,
    231–233, 235

"Data box," 360
Data sequences, leading/lagging aspects
    of, 255–256
DCS (dual change score), 246
DCS model. *See* Dual change score model
Decline scores, 78. *See also* Change scores
Degrees of freedom, 47–48
    and L^2 difference test, 55–56
    in RANOVA, 154, 157
    and single model fit index, 53
    writing models in terms of, 50
Density, of observations, 70
Dependence, statistical, 71
Determinants of behavioral change,
    studying, 23
Development, influences on, 20
Developmental methodologists, 4–5
Difference, in Type A models, 85
Difference in intercepts, 144, 145, 147
Difference in slopes, 30
Difference scores, 76, 369. *See also*
        Change scores
Differential equations models of change
    discrete models vs., 139, 369–370
    latent change score models as, 139
    and latent change scores, 121–122
Differential R (dR) technique, 272
Difficulty factor, 243
DIOG. *See* Dynamic invariance over
        groups
Directional derivatives, 302

Discrete time (DT) approach
   differential equations models of change, 139, 369–370
   and estimation of feedback loops, 299
   in latent change score models, 137–140
   in models of change, 122
Distributed lag models, 137
Disturbance
   in cross-lagged regression models, 257, 275
   residual, 129
   in time-series regression models, 110, 113, 136–137
   in Type A models, 85
Disturbance variance, 137
Doubly repeated measures model, 282–283, 285–286
Dropout, 71, 178, 181
dR (differential R) technique, 272
DT approach. *See* Discrete time approach
Dual change score (DCS), 246
Dual change score (DCS) model, 129–131
   bivariate, 294–297
   expectations with, 123
   with latent basis model, 134–137
   path diagram of, 129, 130
Dual latent changes, common factor models with, 233
Duncan, O. D., 264, 265, 269
Du Toit, S. H. C., 94, 103
Dynamical systems models, 290
Dynamic analysis of between-group differences, 308–309
Dynamic effects, in time-varying covariate models, 288, 289
Dynamic factor analysis models, 362, 363
Dynamic inference, 268
Dynamic influence over groups, 308–309
Dynamic invariance over groups (DIOG), 315–317
   criteria for, 316
   in cross-lagged models, 319–320
   expectations about, 317
   in nonstandard bivariate latent change score models, 320–321
   parameter invariance, 315–316
Dynamic models, 23
   selection of, 368–370
   of statistical power, 57
Dynamic predictors, cross-lagged regression model, 268
Dynamic processes over groups, 307–314
   and establishing factorial invariance over groups, 313–314
   identifying differences in, 308–309
   and latent common factors/factor loading coefficients in parameter invariance over groups, 311–313
   and theorems on parameter invariance over groups, 309–311
Dynamic structure rotation (factorial invariance), 348–350

EFA. *See* Exploratory factor analysis
Effect matrix, 62
Effect size, 55
Empirical science, variation in, 356–357
Empirical time-adjusters, 136
Engle, R., 207
Epstein, D. B., 103
Equal-grade Markov simplex, 115, 116
Equality constraints, cross-lagged regression model with, 263–264
"Equal parameters for equal amounts of time" assumption, 134
Equilibrium, 117
Equivalent-level-only model, 100, 101
Ergodicity assumption, 123, 265
Error(s). *See also* Measurement errors
   correlated, 219, 227, 236, 237
   random, 78, 80
   residual, 28
   standard, 52, 240
"Error in variables" models, 188, 207
Error of measurement score, 236
Error rates
   Type I, 55
   Type II, 53–54
"Error" scores, 100, 101, 236
"Error terms," 356

Error variance
　in latent change score models, 122–123
　for linear regressions, 31
　and specific score variance, 236, 237
　and unreliability of SEM outcomes, 34
Estimated parameters
　from iterative approach, 46–47
　notation for, 85
Estimates. *See also* Maximum likelihood estimate (MLE)
　best linear unbiased, 31, 52
　unique variance, 103–104
Estimation
　of common factor means, 208–209
　of common factor scores, 203–206
　of feedback loops, 298–300
　of independent residual variance, 158
　of intercept for linear regression, 36–37
　iterative approach to, 46–47
　in linear multiple regression, 30–32
　with RANOVA, 158, 330
　of SEM parameters, 46–47
　of thresholds for variables, 249
Estimators
　of asymptotic covariance matrix of the latent correlations, 248
　standard errors for, 240
Expected covariance. *See also* Covariance expectations
　in common factor models, 191–192
　creating, 46
　in latent change score models, 125, 127
　in multiple group models, 171
　notation for, 41
　in time-series regression models, 110–112
Expected covariance expectations
　and multiple factorial invariance over groups, 312
　and multiple factorial invariance over time, 222, 224
Expected means. *See also* Mean expectations
　of bivariate latent change scores, 302
　creating, 46
　in cross-lagged regression models, 262
　in latent change score models, 124, 125, 127
　in multiple group models, 171
　notation for, 41
Expected mean vector expectations
　and multiple factorial invariance over groups, 312
　and multiple factorial invariance over time, 222, 224
"Expected trajectories over time," 7
Expected values, bivariate latent change score, 302–304
Expected variance. *See also* Variance expectations
　for binary measurement model, 243
　in common factor models, 191–192
　in latent change score models, 124, 125, 127
　in time-series regression models, 110, 111
Explained variance
　in multilevel modeling, 162, 165
　in Type A models, 85
Exploration, confirmation vs., 68–69, 72
Exploratory factor analysis (EFA), 188, 198, 200
Exponential constraints, latent growth curve with, 108
External variable models, 159. *See also* Multilevel modeling

Factor analysis, 231–238. *See also related topics, e.g.:* Common factors
　categorical, 239–240
　confirmatory. *See* Confirmatory factor analysis
　curve of factor score models, 231–233
　defined, 188
　exploratory, 188, 198, 200
　factor of curve score models, 233–236
　history of, 189–190
　latent variables in, 358
　limitations on, 196–202
　with multiple factors, 202–203
　of multiple factors with multiple observations, 228–229

INDEX　407

Factor analysis, *continued*
  P-technique, 361–362
  rationales for conducting, 22
  selection in, 310
  with specific covariances, 236–238
  structural, 188, 218–219
  two-occasion data in, 236
  variance for longitudinal factor models, 351–354
Factor analysis models
  bivariate longitudinal, 273
  dynamic, 362, 363
  P-technique, 361–362, 364
Factor change models, 89–90
Factorial invariance, 207–219, 345–350. *See also* Multiple factorial invariance over groups (MFIG); Multiple factorial invariance over time (MFIT)
  and biometric design, 345–346
  and common factor means, 208–210
  cross-lagged latent regression model with, 285
  dynamic structure rotation for, 348–350
  and longitudinal change scores, 215–218
  longitudinal structure rotation for, 346–349
  multilevel modeling for tests of, 354
  over groups, 210–211, 313–314
  path diagrams for, 208, 348–349
  and repeated measures, 207–208
  in scientific inquiry, 358–359
  structural models of, 211–214
  and tests with two occasions of longitudinal data, 218–219
Factor loading coefficients, 311–313
Factor loading invariance, 350, 353–354
Factor model parameters approach to unreliability, 82
Factor of curve score (FOCUS) models, 233–236
Factor rotation
  in common factor model, 200–202
  dynamic, 348–350
  longitudinal, 346–349
  and parameter invariance over groups, 210–211, 310, 314, 347

simple structure as goal of, 203
and structural factor analysis, 188
Factor scores, 89. *See also* Common factor scores
  latent, 155
  specific, 236, 351–352
  unique, 292, 351
Factor variance, 192
Feedback coefficients, 298
Feedback loops
  bias due to, 35, 36
  in LSEM, 298–300
Ferrer, Emilio, x
Filter matrix, 60, 66
FIML (full information maximum likelihood), 178, 344
Firing, 242
Fisher, G. G., 69
Fisher, R. A., 8, 42, 268, 324
Fit, model. *See also* Model fitting
  determining, 55–56
  emphasis on, 48–51
  and model trimming, 68
  searching for best-fitting models, 6
Fixed basis polynomial model, 368
Fixed effects, 47
FOCUS (factor of curve score) models, 233–236
Fratiglioni, L., 341–342
Free basis model, 368
Friendly, M. L., 350
Full information maximum likelihood (FIML), 178, 344
Fully-recursive time-series regression, 112, 114–115
Fully saturated cross-lagged regression, 258, 265
Furby, L., 78, 79

Gain scores, 76, 78, 369. *See also* Change scores
General intelligence, 189, 190
Generality, 28, 355, 358, 361
Generalized learning curve analysis, 22
Generalized least squares (GLS), 48, 52
General linear model, 5, 43, 45, 228
Gerstorf, D., 364
GLS (generalized least squares), 48, 52
Goldberger, A. S., 30, 32–37, 39, 58
Goldberger's biases, 30, 32–37, 58

Gollob, H. F., 265, 269, 353
Goodness-of-fit indices, 6, 48–51
Goodness-of-fit tests, 41, 193, 198, 202
Grand means, fitting MFIT models to, 226
Granger causality, 267–269
Graphics, in RAM notation, 60–63
Greenberg, D. F., 299
Griliches, Z., 207
Grimm, K. J., 125
Grimm, Kevin, x
Group difference dynamic change score models, 371
Group differences. *See also* Between-group differences
    general classes of, 148, 149
    on latent variables in RANOVA, 154–155
    linear models of, 144–146
Grouping variables, 148
Group variables, splitting groups based on, 148
Growth
    and change, x, 29
    joint growth–survival modeling, 341–342
Growth and change models, 106
Growth curve model, parallel, 286
Growth curves
    bivariate latent, 286–287
    latent, with exponential constraints, 108
    parallel, 235
Growth model, for SEM power analyses, 56
Growth scores, 78. *See also* Change scores
Gulliksen, H., 357

Hamagami, E., 338–339
Hamagami, F., 108, 133
Hannan, M. T., 302
Hardy, S. A., 364
Hauser, R. M., 67–68
Hausman, J. A., 207
Heise, D. R., 113, 116, 122, 292
Heritability coefficients, 365
Heterogeneity, unobserved, 71, 300
Hierarchical modeling, 160, 238. *See also* Multilevel modeling

Higher order invariance, 364–365
Higher order models, 137
Hindley, C. B., 18
Hishinuma, E. S., 310
Holtzman, W. H., 362
Homogeneity, of replicates, 53
Horn, J. L., 48, 120, 178, 219, 272, 338, 353, 358
Horn, John, 357
Hypothesis, a priori statement of, 71–72
Hypothesis testing
    about common factors, 188–190
    about multiple factorial invariance over time, 214
    with alternative multivariate models, 178
    in continuous time approach, 139–140
    with RANOVA, 156–158
    with SEM, 41–43

Identification constraint, in common factor models, 192
Idiographic filter, 361, 363–365
Idiosyncrasies, 372
Incomplete data, 177–183. *See also* Planned incompleteness
    about categorical factors, 250–251
    bivariate latent change score model with, 320–321
    confirmatory factor-based analysis of, 340–341
    defining, 181–182
    and masked data, 182–183
    modeling of, 337–340
    and multiple factorial invariance over groups, 178–181
    multiple group modeling with, 325–326
    and randomization of selection, 144
    RANOVA with, 156–158, 329
Independent residual variance, 158
Index for average sums of squares and cross-products, 49
"Indication procedures," 5
Individual, as behavior analysis unit, 357–358
Individual changes, 75–92. *See also specific models*
    calculating observed change scores, 76–78

Individual changes, *continued*
   critique of change scores, 78–82
   identifying, 75
   interindividual differences in, 143–150
   two-occasion models of, 90–92
   Type A models of, 85–87
   Type D models of, 83–84
   Type DR models of, 86–88
   Type Δ and ΔR models of, 88–90
Individual differences approach, 371–372
Individual latent changes, 123
Individual-level heritability coefficients, 365
Individual likelihood, 172
Inference
   causal. *See* Causal inference
   dynamic, 268
Influence(s)
   concurrent, 265
   on development, 20
   dynamic, over groups, 308–309
   instantaneous model of, 265
An Information Criterion (AIC), 50
Initial level, latent curve model, 94
Initial predictors, for groups, 317
Initial scores, as predictors of change, 91
Initial variance, in groups, 326–327
Innovation variance, 137
Instability, score, 267
Instantaneous changes, 370
Instantaneous model of influence, 265
Instantaneous results, 299
Instrumental variables, 324
Intelligence, general, 189, 190
Intensively repeated measures, 355–364
   and centrality of latent variables in psychology, 358
   "data box" for, 360
   dynamic factor analysis, 362, 363, 365
   idiographic filter, 361, 363–365
   and individual as unit of behavior analysis, 357–358
   and invariant relations as objective of scientific inquiry, 358–359
   models for latent variables, 359–365
   P-technique factor analysis, 361–362
   and variation in empirical science, 356–357
Interaction
   in change score models of group differences, 147
   in regression models of group differences, 145, 146
Intercept(s)
   bias in, 36–37
   for change score models of group differences, 146, 147
   common factors of, 235
   for cross-lagged regression models, 262
   difference in, 144, 145, 147
   in linear regressions, 28, 31, 36–37
   for regression models of group difference, 144, 145
   for Type A models, 85
Interindividual differences in intraindividual changes, 143–150
   and assignment of people to groups, 144
   causes of, 23
   direct identification of, 21–22
   general classes of group differences, 148, 149
   resolving, 148–150
   in two-occasion group models, 144–147
Intraindividual changes
   causes/determinants of, 23
   direct identification of, 21
   interindividual differences in, 21–23, 143–150
Intraindividual differences, 9
Intraindividual differences in intraindividual differences, 10
Intraindividual variation, P-technique factor analysis of, 362
Invariance, 58. *See also* Factorial invariance
   factor loading, 350, 353–354
   higher order, 364–365
   over groups, 210–211, 309–316
   parameter, 6, 58, 309–313, 315–316
   partial, 224, 278
Invariant relations, 358–359
Isomorphism, partial, 24

Item-level data
  MFIT for, 246
  one factor model with, 245
Item response factor model, 243, 244
Iterative approach to parameter estimation, 46–47

Jacob, F., 71–72
Jansen, R. A. R. G., 139
Johnson, R. C., 310
Johnston, J., 91
Joint growth–survival modeling, 341–342
Jöreskog, K. G., 45, 76, 113, 115, 116, 122, 172, 178, 200, 201, 273, 274, 292, 310, 351

Kadlec, K. M., 58, 69
Kaiser, H. F., 367
Kenny, D. A., 352
Kessler, R. C., 299
Kline, R., 46
Kroonenberg, P. M., 352

L^2 (likelihood) difference test, 55–56
L^2 (likelihood) index, 170, 172, 179
Lag. *See also* Time lags; *specific cross-lagged models*
  causal, 24–25
  distributed lag models, 137
  P-technique factor analysis of, 362, 363
Lagged effect, cross-lagged regression model, 257
Lagging aspects (data sequences), 255–256
Lagging variables, 260
Latent basis coefficients, 134–136
Latent basis models, 368
  complex growth forms with, 108
  dual change score, 134–137
  and latent time scale, 107
Latent change factors, mean of, 273
Latent changes
  dual, 233
  individual, 123
Latent change score (LCS) models, 119–140, 369. *See also* Bivariate latent change score models
  additive, 123, 126–128, 294, 295
  benefits and limitations of, 370–371

  with categorical outcomes, 247, 248
  for common factors with multiple groups, 279, 280
  continuous time approach in, 138–140
  and definition of latent change scores, 121–123
  discrete time approach in, 137–138
  expectations with, 123–125, 127, 131–132, 333
  fitting observed variables to, 235
  with group differences, 150
  and latent curve models, 119–121, 131
  multiple group model for, 173–174
  path diagrams of, 125–132, 150, 280, 340
  with planned incompleteness, 339–340
  proportional, 123, 129–130
  and RANOVA, 329
  and time-series regression models, 119–121, 131, 136–137
  triple change score models, 134–137
Latent change score regressions, 88, 89
Latent change scores, ix, 80, 124
  among common factors, 89, 90
  bivariate, 301–304
  characteristics of, 88, 89
  cross-lagged regression model expressed as, 266–267
  and cross-lagged regression of common factors, 272
  definition of, 121–123
  multigroup modeling of, 167
  multilevel modeling of, 161, 162, 164
  from multiple factorial invariance over time, 212, 213, 215
  multiple group modeling of, 169
  path diagram, 87
  residual, 88, 89
Latent class analysis, 240
Latent classes, 307
Latent class mixture models, 11
Latent common factors, 311–313
Latent curve models (LCMs), 7, 93–108. *See also* Multilevel modeling
  alternative extensions of, 105–108
  between-persons predictors in, 161

Latent curve models (LCMs), *continued*
  with common factor scores, 284
  complex nonlinear representations with, 108
  with composites/common factors, 286–287
  curve of factor scores models, 231–233
  defining, 94–98
  expectations with, 96–98
  and generalized learning curve analysis, 22
  history of, 93–94
  implied reliability of, 103–104
  and latent change score models, 119–121, 131
  for multiple groups, 169–171
  nonlinear quadratic modeling with, 104–105
  parameters of, 96–98
  path diagrams of, 96, 98–103, 106, 286
  with planned incompleteness, 337–339
  RANOVA vs., 152–154
  time-series regression models vs., 117
  and time-varying covariate models, 288, 290
  and triple change score models, 135
  for twin studies, 346
  unique variance estimates of, 103–104
Latent curves, "summations" of, 105–108
Latent factors
  cross-lagged change score model with, 278
  cross-lagged regression model with, 277
  in factor analysis, 189
Latent factor scores, in RANOVA, 155
Latent groupings, 148
Latent growth model, 56
Latent level (latent curve model), 94
Latent means, 217–218
Latent path model for factor invariance over time, 214
Latent slopes, 126, 128, 287
Latent time scale, 107

Latent transition analysis, 240
"Latent Variable Analysis of Age Trends in Tests of Cognitive Ability in the Health and Retirement Survey 1992-2004" (McArdle, Fisher, and Kadlec), 69
Latent variable covariance expectations, 244, 247
Latent variable mean expectations, 97, 244
Latent variable path models
  in multilevel modeling, 160–161
  without factor score estimates, 204
Latent variables
  binary outcome variables combined with, 241–242
  and common factors, 188
  group differences in, 154–155
  idiographic filter for, 361, 363–365
  models for, 359–365
  in multilevel modeling, 160–161
  in nomothetic models, 368
  nomothetic relations for, 364
  path diagrams with, 29
  in psychology, 358
  on RANOVA, 154–155
  and residual change scores, 92
  in SEM, 6, 69
  in statistical power computation, 56–57
  in time-series regression models, 116
  true change in, 80
Latent variable variance expectations, 97
Lawley, D. N., 171, 309
LCMs. *See* Latent curve models (LCMs)
LCMs (linear change models), 123, 229
LCS models. *See* Latent change score models
Leading aspects (data sequences), 255–256
Leading variables, 260
Learning curve analysis, 22
Least squares estimators, 240
Least squares function, 48
Ledermann, W., 309
Leibniz, Gottfried Wilhelm, 121
Leite, W. L., 57

"Level" scores, latent curve model with, 100, 101
Lewis, C., 49, 51
Life-span developmental processes, 19–20
Likelihood. *See also* Maximum likelihood estimate (MLE)
 full information maximum, 178, 344
 individual, 172
Likelihood (L^2) difference test, 55–56
Likelihood (L^2) index, 170, 172, 179
Likelihood modification test, 56
Likelihood ratio, 50, 53
Linear basis models, fitting latent curve models to, 96
Linear change models (LCMs), 123, 229
Linearity assumption, 53
Linear models of group differences, 144–146
Linear multiple regression, 30–32
Linear regression
 defining, 28
 estimation of, 30–32
 Goldberger's biases in, 30, 32–37, 58
 for group differences, 144–146
 with intercept, 36–37
 path diagram for, 28–30, 33
 in RAM notation, 63–66
 with unreliable predictors, 33, 34
Linear scaling, of latent curve model, 104
Linear structural equations model approach. *See* LISREL approach
LISCOMP, 248
LISREL (linear structural equations model) approach, 40, 41
 and confirmatory factor analysis, 43–45
 expectations in, 59
 model trimming with, 67–68
 path diagram of, 43
 popularity of, 63
 and RAM, 60
 restrictions of, 67
 specifying a general SEM with, 44
Loehlin, J. C., 46
Lohnes, P. R., 5
Longitudinal analyses, planned incompleteness in, 343–344

Longitudinal categorical factors, 239–251
 and common factor model for categorical data, 241–245
 in cross-classification of multivariate models, 239–240
 decision to measure, 250–251
 longitudinal models of binary responses, 245–248
 multiple threshold calculations for, 248–250
 in path diagrams, 245–247
Longitudinal change scores, 215–218
Longitudinal data
 causal inferences from, 267–269
 cross-sectional data combined with, 343
 factor analysis of, 188
 factorial invariance with two occasions of, 218–219
 importance of feedback parameters in, 299
 multiple occasion, 351–354
Longitudinal factor models, variance components for, 351–354
Longitudinal models of binary responses, 245–248
Longitudinal panel data, 7
 benefits and drawbacks of, 70–72
 reasons for change in, 76
 time-series regressions with, 109
Longitudinal research, 17–25
 defined, 18–20
 difficulty of performing, 368
 five rationales for, 21–23
 importance of, 367–368
 randomization in, 323–327
 relationship of theory and methodology in, 23–25
 selecting discrete dynamic models for, 368–370
 selection of people for, 334–337
 statistical power in, 55
Longitudinal structural equation modeling (LSEM)
 analysis of factorial invariance with, 212–214
 benefits and limitations of, 370–371
 feedback loops in, 298–300
 five basic questions of, 3–4

Longitudinal structural equation
modeling (LSEM), *continued*
   importance of, ix
   notation for, 12–14
   randomization in, 325
   RANOVA as, 155
   reasons for using, 7–9
   repeated measures in, 207–208
   uses of, 69–70
Longitudinal structure rotation, 346–349
Lord, F. M., 149–150, 178
Lord's paradox, 149, 150
Loss scores, 78. *See also* Change scores
LSEM. *See* Longitudinal structural equation modeling
Lurking variables, 255

MacCallum, R. C., 56
MANOVA. *See* Multivariate analysis of variance
MAPLE software, 125
MAR data. *See* Missing at random data
Markov simplex, 110, 111
   with equal effects, 115
   equal-grade, 115, 116
Masked data, 182–183, 343
Matrix of moments, 61, 62
Maximum likelihood, full information, 178, 344
Maximum likelihood estimate (MLE), 48, 52
   consistency of, 240
   and incomplete data, 178–180, 182
   MGM-MLE approach, 338
   and multiple factorial invariance over groups, 178
   in multiple group modeling, 170–172
Maximum likelihood estimates–missing at random (MLE-MAR), 182, 248, 251
Max Planck Institute (MPI), x
Maxwell, A. E., 171
MCAR data. *See* Missing completely at random data
McArdle, J. J., 11, 48, 56–58, 61, 62, 69, 94, 97, 103, 108, 120, 123, 125, 133, 138, 153, 172, 178, 189, 201, 204, 208, 211, 212, 216, 221–222, 231, 232, 235, 238, 272, 278, 286, 310, 313, 327, 337–342, 346, 347, 352
McDonald, R. P., 46, 243, 244
McDonald, Roderick P., 59
McLuhan, Marshall, 17
Mean(s)
   of common factors, 200, 208–210, 217
   and covariances, 36–37
   grand, 226
   of initial predictors for groups, 317
   latent, 217–218
   of latent change factors, 273
   in latent curve models, 98, 102
   in models of change, 76
   observed, 41, 242
   in RANOVA, 155
   of slopes, 133
   in time-series regressions, 117
   in Type D models, 83, 84
   in Type Δ models, 89
Mean deviation form (cross-lagged regression model), 257
Mean expectations. *See also* Expected means
   in bivariate latent change score model, 293
   in latent curve models, 96–98
   latent variable, 97, 244
   in multilevel modeling, 163
   in multiple group models, 168
Mean vector expectations
   for common factors, 209
   expected, 222, 224, 312
Measured variables
   factor analysis with, 189
   in models of group differences, 148
Measurement errors
   with composite scores, 206
   in continuous time models, 139
   in cross-lagged regressions of common factors, 275, 276
   in latent curve models, 103–105
   in time-series regression models, 113–114
Measurement invariance (Case I)
   over groups, 311–313
   over time, 222, 223, 226, 227
Measurement models, x
Mediation modeling, 264

Meredith, Bill, 93
Meredith, W., 105, 171, 210–211, 219, 222, 223, 226, 309–314, 347
Meta-analysis, 334
Meta-meter scale, 107
Methodologists, developmental, 4–5
Methodology, relationship of theory and, 23–25
Metric invariance (Case II)
  over groups, 311–313
  over time, 222, 223, 226
MFIG. *See* Multiple factorial invariance over groups
MFIT. *See* Multiple factorial invariance over time
MGM. *See* Multiple group modeling
MGM-MAR (multiple group modeling–missing at random) convergence techniques, 339
MGM-MLE (multiple group modeling–maximum likelihood estimate) approach, 178–180, 338
MGM-SEM. *See* Multiple group modeling–structural equation modeling
Mill, J. S., 17, 18, 24
Millsap, R. E., 309
Misfits
  calculating, 48, 49
  in multiple group modeling, 174
  and multiple invariance over time, 225
Missing at random (MAR) data
  confirmatory-based analysis of, 340
  in contemporary longitudinal studies, 343–344
  defined, 181
  joint growth–survival modeling with, 342
  latent change score models with, 339
  in longitudinal research, 182
  masked data as representation of, 182
  and selection of people in studies, 336
Missing completely at random (MCAR) data, 340
  in bivariate latent change score model, 321
  defined, 181
  in longitudinal research, 182

and selection of people in studies, 336, 337
Missing predictor variable bias, 32–34
Missing variables (unmeasured variables), 255, 264, 276–277
MI (multiple imputation) techniques, 181, 182
Mixed-effects modeling, 7, 69–70, 94, 159. *See also* Multilevel modeling
Mixture modeling, 240
MLE. *See* Maximum likelihood estimate
MLE-MAR. *See* Maximum likelihood estimates–missing at random
MLM. *See* Multilevel modeling
Model expectations
  analysis of variance, 46
  bivariate latent change score model, 293–295
  common factor model, 194, 195, 244
  conditioning of, 342
  creating, 46
  cross-lagged regression model, 258–260
  dual change score model, 123
  and goodness-of-fit indices, 48
  latent change score model, 123–125, 127, 131–132, 333
  latent curve model, 96–98
  in LISREL, 59
  multilevel model, 161, 163
  multiple group model, 168
  in RAMpath notation, 60, 61, 65–66
  time-series regression model, 112
  two-factor model, 193, 195
Model fitting. *See also* Fit, model
  for common factor models, 192, 197–199
  for cross-lagged regression models, 258–262
  and multiple factorial invariance over time, 225–227
  and RANOVA, 330
Model modification indices, 68
Models, RAMpath rules for defining, 61
Model trimming, 67–69
Molenaar, P. C., 207, 358
Molenaar, P. C. M., 363, 365
Monte Carlo simulations, 56
Morality aspect, 357
Movement, score, 267

Moving averages, 110, 112, 113
MPI (Max Planck Institute), x
Mplus, 40
MRSRM (multivariate, replicated, single-subject, repeated measurement) designs, 360, 364
Multilevel modeling (MLM), 159–165
  with cross-lagged change score model, 320
  defined, 161, 162
  explained variance in, 162, 164–165
  identifying differences in dynamic influence over groups with, 308, 309
  latent change scores in, 161, 162, 164
  and latent curve analyses, 94
  latent variables in, 160–161
  limitations of, 161
  model expectations with, 161, 163
  multiple group modeling vs., 160, 169, 173
  of multiple occasion longitudinal data, 352–354
  path diagrams for, 352
  terminology for, 159
Multiple factorial invariance over groups (MFIG)
  bivariate latent change score models with, 320
  and dynamic invariance over groups, 316
  fitting of, 177–178
  history of, 178
  for incomplete data, 178–181
  Meredith's tables of, 312
  and multiple factorial invariance over time, 222–225
  theorems on, 210–211, 309–311
Multiple factorial invariance over time (MFIT), 214, 221–229
  for analyzing multiple factors with multiple observations, 228–229
  bivariate latent change score models with, 293, 320
  cross-lagged regression models with, 256–257, 271–275, 278
  factor of curve scores model without, 233–235
  importance of, ix
  for item-level data, 246
  latent change scores from, 212, 213, 215
  latent curve models with, 231–233
  and latent transition/latent class analysis, 240
  model-fitting strategies for, 225–227
  and multiple factorial invariance over groups, 222–225
  and RANOVA, 227–228
  terminology for, 222–223
  two-occasion model with latent means for, 217–218
Multiple factor models
  factor analysis with, 202–203
  for multiple longitudinal observations, 229
Multiple group modeling (MGM), 167–175
  for biometric design, 345–346
  of changes, 167–171
  factorial invariance in, 211
  identifying differences in dynamic influence over groups with, 308–309
  incomplete data with, 177–183
  maximum likelihood expression in, 170–172
  multilevel modeling vs., 160, 169, 173
  and multiple factorial invariance over groups, 178, 312
  path diagrams for, 168–170, 174, 180, 326
  randomization in, 325–327
  two-group example of, 172–175
Multiple group modeling–maximum likelihood estimate (MGM-MLE) approach, 178–180, 338
Multiple group modeling–missing at random (MGM-MAR) convergence techniques, 339
Multiple group modeling–structural equation modeling (MGM-SEM)
  confirmatory factor-based analysis with, 340–341
  with incomplete data, 178–180
  planned incompleteness in, 336–339

Multiple group regression models, 148, 149
Multiple groups, bivariate latent change score model with, 319–321
Multiple imputation (MI) techniques, 181, 182
Multiple longitudinal outcome scores, 281–290
  cross-lagged models of multiple times for, 284–286
  cross-lagged models with composites/common factors for, 283–285
  doubly repeated measures model for, 282–283
  LCMs with composites/common factors for, 286–287
  time-varying covariate models for, 287–290
Multiple occasion longitudinal data, 351–354
Multiple situation functional analysis of variance, 353
Multiple threshold calculations, 248–250
Multiple variable latent variable model analysis, 232, 233
Multivariate, replicated, single-subject, repeated measurement (MRSRM) designs, 360, 364
Multivariate analysis of variance (MANOVA)
  analysis of factorial invariance with, 212, 214
  analysis of MFIT vs., 227, 228
Multivariate longitudinal data analysis, MFIT in, 225
Multivariate models
  with common factor scores, 284
  cross-classification of, 239–240
  linear structural equations models, 207
  RANOVA as, 156–157
Multivariate perspective on behavior, 22
Muthén, B., 243, 244, 248
Muthén, B. O., 56
Muthén, L. K., 56
Mx, 40, 41
Myamoto, R. H., 310

Nesselroade, J. R., 3–4, 9–11, 18–23, 121, 143, 151, 189, 208, 212, 216, 272, 363–365, 368
Nested models, 55, 56, 68
Nested tests of effects, 226–227
Networks, 307
Newton, Isaac, 121, 122
NMAR data. *See* Not missing at random data
No-changes baseline model, 126, 127
No-growth–no-individual differences model, 99–100
Noise, process, 363
Nomothetic relations, 364
Noncentrality parameter, 56, 57
Nonlinear dynamic models, 94
Nonlinear quadratic modeling, 104–106
Nonlinear representations, latent curve models for, 108
Nonrecursive loops, 298–300
Normal daily variability, 357
Normality
  of outcomes, 240–241
  of residuals, 53
Not missing at random (NMAR) data
  defined, 181
  and MAR corrections, 344
  masked data as representation of, 182, 340
Null model, 193, 194

Oblique constraints, two-factor models with, 197–199
Observational data
  causal inferences from, 8–9
  causal relations in, 255–256, 264, 276–277
Observational studies, controlled-manipulative studies vs., 324
Observed change score models
  defining, 78–80
  for group differences, 146–147
  Type A, 85–86
Observed change scores
  calculating, 76–78
  defining, 77
  reliability of, 81–82
Observed covariance, 41
Observed means, 41, 242
Observed outcomes, notation for, 63

Observed predictors, notation for, 63
Observed scores, RANOVA, 155
Observed variables
  fitting latent change score models to, 235
  RAMpath notation for, 29
Observed variance, with binary response, 242
Observed variance expectations, 112
Occasion-discriminant approach, 353
Occasions (data box), 360
OLS function. *See* Ordinary least squares function
O'Malley, P. M., 91
One-factor models, 193, 194, 245
Oort, F. J., 352
Ordinal measurements
  and LSEM, 7
  multiple threshold calculations for, 248–250
Ordinal scale points, 251
Ordinary least squares (OLS) function, 52, 104, 107
Orthogonal constraints, two-factor models with, 199
Orthogonality, of common and specific factors, 352
Orwell, George, ix
Oud, J. H. L., 139
Outcomes. *See also* Multiple longitudinal outcome scores
  and choice of model for resolving group differences, 148–150
  normality of, 240–241
  observed, 63
  unreliability of, 34, 35
Overaggregation, 300

Panel data. *See* Longitudinal panel data
Parallel change score models, 294, 295
Parallel growth curve model, 286
Parallel growth curves, 235
Parallel proportional profiles, 211, 310, 347
Parameter(s)
  in continuous vs. discrete time approach, 139–140
  estimation of, 46–47
  latent curve model, 97
  meaning of, 52
  in multiple group modeling, 174
  saliency of, 52–53
  in statistical model trimming, 67–68
  unique, 311
Parameter invariance, 6, 58
Parameter invariance over groups
  dynamic, 315–316
  latent common factors/factor loading coefficients in, 311–313
  theorems on, 309–311
Parsimony, 50
Partial adjustment model, 133
Partial invariance, 224, 278
Partial isomorphism, 24
Path diagrams
  additive latent change score model, 126–128
  autoregression model, 146
  binary factor measurement model, 243
  bivariate latent change score model, 292, 296–297
  common factor model, 190, 193, 194, 196–199
  cross-lagged regression model, 257–261, 265, 267, 273–275, 285
  curve of factor scores model, 232
  dual change score model, 129, 130
  dynamic factor analysis model, 363
  for factorial invariance, 208, 348–349
  latent change score model, 125–132, 150, 280, 340
  latent change score regression, 88
  of latent change scores, 87
  latent curve model, 96, 98–104, 106, 286
  linear regression, 28–30, 33
  of LISREL approach, 43
  for models with categorical data, 245–247
  multilevel model, 352
  multiple group model, 168–170, 174, 180, 326
  predictors in, 60
  P-technique factor analysis model, 362
  quadratic polynomial, 104, 106

quasi-Markov simplex, 113
with RAM notation, 63–66
RANOVA, 102, 152, 155
residuals in, 60
time-series regression model, 112, 114–116
time-varying covariate model, 288
triple change score model, 134, 163
two-factor model, 196–199
Type A model, 86
Type D model, 83, 84
Type DR model, 87
Type Δ model, 88
variance in, 29
PCs (principle components), 203–204
Pearson correlations, 250
Person-centered orientation to change, 358
Person-centering technique, 353
Persons × variables data matrix, 359
Phase diagrams, bivariate latent change score, 302
Phi coefficients, 243
Planned incompleteness, 333–344
and confirmatory factor-based analysis of incomplete data, 340–341
in contemporary longitudinal analyses, 343–344
and joint growth–survival modeling, 341–342
and masking of available data, 343
and modeling incomplete data, 337–340
and selection of people for longitudinal studies, 334–337
Planned missing data, 100
Plotting bivariate latent change scores, 301–304
Polychoric correlation, 249–250
Polynomial growth models, 104–106
POM (proportion correct of maximum) scores, 205, 206
Popper, K. R., 202
Power, statistical, 53–57, 341
Practice effects, 338, 339
Predictions
of change scores, 85–86
from time-series regressions, 114
with Type A models, 86

Predictors
dynamic, 268
for groups, 317
initial, 317
initial scores as, 91
missing, 32–34
in multilevel modeling, 162, 165
observed, 63
in path diagrams, 60
second-level, 162, 165
selection based on, 148, 149
in time-series regressions, 115
unreliability of, 33–35
variance of, 63
Pre-experimental studies, 23–24
Prescott, C. A., 204, 346
Pretests, 326, 335
Principle components (PCs), 203–204
Prindle, J. J., 57, 278
Probabilistic model, 243
"Probability of perfect fit," 48, 49
Process noise, 363
Proportional changes, 294, 295
Proportional index of reduced misfit, 49
Proportional latent change score model, 123, 129–130
Proportion correct of maximum (POM) scores, 205, 206
Psychology, latent variables in, 358
P-technique data, 360–362
P-technique factor analysis model, 361–362, 364
p values, statistical power and, 55

Quadratic modeling, nonlinear, 104–106
Quasi-Markov simplex, 113–114, 116, 129

Ram, N., 364
RAMgraph, 62
RAM notation. *See* Reticular action model notation
RAMpath notation, 29–30
model expectations in, 61
regression expectations in, 65–66
specifying regressions in, 63–66
tracing rules for SEM in, 62
RAM specification, 60
Random coefficients model, 159. *See also* Multilevel modeling

Random effects, 47
Random error, 78, 80
Randomization, 323–327
    of assignment to groups, 144
    and causal inference, 8–9, 323, 325
    as condition for causation, 268–269
    in longitudinal contexts, 324–325
    in multiple group modeling, 325–327
    purposes of, 324
Randomized clinical trials (RCTs), 8, 144, 325
RANOVA. *See* Repeated measures analysis of variance
Rao, C. R., 106
Rasch, G., 241, 243
Rasch-type models, 193, 194, 241
RCTs. *See* Randomized clinical trials
Reciprocal causation, 264–265
Reference groups, 209
Reference time, 209
Regime switches, 307
Regression models
    auto-. *See* Autoregression models
    cross-lagged. *See* Cross-lagged regression models
    multiple group, 148, 149
    Type DR, 86–88, 92
Reichardt, C. S., 265, 269
Reliability
    and cross-lagged regression models, 258
    of latent curve models, 103–104
    of latent score models, 97
    of observed change scores, 81–82
    of outcomes, 34, 35
    of predictors, 33–35
Reliability coefficients, 51
Repeated measures, 207–208
Repeated measures analysis of variance (RANOVA), 151–158, 329–330
    analyzing factorial invariance with, 212, 213, 218
    ANCOVA vs., 146, 149–150
    continuous time approaches and, 139
    cross-lagged regression model of common factors vs., 271–273
    doubly repeated measures model, 282–283
    group differences on latent variables in, 154–155
    issues with, 156–158
    latent curve model vs., 152–154
    model fitting for, 330
    and multiple factorial invariance over time, 227–228
    for multiple longitudinal observations, 228
    path diagram for, 102, 152, 155
    popularity of, 330, 334
    SEM path model of, 155
    and "Tuckerized" curve models, 93
Replicates, homogeneity of, 53
Residual change scores, 86, 92
Residual disturbance, 129
Residual error, 28
Residual latent change scores, 88, 89
Residuals
    normality of, 53
    in path diagrams, 60
    in Type DR model, 86
    unobserved, 63
    variance of, 63, 158
Residual scores, Type A model, 85
Reticular action model (RAM) notation, 59–66, 69. *See also* RAMpath notation
    defined, 60, 61
    graphics in, 60–63
    path diagrams with, 63–66
    specifying model expectations in, 60, 61
Rindskopf, D., 178
Root mean square error of approximation (RMSEA), 49, 50, 56–57
Rotation, factor. *See* Factor rotation
Rozeboom, W. W., 218–219, 221
Rubin, D. B., 181

Saliency, parameter, 52–53
Sample selection, 148
Sample size, 55
Saris, W., 56, 341
Satorra, A., 56, 341
Scaling
    of categorical data, 250
    in latent curve model, 95, 104, 107–108
    linear, 104

of slope, 107–108
   variation in, 356–357
Science Directorate (APA), x
Score deviation model, 76, 77
Score transformations, 251
Searches, specification, 68
Second-level predictors, 162, 165
Selection, 144, 148
   and causal inferences, 8–9
   and covariance in groups, 309–310
   in factor analysis, 310
   for longitudinal studies, 334–337
   self-, 178, 317, 324, 343
   and variation in initial predictors for groups, 317
Self-selection, 178, 317, 324, 343
SEM. *See* Structural equation modeling
SEM Trees, 11
Sequences, leading/lagging aspects of, 255–256
Sequential effects, 263–264, 276
"Setting the metric," 192
Sewell, W. H., 67–68
SFA. *See* Structural factor analysis
Shared parameter models, 341–342
Simple structure of common factors
   and factorial invariance over groups, 313–314, 347
   as goal of factor rotation, 202–203
Single model fit index, 53
Size of effect, 55
Skewed variables, 250
Sling matrix, 60
Slope(s), 63
   in change score models of group differences, 146, 147
   common factors of, 235
   correlated, 286–287
   difference in, 30
   latent, 126, 128, 287
   in latent curve models, 98, 107–108
   mean of, 133
   in regression models of group difference, 144, 145
   scaling of, 107–108
   in Type A models, 85
   as variable, 99
Slope loading, in partial adjustment model, 133
Small, B. J., 341–342

Solomon-four group design, 335
Sörbom, D., 76, 171, 178, 210, 211, 273, 274, 309, 310
Spearman, C. E., 189–190
Spearman, Charles, 42
Specification searches, 68
Specific covariances, factor analysis with, 236–238
Specific factor score, 236, 351–352
Specific score variance, 236, 237
Sphericity, 153
SSCP. *See* average sums of squares and cross-products
SSCP (average sums of squares and cross-products) matrix expectation, 61, 62
Stability
   and change, 17
   and cross-lagged regression models, 258
   of factor patterns, 213
   of factor scores, 213, 219
Standard errors, 52, 240
Stanley, J., 23–24
Stapleton, L. M., 57
States, factors representing, 216, 272
Stationarity assumption, 117, 262–263
Statistical adjustment to data, 32
Statistical control, 32
Statistical dependence, 71
Statistical indicators, 47–52
Statistical model trimming, 67–69
Statistical power, 53–57, 341
Statistical significance, 42
Statistical testing, limitations of, 52–53
Statistical vector fields (SVFs), 302–304, 327
Steiger, J. H., 56
Strict invariance (Case IV)
   over groups, 311–313
   over time, 222–224, 226
Strong invariance (Case III)
   over groups, 311–313
   over time, 222, 223, 226
Structural equation modeling (SEM), 27–37, 39–58. *See also specific types of models*
   computer programs, 40–41, 45
   confirmatory factor analysis, 43
   creating model expectations, 46

Structural equation modeling (SEM), *continued*
  current research, 57–58
  defined, 28, 39
  estimation of parameters for, 46–47
  examining theories with, 41–43
  generalization in, 28
  and Goldberger's biases in regression, 30, 32–37
  identifying common factors in, 201–202
  and limitations of statistical testing, 52–53
  LISREL approach, 43–45
  path diagram for linear regression, 28–30
  RAMpath analysis notation for, 29–30
  randomization in, 324–325
  reasons for using, 5–6
  standard estimation of linear multiple regression, 30–32
  statistical indicators in, 47–52
  as theoretical tool and practical tool, 70
  tracing rules for, 62
  uses of, 69–70
Structural factor analysis (SFA), 188, 218–219, 351
Structural models of factorial invariance, 211–214
Substantive importance, 42
Sugwara, H. M., 56
"Summations" of latent curves, 105–108
SVFs (statistical vector fields), 302–304, 327
Symmetry, compound, 153
Systematic bias, 264

TCS models. *See* Triple change score models
Teresi, J. A., 314
Tetrachoric correlation, 249–250
Theory(-ies)
  examining, with SEM, 41–43
  relationship of methodology and, 23–25
Thomas, L., 54
Thomson, G. H., 309
Thresholds, categorical data, 242–243

Thurstone, L. L., 202, 310, 347, 356
Time. *See also* Multiple factorial invariance over time (MFIT)
  change over, 5, 19–20
  common factors measures over, 188–190
  for developmental methodologists, 5
  empirical time-adjusters, 136
  "equal parameters for equal amounts of time" assumption, 134
  factor invariance over, 211–214
  latent time scale, 107
  reference, 209
Time delay
  in latent curve models, 95, 96
  in Type A models, 85
Time-forward predictions, 86
Time-lag delays, 337–338
Time lags
  in cross-lagged regression models, 264–265, 269
  as dimension under study, 138
  in time-series regression models, 110, 115, 116, 137
  in time-varying covariate models, 290
Time points
  cross-lagged models of multiple, 284–286
  in time-series regressions, 117
Time series-based autoregression models, 29
Time-series data, 70
Time-series regression, fully-recursive, 112, 114–115
Time-series regression (TSR) models, 109–117
  advanced, 112
  assumptions with, 117
  defining, 110–114
  as latent change models, 123
  merging latent curve models and, 119–121, 131
  path diagrams of, 112, 114–116
Time-to-time prediction of change scores, 85–86
Time-varying covariate (TVC) models, 287–290
Timing, estimation of feedback loops and, 299

Tisak, J., 105
Tracing rules, 62
Traits, factors representing, 216, 272
Trajectory(-ies)
   autoregressive latent trajectory approach, 120
   expected trajectories over time, 7
   in latent change score models, 121
   in latent curve models, 94, 95
   multiple, 239
Transient factors, 221
Traub, R. E., 219
Triple change score (TCS) models, 134–137
   and bivariate latent change score models, 294, 298
   with multilevel modeling of group differences, 162, 163
   path diagrams for, 134, 163
"True models," 6
"True scores," change in, 78, 80–82
Tsai, S.-L., 67–68
TSR models. *See* Time-series regression models
Tucker, L., 93, 106
Tucker, L. R., 22, 49, 51
"Tuckerized" curve models, 93
Tukey, John, 5
Tuma, N. B., 302
TVC (time-varying covariate) models, 287–290
Twin research, common factors in, 345–346
Two-factor models, 245
   expectations, 193, 195
   limitations with, 196–199
   path diagrams for, 196–199
Two-occasion data
   and dynamic structure rotation, 348–350
   factor analysis in, 236
   and longitudinal structure rotation, 346–348
Two-occasion models
   factor of changes, 216–217
   for groups, 144–147
   of individual changes, 90–92
   for metric factor invariance over time covariance, 208
   for multiple factorial invariance over time with latent means, 217–218
Two-occasion tests of factorial invariance, 218–219
Type A autoregression models, 85–87
Type D change score models, 83–84, 86
Type DR change regression models, 86–88, 92
Type Δ change score models, 88–90
Type Δ factor change models, 89–90
Type ΔR change score models, 88–90
Type I error rate, 55
Type II error rate, 53–54

Unbalanced constraints, two-factor models with, 196–197
Unbalanced data, 99–100, 117
Unconditional latent curve model, 94, 95
Unique factors, 236
Unique factor scores, 292, 351
Uniqueness, equality of, 133–134
Unique parameters, invariance in groups over, 311
Unique variance
   for categorical factors, 246
   estimates of, 103–104
   in latent curve model, 97, 103–104
   in multiple group models, 171, 173
   tests of invariance based on, 219
Unit constant, latent curve model, 99
Unmeasured variables, 255, 264, 276–277
Unobserved heterogeneity, 71, 300
Unobserved residuals, 63
Unobserved variables, 29, 43
Unreliability
   of outcomes, 34, 35
   of predictors, 33–35

Variability, 18
Variables. *See also specific types*
   cross-variable covariance, 224
   "error in," 188, 207
   identifying common factors from, 200–202

Variance. *See also* Analysis of variance (ANOVA); Invariance
  in common factor models, 190–192
  of common factors, 208
  disturbance, 137
  error. *See* Error variance
  estimates of, 103–104
  explained, 85, 162, 165
  factor, 192
  in groups, 326–327
  initial, 326–327
  of initial predictors, 317
  innovation, 137
  in latent curve models, 98, 103–104
  in longitudinal factor models, 351–354
  in multilevel modeling, 161, 169, 173
  in multiple group modeling, 172–173
  observed, 242
  in path diagrams, 29
  of predictors, 63, 317
  in RANOVA, 155, 330
  of residuals, 63, 158
  specific score, 236, 237
  and stationarity assumptions in cross-lagged regression model, 262–263
  unique. *See* Unique variance
Variance expectations. *See also* Expected variance
  in common factor models, 194, 195
  in latent curve models, 96–98
  latent variable, 97
  in multilevel modeling, 163
  observed, 112
Variation, in empirical science, 356–357
Vector fields, 302–304, 327

Wald test, 56
Watson, M., 207
Weak invariance (Case II)
  over groups, 311–313
  over time, 222, 223, 226
Wiley, D. E., 113, 114, 116, 122
Wiley, J. A., 113, 114, 116, 122
Wishart, J., 104, 368
Within components, in multilevel modeling, 354
Within groups (term), 151
Within-person changes, 9, 10
Wohlwill, Joachim F., 24
Woodcock, R. W., 138, 238, 337, 352
Wright, S., 62
Wright, Sewell, 29, 42, 298

Zautra, A., 352
Zazzo, R., 18
Zero common factor models, 192–194
Zhang, G., 363
Zhang, Z., 364–365

ABOUT THE AUTHORS

John J. (Jack) McArdle, PhD, is senior professor of psychology at the University of Southern California (USC), where he heads the Quantitative Methods Area and has been chair of the USC Research Committee. He received a BA degree from Franklin & Marshall College (1973; Lancaster, PA) and both MA and PhD degrees from Hofstra University (1975, 1977; Hempstead, NY). He now teaches classes in psychometrics, multivariate analysis, longitudinal data analysis, exploratory data mining, and structural equation modeling at USC. His research was initially focused on traditional repeated measures analyses and moved toward age-sensitive methods for psychological and educational measurement and longitudinal data analysis, including publications in factor analysis, growth curve analysis, and dynamic modeling of abilities.

Dr. McArdle is a fellow of the American Association for the Advancement of Science (AAAS). He served as president of the Society of Multivariate Experimental Psychology (SMEP, 1992–1993) and the Federation of Behavioral, Cognitive, and Social Sciences (1996–1999). A few other honors include the 1987 R. B. Cattell Award for Distinguished Multivariate Research from SMEP. Dr. McArdle was recently awarded a National Institutes of Health-MERIT grant from the National Institute on Aging for his work, "Longitudinal and Adaptive Testing of Adult Cognition" (2005–2015), where he is working on new adaptive tests procedures to measure higher order cognition as a part of large-scale surveys (e.g., the Health and Retirement Study). Working with the American Psychological Association (APA), he has created and led the Advanced Training Institute on Longitudinal Structural Equation Modeling (2000–2012), and he also teaches a newer one, Exploratory Data Mining (2009–2014).

John R. Nesselroade, PhD, earned his BS degree in mathematics (Marietta College, Marietta, OH, 1961) and MA and PhD degrees in psychology (University of Illinois at Urbana–Champaign, 1965, 1967). Prior to moving to the University of Virginia in 1991, Dr. Nesselroade spent 5 years at West Virginia University and 19 years at The Pennsylvania State University. He has been a frequent visiting scientist at the Max Planck Institute for Human Development, Berlin. He is a past-president of APA's Division 20 (1982–1983) and of SMEP (1999–2000).

Dr. Nesselroade is a fellow of the AAAS, the APA, the Association for Psychological Science, and the Gerontological Society of America. Other honors include the R. B. Cattell Award for Distinguished Multivariate Research and the S. B. Sells Award for Distinguished Lifetime Achievement from SMEP. Dr. Nesselroade has also won the Gerontological Society of America's Robert F. Kleemeier Award. In 2010, he received an Honorary Doctorate from Berlin's Humboldt University. He is currently working on the further integration of individual level analyses into mainstream behavioral research.

The two authors have worked together in enjoyable collaborations for more than 25 years.